Counting Americans

Counting Americans

How the US Census Classified the Nation

PAUL SCHOR

TRANSLATED BY LYS ANN WEISS

OXFORD
UNIVERSITY PRESS

OXFORD

UNIVERSITY PRESS

Oxford University Press is a department of the University of Oxford. It furthers
the University's objective of excellence in research, scholarship, and education
by publishing worldwide. Oxford is a registered trade mark of Oxford University
Press in the UK and certain other countries.

Published in the United States of America by Oxford University Press
198 Madison Avenue, New York, NY 10016, United States of America.

*Compter et classer. Histoire des recensements
américains.* by Paul Schor © Éditions de l'École des hautes études en sciences sociales, Paris, 2009

English translation © Oxford University Press 2017

First issued as an Oxford University Press paperback, 2020

The translation of this work was made possible through the financial support of the Centre National du
Livre; the Université Paris Diderot, UMR 8225 LARCA; the Institut des Amériques; and the Mission
Culturelle et Universitaire Française aux Etats-Unis.

Library of Congress Cataloging-in-Publication Data
Names: Schor, Paul, author.
Title: Counting Americans : how the US Census classified the nation /
Paul Schor ; translated by Lys Ann Weiss.
Other titles: Compter et classer. English
Description: New York, NY : Oxford University Press, [2017] | First published as:
Compter et classer : Histoire des recensements américains by Paul
Schor, Éditions de l'École des hautes études en sciences sociales,
Paris, 2009. | Includes bibliographical references and index.
Identifiers: LCCN 2016053521 (print) | LCCN 2017013971 (ebook) |
ISBN 9780199917860 (Updf) | ISBN 9780190670849 (Epub) |
ISBN 9780199917853 (hardcover : alk. paper) | ISBN 9780190092474 (paperback : alk. paper)
Subjects: LCSH: United States—Census—History. |
Race—Classification—History. | Ethnicity—United
States—Classification—History.
Classification: LCC HA181 (ebook) | LCC HA181 .S3413 2017 (print) |
DDC 317.3072/3—dc23
LC record available at https://lccn.loc.gov/2016053521

CONTENTS

ACKNOWLEDGMENTS

In the course of years of research and writing that resulted in this book and then its new life in English, I have had the good fortune to benefit from the help and advice of many individuals and institutions in the United States and France. At the National Archives in Washington, I am especially grateful to Rod Ross, Bill Creech, and Jane Fitzgerald. This study has benefited from conversations and exchanges with colleagues too numerous to all be mentioned here, but special thanks is due to Margo Anderson, who believed in my project when I was just starting this research and who years later encouraged me to publish the book in the United States.

I would like to thank the members of the Organization of American Historians committee who gave the French edition of the book its 2011 Willi Paul Adams Award.

When working on the American edition, I benefited from the help, material and intellectual, of my department and colleagues at UMR LARCA at the Université Paris Diderot.

At Oxford University Press, I benefited from the skills of Susan Ferber, Alexandra Dauler, and Julie Mullins, to navigate the manuscript from the moment Susan accepted the proposal to its final stages of production.

Lys Weiss has done a superb job translating the book, making the text clear and elegant.

The translation was made possible through the generous support of the Centre National du Livre; the Université Paris Diderot, UMR 8225 LARCA; the Institut des Amériques; and the Hemingway Grant from the Cultural Services of the French Embassy in the United States.

Thank you, Martha Egas and Pablo Yanez, for welcoming me in your home during my trips to the archives.

And last but not least, thanks to Flor, Gabriela, and Joe who have been waiting for this to happen.

NOTE ON ILLUSTRATIONS

Unless otherwise indicated, illustrations come from the series RG 29 (Census) of the National Archives of the United States. 29-C is the reference of the photographic archives of the census in the National Archives at College Park, Maryland. The documents reproduced in this work which come from the National Archives and the Library of Congress are in the public domain.

29/xxx/xxx is the reference used for the administrative archives of the census in the National Archives in Washington, DC. RG 29/215 is the series of archives of publicity activities of the Census Bureau.

Photos coming from the photographic archives of the census, in College Park, were gathered for informational campaigns and publicity for the 1940 census, including older photos.

LIST OF TABLES

NOTE ON TERMINOLOGY

In this book, racial terms are used without quotation marks or italics, which is not intended to give them substance but instead refers to the concepts as used by historical actors. Lowercase style has been used for the adjectives "white" and "black." Terms used by the census that do not correspond to social groups, such as "mulatto" or "quadroon," are also lowercased. The term "Negro population" is the generic term used by the census to include all black people.

Counting Americans

Introduction

When people think of the census, they tend to imagine endless tables, line after line of numbers, and dull technical and repetitive operations, detached from their lives and from the larger history of the country. This is not what this book is about.

It is about the invention and the building of a nation, and the census, as a representation of the nation and as a policy tool, has played a crucial, if too often obscure, role in that history. This is particularly true in the case of the United States, where questions of population have been from the beginning the object of policy and debate, be it slavery, immigration, or the unequal distribution of the population and resources across the states.

This book studies the population categories constructed and utilized every ten years by the US Census, which is a political, administrative, and scientific instrument. Approaching these categories from a historical perspective rather than a strictly sociological or political one permits their analysis as sites of internal and external mobilization. It also brings to light the hidden evolutions by which the contents of seemingly stable categories change while the definitions remain the same. Categories that have long been in use, such as white or black, have varied dramatically across periods and regions, to the point that the same individual would be classified differently depending on the year and location of the census. Based on the distinctions of origin and status operating at the heart of the American population—between free and slave, white and non-white, native-born Americans and immigrants or children of immigrants—over a period of a century and a half, from the creation of the federal census in 1790 to the 1940s, this study retraces the genealogy and evolution of these categories.

In the American context, the focus on race and, secondarily, on ethnicity since the second half of the twentieth century has produced research and analyses that highlight the porosity of these categories, but that often seem to indicate that this porosity is a recent phenomenon. Thus, since the 2000 census, US residents can choose to identify themselves with more than one race at a time, something that was not possible before. The novelty lies in offering the choice of multiple affiliation, but it must not obscure the fact that these categories in the past were the object of negotiation, as much by those who designed the census as by the actual investigators and the population itself. This is what this book highlights by examining the fieldwork of the investigators and the difficulties they encountered, both in contacting the population and in codifying and collating the findings.

In both the United States and Europe, recent decades have seen the mushrooming of studies on the history of statistics[1] and of works on the history of "race" as a social construction—two very different areas of historiography. The effort to reintegrate the history of statistics into a larger social and political context has been characterized by greater attention paid to different actors, situating the history of statistics at the intersection of the history of the social sciences and the history of the tools of governance or the management of society.[2] The census forms only a part of social statistics, often the oldest part, and it holds only slight interest for scientific innovation. In contrast, the census plays a central role in the diffusion of quantification and statistical reasoning, being both exhaustive and conducted by nation-states. In this respect, it is indeed a mirror in which nations see themselves. This function can be clearly seen in the United States in the first half of the nineteenth century, when the results of each census were awaited as confirmation of the exceptional destiny of the nation, signaled by its demographic vitality. But if the census participated in this process of construction of the United States, by dividing up the population according to categories, it contributed equally to the ordering and hierarchizing of the social world, or at least, to codifying the existing hierarchies.

Studying the history of the population categories utilized by the US census also means analyzing the actual process by which the American population was defined by the state. American history presents the distinctive trait, often put forward, that the nation was formed not from a territory or a people, but from principles expressed in legal and political documents. The US census was created by the American Constitution to divide up taxes and congressional seats among the federated states, and for that reason it was organized around a fundamental division of Americans into three groups: free residents, counted in full; slaves, whose numbers were adjusted by a coefficient that reduced their numerical importance; and Indians, who were excluded from the count. As a result, the administrative categories of the census, though they lack the force of legal norms, nonetheless had a leading role in the measurement and definition of the American population and its composition.

This work is guided by the idea that the population does not preexist the census, that the census participates in the production of the national community defined by the inclusion of some and the exclusion of others.[3] Following in the footsteps of other works on the construction of the nation, it highlights the processes and negotiations that mobilized very diverse actors, whether institutions such as Congress, which regulated the US census through legislation, the directors and agents of the census, the spokespeople of groups or collectives, or the residents themselves.[4]

Even though socioprofessional categories and statistics concerning professions deserve attention, this book focuses only on the categories that distinguish human groups by their race or origin.[5] By concentrating on racial and ethnic categories, this study aims also to reunite two historiographical fields that in the United States are seen as separate: studies on race and studies on immigration and ethnicity.

Examining the history of population categories in the US census serves a dual purpose, both investigating the importance of the census in the production of social categories, especially as a norm for other actors, and looking at the importance of racial and ethnic categories in American society. The fact that American ethnic and racial statistics have been used as a reference in other countries adds to the value of a research project based on the idea that these categories can only be understood in their historical context.[6] Race has long been a category of analysis in American social sciences, even if it has become a truism to call it a socially constructed category freed from its origins in biology. A detailed examination of the social and scientific usages of racial categories, as they have been produced and mobilized by public statistics in the American context over the past two centuries, allows for some discussion of the relevance of the comparison and of the importation of categories in a different national context. The history of the categories of the US census here comes down to a history of the construction of the American nation and of the division of the national community into different populations, as well as to a history of the intellectual, technical, administrative, and social practices involved.

The study of statistics leads almost naturally to the study of the processes by which elites objectify other classes of the population, as the historian Theodore Porter noted in connection with the development of social statistics in the nineteenth century, whether in the United States or in Europe, with numbers becoming the privileged means of study of the lower classes.[7]

The US census fits well in this process of constituting groups of individuals as social problems—especially from 1840 on, when it aimed to find answers to the big political questions about the population, such as slavery and the harmfulness of freedom for blacks, the inassimilability of new immigrants and the "racial suicide" of Anglo-Saxons, racial mixing, hybridization, and the degeneracy of blacks. This is revealed in the multiplication of racial categories to distinguish groups that sometimes were numerically insignificant; thus the 2,039 Japanese enumerated in 1890 contrasts with the treatment of the white race, which was never defined during the entirety of the period under study. The most blatant illustration of this absence of investigation of the white race occurs in the census of 1850, the first to separately identify each individual: color only needed to be noted by the name of each resident if he was not white; when the space was left blank, it meant that the person was white. This, at a time when legislators regularly expressed their concern over the fact that the appropriate instruments to identify all the members of other groups were not available. Pushing this line of reasoning further, one might almost say that the whites distinguish themselves precisely by the fact that they are not racial subjects and that the aim of the census is not to identify all residents, but only those who differ from the implicit norm.

Historians have shown the extent to which the definition of whites was negative, how they were defined by what they were not, and above all by the fact of not being black. Recently, whiteness has become an important topic of historical study, permitting the class and ethnicity of new immigrants to be linked with race.[8] What characterizes the long period studied here is the absence of explicit reflection and of efforts to define whiteness. White identity was constructed as constantly threatened with corruption by non-whiteness, and the statistical apparatus was an apparatus for the protection of the purity of the white race. As such, the category of the white race escaped all reflexive investigation on the part of the census, expressing the gaze of white Americans on other inhabitants. The constancy with which mulattoes (those of mixed white and black blood) were defined by the census without explicit reference to their white heritage is only the most successful case of this denial.

The census indeed objectifies individuals who only "count" to the extent that they are a social problem. Its history is characterized by the development of ever greater numbers of categories investigating the specifics of those who maintained the greatest social distance from the milieux that gave rise to the census officials. Studying the categories of the population census, once they went beyond description, amounts to discerning the way one part of the population was constituted as an object of knowledge. This had different impacts and different consequences, depending on whether the otherness in question was racial or ethnic.[9] For the census, division by color or by race preceded by sixty years accounting for the country of birth, and it remains the fundamental distinction throughout the history of the US census. But recording the country of birth of residents (1850), that of their parents (1880), and then their native language (1910) share equally in this enterprise of distancing from the other by means of objectification through categories and numbers. This is even more the case because the desire for knowledge is driven by a political aim that is, in the final analysis, simple: to identify and count those who are surplus. This is why this study can only be a study of categories of difference, which blends social, political, cultural, anthropological, and biological dimensions. On this level, it aspires to be a contribution to the history of race, of racism, and of whiteness.

Studies on the construction of race in the United States often mention census categories, either as an indication of the stages of its evolution or to emphasize the federal government's participation in the process. But the racial categories of the census are most often perceived as a sign of racism at work in society, rather than the subject of a more in-depth investigation. More specifically, most of the studies that refer to the racial categories of the census are limited to picking up the taxonomies that appear in the published volumes, without examining the rules and practices of the census. One question has been explored in greater depth—that of racial mixing since the census created national norms, while the racial laws on which it was based were adopted at the state level. A number of works have reconstructed the procedures of attribution of racial categories in the case of "mulattoes." Three studies have contributed to showing how the racial categories of the census were applied and how they were the product of numerous, often contradictory, factors.[10] But their chief limitation comes from the fact that they are essentially concerned with categories of race and color, and especially the opposition between white and black, and that they ignored ethnic categories or treated them in passing. This separation between the field of racial studies, which has as its object racial minorities and the history of their identification for purposes of their exclusion, and that of ethnic studies, which originated in the history of European immigrants and their descendants, prevents us from seeing how, for the US census, population categories constituted a system whose foundation was the distinction between blacks and whites, but whose classifications were profoundly influenced by the existence of this fundamental difference. One of the aims of this book is to show that dissociating categories of color or race from categories of national origin and ethnicity is an arbitrary choice, imposed by the division of research into distinct fields, which obscures the borrowings of method and reasoning that, for the Census Bureau, characterized the elaboration of these two sets of categories.[11]

This distinction between racial minorities and ethnic groups, which Hannah Arendt formulated as an opposition between "visible minorities" and "audible minorities," is found just as much in historical research as in the history of the treatment of these groups by American society, as well as in the practices of the census.[12] *Counting Americans* hopes to show that, even if these two things were distinct for the census, they were not necessarily independent of each other. To take just one example, the procedure for attributing the national origin of the parents to a child born in the United States of immigrant parents flows directly from the rules for attributing the racial categories of the parents to their children, even if the categories of origin lack the characteristic of permanence without limit by generation. The child of an immigrant parent and a native-born parent would be classified as belonging to the population of foreign parentage, a procedure reminiscent of the practice of including mixed-race children in the black population and not allowing space for an in-between group. By analyzing the procedures, working methods, argumentation, and critiques of the workings of the census, one can document the link that exists between accounting for race and accounting for ethnicity and thus transcend this artificial divide.

Racial categories were indeed more important in census-taking than categories of origin. This is why nearly all social statistics in the census publications of the second half of the nineteenth century are presented by race—that is to say, in the vast majority of cases, with whites on one side and blacks on the other, while the categories of national origin play a much more limited role, which varies according to the importance of the immigration question in political debates. But the study of the two types of categories, which correspond in principle to two different methods—visual observation for race, and the response to a question for national origin—have enough shared features for them to be analyzed together.

Studies devoted to the history of the Census Bureau have addressed the question of categories of race or color, and that of slavery, as well as the role played by the census in taking account of immigration, in light of the considerable importance of public debates about the census.[13] But these studies did not take as their central subject the study of population categories, and they only addressed the question when these categories came to the fore in public debates over the census.

This study proceeds by more or less faithful borrowings from different methodologies—the history of race, the history of immigration and ethnicity, and the history of statistics. But since this kind of methodological *bricolage* is characteristic of the census itself, this approach seems the one best suited to the subject. Thus, the analysis of the place of black slaves in census statistics inevitably leads to the evoking of both the hierarchy of racial categories and the epistemological and general anthropological issues that it raises. Knowing whether the name of each slave should or should not be picked up by the census, as it was for other Americans, or whether a number would suffice, leads to the consideration of the role of census data in the creation of social facts—a question that can be extended to other categories.

Since these terms are critical to the study, it is important to clarify exactly how "race" and "ethnicity" are used in this book. The term *race* is used only in reference to census practice and to the content given by the collection and treatment of personal data. For this purpose, *race* has no meaning until the perforated card on which it was written had been processed by the tabulating machine. It is understood that race is a category, the product of a social convention, whose importance comes uniquely from the importance that it is accorded by the society studied. The refutation of the biological or anthropometric bases for racial distinctions has not led to the demise of the use of race as a social category. While the census may have helped give race a social and historical depth that allowed the category to survive the disappearance of its theoretical foundation, *ethnicity* is a term that does not appear in the censuses of the period. The expression "ethnic groups," used to designate the populations issuing from recent immigration, appears only at the end of the period under consideration, notably after the system of national origins was instituted in 1928. On an analytical level, the notion of ethnic groups explains the shift from the collection of biographical facts, linked to country of origin (place of birth, mother tongue), to the production of social characteristics that permit individuals to be inscribed in the social fabric of the welcoming society, while the notion of national origins does not effectively account for this displacement. The precise content of the concept will be specified in different stages of the analysis. While the census considers the national origins of certain categories of immigrants, it produces through the taking of the census an ethnicity that did not previously exist. No identity, whether racial or ethnic, exists outside of a social interaction, and it follows as a matter of course that one of the purposes of this study, in recontextualizing the categories used by the census, is to contribute to the weakening of the essentialist interpretations of racial categories, for which the census was able to supply content.

This study involves paying attention to the empirical practices of classification rather than to taxonomies alone and, as much as possible, refraining from introducing an ideological coherence that was lacking at the time for the categories and statistical procedures that followed the collection of the data. The fact that the meaning of the terms of "race," "nationality," "people" were never stable or coherent presents no obstacle to research but is precisely its point. The goal here is not to study a discourse, still less an ideology, but rather to examine the practices in which ideology and vocabulary are two factors among others. For this reason the study is attentive not only to the terms and the variations in their interpretation, but also to the rules of consolidation or invalidation of responses, and to the procedures used for assignment of unclear cases. In many cases, technical imperatives, such as cost or space limitations on one sheet or card, influenced how responses were treated.

To the extent that the sources permit, analysis follows the categories, from the discussions that accompanied their introduction or modification, to the interpretations of findings published in the reports of the census, while noting anything knowable about the moment of the interaction between the census agent and the population and about the procedures of correction and arrangement of the data. Examining the rules for correction of individual data points before their statistical processing shows how certain responses from residents were invalidated by the staff charged with the mechanical processing of the data. These norms are often more precise than the instructions given to agents in the field, and in certain cases they serve to bring individual data points into line with the expected patterns.

Intervention of the public was diverse, rare, and above all the act of experts during the first part of the nineteenth century; they were later more numerous, and were organized into effective pressure groups from the early years of the twentieth century on. The stakes of classification or of reclassification also vary, from the mobilization of pure prestige, as in the recognition of national minorities of the Austro-Hungarian Empire by language, to the mobilization of American citizens of Mexican origin for the suppression of the "Mexican" race in the census, which risked furnishing legal arguments for the segregation of their children in Texas schools. It will become apparent that the Census Bureau tried to follow a consensual path, demonstrating its concern with obtaining cooperation from all residents, but was often constrained by Congress to respond to specific demands, as in the case of the introduction in 1890 of subcategories for blacks (*black, mulatto, quadroon, octoroon*), against the wishes of the directors of the census. The weakness of the Census Bureau in the federal bureaucracy, as an administrative agency subjected to numerous political demands, also made it a sounding board for certain claims, which have to be interpreted cautiously because the success or failure of the demands depended on multiple factors. The hazards of classification express a climate more than a political will. Finally, individual cases of resistance, unexplained variations, the spontaneous creation of categories by agents, and failures in the field furnish rich materials which allow for interpretive hypotheses where certainty is lacking.

The available sources are very unequally distributed over the period of study. Archives are rare for the period before 1900, while the belated creation in 1902 of a permanent Census Bureau produced sources for the period from 1900 to 1940. The main source—and, for the early period, practically the only source—consists of laws passed by Congress and the debates in the House of Representatives and the Senate. In some cases, it is possible to reconstitute some of the legislators' intentions. In contrast, before 1850, the published volumes of the census provide little information, since they do not include any explanatory text and consist of a simple compilation of the data from the questionnaires. From 1849 onward, the sources are more numerous and more fruitful, especially the reports of the census directors, the numerous official statistical publications with lengthy introductions, and the archives of the congressional committees that prepared the censuses. The archives of the Department of Interior have preserved a portion of the archives of the Census Office beginning in 1870. They consist largely of the superintendents' correspondence, but the documents rarely address questions of method. The administrative archives of the Bureau of the Census, beginning in the late nineteenth century, are quite rich in this respect and furnish the key information for the sources used for the first half of the twentieth century.

The stages of development of the census translate into the creation of more abundant and better quality archives. Over a period as long as that studied here, the changes in the census are significant. Thus it was essential to organize this work in chronological parts, especially since the formation of categories was a cumulative process through which the existing categories were constantly redefined by new contexts and practices. The first part of this book, covering the period from 1790 to 1840, addresses the foundation of the census as a political instrument and the dominance of the slavery issue. This first period, marked by significant natural increase in the population, is distinguished by the summary character of the census and of debates over population questions. Despite the paucity of sources, the period deserves discussion because the categories put in place at that time formed the basis of later censuses. The first census divided the population into three types of inhabitants: free whites, distinguished by gender and by age; slaves and free blacks, placed in a single group without regard to age or sex; and Indians, who were excluded from the count. The political division foreseen by the Constitution (free, slaves, and Indians) was from the start crosscut by a distinction of color—although the Constitution carefully avoids the issue and is a "color blind" document—whites were called free, while the freedom of blacks who were not slaves was passed over in silence.

The year 1850 marked the beginning of the second stage of the census, when residents were all counted individually. The use of no fewer than six questionnaires facilitated collection of a mass of statistics completely disproportionate to those collected for previously published volumes. The importance of the slavery question, the most burning political issue of the day, led to the creation of a special questionnaire devoted to slaves in 1850 and 1860. Taking slaves into account as persons was extremely problematic, and the solution adopted, which consisted of attributing numbers to slaves rather than naming them, highlights the anthropological dimension of the population census. By returning to the debates in Congress and the rules of attribution of the categories "black" and "mulatto," this part aims both to contribute to the history of racism in American social sciences, and to analyze the production of the data that provides the only population-level statistics historians have on the extent of mixing between whites and blacks in the context of slavery. This part helps clarify the matrix of the system for taking account of racial mixing in American public statistics, or rather of its persistent denial, by assigning children of mixed couples only to the subordinate group.

The third part covers the period opened up by the reorganization of the census in 1850 and goes up to the establishment of the permanent Census Bureau at the turn of the century. This period was marked by the importance of statistics on immigration, a development that is connected to racial statistics. The 1850 census was the first to register the birthplace of free inhabitants, which was further extended by the question on the birthplace of the parents (1870 and 1880), and also by counting as nationalities birth in states that were defunct but seemed pertinent to characterize the immigrants from those places then living in the United States. This lack of interest in the situation of the country of departure, which was also manifested by the absence of any reference to the citizenship of origin, can be understood as the beginning of the long transition from geographical statistics to ethnic statistics. This section also shows how the census, in spite of its connections to the international statistical community, remained dependent on US debates over population.

The next period, 1900–1940, is divided into two parts: the fourth section of the book focuses on the rise and fall of ethnic statistics and the fifth and last on the modernization of the census and its relation to various segments of the population that became associated to the operation of the census. The US Census remained a political instrument and continued to have as its goal the establishment of the "constitutional" population of the United States, that is to say, the figure that enters into the calculus of the division of congressional seats in the House of Representatives. But it is in this period, when the Census Bureau was asked to produce immigration quotas, that the political dimension of its activity came to the fore. During this period certain categories appeared to be maladjusted or rejected by those to whom they were applied, whether it was a question of racial classifications that tried to measure racial mixing or of the ephemeral "Mexican race."

This book does not cover local censuses, those of cities, of territories, or of special populations, whether they were taken under the authority of the federal Census Bureau or, a fortiori, of other institutions. It focuses on the federal census, at once a political instrument, a means of demographic inquiry, and a locus for assigning collective identities to individuals in a national context. It is in no way a history of demographic or administrative inquiries in the United States. However, the censuses of outlying territories that remained American during the entire period concerned are included.[14] Although they did not form part of the "constitutional" population, they shed light on the difficulties of exporting the categories forged on the continent. These categories were revealed as poorly adapted to populations that did not have the same history of racial or ethnic relations, and the fact that these censuses were not strictly limited by the terms of the legislation voted by Congress permitted important adaptations opening a more flexible way than on the US mainland. The attention brought to bear on colonial censuses of the United States, which have been little studied, allows for the American census to be shown in a larger context, to underscore the national history of the census, and to compensate for the exceptionalist bias that characterizes some of the American studies on the history of the social construction of race.[15]

The transformation of the temporary bureau into a permanent institution, called for by the census leaders since 1850, gave it an institutional existence that made it the unmediated partner of all those who took an interest in the census of the population. Thanks to the bureau's archives, it is possible to show the different stages of decision-making of an organization subject to multiple pressures, whether the traditional ones of Congress or those of other government agencies: pressure groups that wanted to influence the classification of those whom they represented, such as the representatives of Central European immigrants who in 1910 imposed the practice of taking account of mother tongue, or groups that expected the census to furnish data that would feed their campaigns in favor of the exclusion of certain categories of inhabitants. This period is marked by the central role played by the census in the conception and production of means of restricting immigration starting in 1921, but it is also distinguished by the efforts made by the bureau to identify and ensure the cooperation of populations that it considered the most resistant to census-taking, which posed once again the question of the political uses of population statistics. The increasing connection between the population and the "users of statistics," to use an expression of the census director of the day, in the conception and progress of the census furnishes sources for a social history of the census that would make it a site for mobilization as much as a locus for decision.

The book's end date of 1940 is justified by the general context of racial and ethnic relations and by the evolution of the Census Bureau. The American racial system had come under serious attacks since the beginning of the twentieth century, whether on the theoretical level with the critique of the scientific foundations of racism led by Franz Boas and his disciples, or on the legal level with the NAACP's struggle for desegregation, to cite only the most obvious aspects. But the comparison with Nazism and later the imperatives of the Cold War led larger and larger sectors of American society to reject the very foundations of distinction by race, to identify distinction by race with racism. Before World War II, the fact that the census classified inhabitants by race had never provoked direct criticism on American soil. From 1965 on, census data would serve as a framework for the politics of affirmative action, while from 1970 onward, the symbolic stakes themselves would be transformed by self-identification and the context of the "ethnic revival."[16] Finally, the inversion of the politics of immigration in 1965 reinvigorated interest in statistics on national origin that had been lost since the 1930s. These changes explain why the racial and ethnic classifications of the postwar censuses have been the object of numerous investigations on the part of historians, sociologists, political scientists, and legal scholars, while the history of the formation of these categories up to 1940 has not received even a fraction of this attention.

After the war, the Census Bureau acquired a historical service, which produced what in the bureau's terms is called a "procedural history," taking minute account of the planning, the progress, and the cost of each census since 1950. This internal history differs in its goals and means from the type of history practiced by academic historians, but it assumes part of the work that only the latter have done for the earlier period. On the other hand, within the bureau, the 1940s saw a process that began in the 1920s come to fruition, but it only showed its effects in the second half of the following decade: the replacement of the older generation of statisticians, trained for the task and for whom the census was limited to gathering administrative statistics to which they applied simple treatments, by a generation of university-trained statisticians who transformed the bureau's working methods. One consequence was the growth of internal discussions devoted to the improvement of statistical methods and the corresponding decrease of the place of political stakes in the census. Along with the strict limitation on immigration, the disappearance of the "mulatto" category, and the growing importance of economic statistics since the Great Depression, the declining importance of population questions likewise justifies the chronological limit of this study.

To understand the current and future stakes of census-taking in the United States as well as the specific role population questions have played in the building of this nation, the past needs to be explained, and this is what this book intends to do.

PART I

THE ORIGINS OF
THE US CENSUS

From Enumeration of Voters and Taxpayers
to "Social Statistics," 1790–1840

The United States Census, created by the Constitution as a way to apportion the taxes and representatives of the federated states, is at its core neither a scientific investigation nor an enumeration for fiscal purposes. Rather, it is a novel mechanism to enable the balancing of powers. It also differs from European enumerations in its regular schedule of every ten years. In both these respects—its breadth and its regularity—it stands apart from earlier experiments, whether American or European. Still, it owes something to the colonial censuses that preceded it, some of which posed the same questions as those that inaugurated the American statistical tradition in 1790. It is also the beneficiary of the census proposals that accompanied the constitutional projects of the Continental Congress. The American census was organized to serve constitutional needs; it was created within a conceptual framework that was already in existence at the time the Constitution was composed—something that in no way lessens its novelty. Several solutions were available to the Founders. The one they chose was not particularly remarkable in and of itself, but was notable for its constitutional role, which made demographic weight one of the sources of democratic power. But even though its principle was that of the proportionality of representation to number of residents, from the beginning the US census, in counting all residents, counted them unequally.

From 1790 to 1840, the census became the popular barometer of the exceptional demographic growth of the young nation. This development gave it the status of an instrument for ascertaining the state of the population and, more broadly, of the country. The history of the first six federal censuses, which concluded with the failures of the 1840 census, is also the history of a nation that learned about itself as it learned to use statistical information as a reflection of its progress.

1

The Creation of the Federal Census by the Constitution of the United States

A Political Instrument

> Representatives and direct Taxes shall be apportioned among the several States which may be included within this Union, according to their respective Numbers, which shall be determined by adding to the whole Number of free Persons, including those bound to Service for a Term of Years, and excluding Indians not taxed, three fifths of all other Persons.
>
> (US Constitution, Article I, Section 2, para. 3.)

The United States Constitution is characterized by the balance of powers that limit each other, known as the system of checks and balances. The US census was created to put this principle into operation. It attributes to each state, in proportion to its population, a number of representatives and also a level of contribution, with the idea that linking the two would encourage the states not to attempt to either inflate or diminish the numbers. In this way it would permit the proportional division of the legislative power among the states while at the same time containing an internal mechanism of control that aimed at preventing manipulation of the figures. A state that inflated its population would gain more representatives but would have to pay more taxes. Conversely, a state that sought to reduce its contribution by lowering the population figure would see its representation lessened. In 1787, Americans were already aware that their rapid demographic growth would be a source of imbalance, especially because of the different patterns across regions. The young republic thus distinguished itself by being the first modern nation after Sweden to provide for a national census at regular intervals. Above all, it made the census an instrument for the balancing of powers between the federal government, the states, and individuals. The historical publications of the Census Bureau in the twentieth century proudly called out this precocious aspect of the American statistical tradition.[1]

The paragraph of the Constitution creating the census was one of the least debated and least commented-upon parts of the document, both at that time and later.[2] Yet this paragraph carried within it the seed of several important developments, such as control by the federal government and its agents over population statistics, in an era when the federal government only rarely acted on the local level. It is true that the Continental Congress, which preceded the Congress created by the Constitution in 1787, had experienced difficulty in obtaining valid figures for apportionment when this task was left to the states. Apportionment, the mechanism that distributes costs and benefits among the states in proportion to their population or their wealth, was a difficult exercise because it lay at the heart of the balancing of powers among the states. The states made use of this mechanism as soon as the problem arose of financing the national government. It was also used to divide up seats in the state legislatures, with rules that varied from state to state. Its inclusion in the Constitution was the practical, arithmetic translation of the fundamental principle of proportional representation at the basis of the democratic regime. However, as with the Electoral College, proportional representation did not mean the strict arithmetical equality of all. Everyone counted, but not with the same weight. Above all, given that the main function of the census was to assign seats in Congress, Congress understandably wanted to maintain control over the operation. The assignment of seats would continue to be the object of the fiercest negotiations. In other words, most members of the House of Representatives would concern themselves with the method only insofar as it affected the result in a predictable manner.[3]

The Constitution distinguished three categories of residents, according to their legal and political status: free persons, who were fully enumerated, including indentured servants; black slaves, who were not named but rather designated negatively by the formula "all other Persons"; and Indians, excluded from the census because they were not taxed and were outside of the national community.[4] The knotty problem was the inclusion of slaves in the calculation, because the device was at once political and fiscal, and because the slaves were not only part of the population but also taxable property.

The inclusion of slaves in the calculation of the apportionment of seats in the House of Representatives and of the taxes paid by the states raised several complex problems relating to the source of the new power. The principle of representation proportional to population, rather than equal representation of the states or representation based on real property, clearly favored the republican position, that is, the national government. Slaves found themselves at the heart of the problem—a question that was resolved by the Three-Fifths Compromise.

This solution, proposed by James Wilson of Pennsylvania, grew out of a proposition that had been made in 1783 to replace Article 8 of the Confederation. If political representation was proportional to population, contributions needed to be established in proportion to the wealth of the states. But it was much harder to measure wealth than the number of residents. The slave states did not count their slaves for the apportionment of legislators in the state assemblies, but to exclude slaves from the apportionment of taxes at the federal level would have given those states an unfair advantage. The problem posed by slavery at that time was not only that of representation but a fiscal problem, arising from the ambivalence of slave status. The southern states had an interest in slaves being taken into account, in order to have equal weight with their northern counterparts in the House of Representatives. Other delegates to the constitutional convention held that this representation was not legitimate.

The compromise that was reached consisted of basing both representation and taxes solely on the number of the population, while assigning slaves a three-fifths coefficient that reduced their weight in the population calculation. The consequence of this choice was to inscribe in the federal census the distinction between two general categories of residents: free persons, and those who counted as only three-fifths of a free person, who were partly people and partly property, which amounted to an implicit recognition of the existence of slavery.[5] The Constitution did not distinguish by color or race, but by requiring the census to count slaves separately, it opened the path to a different distinction, not of status but of color, which appeared as early as the first census even though it was absent from the Constitution.

The arbitrary character of the choice of three-fifths, as opposed to a half (as had once been considered) or any other fraction, had been pointed out by James Madison and Alexander Hamilton. It was an expression of a political compromise rather than that of a scientific choice. From its origin, the census was subject to tension between technical and scientific imperatives and political compromise. The history of the US census over the following two centuries would be largely bound up with the history of this tension.

From Status to Color: Free, Slaves, Whites, and Blacks in the Constitutional Debates

The text of the Constitution refers to slavery only implicitly and is silent on color—in current parlance, color-blind. Yet, from the very first census, free blacks were distinguished from free whites, thus following the practices of the colonial period and the attempt to establish a national census for fiscal purposes as early as 1775. Debates mention the color of residents, whether to include "negroes and mulattoes" indifferently to their status (1775)[6] or to say that they would be evaluated quantitatively but that the deduction would show the number of white residents. The question of color was always linked to that of status, to the point that, in the text of a report of 12 July 1776 on the draft of the Confederation Articles, a note indicates that the term "white Inhabitants" has been introduced to replace the phrase "who are not slaves."[7] Some delegates explicitly invoked the equality of all men, affirmed in the Declaration of Independence, to argue that quotas should not be based only on the number of white residents of each colony, demanding that "persons of a different colour . . . be reckoned in the account of the inhabitants in the present instance."[8]

The different rehashes of the paragraph of the Constitution of 1787 that created the census were characterized by confusion between color and condition. The most significant text is a report presented on 18 March 1783, very close to the final wording. It took up again the idea of linking the number of men required for militia service to the area and the number of residents, here expressed as

> in proportion to the whole number of white and other free citizens and inhabitants of every age, sex and condition, including those bound to servitude for a term of years and three-fifths of all other persons not comprehended in the foregoing description, except Indians not paying taxes.

On 28 March 1783, a new change to Article 8 of the Articles of Confederation firmed up the text that would be taken over in the Constitution:

> in proportion of free ~~white~~ inhabitants, and ~~one half~~ three-fifths of the number of all other inhabitants of every sex and condition, except Indians not paying taxes.[9]

The variant that had at one time been considered substituted "whites" for free "persons." The other residents, in this version of the text, thus were not only slaves but all blacks. The distinction was not one of status, but of color. Had this version been adopted, the separation of slaves from the rest of the population on the grounds that they were at once property and persons would no longer have been needed, and the racial distinction would have been inscribed in the Constitution, without any explicit basis.[10]

However that may be, the different states of the text bear witness to the mix of status (free or slave) and race (white or colored). It was not always clear at that time that "white" necessarily implied "free." Still, the process of confusion of color and status, identifying white with free and black with dependent, which recurred in the first half of the nineteenth century, was already at work. With respect to the Three-Fifths Compromise, Madison observed that this formula treated slaves "as inhabitants, but as debased by servitude below the equal level of free inhabitants, which regards the *slave* as divested of two fifths of the *man*."[11] Paradoxically, it was more often the delegates of free states or those in the process of eliminating slavery who defended the distinction, such as the Pennsylvania delegate Gouverneur Morris, who declared in the course of the debates that the people of Pennsylvania would revolt on being placed on an equal footing with slaves.[12] The paradox is only apparent, however, since it was in the interest of the states where slaves were numerous that slaves should have as much weight as possible so that their delegates might protect their own interests, with slavery rapidly moving to the top of the list.

The First National Census of the American Population (1790): Free Men, Slaves, and Other Persons

The first census of the young American nation took place in 1790, on the date envisioned by the Constitution. As intended, the census, directed by the president, was framed by a law passed by Congress, the First Census Act.[13] This law inaugurated a tradition that continued up to the census of 1930: the list, the order, and the text of the questions on the questionnaires closely followed the text of the law, which means that Congress played a central role in the preparation of the census. Madison had proposed to Congress a rather complete questionnaire that would have classified the population by age, sex, color, and profession. Congress accepted the inclusion of simple distinctions by age and sex, aware that by so doing the census would facilitate knowledge of the military potential of the nation, but it did not wish to use the census to chart the state of society. The Senate rejected the enumeration of professions, accepted by the House of Representatives, because, as Madison reported to Jefferson, the senators felt it would be "a waste of trouble and supplying material for idle people to make a book."[14] The historian Patricia Cline Cohen notes that such distinctions were not unusual, since many colonial censuses included at least that much information. The distinctions proposed by Madison and retained by Congress permitted the identification of the most important group: free adult white men, that is, the soldiers and citizens of the nation.

The text of the First Census Act of 1 March 1790 actually went beyond the requirements of the Constitution, to the extent that it required the count of residents omitting in such enumeration Indians not taxed, and distinguishing free persons, including those bound to service for a term of years, from all others; distinguishing also the sexes and colors of free persons; and the free males of 16 years and upward from those under that age.

The question concerning color of free persons and the distinction between two age classes of free men were not required by the terms of the Constitution; in fact, they bore witness to Madison's efforts to broaden the field of the census. The text of the law does not indicate—as the questionnaire for the census would do—that free persons are white. From 1787 to 1790, from the adoption of the Constitution to the first census, including the First Census Act, each stage made more explicit the racial dimension of the separation of slaves from the rest of the population. A few census agents applied the text of the First Census Act to the letter, no doubt ignoring later oral instructions, for they distinguished on their questionnaires the free persons of color of more or less than sixteen years of age, as if the implicit racial awareness that restricted this question to free whites only had not influenced them as it had for the vast majority of census workers.[15]

The law passed at the start of the year 1790 provided that the census would begin in August and that it would take the US marshals[16] and their 650 assistants nine months to collect the information.[17] Once the questionnaires were completed, the assistants were to post them in two public places so that the population might verify their accuracy, and then transmit them to the marshals, who were to place them in the care of the federal district courts, add up the results, and then present to the president the total number of residents of their districts. In reality, it took eighteen months to enumerate the 3.9 million people counted in the first United States census.[18]

In October 1791, President Washington reported the results to Congress, which then began to draw up a law of apportionment. This began a long series of discussion and bargaining that would repeat itself every ten years, after the publication of each census. While the division of contributions among the states could be made without difficulty, seats by definition were indivisible and could not be fractional, an unexpected problem that inevitably entailed gains for some states and losses for others. From this date onward, debates concerning apportionment would revolve mainly around the number of seats of representatives allotted to each state.

The first federal census asked only five questions, which is why the questionnaires composed by hand by the census agents in the different states had only five columns. Only with the census of 1830 did the government begin to distribute printed questionnaires. Over the course of the four first censuses, the form and dimensions of the questions, drawn up by hand, varied by region and even, in 1790, by agent.[19] Following the names of household heads, the five categories used in 1790 were

- Names of heads of families
- Free white males of sixteen years and upwards, including "heads"
- Free white males under sixteen
- Free white females, including "heads"
- All other free
- Slaves

The column titles echoed the terms of the First Census Act, with at least one major modification, which made more explicit the racial character of these categories: where the law spoke of "free males" or "females," the census counted the "free white males" and "free white females" and added free blacks ("all other free") and slaves. Actually, since the term "slaves" did not appear anywhere in the Constitution, the census did no more than make explicit what had been implicit. This slippage is very significant, because it gave rise to a separate category for free blacks. While the phrase "all other persons" of the Constitution designated slaves, in 1790 the phrase "all other free," just before the slaves, referred to free blacks. The authors of the Constitution eschewed use of the words "slave" or "slavery" in the fundamental text, but in practice, they had to avoid risk of confusion. Congress, in passing the First Census Act, had no such scruples.[20]

The purpose of this first questionnaire was to provide the information required by the Constitution or considered useful to the government, such as determining the number of white men old enough to bear arms, while women were not distinguished by age. On the other hand, free blacks and even slaves could be heads of family, like white women, even if that was not made explicit in the questionnaires. But there again, uniformity was not the rule, and slaves were sometimes listed as members of the family, sometimes as a separate family. Free persons of color who were heads of families were often designated as being "free": for example, "Ruth, Free negro" or "Brown, John (free mulatto)."[21]

In one way, all the other categories were constructed negatively with respect to the one that defined the body politic par excellence—free white men of sixteen years and older. Thus, the other inhabitants were free white men of less than sixteen, men and women who were not white, those who were not free (of whom it is pointless to say that they were also not white), and residents who were not men, that is, (white) women of any age. This is why the questionnaire is deeply unbalanced: neither free blacks nor slaves were distinguished by age or sex.

Finally, up to and including the census of 1840, the fact that all the censuses were familial and not individual made it impossible to cross-tabulate within families. There was only one line per family, and only the name of the head of family appeared on the census page, while the number of members of the family of each category was indicated in the corresponding column. Some families were very large, especially when the count included domestic servants and slaves.

The questionnaires did not lend themselves to statistical exploitation, the field agents had no specific training, and they interpreted the rules and definitions differently. Nonetheless, out of these first, rudimentary distinctions there slowly developed the categories that permitted a more fine-grained knowledge of the American population.

2

The First Developments of
the National Census (1800–1830)

As the census of 1800 approached, Congress took note of two documents composed by learned societies, proposing changes in the direction of a broader investigation of the state of the American population, which had been rejected in 1790. The first of these was addressed to the Senate and composed by Vice President Thomas Jefferson, on behalf of the American Philosophical Society, of which he was a member. It proposed, among other things, distinguishing the number of native citizens, citizens of foreign birth, and aliens. The second, from Timothy Dwight of the Connecticut Academy of Arts and Sciences, likewise tended toward a census that would serve demographic science and whose findings would allow comparisons between different categories of the population.[1]

The two learned societies both hoped to know the age of residents, in order to establish the structure of the population by age and to construct actuarial tables, and their professions, picking up on Madison's proposal for the first census. The congressional committees charged with census laws between 1800 and 1810 retained only some of these suggestions. Yet however modest, these developments moved in the direction of broadening the field of the census beyond its constitutional mission.

The questionnaire of 1800 differed from that of 1790 only in classifying white men and women into five classes by age: less than ten years old; ten to under sixteen; sixteen to twenty-six; twenty-six to forty-four; and over forty-five. No distinction by age was made for free blacks—"all other free persons (except Indians not taxed)," as was specified for the first time—nor for slaves, who were thus counted only for the needs of apportionment, and not out of concern for collecting demographic information on this part of the population.[2] Even though these were not regular age classes, which would have permitted a better understanding of the age structure of the population, it is noteworthy that while remaining organized around the age of sixteen for men—that is, the age for militia service—these new divisions existed only to satisfy the scientific curiosity of those interested in the study of the population of the young republic. In order to know the potential numbers of soldiers or citizens, there was no need to ask about the age of white women. Since the age classes of the black population were different, it was a piece of good fortune that Congress should have decided to rigorously use the same classes for white women as for white men.

The 1810 questionnaire was identical to that of 1800, as the modifications introduced by the legislators were concerned with process rather than content. Thus, it was specified that the census agents, assistants to the marshals, had to be residents of the area where the census was taken, and they had to go in person to each home to gather the information. Moreover, for the first time, the population census was accompanied by a census of national production—a difficult experiment that was repeated in 1820, with inconclusive results, before being provisionally abandoned in 1830.[3]

The census of 1820, the fourth federal investigation of this sort, marked an initial break with the tradition begun in 1790, as a result of the decisive intervention of John Quincy Adams, who asked Congress to finance a more comprehensive census. The Instructions to the marshals for 1820 made plain that beyond the enumeration they should

> ascertain in detail the proportional numbers of which it is composed, according to the circumstances of sex, color, age, condition of life, as heads or members of families, as free or slaves, as citizens or foreigners, and particularly of the classes (including slaves) engaged in agriculture, commerce, and manufactures.[4]

The division by age classes made it possible to know the structure by age and by sex of the population of free blacks and slaves, thirty years after the first census had collected this for the rest of the population. Patricia Cline Cohen, seeing the census as a reflection of the concerns of the era, noted that this reveals the lack of interest before 1820 in the black population, whether free or slave.[5]

Up to 1820, slaves were objects statistically as well as legally, attached to the head of the family. But the same lack of interest applied to free blacks, who were not distinguished in the census, even though they were legally persons. Lack of interest in the black population, combined with a general lack of sophistication in the early censuses, thus seems to have been the case for this first period.

The problem of age classes applied to free blacks or to slaves was that these classes did not conform to those used for whites, thereby reinforcing the impression that these were two distinct populations, subject to different evolutionary paths. The four classes used for blacks, with men and women distinguished for the first time, were: less than fourteen years of age; fourteen to under twenty-six; twenty-six to forty-five; and over forty-five. These distinctions may have

corresponded to the economic utility of these persons. Just as for the white population, the age of forty-five would mark the onset of old age, and the threshold
of a lessened work force, fourteen would correspond to black inhabitants' entry
into active life.

The white population remained grouped according to the five classes used in
1800 and 1810, with the exception that, for white men only, one new category
had been introduced, distinguishing those between sixteen and eighteen years
of age.[6] Thus, if the classes over twenty-six were comparable, the others were
not, which makes it impossible to compare the structure by age of whites and
blacks—a situation that would last until the census of 1850 recorded the exact
age of each individual. One of the first to have perceived the considerable importance of the census for the study of population movement, Archibald Russell, a
New Yorker of Scottish origin and a geographer, bitterly lamented this fact in
1839. The legislators of 1840 did not listen to him, for the discordance worsened
in the next census, in which the divisions did not agree in any case after the age of
ten.[7] An isolated attempt by one representative to gain better knowledge of the
age structure of the black populations in 1839 was rejected without even being
put to a vote.[8]

If the concept already existed, the term "color" appeared on questionnaires
for the first time in 1820, as free blacks were counted under the label of "Free
colored persons" next to slaves, while there was a single column at the end of the
questionnaire for "All other persons except Indians not taxed." "All other persons" were not distinguished by either sex or age in 1820. Some people whose
classification had fluctuated in the censuses may have chosen to opt out of the
census from 1820 onward in order not be stigmatized by the term "color" and
risk losing their rights, a hypothesis advanced in a study of the variations in size
of this category.[9]

It is hard to know who the 4,631 persons included in this category were,
as the heading seems to have survived by accident and was abolished in 1830.
Probably some were Indians who paid taxes because they lived among the
rest of the population of the states. The small number supports this hypothesis: there were 4,631 "all other free, except Indians, not taxed" out of a total of
9,638,453 residents, of whom 7,862,166 were whites and 1,771,656 were blacks.
This breakdown shows that these individuals were neither black nor white. This
also appears from an analysis of the archived manuscripts and documents done
in 1900 by William Rossiter, who noted explicitly that "taxed Indians" were
included among the "free colored."[10] This category may also have included people whose status had not been determined by the census worker, who at that
time assigned a color to the families he enumerated.

Blacks were thus defined by the fact of being colored, of possessing a physical
attribute that distinguished them from the rest of the population, who did not

have color. They were no longer simply "other persons." The term "black" had not yet appeared, although the term "white" is found in all the questionnaires from 1790 through 1840, in the labels "Free white males" and "Free white females." "Colored" is at once a euphemism to designate blacks and eventually mulattoes, and also to indicate the negative character of that which is not white, without further details. There was no point in stating their color, in part because "colored" in the language of the day designated blacks, and in part because what was important was that they be distinguished from whites. For the census, "white" was not so much a color as the absence of color, to the point that in the 1850 census, agents were instructed to indicate in the column "Color" a "B" for blacks, "M" for mulattoes, and to leave the column blank if the person was white.[11] It was still a question of a negative definition, even if it was more explicit. When the census began to enumerate other races, they were always grouped under the term "non white races."

At the same time, in the language of the day, the terms *free* and *freeman* were no longer merely a designation of free status, but became associated with a race—white—as the historian David Roediger has pointed out. In other words, beginning in the 1830s, the terms *free* and *freeman* denoted not only status but also race.[12]

For the first time, based on an earlier request by those who favored extending the scope of census-taking, the census distinguished non-naturalized foreigners. This was a clear sign of the desire to know the role played by immigration in the strong demographic growth that was beginning to be seen, thanks to the censuses, as a national characteristic. In this domain as well, the census proceeded by cautious experimentation, reflecting the uncertainty and inexperience of legislators confronting a new phenomenon. This question was only posed to whites; the importation of slaves having been abolished in 1808, it was obvious to Congress that only Europeans could immigrate to the United States, and this corresponded generally to the reality of the situation.

In another respect, this census acknowledged the validity of the demands made in vain by Madison and others, on the occasion of each preceding census, that this unique tool should be used to learn about the activities of Americans. Adult residents were grouped into three categories of economic activity: agriculture, commerce, and manufacturing. These questions applied to all men, white and black, American and foreign, free and slave—but not, it appears, to women. Neither the form of the questionnaire nor the instructions were altogether clear on this point, but in all probability, and judging by the later difficulties in measuring women's activity, the question did not apply to them.

In 1820, for the first time, written instructions were distributed to the marshals, who were to use them as the basis for their questionnaire. While this reflects progress in the attempt to regularize questionnaires and procedures, this progress was limited. The decision to print instructions that diffused but also interpreted the text of the law can be understood as the beginning of stronger control by the executive branch over the census. There were as yet no government employees specifically charged with preparing the census, and the results were still compiled in the field by the marshals. But for the first time the secretary of state had hired workers to prepare the publication of the report.[13] Up until then, the president or the secretary of state themselves had transmitted the results to Congress, and the printed reports were prepared by the existing services of the executive branch.[14]

The development of the federal government in this period equally concerned the census, which created its own demands on manpower. Instructions were necessitated by the fact that the required tasks had become more complex, in a period when the arithmetical competence of the majority of Americans, including members of Congress, was limited. For the first time, because of the questions concerning foreigners and professions, census workers could no longer put on one line the total of all the individuals enumerated in each family. The instructions, which were themselves complex, expressed this new challenge in the work of the census agents by suggesting that they put a box in red ink around the columns of subtotals, "which may keep them separate from the others, by a sensible impression constantly operating upon the mind."[15]

Secretary of State John Quincy Adams took care to be very precise, even didactic, in this development of the investigation. From this time on, the census posed qualitative, and therefore potentially ambiguous, questions, which required the marshal's assistant who asked these questions door-to-door to engage in some reflection and interpretation. The same was required of the member of the family who responded. At the same time, the secretary of state, in order to facilitate the work of compilation done in the field, provided a method for compiling and filling out the questionnaires. Printed questionnaires did not appear until the following census, but already the proposed model shows a desire for uniformity reiterated in the text of the instructions. It is clear that in 1820, at the moment when Congress recognized its own interest in broadening the field of investigation of the census, the status of the statistics changed. From a political instrument, they were in the process of becoming an object worthy of scientific interest as well as public curiosity.

In the questionnaires for the census of 1830—the first to be printed and distributed uniformly by the government—the three categories for professional activity were abandoned. Instead there appeared the first personal questions. At the end of the questionnaires, which were still organized by family and not by individuals, there were three categories for deaf-mutes, grouped by age and then by color: white deaf-mutes of less than fourteen years of age, from fourteen to twenty-five, and more than twenty-five years old. Next to this was a column for enumerating blind persons, and still under the heading of "white persons included in the foregoing," the column distinguishing foreigners. Then, under the heading "Slaves and colored persons included in foregoing," were four columns of statistics of infirmity, identical to those for whites.[16] The end-of-line placement of these questions, which counted certain individuals twice, was a way of limiting the kinds of errors that had cropped up in 1820 with the professional statistics, since the total had to be written down before completing these columns. Doubling these statistics, like those for age, produced a double body of demographic and physical data, which facilitated treating the two series, the white population and the black, as two phenomena with different paths of development.

While color is a central element in the American statistical apparatus, the first question that allowed the enumeration of foreigners did not appear until the fourth census, in 1820. That question distinguished "foreigners not naturalized." The 1830 census retained the same question, under the category "Aliens—foreigners not naturalized," that is to say, foreigners in the legal sense of the term, non-citizens, coming from another country. These distinctions, introduced by Congress, which fixed by law the list of questions to be asked, had no consequences for the calculation of political representation. While slaves counted for only three-fifths of free persons, immigrant aliens were an integral part of the constitutional population. The American census has always been a de facto census and not de jure: it counted as residents all those persons present in the country at the date of the census. The value of this question was more a matter of information, in knowing the composition of the population, than one of practical utility—all the more because at this time there was no federal legislation on immigration, as entry into and departure from the country happened freely up to 1875. The responses to the question also did not serve to measure the share of immigration in the population, since naturalized immigrants were not distinguished from the rest of the population. Given the state of tabulation techniques, it also did not permit establishment of the number of citizens, since to do so would have involved cross-checking responses with sex and age. In any case, this would not have yielded the number of potential voters, or of active citizens, since a large number of American men of more than twenty-one years of age did not yet have the right to vote due to various restrictions on suffrage imposed by the states. It was a matter of curiosity rather than the desire to produce data that could be used to redefine the political community.

As in 1820, the question on nationality applied only to whites. This was made explicit in the questionnaire: after the age categories, whose number had increased for whites as for free blacks and slaves, yet still without agreement, and the total number of residents, came five columns for "white persons included in the foregoing" and only four columns concerning "Slaves and colored persons included in foregoing."

This nationality question, relegated to the end of the questionnaire, seems to have been judged sufficiently unimportant by the legislators of 1840 that it disappeared from the list that year, even though it had seen an unprecedented growth of its categories. Not until the 1850 census, generally considered the first American census with a "scientific" character, did immigration appear as the object of official statistics. These forms, which were very detailed, covered a large number of social and economic questions, such as profession, education, and property, and took up the question from a different angle than in 1820 or 1830. The 1850 forms, like those of 1860, for the first time posed the question of place of birth and not of legal status—that is, they were concerned with nationality, in the American sense of the term, national origin, and not with citizenship.

3

The Census of 1840

Science, Politics, and "Insanity" of Free Blacks

In what may seem a paradoxical fashion, the census of 1840, later rated as "a humiliating failure," was conducted in a more favorable context than any preceding census: the power of the superintendent had grown, and already there existed the nucleus of a community of scientific experts.[1]

Patricia Cline Cohen, in one of the few works to analyze the spread of arithmetical knowledge in the colonies and the young republic, dates the awareness of the importance of accumulating and understanding quantifiable facts of all kinds to the 1790s. She sees the introduction of the question on professions in 1820 as the reflection of a change in American society. On the one hand, the idea had spread that there existed different classes within the population and that they could be identified—in other words, artisanal activities had left the farm for the workshop or the factory. Thus, it had been conceivable and even possible to ask participants to define themselves by their principal activity. On the other hand, a profound cultural change had taken place in the course of the 1810s, as gazettes and popular almanacs appeared, stuffed full of figures, and the teaching of arithmetic in the United States was transformed.[2]

These converging phenomena meant that, in just a few decades, statistical data and the capacity to understand them had become indispensable to anyone who claimed to speak seriously about national affairs. This was a significant change, for up to this time, the old political arithmetic had been disdained in the United States as a science of government, partly for lack of interest but also for lack of national data.

The census itself played a crucial role in this transition. With the volumes for 1790 and 1800, and especially after the publication of the 1810 report, it became possible to calculate the rate of growth of the population and to project, on the basis of the past, the curve of the population for the future.

Such information about the characteristics of the population undoubtedly had pedagogical value and must have aroused public interest. The first three censuses demonstrated that the American population was growing at a rate of 35 percent per decade. The historian Margo Anderson has shown that when these figures were compared to the English censuses of 1801 and 1811, it became apparent that the new country was quickly going to overtake and surpass the mother country.[3] At a time when the belief that a country's population was its main source of wealth was widely shared, these figures made the American nation conspicuous for its vigorous demographic growth. The population movement revealed by the census became a source of patriotic pride. The European reception of American statistical works attributed the recourse to figures to the American national character. The *Edinburgh Review* called Adam Seybert's *Statistical Annals*, published in 1818, pretentious and jingoistic, with its tables all showing the economic and demographic dynamism of the young nation. By converting data into percentages and simple growth rates, Seybert popularized a type of quantitative reasoning that nourished simultaneously both patriotism and the fad for figures that made it possible to rank regions and nations by performance. The Scottish critic added that the typical American was "vulgar and arithmetical," lacking precisely what could not be quantified in these tables: culture, genius, science, and art.[4] For its part, the US Congress saw enough value in Seybert's work to finance its publication and wide distribution.[5]

Statistical publications of all kinds multiplied throughout the 1820s and 1830s. The growing public interest in what would come to be called moral statistics, on the poor and disabled, was fed by the growth of the movement for reform of public health. The public and private production of such statistics reinforced this trend, which was also visible in the 1840 census.

This first period ended in 1839 with the founding, under the leadership of Lemuel Shattuck, of the American Statistical Association in Boston, even though the event had few immediate consequences. In the beginning, it was an association uniting those individuals interested in statistics for various reasons. Among them were a significant number of physicians seeking statistics on mortality and life expectancy, who rubbed elbows with other "statisticians" more preoccupied with collecting varied data on the past. These antiquarians cared about things like the number of horse-drawn carriages in such-and-such a county of New England in the colonial era. The flaws that marked the 1840 census led the American Statistical Association to become an expert lobby to the government, consulting on and overseeing the census, which thus entered into its scientific era.

The Beginnings of the Politicization of the Statistical Debate on Slavery

The 1840 census was the first to be carried out under the direction of a "Superintendent of the Census" rather than under the direct supervision of the president or the secretary of state.[6] The first man to hold the superintendent post was William A. Weaver. This change marked a new stage in the development of the federal statistical apparatus, now with its own staff. But Weaver's personality and the errors made in the published results struck a fatal blow to the "numerical gullibility" that characterized American enthusiasm for statistics of all kinds.[7]

Weaver's background had in no way prepared him for this task: he had been obliged to leave the Navy and had then made unsuccessful bids for a diplomatic post in Havana and in the Balearic Islands. In the month following his nomination he engaged two assistants, as authorized by the law: one was his own brother, the other a young relative of a State Department accountant. Between April and December 1839, Weaver and his two staff members compiled questionnaires, obtained the president's endorsement, and had the new questionnaires printed and sent to the marshals.[8] The new questionnaires were extremely ambitious in the extent of the data they planned to collect, going well beyond what had been started in 1820.

In each census, new questions had been added, but in 1840, in the context of a widespread demand for statistics of all kinds, Weaver increased to seven the number of columns on professional activities; added two columns in the middle of the questionnaire to take down the name and age of veterans receiving government pensions (in order to purge the lists of fraud); and added at the end of the questionnaire columns for information on schools and universities, as well as one reporting the number of white persons more than twenty years of age who did not know how to read or write. In addition to the many columns on age, this made for a questionnaire of seventy-four columns, not counting the marginal ones.[9]

The problems embedded in the questionnaires, and the fact that Weaver himself remained aloof from the actual conduct of the census in the field, became evident only after the compilation and publication of the census findings. The change of presidential administration raised Daniel Webster to the post of secretary of state, and one of the consequences of this development was that the contract for printing the census was withdrawn from the usual printer for Congress, Blair & Rives, and was awarded in September 1841 to a printer close to the Whigs, Thomas Allen, even though the rivals had already begun the work of printing. Weaver, who held the copyright on the Blair & Rives edition, continued to provide them with data; Blair & Rives, believing that they still had the legal contract, went on with the job. This meant that the census of 1840 was published in two editions.[10] Weaver had taken sides with Blair & Rives against Webster and was thus forced to step down in the spring of 1842. It was in these unfavorable circumstances that the results of the sixth census of the United States appeared. Reading the reports by Congress on the conflict between the printers allowed Patricia Cohen to see at what stage errors crept into the published results, since the reports provide an exceptionally detailed picture of the stages of the work of compilation. She showed that the errors came mainly from the transcription of the original questionnaires onto lists prepared for the published volumes, in which the column headings were slightly different, while the state of mathematical knowledge of the period did not permit an understanding of how errors on a limited number of individuals had been amplified. Contemporary critics advanced the hypothesis of fraud or carelessness at the time the data were recorded.[11]

The most egregious errors concerned the insanity statistics for blacks of the northern states, blacks who were all free by this date. Following the other questions on the "dependent classes," Weaver had added questions on the number of "insane or idiot" persons, separated by color. Among whites, without distinction of gender, there were deaf-mutes, blind persons, "insane and idiots at public charge," and "insane and idiots at private charge"; in the following columns appeared the same categories for the "colored persons" counted in the preceding columns, with no distinction between free blacks and slaves. These columns fell at the end of the second page of the questionnaire, which was printed on the verso of the first page, and this made it easy to put in numbers inconsistent with those on the recto.[12]

The numerous and egregious errors were pointed out as early as the summer of 1842 by Dr. Edward Jarvis, a specialist in insanity who was familiar with medical statistics, being a member of the young American Statistical Association. He was surprised to read the figures on insanity as published in the Blair & Rives edition. It appeared that northern blacks suffered a rate of insanity ten times higher than that for southern blacks, and what was especially remarkable, the rate increased the farther north one went. Jarvis calculated these rates by comparing the number of insane blacks to the total number of blacks in the state. Altogether, the rate in the North was 1 "insane or idiot" black per 162.4, while in the South, the rate was 1 in 1,558. The rate for whites scarcely varied between the North (1 in 970) and the South (1 in 945.3).[13] This finding was surprising, but it generally conformed to the widespread opinion of the time, according to which northern blacks suffered from being left to their own devices, while in the South slavery protected them from these worries.

But in a second article, published in September 1842 in the same journal, Jarvis reviewed the figures in greater detail and showed that it was a question of blatant errors. For example, Worcester, Massachusetts was stated to have 133 insane blacks, while in fact the city had no blacks at all, as one might see by looking at the line total for the city, even though the city did have a mental asylum with which Jarvis, as a Massachusetts resident and as a doctor, was well acquainted. This finding led him to systematically search for other, less obvious errors, which turned out to be numerous. His conclusion left no room for doubt: the mistakes had been made in Washington, at the Census Bureau, as the returns from the marshals were being combined and totaled.[14]

Actually, the errors were easy to find for anyone willing to take the trouble to look for them. Thus, in the Thomas Allen edition, which presented the data by counties and by major cities, there were instances of flagrant errors in the presentation of statistics on the insanity of blacks in the northern states. In the state of Maine, Somerset County had five "colored insane at private charge" and five "colored insane at public charge," which made ten blacks afflicted with insanity, yet the county had only sixteen black men and six black women. The statistics by city had the greatest number of inconsistencies. In Biddeford, Maine there was only one black person, a woman between the ages of thirty-six and fifty-five, but two "insane colored persons." In Danvers, Massachusetts there were no blacks, but there were stated to be two insane blacks.[15]

These results gave rise to two diametrically opposed interpretations: on the one hand, the spokesmen of the South, defending slavery, found in the 1840 census the mathematical proof of the inability of blacks to adapt to freedom; on the other, readers challenged the census findings, either out of statistical rigor or out of opposition to slavery. The lengthy debate that followed constitutes the first important occasion when census findings lay at the heart of a political controversy. On both sides, the credibility of the figures was a function of partisan choice more often than of mathematical competence, especially because the debate revolved around figures reprinted in almanacs and reviews, with readers and writers alike seldom taking the trouble to consult the complete census volumes, even though this would have allowed them to find flagrant errors.[16] To make such an effort would presuppose a degree of skepticism that was still rare with regard to official figures and tables reprinted in the reviews, and the effort would be still greater insofar as the data, by establishing a proportional relationship between the rate of insanity among blacks and their geographical location as one went north, only served to support widely held views.

After 1842, the existence of the errors had been demonstrated for anyone willing to admit it, but the rigorous proofs of Jarvis and other experts carried little force in the face of the motivations that led partisans of slavery to buttress themselves with these figures in the context of defending the "peculiar institution."

Census officials fiercely refused to admit that errors had occurred in the compilation of the findings. Weaver was particularly defensive because his reputation and income were at stake. The new secretary of state John C. Calhoun, who had charge of the census and who was unquestionably the most important southern politician of the day, was defensive because he had relied heavily on data from the 1840 census to defend slavery.[17] These statistics came in just in time to prove the physical and moral degeneration of freed blacks, as seen in an anonymous article in the *Southern Literary Messenger* of June 1843. Commenting on the insanity statistics for blacks, which corroborated other statistics such as their higher rate of imprisonment, their higher mortality, or the poverty that affected them in greater numbers, the author concluded: "The free negroes of the northern states are the most vicious persons on this continent, perhaps on the earth."[18]

The publication of this article marked a turning point in the debate, pitting the defenders of slavery against the statisticians grouped around Jarvis and other members of the American Statistical Association. After the appearance of this piece in the *Southern Literary Messenger*, Jarvis demanded publicly that Congress investigate these absurd findings, in deference to "the honor of our country, to medical science, and to truth."[19] From this moment on, the issue became a polemic in Congress between southern representatives and northern abolitionists, all proclaiming a basis of scientific truth that few were capable of, or interested in, verifying for themselves. The importance of this polemic, over what was in the end a minor point in the census data, was that quantitative data were thereafter a major element in the debate over slavery, which until that time had been argued in moral terms by the abolitionists.

The authority of the figures and that of the official US census were invoked throughout the decade and beyond by the defenders of slavery, foreshadowing the use that would be made of differential mortality statistics for whites, blacks, and mulattoes in the following decades.[20] The quarrel over the figures allowed a new rhetoric—a mix of statistical expertise and of ideological and moral commitment—to enter the political debate. The partisans of slavery most often took the most categorical positions, presenting, with the aid of the figures, proofs of the degeneracy of blacks, while the critics of the results of the 1840 census spoke in a more measured tone. Whether it was Jarvis himself or the other statisticians of the American Statistical Association, such as Archibald Russell, their tone was that of experts who methodically pointed out errors without directly blaming pro-slavery ideology for them. But these two positions were not the only ones, and other actors, often less well known, intervened in the controversy.

Representatives of the black community addressed petitions and memorials to Congress on the subject of the shocking statistics. What is remarkable about this mobilization is that the petitions functioned at two levels, that of expertise and that of morality: they noted factual errors in the census and at the same time proved, by their very composition, that the black community was not degenerate. A notable example was the memorial written by Dr. James McCune Smith,

a well-known black doctor in New York, who also compiled several rigorous statistical articles to refute the southern claims.[21] Another notable memorial, which
was preserved in the Senate archives, was signed by a group of black citizens of
the state of New York on 25 May 1844. It is worthy of attention for showing
how quantitative rhetoric became central to the discussion of slavery and the
advancement of the free black population. Secretary of State Calhoun, in a letter
to a member of Congress dated 18 April 1844, buttressing himself with the figures of the 1840 census, wrote that after their emancipation in the North, "the
African race has sunken into vice and pauperism." In this petition, these citizens
denounced Calhoun's claims that while "in all other States that have retained the
ancient relations (the slave States, meaning,) between them (the races, meaning), they (the slaves, meaning,) have improved greatly in every respect, in number, comfort, intelligence and morals." Refuting Calhoun's arguments point by
point, the "free colored citizens of the city and county of New York" made clear
that the demonstration of the internal contradiction of this reasoning was found
in the statistical tables, for whoever wanted to take the trouble to examine them.
The petitioners concluded their protest with an exhaustive table of states and
cities where the population of color was equal to zero and where the number of
insane persons of color was greater than zero.[22] It is remarkable that these citizens showed perfect mastery of quantitative rhetoric, including tabular presentation, which reveals a degree of familiarity with statistical methods that was far
from typical of the majority of their interlocutors.

Going beyond the simple identification and refutation of errors, the writers undertook to present figures in support of the progress of the black population in the North. For example, they showed that northern blacks had a ratio
of churches to residents significantly higher than in the South. Making use of
the same quantitative rhetoric as the less scrupulous users of the 1840 census
results, the writers refuted their claims by producing statistics, drawn from the
census and other sources, comparing mortality rates and educational statistics
for blacks of the North and South, free and slave.[23]

Finally, the petition flatly rejected Calhoun's comments on the degeneracy
of blacks—a political battleground on which the experts had not engaged. It
criticized the very concept of the census, in how questionnaires and reports isolated the social problems of blacks from other social questions. In conclusion,
it demanded that the 1840 census should become the object of an inquiry; that
a General Office of Registration be set up in Washington "with a proper officer
at its head"; and that the 1850 census should record the number of adults who
could not read or write among "the whites, the slaves, and the free persons of
color in every county of the United States."[24]

These black citizens of New York were not opposed to the idea that blacks
should form a distinct class of residents in the census. On the contrary, what

they demanded was equality in the type of statistical treatment applied to blacks and whites. From this point of view, their criticisms were intended to improve the work of the census. Although severe, the criticisms were aimed at Weaver's census and not at the institution that had established the practice of producing separate data for whites and blacks. In this they espoused the demands of Jarvis, Archibald Russell, and, more generally, of the experts united around the young American Statistical Association, to which they added their own political demands. Perhaps they were in contact with members of this group, and especially with Russell, who was a fellow New Yorker and head of the American Geographical and Statistical Society.[25] While this is not known, this group of black abolitionists, as early as 1844, had taken up quantitative rhetoric and its techniques, expecting that the following census would prove the opposite of the thesis held by Calhoun—that is, that it would measure the progress of the black population, in order to contradict the figures supporting those interpretations of the 1840 census.

Another, similar petition was addressed to Congress by a group of Pennsylvania citizens. The Select Committee of Congress responded that, four years after the facts, there was not much that could be done.[26] These petitions, like all the other efforts in this direction, whether the work of figures of the black community in the northern states or of statistical experts who found in this a means to reinforce their scientific legitimacy, met with only partial success.[27] Congress recognized that the 1840 census contained numerous and serious errors, but it refused to have it officially revised or to publish corrected figures. However, these errors led Congress to place the 1850 census under the supervision of a Census Board composed of three experts. Everyone agreed that the census of 1850 was of much better quality than that of 1840, which did not prevent the two camps from immediately latching onto the new figures on the respective conditions of slaves and free blacks, especially the statistics showing their differential rates of mortality.

The polemic was not stifled by these scientific refutations, because the defenders of the 1840 census clung to these providential results. Weaver himself responded with extremely weak arguments to demonstrations of the incoherence of the data on the insanity of blacks.

We now know how the errors slipped into the published volumes: the slight differences between the manuscript questionnaires and tables compiled in Washington by Weaver and his aides for purposes of publication were the primary source of error, since the data were thus reported in incorrect lines and columns. In the case of the statistics on the insanity of free blacks, which was far from the most serious error, it appears from a rereading of the manuscripts that a goodly number of elderly or aged persons, white or black, were listed as "idiot" by the census agents, which is to say that senility was assimilated to insanity.

These persons were frequently added by mistake as "insane" and black, due to the proximity of the columns in the tables prepared for publication.

The problem arises not so much from the material source of errors, which scholars like Patricia Cline Cohen have been able to retrace a century and a half later, as from the impossibility at that time of correcting demonstrable errors—an impossibility fostered by the incompetence of the officials who felt they were being personally accused, Weaver first and foremost, and also by the blindness that allowed them to view these results as plausible. Together, these factors permitted propagators of theories on the inferiority of blacks to continue to use the official census of the United States as their warranty.

The last census of this first period lived on as the synonym for the gravest errors committed by the American census, to the point that Edward Jarvis, writing twenty-five years later to James Garfield concerning the preparation of the census of 1870, returned to the data on insanity as an example of good and bad statistics.[28] Jarvis gave the example to show how manifest errors could be upheld for reasons of anti-abolitionist propaganda.

The history of the census of the population, which is entwined with that of the diffusion of statistics and numbers among the American population, was marked in this period by efforts to know the composition of the population by making finer and finer distinctions among residents, by sex, by age, and by profession and disability, while maintaining two separate statistical populations according to race. For contemporaries, the fact that the early censuses, even when their questionnaires were quite brief, divided the population into two large groups, blacks and whites, was not a cause for comment. The federal census was far from being the only source to present these first statistics in this way. The idea that blacks and whites, in the federal census, constituted in a sense two separate types of humanity signals one of the causes of the errors that marked the results of the 1840 census. But at this time, population statistics, which more and more authors and readers anticipated and commented upon (without always having the necessary competence), had become part of the stakes in the conflict between North and South. This instrumentalization of the census facilitated the growth of a community of statistical experts who, through their close involvement in the preparation of the 1850 census, brought the federal census out of its period of infancy.

PART II

SLAVES, FORMER SLAVES, BLACKS, AND MULATTOES

Identification of the Individual and the Statistical Segregation of Populations (1850–1865)

On 9 April 1850, as they had done every ten years since 1790, the members of Congress were to discuss the upcoming census. For the first time, the plan for the census proposed collecting, for each individual, information about age, name, and color, including for slaves, who were to be enumerated on a separate, shorter questionnaire. From the start of the Senate's examination of the questionnaires prepared by the Census Board, Senator King of Alabama proposed to amend the text concerning the second questionnaire, in order to eliminate the question on the place of birth for slaves. Since slaves were frequently sold, he proposed instead simply to count them, rather than to record the name of each individual as was done for free residents, by replacing the word "names" with "numbers" in the article of the law.[1]

To the objection raised by the defenders of the new questionnaires, who maintained that to obtain the names of slaves like those of other residents would limit the risk of error, especially the risk of double-counting, the southern senators responded with derision:

SEN. BADGER [NORTH CAROLINA]: What do you want of such names as Big Cuff and Little Cuff?

SEN. BUTLER: Or Little Jonah and Big Jonah? [Laughter]

SEN. UNDERWOOD:[2] I have no particular anxiety to see these classical names that have been suggested, and whether it be Cicero or Cuff, it makes no difference to me.[3]

Behind this seemingly light dialogue were two key issues concerning the census and the balance of powers between the federal government and the states, especially the southern states. The first was whether slaves were residents or property. The second issue was whether government had the authority to collect in the states social statistics that went well beyond its constitutional mandate of counting residents for the purpose of apportioning representatives' seats and taxes. The question of the enumeration of slaves would disappear with Emancipation, but its legacy was still an issue in the census of 1870, one of whose tasks was to count the former slaves whose right to vote had been denied. The question of the federal government's right to collect general statistics on various subjects outside of its constitutional mission would continue to unite the defenders of states' rights. But in the course of the stormy and often confused debates of the years 1849 and 1850 over the census, the US census entered into its adulthood while the Union entered its gravest crisis. The history of the census during the decades spanning from the sectional crisis to Reconstruction thus inevitably involves the political history of this period of crisis. Its legacy can still be seen today in the debates over the use of the census to correct racial inequalities.

The census, in the context of the growing strain between North and South, was certainly not the most important issue debated by Congress. But the censuses of 1850, 1860, and 1870 were conceived and conducted in this context by the legislative and executive branches, while the results—especially the data on free blacks and slaves—were exploited by both camps, even in the official reports, for propaganda. If the slavery issue provoked the biggest arguments, the enumeration of all individuals beginning in 1850 also revealed the rapid demographic changes taking place since the 1840s. First and foremost was the new immigration, which by its size and origin would become the main focus of the census after Emancipation. The perfecting of techniques, coinciding with the arrival of new immigrants, first Irish and then Asians (much less numerous but more noticeable), would bring about increasing sophistication of data on origins. This involved a double movement of racialization of origins of non-European immigrants and progressive ethnicization of European immigrants, largely upon their own impulse. This section shows how the detailed identification of each free individual lay at the heart of this modernization, while slaves remained separate. The census of 1870, the first after the abolition of slavery, was charged with settling this matter. At the same time the disappearance of slaves coincided with the multiplication of racial categories, a development in reaction to the first massive wave of immigration, which began in the 1840s.

These decades constituted an important turning point, a second foundation of the federal statistical apparatus. The classification of slaves was the model for other kinds of distinctions made by the census in the second half of the nineteenth century. For this reason, this section is devoted to American slaves and their descendants in the only two censuses that provided precise information on them before Emancipation.

4

Whether to Name or Count Slaves

The Refusal of Identification

In the context of the crisis between sections that had become increasingly bitter since the Missouri Compromise of 1820, the place of slaves in the census was an extremely sensitive question because it involved, beyond the comparative merits of free or slave societies, the division of powers between the federal government and the states, as well as between the executive power and Congress.[1] As a result, the resolutions achieved through these debates came through political compromises that often overshadowed scientific arguments. But due to the emergence of experts in the 1840s, even if the text of the law remained under political control, the conduct of the census, the compilation of the data, and their interpretation thereafter left room for the technicians, who strengthened their authority beginning with the preparation of the census of 1850.

The Census Board of 1849, First Victory of the Experts

The 1850 census, heralded as the "first scientific census" of the United States, made a clean break with its predecessors of the first half of the century and solidified the influence of the reformer statisticians, who found in it a way to make up for the catastrophic census of 1840.[2] But they did not win their victory easily, given the degree of distrust of the federal government. Many members of Congress, especially those from the South, relayed these concerns, advancing political and legal arguments on the limits of the federal executive power. On 1 March 1849, when the 1850 census was broached for the first time in the Senate, there were forceful objections to the plan proposed by Senator Davis to greatly broaden the field of investigation of the census. Senators Westcott and Calhoun competed in the eloquence of their attacks on the waste of public money to obtain information that they believed was useless, such as the number of barn-yard animals or the differing cost of labor between slaves and free men.

For Senator James Westcott of Florida, Congress had exceeded its constitu-tional mandate, which limited the census to the enumeration of residents:

> Congress, they [voters and taxpayers] will say, has no right to take the public money and employ the public officers in getting philosophical and medical and physiological information about the slave laborers or about free laborers.[3]

John C. Calhoun of South Carolina, the great defender of states' rights and of the South against the federal government, outdid Westcott in viewing the census as an attempt to concentrate power, just like the creation of the Patent Office: "Ours is a Federal Government, not a National Government." What riled him was not so much the standardization on a national scale as the abuse of power. For him, information other than basic demographic data should be collected by statistical investigations conducted by the states. In order to place limits on the jurisdic-tion of the federal government in this domain as in others, he proposed return-ing to the first census law, that of 1790, which effectively limited the information collected to the areas specifically mentioned in the Constitution.

On the other side were the partisans of the extension of the census. These men came mainly from the northern states, like Davis, who emphasized the importance of economic information for the enlightened conduct of affairs of state. Senator Badger made a distinction between the census, which was neces-sary, and "statistics," by which he meant vague economic data, which should be the object of a separate process. Badger was not hostile to the proposed inves-tigations, but he thought their proper place was not as part of the census. The political origin of the census in the Constitution was the central argument of those who wanted to limit its scope, because the census was at that time the only statistical apparatus for collecting demographic or economic data on the national scale; the only other type of data systematically collected and published by the federal government at this time was the annual figures on import taxes.[4]

The most determined proponent of broadening the scope of the census was Robert M. T. Hunter of Virginia:

> Sir, I know of nothing which has contributed more to the advance of political science than the increased attention which has been paid to statistics, and the opportunity which has thus been accorded of test-ing theory according to experience. Especially it is important for the American statesman to obtain a full and accurate view of all the parts of the vast society whose machinery he directs. He should have all

possible facilities for studying our progress, and tracing the connection between cause and effect.[5]

This rhetoric, which makes the art of government into a science and the president of the United States into a great social engineer, was completely opposed to the defense of states' rights preached by the members who spoke for the South.[6]

Tied to the question of the broadening of the scope of the census was that of the growth of the federal government. The initial plan envisioned entrusting the conception and the realization of the census to a group consisting of the secretaries of state, treasury, and interior; in a second version, this task was delegated to a Census Board, issuing from the executive power. At this time, the Department of Interior did not yet exist, and the plan for the census law was among the factors working in favor of the creation of this new department. Senator Westcott immediately denounced this plan, which entrusted three government officials with preparing the law that would be submitted to Congress in the following session, as a transfer of powers in favor of the executive branch, and in this he was not wrong. He also repeated that if the various statistics sought by the project were necessary, it would fall to the states to collect them. Nonetheless, the plan calling for the creation of the Census Board was adopted by the majority of the senators, and the board was ordered to prepare and present a detailed plan for the session of 1849–50.[7]

The most important change introduced by this wide-ranging project of demographic, economic, and social statistical investigation was the shift from the familial level for collection of information, which had been used since 1790, to individual data. From then on, it was no longer a question simply of counting the members of each family and noting their number in the different categories. Rather, it was a question of devoting to each individual, with his first and last names, a whole line of the principal schedule. This made it possible to know which characteristics corresponded to each individual, and opened the possibility of cross-checking the figures, even if that would not be put into effect until thirty years later.

The other great innovation was the division of the census into six separate schedules, as follows: (1) free inhabitants; (2) slaves; (3) mortality (information on persons who had died during the past year); (4) agriculture; (5) manufactures; and (6) social statistics (taxes; numbers of schools, of newspapers, of churches; criminality; and libraries within the district).

Finally, the labor of tabulating the data, compiled from handwritten schedules onto printed forms prepared by the Census Office, would be centralized in Washington instead of taking place at the level of the marshals who up until then had transmitted to Washington the data aggregated by themselves.

These major changes were attained by J. C. G. Kennedy, who was named secretary of the Census Board by the Whig president Zachary Taylor by May 1849, before being confirmed by Congress as superintendent a year later. They were conceived and organized by the two experts whom Kennedy brought to the Census Board: Lemuel Shattuck of the American Statistical Association and Archibald Russell of the American Geographical Association.[8] Three other important statisticians of the period also offered their services and submitted their plans to the Census Board: Jesse Chickering, who compiled the first solid statistics on immigration; Nahum Capen; and Edward Jarvis.[9] The Census Board, which consolidated the importance of the experts, was created thanks to the action of Senator Davis, who was able to convince his skeptical colleagues of the necessity of advance planning for this vast enterprise, indispensable to the smooth progress of public affairs. It was composed of three members: the secretary of state; the secretary of the interior, a new authority over the census; and the postmaster general. The real power lay in the hands of the secretary of the Census Board, Joseph Camp Griffith Kennedy, a thirty-six-year-old Pennsylvanian who owed his nomination to his affiliation with the president's Whig party, and the two experts he had called to his side, Shattuck and Russell.[10] Together, the three men formulated in detail and prepared the six schedules presented to the Senate's Select Committee on the Census in January 1850.[11] The six schedules were not particularly complex in themselves, but their length and the shift to individual data, as opposed to data at the household level, created more work for the marshals' assistants in the field and made it necessary to carry out the rationalization and centralization of the treatment of the manuscript forms in Washington.

From its announcement in the report of the Census Board and then in the president's message to Congress, this ambitious program, developed over several months by highly motivated experts, provoked a serious conflict of authority with the Select Committee on the Census, formed by the Senate. According to tradition, the senators thought that it would be up to them to draft the questions on the form, and they had charged this committee with preparing it, although the preceding session appeared to have settled this point once and for all. Meanwhile Kennedy had submitted to them in January 1850 the schedules as established by the Census Board—which issued from the executive power—complete and ready to be printed and utilized. The Select Committee on the Census believed that its task was not only to draw up the law defining the census but also to write the schedules. Kennedy, thinking in good faith that the Census Board had been created precisely for this purpose, had sent the six schedules to the printer by January 1850. Finally, after a sometimes tense debate on the respective jurisdictions of the legislative and the executive powers—since Kennedy reported to the secretary of the interior and was not directly under the authority of Congress—the law was adopted, largely in the terms prepared by Shattuck, Russell, and Kennedy, on 23 May 1850, just one week before the start of the census.[12]

The senators' first reaction was an attempt to drain Kennedy's plan of its substance by amending the essence of the innovations. Some senators even proposed returning to the law of 1840, denying to the executive the right to conduct such a detailed inquiry on the population and economy of the states. It is in this context, in the midst of the crisis over the Compromise of 1850, that the law organizing the 1850 census made its way laboriously through the two chambers. Kennedy and his defenders in Congress succeeded in preserving the essence of the progress proposed by the Census Board, but the Slave Schedule had several categories deleted after vigorous debates. These fears were not the only ones, though they were the strongest; the question of slavery naturally crystallized the tensions between the defenders of states' rights and the partisans of greater efficacy of the federal government.

Another widespread fear concerned the use of the census for fiscal purposes, as well as the fear of a census of religious affiliations. This theme cropped up anew in the House in the speech of Rep. David S. Kaufman of Texas, who maintained that broadening the investigative scope of the census was contrary to both the letter and the spirit of the Constitution.[13] Making a distinction between "enumeration," the term used in the laws of the first censuses as well as in the publications, and "census," a term that in his view applied to property, he stated:

> This bill proposes to take an account of all the property in the United States. Now it is *population* and not *property*, except slave property, that is the basis of taxation and representation under the Constitution of the United States.[14]

Since slaves were at the same time both inhabitants and property, this would complicate any statistical inquiry that was both demographic and economic. In one way, the three-fifths compromise by which the Constitution had organized the census had solved the problem as long as the schedules did not identify everyone individually. The three-fifths rule was upheld for the calculation of apportionment while slavery lasted, but the new possibility of distinguishing each person raised the problem in a different way.[15]

Several interventions by northern representatives suggested taking advantage of the census in order to gather detailed data on slaves. Charles E. Clarke of New York, for example, proposed using the census to get a better idea of their number and to see whether certain states had admitted them as contraband after the interdiction of the slave trade in 1808, by recording the place of birth of slaves as was done for free people.

A South Carolina representative responded to this suggestion by stating that the purpose of several amendments and that of the whole plan for the new census was solely to create abolitionist propaganda and to point a finger at the flaws of southern society. This opinion seems to have been widely shared by the southern representatives, who viewed the census as an engine of war of the North against the South. In reality, once the results were published, the pamphleteers of the South were as quick as those of the North to use the statistics on slavery and the data on the poor and poverty in the North to help plead their cause. Finally, to pour oil on the troubled waters, Rep. Cartter of Ohio pointed out that in the South the census would be conducted by Southerners:

> The marshals of the several States are charged with the duty of taking the census of their respective States; they appoint the deputies, those deputies sustain neighborhood relation to the fields of their duty, imbued with all the sympathies, and possessed with all the prejudices peculiar to the institution and interests of their locality—as far as their labor is connected with slavery and its effects.[16]

On this question as for others, political patronage guaranteed a local interpretation of orders, which certainly influenced the results.[17] In general, it seems that many southern representatives saw in the extension of the census a gain in power by the federal government and thus a threat to the "peculiar institution." The plan prepared by the reformers who wanted to modernize the census was thus debated in a context where modernization of tools of the federal government was perceived not as progress from which all would benefit, but rather as an attempt to strengthen the power of the federal government to the detriment of the South and its traditions. This explains why the most hotly debated questions were those bearing on property in general and especially on that form of private property that consisted of slaves.

Slaves: Numbers Without Voice nor Memory

The debate in the Senate in May 1850 is worth reconstructing in detail, since it focused on the burning questions of slavery and, more broadly, the difference between races. The second schedule of 1850, reserved for slaves and much shorter than the first schedule which concerned free inhabitants, unleashed passions as no earlier census law ever had. In the initial plan, the second schedule was supposed to resemble that for free people, but in the course of the debates it was considerably shortened.

The condescending tone of the exchange cited earlier on the first names of slaves is a hint of the paternalism that characterized slavery as practiced in the American South. Cuff, Jonah, and Cicero were in wide use as first names among slaves, but they had different symbolic value. While the senators appear to indicate that the first names of slaves are interchangeable and to some extent unimportant, the three examples given show at least empirical knowledge of the rules for naming slaves, which owed nothing to chance. In this irony lay the desire to dispossess slaves of the power of choosing their own names, or even the will to deny them the intellectual capacity to do so.

Even in anglicized form, Cuff retains a link with the languages and names of Africa, while biblical names like Jonah spread along with the evangelization of slaves. Classical names like Cicero testify to the acculturation of slaves within the Anglo-American society of the American South and may refer to other practices for the transmission of first names, whose meaning might have escaped white observers.[18] Ridiculed by the senators, these examples deny slaves the aptitude for consciously expressing rootedness, the transmission of a familial or cultural heritage that could not be completely mastered by the masters. What is at play here is at once the possibility for slaves to choose the names of their children and their status as human beings endowed with a personality, an identity, and a history. In denying all this as well as the existence of a stock of names having rules and symbols, Senators Badger and Butler hint at removing slaves' humanity, a theme that would develop throughout the debates.

By proposing to replace the word "names" with "numbers" in the plan submitted by Kennedy—that is to say, to count and enumerate slaves rather than to name them—they returned slaves to their status as property, or "chattel" to use an expression often employed. "Numbers" here signifies both quantity and numbering, thus making slaves literally into numbers. While schedule no. 1, reserved for free inhabitants, recorded line by line "the name of every person whose usual place of abode on the 1st day of June, 1850, was in this family," schedule no. 2, for "Slave Inhabitants," reported on each line the name of the slave owner and, in the seven following columns, information concerning the slaves he owned. The debate thus concerned a relatively minor point in the work of the census, whether in column 2 of this schedule the census agent would record the names of the slaves or assign them numbers. While this would not require any substantial modification of the form, it carried a heavy political or even philosophical or anthropological weight, since what was at stake in the polemic was whether or not to name slaves like the persons (free individuals) on schedule no. 1.[19]

Senator Davis of Massachusetts showed the greatest concern for the improvement of the census. He had no objection in principle to the substitution of "numbers" for "names" in the text of the law. Rather, his argument was technical. He did not respond on a political or philosophical level, but put forward the imperative of the smooth running of the census. Emphasizing technical neutrality and defending effectiveness will always be the preferred position of reformers, while their adversaries are in general more inclined to use political arguments. Thus, he pointed out that "names" had been used for more precise information and in order to reduce the possibility of fraud. Taking up an even more defensive position, Senator Butler replied that he did not see the point of obtaining names of slaves, since it had not been done before, thus openly indicating that the improvement of the quality of the census was not his first concern, even though he was a member of the Select Committee on the Census.[20] Following up on this, he remarked that on large plantations with several hundred slaves, there would be many who would have the same name and would only be known by nicknames or last names. Davis and Underwood once again explained that the best and surest way of knowing how many slaves an owner possessed was to enumerate them by their names, which would limit the risk of double counts or omissions.[21]

Underwood tried to reassure his colleagues by reminding them that the names would not be published: "The names of the white population are not proposed to be published, nor are the names of the blacks."[22] He even stated, presenting himself as a recent convert to the usefulness of statistics, that early on the idea that the government would have a list of names of inhabitants had struck him as being a "monstrous sort of proposition," but that he later became convinced this would be the best way to do the count. The agents would be able to work more quickly and to furnish reliable data for the calculations.[23]

Senator Clemens of Alabama raised the objection that the owners of large plantations could not possibly know the names of all their slaves, which would oblige the agents to go to the slave quarters themselves, an idea implicitly rejected as shocking and absurd. Underwood, himself the senator of a slave state, remarked that in his home state of Kentucky, there were no big plantations and that, in his experience, if masters knew the age of their slaves there was no reason why they would not know their names. The question of knowing how many children female slaves had gave rise to an exchange that bluntly revealed the political lines of fracture.

All these arguments—often sound or made in the name of the progress of knowledge—did not cause the southern members to give in, and the amendment replacing "names" by "numbers" in the law was finally passed. Thus, while the most important innovation introduced in the 1850 census was the individualization of data, slaves benefited only partially from this progress in the methods of the census. The southern members were anxious to know the situation of slaves, gaining in the committee the introduction of supplementary questions such as the number of freed or fugitive slaves, from which they hoped to build arguments for the defense of southern interests.[24] As part of this concern, personal questions concerning slaves were retained but in a form that preserved the political compromise by treating slaves more as property than as human beings.

In accordance with the law adopted at the conclusion of the debates, the Instructions to the assistant marshals instructed them very precisely in how to complete schedule no. 2, emphasizing that "in the case of slaves, numbers are to be substituted for names,"[25] which might lead to the conclusion that this method was not to be taken for granted. Columns 3 and 4 (age and sex) were identical to columns 5 and 6 of schedule no. 1. For the first time, for slaves and free persons alike, the exact age of each individual would be known, making possible precise comparisons of their longevity. Following the amendments proposed in the Senate in May, out of the eight columns of the schedule, two concerned slaves who, during the past year, had disappeared and not been returned (column 6) or who had been freed (column 7).[26] Column 8 took account of slaves who were "deaf and dumb, blind, insane, or idiotic." Although not noted in the heading of the column, the instructions stated that if the slaves were imprisoned at the date of the census, the nature of the crime should be listed in column 8 and opposite this, under the name of the owner, the date of imprisonment. This procedure was the same as for free persons (column 13 of schedule no. 1), with the difference that in the case of free persons the heading of the column was more detailed: "Deaf and dumb, blind, insane, idiotic, pauper, or convict." By definition, slaves could not fall into the category of paupers. Strangely, the instructions for column 8 of the schedule for slaves stated that in the event that the assistant marshal encountered slaves afflicted with one of these infirmities, he should note, opposite the name or number of this slave, the term "deaf and dumb," "blind," "insane," or "idiotic," as appropriate. The mention of "name or number" is surprising and in contradiction to the rest of the instructions, which eliminated slaves' names from the census. Perhaps it was a holdover from an earlier version of the instructions.[27]

Finally, as for schedule no. 1, the individual format of the data gave rise to a column for noting the "color" of slaves, a choice made possible by the distinction, newly adopted in 1850 by the US census, between "black" and "mulatto," which presumed that slaves could not, in principle, be either whites or Indians.

Color, Race, and Origin of Slaves and Free Persons

"White," "Black," and "Mulatto" in the Censuses of 1850 and 1860

The census of 1860, save for some inconsequential changes, followed the format of the 1850 census, given the lack of agreement on a new law in 1860. The schedules and the instructions were thus virtually identical to those of 1850. This is why the debates that took place in 1849 and 1850 are essential, since they determined the racial classification of slaves and free persons until the census of 1870, the first census after Emancipation. This amounts to saying that the source of the most complete set of quantitative data on slaves available to historians was determined by the debates of 1850, and that the categories that were adopted and the procedures put in place in the field at this time defined the statistical population of black slaves, divided into two groups of different size, blacks and mulattoes. This distinction of color, also made for free blacks, was in part the consequence of the possibilities opened up by the individual schedule in which the question of color was raised, with three answers proposed for free persons and two for slaves.[1]

That there were two possible responses for slaves—black and mulatto—while there was no provision for "white" had two lasting implications for the American statistical apparatus and, more generally, for the definition of racial groups in American society: black individuals could be divided into two groups, and only two groups.[2] Whatever the definition adopted for those who visibly were the product of a mixing between blacks and whites, all such individuals remained within the confines of the black population, and they in no way occupied an intermediary position between the two races.[3] The new possibilities of choices offered by the individual schedule remained strictly limited in the case of "color" by what will later be called the one drop rule, that rule coming from the strictest slaveholding states, according to which a single drop of black blood sufficed to legally define an individual as black.[4]

While schedule no. 1 for free inhabitants also distinguished between black and mulatto, debates on this point concerned only the schedule for slaves. Yet the instructions for schedule no. 1 emphasized the importance of this distinction of color, unlike the instructions for schedule no. 2, the Slave Schedule:

> Schedule no. 1. Free inhabitants. 6. Under heading 6, entitled "Color," in all cases where the person is white, leave the space blank; in all cases where the person is black, insert the letter B; if mulatto, insert M. It is very desirable that these particulars be carefully regarded.
>
> Schedule no. 2. Slave inhabitants. 5. Under heading 5, entitled "Color," insert in all cases, when the slave is black, the letter B; when he or she is mulatto, insert M. The color of all slaves should be noted.[5]

If we do not find for slaves the same reminder about the importance of these distinctions, it is nonetheless remarkable that the instructions show clearly that slaves are not all of the same color for the census from 1850 on, and that it is possible and desirable to register their distribution by color.[6] It goes without saying that slaves could only be black or mulatto. On schedule no. 1 the wording printed in column 6 is "Color—White, Black, or Mulatto," while in schedule no. 2 we find only "Color" without a reminder of the proposed choices.

While this distinction figured for the first time in the census, and while the instructions for 1850 were richer in definitions for the terms employed than had been the case in previous censuses, the term *mulatto* was nowhere defined, and how to distinguish a mulatto from a black is not explained.[7] The point, however, is to know the distance of the mulatto from the black and from the white since, whatever the definition adopted, the mulatto was the product of a mixture between these two groups. But white legislators and officials found it impossible to recognize white men's paternity in this phenomenon. This difficulty lay at the heart of the congressional debates on the question.

The mulatto category was introduced into the census, at first in schedule no. 2, by Senator Underwood, but his proposition was heatedly discussed and amended. Originally, the schedule was to have included, beyond color, a question on the "degree of removal from pure blood," which would have provided a way to measure the importance of interracial unions and to situate them in terms of generations.

In the Senate, on 9 April 1850, in the continuation of the debates over schedule no. 2 and after winning agreement on elimination of the question on the birthplace of slaves, Senator William King, Democrat of Alabama, proposed an amendment to delete the question, which was to be asked only for slaves, "If a female, the number of children she has had, known to be alive, known to be dead." Once again, King resorted to ridicule to eliminate a question that he felt was useless and too intrusive about the condition of slaves:

> The woman herself, in nine out of ten cases, when she has had ten or fifteen children does not know how many she actually had. [Laughter]. No sir, she cannot tell. The owner certainly does not know; the manager of the estate does not know, because managers are frequently changed.[8]

Underwood's response to this remark was lengthy and of interest. Once again, he attempted to place scientific interest in opposition to politically motivated obstruction. He emphasized how much this data, if collected, would contribute to the comparison of the two races, especially with an eye to constructing actuarial tables. This argument in support of the economic utility of fine-grained demographic data would recur frequently later on, but in 1850 it clearly identified Underwood as someone open to the arguments of the experts who upheld the plan. He also noted, in order to defuse the highly charged nature of the subject, and deliberately remaining somewhat vague, that these questions had been proposed to the Senate committee by Southerners:

> You will find in these tables that we require, not only the age and sex, but the color of the person; and we find in another column the degree of removal from pure blood is required to be stated; and this inquiry, in reference to the number of children which each woman may have had, I can inform my honorable friend, was inserted, as far as I know, at the instance of a southern gentleman, with a view to ascertain certain facts which he told me, but which I do not think necessary to go into here. Now, the question is, are you willing to take all this information, with a view to ascertain the laws of longevity between the two races—the degrees of blood and other physical laws of the races?[9]

What Underwood was referring to without naming it—as all those present would have known—was the phenomenon that from the Civil War on will be known as miscegenation: interracial unions, and specifically unions between slave women and white men, a supremely sensitive subject. The number of mulattoes would thus be an indicator of the frequency of interracial unions.[10] His arguments in favor of a scientific census, like the similar ones made by Davis, only aggravated the opposition of Southerners over the expansion of the schedule on slaves.

To the objection raised by Solon Borland, Democrat of Arkansas, for whom the purpose of the census was not to launch into scientific research but simply to enumerate inhabitants, Underwood replied that it was precisely a question of collecting simple facts:

> It is not a matter of scientific investigation at all, but a mere inquiry as to facts—whether an individual is a quadroon, a mulatto or any proportion of blood. . . . And certainly it concerns the public, as well as the government, to know the actual *relative* condition of the different classes of population.[11]

By the time the Whig senator from New York, William Seward, one of the strongest critics of slavery in the Senate, explicitly drew conclusions from these changes, southern opposition to the plan had risen to the point that some opponents took advantage of the occasion to eliminate, by amendment, all these novelties and return to the schedule of 1840.

Seward, likewise making use of irony, deliberately put his finger on everything about these questions that could frighten those senators who defended slavery. He could not believe that a woman, whatever her race (and the mere fact of using the expression "a woman, whatever her race" placed Seward squarely in the abolitionist camp), could forget how many children she had had. Not content with placing slave women and white women on the same level, Seward continued his provocation by invoking ironically the traditional argument of defenders of slavery: that slavery was necessary and beneficial to slaves of African origin. If such women existed, he said, he would like to know their number in all races.

> I should like to ascertain the number of such that there are of all races. And I desire this information because we have all cherished a hope that the condition of African servitude in this country was a stage of transition from a state of barbarism to a state of improvement thereafter. I wish to know how rapid that progress is.

He suggested that they ascertain the degree of education of slaves in order to measure their progress toward a better condition, which constituted "the only excuse, as I understand, we have for holding them in servitude."[12]

At this point in the debate, for many of the senators, the census was no longer anything but a pretext for debating slavery and a means of calling it into question. This is the meaning of the response of another southern senator, Thomas Jefferson Rusk, and of the Democratic senator from South Carolina, Andrew Butler:

> Now, sir, he proposes to acquire this information with a view to use it in Congress, of course in reference to this species of population. Does the

gentleman assume that he has a right to legislate upon the social condition of slavery in the southern States? Does he wish for the information
as a mere matter of curiosity or for a purpose?

Butler, emphasizing the distance that for him separated the questions asked of
slaves from those asked of whites, demanded to know whether Seward would
approve of having white women in New York asked such indiscreet questions as
how many children they had had—to which Seward replied with malice that he
himself would have no objection whatsoever.

   Given the turn the debate had taken, Underwood attempted to save what
he could by detailing the reasoning that he had not explained and expos-
ing the Southerner's intentions behind the questions on the degree of racial
purity.

> He believed that a certain class of colored people had fewer children
> than a certain other class; and he believed that the average duration of
> the lives of the children of the darker class was longer than that of the
> children of the lighter colored class, or the mixed.[13]

At once the group of senators ended their opposition, commenting on the differences between mulattoes and blacks. Dayton, taking up what King had said
about members of "the really black race" having greater resistance, concluded
"that, in a word, the mulatto in a certain degree is a *hybrid*!" by which his hear-
ers were to understand that they were a species less "prolific" and less robust.
These discussions in 1850 took place in a new scientific context: while in the first
half of the century the strict interpretation of Christian doctrine forbade doubt
over the divine creation of a single first man, this restriction was now lifting.
Henceforth it would be possible to profess polygenism without being immediately accused of a crime against religion.[14]

   The popularity of polygenism in the United States translated politically into
the idea that blacks did not have the same origin as whites. They thus did not
have the same claim to constitutional protection, so it appeared logical to forbid
or condemn unions between blacks and whites. Borrowings from Lamarckian
theory on species made it possible to claim that mulattoes were hybrids who, if
they were not sterile, were at least less fecund. Over the decade preceding the
census of 1850, the idea of evolution had been rejected, while the application to
human races of the Linnaean model of classification of species remained dominant, if not exclusive.[15] In this context, bringing to bear the statistical research
of the Belgian statistician Adolphe Quételet made it possible for the census to
become the hoped-for place to prove the irreducible difference between blacks
and whites.[16]

Based on Quételet's concept of the average man, the idea arose that the American population, subjected to the extensive quantitative analysis of the census, would reveal not one but several "average men," according to race, for each of whom the measurements (longevity, morbidity, crime, poverty) would corroborate the necessarily more limited studies of anthropometry. Thus, within ten years from the fantasy statistics on the insanity of free blacks in 1840, the combined progress of statistical techniques, of the natural sciences, and of the census itself was such that the census results were awaited in a new scientific and intellectual context.[17] From this time on, quantitative analysis would participate in a vast scientific program, whereas the 1840 figures had been brought to light by accident.[18]

Polygenism's popularity, and slavery partisans' hopes for the census of 1850, were set forth regularly and with great clarity in the prestigious publications of J. D. B. DeBow, especially in the volumes of his *Encyclopaedia of the Trade and Commerce of the United States, More Particularly of the Southern and Western States*, and the influential *DeBow's Review*.[19] James Dunwoody Brownson DeBow was a well-known statistician and professor of political economy at the University of Louisiana (now Tulane University). As the *Review*'s editor, he repeatedly expressed in its pages his enthusiasm for polygenism.

Both the *Encyclopaedia* and *DeBow's Review* were serious publications aimed at informing the cultivated public of the South. They contained a large number of diverse statistics on southern economy and society, and detailed reviews of technical and scientific works. They were also publications that their editor used to fiercely defend the cause of the South in general, and slavery in particular. This explains why we find, side by side with economic or political essays or statistical compilations on cotton, apparently scientific articles that give the impressions that there existed a southern science and that the racial question contaminated all others. For example, a doctor from New Orleans, Dr. Cartwright, published in the *Encyclopaedia* an astonishing and oft-quoted article on the illnesses specific to blacks. Besides a form of tuberculosis specific to blacks, he found among that population an original illness, for which he coined the term *drapetomania*, defined as the illness that causes blacks to run away:

> Drapetomania is from δραπετης, a runaway slave, and μανια, mad or crazy. . . . The cause in the most of cases, that induces the negro to run away from service, is as much a disease of the mind as any other species of mental alienation, and much more curable, as a general rule.[20]

In the 1850 volume of the *Encyclopaedia*, DeBow stated, in an extremely favorable review of a work on the inequality of human races, that "we, in common with our author, consider the diversity of origin proved beyond dispute" and simply expressed regret that the author had not cited "the great Agassiz." The review went so far as to claim that the program for ameliorating the condition of blacks, known as "negro improvement," frequently trotted out as a justification for slavery, could only lead to the degradation of the white man and that the differences between races were intended by God, so that it would be impious as well as stupid to wish to change them.[21]

DeBow's *Encyclopaedia*, in the article on "Negroes.—Black and Mulatto Population of the South," explained in detail how the coming census would demonstrate once and for all, statistically, the benefits of slavery and the degeneracy of mulattoes:[22]

> The Hon. Mr. Clingman, of North Carolina, has addressed a letter to the census board, urging the importance of more accurate information than has hitherto been elicited with reference to the black race, and especially to that portion of it in which there is a mixture between the black and white races. The last census [1840] was notoriously faulty in this respect, and, owing to the conflicting extremes of opinion and assertion which have been adduced by the parties who are associated most intimately with the interests of the negro population, nothing like a true knowledge of the state of the black race in the United States has been arrived at. In the south, the negro is described as hardly human— incapable of refinement or intellectual advance; while the abolitionists extol him as naturally the equal of the white man, physically and mentally. So that it is a mooted question whether slavery has degenerated, or freedom at the north has improved the negro.

The author of the review went on to explain that the "mixed race" showed abilities more apt to cultivation than those of the pure African, taking as an example the facts that in the South they were chosen for more complex tasks than those assigned to the simple "field negro," and that in the North everyday observation showed that the mulatto was endowed with "mental gifts superior to those of his black brother." But "whether the mulatto deteriorates physically in proportion as he ascends in the intellectual scale, is the question of highest importance, considering the ratio in which this portion of our population is increasing."

DeBow's *Encyclopaedia* relied on statistics, and in the case here on the census alone, to resolve this debate:

> It has been lately asserted, by men who have made this branch of science their study, that the hybridity of animals, is, in course of time, fatal to their powers of procreation; and that after two or three generations, the mulatto (the hybrid man) loses this power as does the mule. This

theory argues a diversity of the human race, and is of course violently opposed by the advocates of its unity; but hypothesis and controversy are alike powerless to elucidate a truth which depends upon statistics for its developments. Hence the importance of Mr. Clingman's suggestion to ascertain not only the number of all such persons, whether free or slaves, of extending inquiries as to the parents of the mulatto population, whether they are black, white, or mixed—and going on still further back, where necessary, until the pedigree is traced back to the individual white and black races.[23]

The plan defended by Rep. Clingman went much further into the investigation of racial mixing than the one that was finally retained by the senators. In order to defuse the criticisms of the southern senators, Underwood had to tell them where this suggestion came from. To go back through the generations until one found pure races was as unrealistic technically as it was politically. The arguments here, which are those of Rep. Clingman, reveal clearly the motivations that remained implicit in some of the interventions in Congress. It is true that the polygenism and scientific racism that underlay the theory of hybridity were not shared by all the defenders of slavery, but they represented the most developed and theorized form of the shared belief in the natural inferiority of blacks.[24] The debate revolved around the question of knowing whether this inferiority was or was not susceptible of evolution. DeBow's *Encyclopaedia* article laid out what was known on this issue, arriving eventually at a political conclusion to this scientific argumentation. It relied for support on an article from the *Boston Medical Journal* which set forth "the following facts, which are said to have been collected from authentic statistics" showing that the African had the greatest longevity of the human species, the African-Caucasian hybrid the shortest, and

> That the mortality of the free people of color in the United States is more than one hundred per cent greater than that of the slaves.
>
> It is questionable whether the negro will care about a change to freedom, if its only benefit is *a short cut to the grave*. There is no question but slavery is an evil, but statistics of mortality prove that, as far as the negro is concerned, poverty is *one hundred* fold the greater evil.[25]

The conclusion of the article took up again the arguments that had been advanced by the proponents of slavery on the subject of the 1840 statistics on the insanity of free blacks, but on another level and in a context where polygenism became a recognized scientific guarantee. This desire for knowledge signals a hardening of relations between whites and mulattoes. This is the thesis of the historian Joel Williamson, who notes that the statutes concerning mulattoes were more flexible at the time of independence and that the crisis between sections made the question more sensitive.[26] The mulattoes, who were the living proof of past sexual relations between whites and blacks and between free and slave, were at the heart of the debate on the difference between races in its new scientific form. There was also a moral dimension to the hypothesis of the natural extinction of mulattoes. They were the visible trace of the sin committed by white men with black women, slaves rather than free, frequently in the form of adulterous relations gained by force. Thus, to predict their extinction was also to hope to erase the visible trace of these relations of which society disapproved.[27]

In this context, the question of "degree of distance from the pure race" was indeed a philosophical question, as the senators said. In their heads, the census would provide elements of the response to the question of whether blacks and whites belonged to a single species. Clearly, slavery proponents could only congratulate themselves on the direction taken by the American School of polygenists, since to demonstrate that black slaves were not of the same species as the whites who enjoyed a natural right to liberty would have paid off a moral mortgage on slavery.[28]

Compared to the studies of craniology or comparative anthropometry that developed from the 1840s, the census could by no means go into the same degree of detail, and the solution adopted—to distinguish two types only within the black population—was more limited. The census, which concerned the entirety of the population, addressed several needs, and "scientific" need was neither the sole nor the first of these, even if the editors of the census volumes had every interest in presenting their results as purely scientific. The same distinction applied to slaves and free may not have had exactly the same meaning, since free "hybrids" would have constituted an intermediary group between whites and blacks. But the fact that there were "mulatto" slaves decided the issue: mulattoes could only be black.[29]

The comparison of data on free and slave "mulattoes" shows nonetheless that there were real differences of status between blacks and mulattoes, to the extent that the individuals who happened to be enumerated as mulattoes fit the known meaning of that category of the population.

Color and Status of Slaves

Legal Definition and Census Practice

The history of the legal construction of race shows that, for legislators as for the courts, the definition of race varied over time; it also remained uncertain in a number of individual cases judged by the courts. Several studies have shown how, in the 1850s, invocation of membership in the white race was an argument that could be made in court to obtain liberty, since a white man or woman (most of the judgments in demands of freedom involved women) could not be a slave.[1] Legal status did not rest on the same forms of proof as the census, which relied basically on good faith and reputation, but the two perspectives overlapped.[2]

The legal criteria for race were determined differently by the different slave states and according to the rules of common law. Moreover, the legal presumption also varied. For example, while in all the southern states, custom established a presumption of freedom for persons who appeared white and a presumption of slavery for those who appeared black, in Louisiana and North Carolina, a mulatto appearance did not carry a presumption of slavery, though in Kentucky it did.[3] Walter Johnson, in his study of the New Orleans slave market, notes that the rules for legal presumption rested on two different foundations according to the state: one method, similar to that of the census, assigned status on the basis of observation and reputation; the other, more widespread, sought to establish the legal presumption of freedom based upon "fractions of 'black blood': halves, fourths, eighths, sixteenths, and so on down to one drop, which was the standard only in Arkansas during the antebellum period." Other forms of proof could take precedence over these rules of presumption, especially the personal history of the individual if it was known that she had been held in slavery or had been born of a slave mother. Johnson notes that these different rules existed concurrently and that their shape was fluid; in his view, legal writers made use of three methods which often overlapped: "Personal history, race science based on discerning 'black blood,' and performance—the amalgam of appearance and reputation, of body, behavior, and scripted social role."[4]

Johnson analyzes the case of Alexina Morrisson, a young woman who was sold as a slave and who took the slave dealer to court on the grounds that being white, she could not be a slave. To shed light on the courts' decisions, Johnson turned to one of the few sources that could illuminate the image that Alexina Morrisson had of herself prior to the case—the 1850 census, a source external to the case. According to him, Alexina Morrisson was categorized as mulatto in the census. This example reveals at one and the same time the role played by these categories and the difficulty of attaching racial data from the census to non-ambiguous identities.

As Johnson remarks, these are only indications. He notes that it was not impossible for a person to appear as "black" or, more probably, "mulatto" in one census and as "white" in another. He sees the census worker's visit as one of those moments that could bring people back to a forgotten or repressed perception of their own identity.

In Johnson's view, the interaction between the census agent and slaves or their owners constituted a formative moment for their racial identity, or even a moment when uncertain identities could be revealed. But it is difficult to view the census as a criterion of truth, when the information collected could be conditional upon the context. We need to maintain caution with respect to the performative agency of the census in the construction of identities. There is nothing to indicate that Alexina Morrisson or her mother had any knowledge of their classification as mulatto rather than as black by the census agent for Matagorda County, Texas, in 1850. Yet this young woman could not be ignorant of the fact that in some people's eyes she was black, while others saw her as white. And, of course, the historian remains dependent on the framework put in place by the law of the 1850 census. The household of Moses Morrisson, the slave owner who left his family name to his slaves, included at the time of the census agent's visit in 1850, in addition to Moses Morrisson himself:

> Three other white men, and, listed separately on the slave schedule, a woman aged thirty and labeled mulatto, five children aged between one and thirteen, also labeled mulatto, and an enslaved man, listed beneath this apparent slave family, aged thirty-eight and labeled black. Of the children, one was a seven-year-old girl, most likely Alexina Morrisson. That the children were listed as mulatto like their mother and that the only enslaved man in the household was not suggests that their father was white—perhaps Moses Morrisson or one of the men who boarded with him.[5]

The census manuscripts here appear as a precious source, since they provide the only trace of the recorded identity of the slaves other than the sales records that included detailed descriptions of them.[6] In her sales record submitted to the court, Alexina Morrisson was described as "yellow," meaning a very light-skinned mixed-race individual. We see the limits imposed on the interpretation of census manuscripts by the cloak of anonymity thrown over the Slave Schedule by the senators. We may guess with some degree of confidence that the woman is the mother of the children; however, in contrast to schedule no. 1, on the Slave Schedule family relations were not taken into account and the names of the slaves do not appear.[7] We must therefore reconstruct the family structures on the basis of the indications that we do have, which leaves a great deal of room for conjecture. Accordingly, relationship is here deduced by the category "black" or "mulatto" and from tenuous indications such as the order of enumeration of individuals on the schedule. Mulatto children, whose mother is also mulatto, could just as easily have a white father as a black or a mulatto. At this time there was no written rule on the classification of children of parents who were categorized differently, since such cases had not been foreseen. The category "mulatto" had been conceived as a marker of former unions, which had taken place and ended sometime in the past. It is also not impossible that the census agent never saw the children and simply extended to them the classification of their mother, or even that this had been indicated by the head of household and slave owner himself.[8] This being said, since here it was a question of a household and not a big plantation, it is plausible that everyone lived in close proximity if not in the same building, and that the census agent may have met the different members of the household. Knowing Alexina Morrisson's age and her physical description, Johnson was able to identify her on the questionnaire, but finding individual slaves on the Slave Schedule presupposes that we know from other sources their age, their sex, and the name of their owner. For the historian, the racial categories applied to slaves in 1850 form part of a bundle of indicators, but we see that they do not suffice to pin down the racial identity of individuals, even if we confine ourselves to a concept of identity existing at a given moment without prejudging what it might have been before or after.

A comparison of the procedures for determining the legal status of slaves with the procedure adopted by the census for assigning, if not actually determining, the racial category of individuals, shows the profound ambiguity of the latter. The language used by the legislators in 1850 and then retained until the end of the century was clearly that of the scientific rules then in favor, which amounts to a calculation of the parts of black blood and of genealogy. The practice was quite the opposite, since individuals were not viewed in terms of their genealogy but rather by their appearance. The census itself did not define the terms "black" and "mulatto" until 1870, but the debates in Congress highlight that it was a question of fitting into a system of fractions and tracking the purity of blood. In practice the census could only follow the reputation and the performance of race, to use the expression of the historian Ariela Gross. This contradiction would never be resolved and would last until the category "mulatto" was dropped after the 1920 census. It was surely one of the reasons why the category was dropped, and was explicitly the reason for eliminating the fraction-of-black-blood standard after the attempt made in 1890 to group blacks into four sub-categories by color.

The idea of race as a performance, as a presentation of self rather than as a biological essence, here takes on its full force. The legal cases that have been studied similarly show the importance of gender in the determination of race. In spite of appearing white, or at least having very light skin and blond hair, Alexina Morrisson was revealed as black to the eyes of the other side when she submitted to being publicly examined undressed to the waist, which a southern white woman was never supposed to agree to unless she were a prostitute, while such displays were common on the platforms of the slave markets.[9] Being white in the South in the 1850s and 1860s was not only a question of skin color or origin but also one of behavior and manner.[10]

This notion of race as performance comes into play in the 1850s and undoubtedly was there from the start, perhaps even before the arrival of the first Europeans on American soil.[11] It brings into question the classic interpretations of the emergence of racism in America, as Ariela Gross emphasizes:

> The "laws" of race could be subverted by people who followed all the rules of whiteness but "hid" their intrinsic blackness. Law, which provided the forum for these challenges, made a discourse of race as performance especially salient.
>
> Recognizing that this discourse of performance rose together with "scientific" ways of thinking about race may unsettle the comfortable certainty that race was "that way then, and this way now." Many contemporary arguments about race on both sides of the political spectrum depend on a view of racism in the past as biological essentialism.[12]

What is in play in the case of the lawsuits studied by Ariela Gross and Walter Johnson, as in the history of the racial classifications used by the census, is the historical value of the opposition between essentialism and constructivism, between scientific racism and cultural identity. It is possible to draw up a list of all the "scientific" rules of racism in the nineteenth century in order to show that the United States has left that period behind, and there is abundant documentation for this. But for judicial procedure as for the census, on the level of how the well-organized categories on paper were actually put into practice, the experience was very different.

As for the study of how racial statistical categories were applied to real individuals, which has always been seen to be complexly linked to legal norms, the conclusions run in the same direction. Not only did the definitions vary across time (as has been known for a long time), but their application was never simple or univocal. Attempting to oppose a period when racism was purely essentialist, when both experts and society in general knew the essence of the black race and the white race, to our own era when these barriers have become fluid, amounts to treating the nineteenth century's normative discourse on scientific racism as an effective social norm, which it was not. Paradoxically, the analyses that have described a discourse on essences may have given them more substance than they actually had in their context.[13] For the statistics on slaves and free blacks in the last years of slavery, as for the law, the transposition of theories of scientific racism into practices and procedures was more a formalization of existing practices than an invention—that is, that people integrated practices that were already current into a new theoretical perspective. This theorizing was done at the time and, in a different way, by late twentieth-century historians. Still, it seems that in many cases the new paradigm of the second half of the nineteenth century facilitated the interpretation of the statistics, without necessarily having influenced the collection of the data.

Census Data for 1850 and 1860 and the Defeat of the South

The figures for the 1860 census and their compilation by agents of the Census Office under the direction of J. C. G. Kennedy played a solid role in the military defeat of the South since, from January 1862, the resources and employees of the census were placed at the disposition of the secretary of war. The main innovation of the eighth census was the cartographic presentation of the data. As Margo Anderson relates, on the existing maps of southern postal routes, the agents of the Census Office reported, county by county, the results of the census of 1860. Thus, northern generals had access to data on cultivated acres, the numbers of horses and mules, and the quantities of wheat, corn, oats, and other crops, as well as on the numbers of whites, free blacks, and slaves in each county. The logistical significance of the agricultural data and the political significance of the demographic data become apparent in light of certain northern generals having taken the initiative of freeing the slaves in conquered territory, and even of enlisting former slaves, making it impossible to return to a previous stage.[1]

> General William Tecumseh Sherman made the most notable use of such statistical information in his march through Georgia to the sea. Sherman acknowledged the debt he had to the Census Office for the information both at the time of the march in 1864 and after the war. "No military expedition was ever based on sounder or surer data," he wrote to his daughter Ellen. The data made it possible for northern commanders to operate with short or no supply lines, to live off the land, and thus to move faster than traditional armies.[2]

The volumes of the 1860 census included numerous maps of the United States, and the Census Office widely distributed some of them separately, such as the one showing the distribution of the slave population in the southern states, published in 1861.[3] The published collections of the censuses of 1850 and 1860 also played an indirect yet important role in the ideological conflict between North and South. This aspect, though well studied by historians, is still worth recalling since the data of the 1850 and 1860 censuses on slaves and free blacks played a central role in the polemics between slavery proponents and abolitionists, and even more because in March 1853 J. D. B. DeBow replaced Kennedy as superintendent of the census, with the intention of using census data as an instrument of southern propaganda.

DeBow's nomination, following the Democratic victory at the polls in November 1852, would reassure southerners concerned that the published volumes would represent their region solely as economically and socially backward. In reality, when DeBow took up his duties, Kennedy's team had already completed the basic work of preparing the volumes. If it was DeBow's name that figured on the title pages, most of the rest was ready in advance. Neither Kennedy nor DeBow allowed their partisan views to appear in the presentation of the results or the accompanying commentary. However, DeBow placed the full weight of his position as census superintendent behind his activity as a pro-South advocate. Thus, although he restrained himself in the official census volumes, more partisan interpretations appeared in *DeBow's Review* in 1853 and 1854, and DeBow was identified as "Superintendent US Census" on the title page of the publication.

The review would take up word for word the census data and commentaries on the black and white populations, sometimes without adding anything and other times placing them into perspective in an article emphasizing the degeneracy of free blacks. An article of January 1853 on the colored population of the North recalled the themes of 1840.[4] In contrast, Kennedy as well as DeBow employed a nationalist rhetoric in the official census reports, eschewing comparisons between North and South.[5] In the end, the 1850 census itself contained little data on slavery. Regardless, at the end of the 1850s, partisans and adversaries of slavery used and abused statistics pulled from the census to defend their cause, without ever convincing their opponents, whom they systematically accused of distorting and making biased use of the data. The relative sparsity of overall data on slaves and free blacks meant that all parties had to use the same source, so that they were forced to denounce the other side's use of data as the ultimate criterion of truth.

The best-known case, and the best example, is the work of Hinton Rowan Helper, *The Impending Crisis of the South* (1857). Helper reorganized the statistics on slave states and non-slave states published in the volumes of the 1850 census in such a way as to make a quantitative comparison of the economic and social advancement of the two sections of the country. He compiled more than fifty tables comparing the states, and in all of them, without exception, the North came out ahead in the comparison, whether it was a question of the number of canals, of roads, of the volume of agricultural production, or of social progress. His explanation was summed up in one word: slavery. It had held down southern whites and had benefited only the elite.[6] Faced with this offensive use of statistics, many southern orators replied by using census data for their own purposes, especially to show the sorry fate of free laborers in the North.[7] Helper's arguments, like many of those of his detractors, were based on rather sloppy use of the data, which were not generally checked against the figures for the local population.[8] Nonetheless, within ten years, scientific arguments had made progress, though this did not prevent the strictest observers from continuing to demand corrections by other users of census data who lacked their scruples.[9]

The debate over the comparative merits of the North and South was fueled by the 1850 census statistics, but was never resolved because neither camp would accept adverse arguments, and above all because the war finally put an end to such propaganda. It took on new life, however, following the work of the economic historians Robert Fogel and Stanley Engerman, when historians specializing in the slavery question in their turn engaged in a statistical fight. Accusations of lack of scientific rigor and of extrapolation based on incomplete data at times recalled the polemics that had raged more than a century earlier. At the heart of the debate was the question of the economic profitability of slavery. Fogel and Engerman defended the thesis, at that time iconoclastic, according to which slavery was not condemned to economic failure and plantations were run efficiently rather than with cruelty.[10] This debate, which flourished in the 1970s, was largely based on the econometric aspects of the study and on its sources, especially plantation account books.[11] But the authors of *Time on the Cross* also made use of the demographic data on slaves collected by the census in 1850 and 1860, in particular on a point we shall return to here: the data on mulattoes and the attempts to evaluate the frequency of unions between white men and slave women that were responsible for most of these births.

Fogel and Engerman proposed a model to take account of the presence and growth of the mulatto population among slaves, leaving aside the question of free mulattoes. The distribution of free and slave mulattoes is quite problematic, since the basis for the separation is difficult to explain, except hypothetically. The generally accepted idea for explaining why the proportion of blacks counted as mulattoes was much larger among the free than among slaves was that the masters showed a greater tendency to emancipate mulattoes.

The census data, for the country as well as for certain cities, where the free were generally more numerous than in rural areas, show that color and status were strongly linked as can be seen in tables 7.1–7.5.[12]

A comparison of the data for free and enslaved mulattoes shows real differences in status. It appears that slaveholders tended to emancipate lighter-skinned slaves. The question of the origin of mulattoes, reformulated in the form

Table 7.1. **Number and Relative Proportion of Different Classes of Black Population in Several Southern Cities, 1850 Census**

Cities (1850)		Richmond, Virginia	Charleston, S. Carolina	Savannah, Georgia	Mobile, Alabama	New Orleans	Total
Free colored	Black	1,550	887	206	98	1,727	4,468
	Mulatto	819	2,554	480	617	7,357	11,827
	Total	2,369	3,441	686	715	9,084	16,295
Slaves	Black	8,222	18,225	5,123	5,549	12,243	49,362
	Mulatto	1,705	1,307	1,108	1,264	4,602	9,986
	Total	9,927	19,532	6,231	6,813	16,845	59,348
Total		12,296	22,973	6,917	7,528	25,929	75,643
Free colored	% black	65.43*	25.78	30.03	13.71	19.01	27.42
	% mulatto	34.57	74.22	69.97	86.29	80.99	2.58
Slaves	% black	82.82	93.31	82.22	81.45	72.69	83.17
	% mulatto	17.18	6.69	17.78	18.55	27.31	16.83
Percent of total mulatto to aggregate population		20.53	16.81	22.96	24.99	46.12	28.84

* The table reads 56.43%, a typographical error that I have corrected.

Source: "Proportions of the different classes to each other. Census of 1850." *Eighth Census,* 1860, 1:xiii.

of the question about their paternity, divided contemporaries and historians, especially over the systematic nature of the unions imposed by masters or their employees on the women of the plantation.

Following on the work of Fogel and Engerman, a number of quantitative studies took up the census data from 1850 and 1860 in order to form a response to the question. In *Time on the Cross,* Fogel and Engerman developed an intergenerational model of the growth of the mulatto population among slaves, in order to give a quantitative response based on available data. They formulated the hypothesis that for each generation of slaves, 1 percent of the children were the issue of a union between a female slave, black or mulatto, and a white man.

Table 7.2. **Number and Relative Proportion of Different Classes of Black Population in Several Southern Cities, 1860 Census**

Cities (1850)		Richmond, Virginia	Charleston, S. Carolina.	Savannah, Georgia	Mobile, Alabama	New Orleans	Total
Free colored	Black	1,461	891	295	99	2,365	5,111
	Mulatto	1,115	4,587	410	718	8,324	15,154
	Total	2,576	5,478	705	817	10,689	20,265
Slaves	Black	9,753	20,793	6,595	6,069	9,937	53,147
	Mulatto	1,946	2,736	1,117	1,518	3,448	10,765
	Total	11,699	23,529	7,712	7,587	13,385	63,912
Total		14,275	29,007	8,417	8,404	24,074	84,177
Free colored	% black	56.72	16.26	41.84	12.12	22.13	25.22
	% mulatto	43.28	83.74	58.16	87.88	77.87	74.78
Slaves	% black	83.37	88.37	85.52	79.99	74.24	83.16
	% mulatto	16.63	11.63	14.48	20.01	25.76	16.84
Percent of total mulatto to aggregate population		21.44	25.25	18.14	26.61	48.90	30.79

Source: *Eighth Census*, 1860, vol. 1, p. xiii.

They showed that if this practice had remained constant from 1620 (the date of the arrival of the first African slaves on American soil) to the eighth generation, around 1860, there would be between 7 percent and 15 percent mulattoes among slaves, a finding consistent with the data from the 1860 census. This meant that the majority of mulattoes in 1850 or 1860 were at some remote degree removed from the descendants of a white ancestor, but were immediately the children of slaves, black and mulatto, because individuals born of unions between blacks and mulattoes were themselves classed among blacks or mulattoes. The authors thus concluded that slave rape or forced concubinage were in no way systematic and that the large majority of mulattoes of the census were not the children of a white father.[13]

According to the working rules of the census, none of the descendants of these unions could leave the group and become white, in theory, so they all boosted the size of the black population. But these rules were not defined until the end of the century, and in 1850 and 1860, there was no definition of "mulatto." This

Table 7.3. **Percentage of Mulattoes for Selected Southern and Northern Cities Compared to Total Negro Population, 1860**

State	Area	Rest of State
Georgia	Savannah City: 18.1	8.2
Louisiana	New Orleans City: 48.9	11.0
South Carolina	Charleston: 25.2	5.5
Kentucky	Jefferson Co. (Louisville): 21.8	20.0
Missouri	St. Louis Co. (St. Louis) 32.7	19.2
Virginia	Richmond: 21.4	16.9
New York	Kings Co. (Brooklyn): 19.5	20.3 (New York City 3.3)
Illinois	Cook Co. (Chicago): 49.3	46.8
Massachusetts	Suffolk Co. (Boston): 38.3	29.9

Source: Based on US Bureau of the Census, Negroes in the United States, Census Bulletin no. 8 (Washington, DC: Government Printing Office, 1904), Table IV, p. 17, "Percent mulatto in total negro population 1860 and 1850."

provided fodder for some of the critics who greeted the publication of *Time on the Cross*, especially Herbert Gutman and Richard Sutch. They pointed out that neither *mulatto* nor *black* had yet been defined by the Census Office at this time and that the information on skin color of slaves was provided by their owners, while that of free blacks was determined by the visual observation of the census worker, which obviously made it a delicate matter to compare the distributions of mulattoes among slaves and free blacks.[14] In Gutman's view, Fogel and Engerman's figures on mulattoes were too low, and contacts between whites and blacks were much more frequent than they had proposed, while for the authors of *Time on the Cross*, mulattoes were rare on the plantations while female mulattoes were proportionally more numerous in cities.

The problem, of course, stems from the poor quality of the data. Some studies confirm the thesis defended by Fogel and Engerman, while others challenge it, but there again comparisons are thorny, since the persons known as "mulatto" were not always classed as such by the census. Further, slave narratives and those of slave descendants testifying to relations between slaves and their masters can only with difficulty be extrapolated to the level of the state or the country.[15]

Fogel and Engerman's model is seductive, but its weakness lies in the fact that they count as the product of interracial unions with slaves only persons who themselves were slaves and who were enumerated as mulattoes in 1850 and 1860. However, there were at least two ways of exiting that population; while

Table 7.4. **Proportion of Mulattoes in Black Population ("Negro population"),**
         1850–1920

	Total (Negro population)	Black	Mulatto number	Mulatto %	Mulattoes to 1,000 blacks
1920	10,463,131	8,802,577	1,660,554	15.9	189
1910	9,827,763	7,777,077	2,050,686	20.9	264
1900	8,833,994	-	-	-	-
1890	7,448,676	6,337,980	1,132,060	15.2	179
1880	6,580,793	-	-	-	-
1870	4,880,009	4,295,960	584,049	12	136
1860	4,441,830	3,853,467	588,363	13.2	153
1850	3,638,808	3,233,057	405,751	11.2	126

Note: How to read this table: The percentage of "mulatto" is the percentage of the black population ("Negro") obtained by adding "black" and "mulatto." e.g., in 1910, 2,050,689 mulattoes represent 20.866% of 9,827,763 (Negro) whereas 1000/8,802,777*1,660,554 = 189.

In 1880 the data for "black" and "mulatto" were collected but were neither compiled nor published. In 1900 this distinction was not used by the Census.

In 1890, among the total 7,488,676, there were 18,636 blacks ("Negroes") counted on the special schedule for the Indian Territory without distinction.

Source: US Bureau of the Census, *Negro Population, 1790–1915* (1918), p. 208; and US Bureau of the Census, *The Fourteenth Census of the United States* (Washington, DC: Government Printing Office, 1920), vol. 2, p. 35.

their proportions are unknown, there is evidence for both. The first was emancipation (of slaves themselves or of their children), the second was the fact that some persons who were the issue of these interracial unions were enumerated as white. The finding that mulattoes were more numerous among the free is a sure sign of this exit route. In the absence of firmer data, these unions may have occurred at a constant rate across time, but they were more strongly disapproved of after the middle of the nineteenth century. Finally, this general model does not take account of significant regional variations in the distribution of mulattoes. As Table 7.3 shows, mulattoes made up nearly half of the black population of New Orleans in 1860, while representing only 11 percent of that population at state level. The problem stems from the inherent difficulty of constructing a national model based on data of varying quality.

Even if the analyses depend on uncertain definitions, some of the conclusions based on the data of these two censuses can hold—the only individual data available for all slaves and which show, despite these reservations, the central importance of the data furnished by the censuses of 1850 and 1860.[16]

Table 7.5. **Rate of Growth of Black Population, Black and Mulatto, 1850–1920**

	Negro		Black		Mulatto	
	Growth rate over 10 years	Growth rate over 20 years	Growth rate over 10 years	Growth rate over 20 years	Growth rate over 10 years	Growth rate over 20 years
1920	6.47%	18.44%	13.19%		-19.02%	
1910	11.25%	31.94%		22.71%		81.15%
1900	18.60%	34.24%				
1890	13.19%	52.64%		47.53%		93.83%
1880	34.85%	48.15%				
1870	9.86%	34.11%	11.48%	32.88%	-0.73%	43.94%
1860	22.07%		19.19%		45.01%	

Note: Rates are calculated based on previous period, whether 10 or 20 years. The number of people enumerated as "black" increased by 22.71% from 1890 to 1910, whereas the total number of black people ("Negro") rose 31.94% over the same period, the difference being explained by the higher growth observed in the "mulatto" category. When numbers were lacking for 20-year periods, I derived them from the 10-year rates given by the census (31.94% for 1910 is the result of applying the 10-year growth rate of 11.25% to the previous 10-year growth rate of 18.60%). Numbers were published for 20-year periods from 1890 to 1910 and 1870 to 1890, for 10-year periods between 1850 and 1870.

Source: US Bureau of the Census, *Negro Population, 1790–1915* (1918), 208.

Following on the work of Robert Fogel, other historians have used these data in an attempt to establish standard-of-living indexes, in the belief that the extant physical data, thanks to the census and to the anthropometric works of the era, permit the formation of hypotheses on the comparative standard of living of slaves, free blacks, and free whites.[17]

In his study, the economist Richard Steckel combined two traditions of measuring development: economic development, on the one hand, and physical measurements indicating the well-being of individuals, on the other.[18] He was thus able to take differences in the height of children and adults between slave and free, Northerners and Southerners, and place them into a broader context of quantification of inequalities that gave new results.[19] He returned to the question of mulattoes in the questionnaires reserved for slaves in 1850 and 1860, and without rejecting Fogel and Engerman's 1974 model, he formed another, more developed model that took into account regional and local variations, especially the presence of men who could have been the fathers of mulatto children in the county:

The probability that a child was mulatto decreased with the size of the holding and increased with the proportion of adults aged 15–19 who were mulatto. The probability was higher on small holdings where no slave dwellings were listed and declined with the number of slaves per dwelling. The frequency of mulatto children increased with the proportion of whites among males 15–49 in the county.[20]

Steckel's use of a regression model allowed him to state that regional variations in the definition of the term *mulatto*, if they existed, did not weaken the overall results, that is to say, the small number of mulatto children whose paternity was very likely due to their mother's owner.[21]

This study tends to show, like *Time on the Cross*, that sexual relations with the slaveowner, by force or by consent, were not the norm and thus helps refute the image of the plantation owner as a sexual predator. At the same time, it permits a critique of the importance of unions between blacks and mulattoes in the construction of the intergenerational model of Fogel and Engerman, which were apparently overestimated, while the role of whites outside the property was underestimated.

The interpretation of the data on mulattoes in the 1850 and 1860 censuses remains a sensitive issue, and there is no consensus on the question because at that date the census had not adopted any definition of these terms. Appearance seems to have been the main criterion of determination of census workers, when they saw each individual.

The end of slavery and the census of 1870 brought about a thorough reformulation of these categories and of the role of blacks in the construction of the definition of whites, but with some degree of continuity with the preceding period. The introduction of the category of "mulatto," rather than broadening the range of possibilities of identification, was conceived of as a way to reinforce racial discrimination in the statistics. The separate identification of each individual on the questionnaire of the population opened the way, from 1850 on, to the multiplication of categories, whether of race or of national origin. Yet the black-and-white model remained at the heart of the system of classification of US residents.

PART III

THE RISE OF IMMIGRATION AND THE RACIALIZATION OF SOCIETY

The Adaptation of the Census to the Diversity of the American Population (1850–1900)

The 1850 census marked the start of a new era, one in which the unprecedented development of questionnaires and the transition to individual data finally made the federal census what Madison had envisioned at the turn of the century: the most complete document in existence on the society, population, and economy of the United States. The ambition of the guiding spirits of the new US census was such that they had no hesitation in proclaiming that the document was the broadest and most indepth statistical investigation in the world.

J. C. G. Kennedy, superintendent of the census for 1850 and 1860, traveled to Europe to meet his counterparts at the international statistical congresses, not only to absorb the rapid progress made on that continent, but also to showcase the progress that the US census had made since he had become its head. In this new perspective of international comparison, the American delegates to the international congresses could rightfully be proud of the progress that had been made since the 1850 census, but they still felt the constraints they operated under, most of all in the political demands emanating from Congress and the executive branch. Moreover, the US census aimed to document the specific movements of the American population, of which the most important (which would be the big question of the census for almost a century) was the massive immigration that had begun during the 1840s. In publications at home, as well as on their visits to Europe, the American statisticians promoted not only the rapid progress of statistical methods put into effect by the office and the scope of its work in each decade, but also the strong demographic growth of the nation, confirmed in each census. This growth allowed them to present the United States as the nation of human progress, while the old continent remained the reference in scientific matters. It was in this period, after the 1860 census, that American statisticians began to take their own statistical history as their principal model, rather than the one borrowed from England, which they had used since the mid-nineteenth century. This new self-assurance was nourished by the incontestable progress of American statistics, as well as by the idea that the American population growth had no comparison with the European demography. From this point of view, the census became more and more its own source of legitimacy.

Meanwhile, the abolition of slavery, coinciding with a larger place being given to immigration in the questionnaires and in the published reports, did not result in the disappearance of the racial categories of the American census along with the suppression of the three-fifths mechanism. On the contrary, the arrival of the first Asian immigrants on western shores and the uneasiness aroused by the "Celtic race" represented by Irish immigrants only served to reinforce the importance of the racial categories that, for the first time, were about to partially cross-cut those of immigration (in the case first of the Chinese and then of the Japanese). The second half-century of the history of the US census unfolds under the double aegis of the difficult modernization of the statistical apparatus and of an increasingly absorbing preoccupation with immigration. To determine and measure the share of national origins in the composition of the population would thus become the major contribution of census statisticians to the definition of the American identity.

In parallel, the development of scientific racism, the failure of Reconstruction, and the development of segregation would assign a new task to the census: to document the fate of the black race, a population whose inevitable extinction by the twentieth century would be predicted in census reports, preceded by that of American Indians and other indigenous peoples. The demography imagined by the successive censuses would develop along two lines: registration of the decline of populations that were not of European origin, and a growing racialization of more recent immigrants. Both the American statistical tradition and the main currents of American sociology and historiography are structured by an opposition between the treatment of racial minorities and that of ethnic minorities, the descendants of slaves and aboriginals or the descendants of immigrants. Unquestionably, the concepts and methods applied by the census to measure their respective shares were different, but, as this section will show, these two simultaneous movements need to be analytically reunited. The study of the rules for assigning characteristics of parents to their children, in particular, will highlight the differences but also shed light on how the concepts, methods, and practices of racial classification influenced what I call ethnic statistics.

Modernization, Standardization, and Internationalization

From the Censuses of J. C. G. Kennedy (1850 and 1860) to the First Census of Francis A. Walker (1870)

In 1853, at the initiative of Adolphe Quételet, the first international statistical congress took place in Brussels. The event inaugurated a series of conferences that took place in various European capitals through 1878. In 1885 these were succeeded by the formation of the International Statistical Institute.[1] The United States sent delegates to each of these congresses, with the exception of 1857 and 1867. J. C. G. Kennedy, even after he had been replaced by DeBow as head of the census, succeeded in being named by the government as its representative at Brussels in 1853 and at the congress in Paris in 1855. Edward Jarvis was the American representative in 1860 and 1869.[2] The superintendents of the census touted their presence at these congresses as evidence of their seriousness and as a way of affirming a scientific legitimacy in addition to their essentially political legitimacy.

This is apparent as early as the 1853 report by DeBow, who in his introduction went so far as to reproduce the 20 May 1853 circular of Quételet containing the recommendations for holding a congress at Brussels and the list of questions that ought to be asked in all countries with the goal of facilitating international comparisons.[3] In reality, the United States' vaunted goal of internationalism remained largely limited to the British example. In his brief overview of the "European census system," DeBow limited detailed comparison to the British census, from its origin up to 1851.[4] Some of the American statistical results were presented alongside the British equivalent; thus, for example, the tables on the age distribution of the white, slave, and free colored population were accompanied by the age distribution of the British population (excluding Ireland) in 1851.[5]

These comparisons were not fortuitous. The 1850 census was the first whose published volumes included text, and DeBow's long introduction can be read equally as a spirited defense of his work (even if it was not actually his) and as a stirring patriotic speech on the vitality of the nation. On this last point, the data were expected to demonstrate national progress—no longer just by population growth, but also by its residents' characteristics, which the 1850 reform made it possible to identify as never before. To the national pride in having been among the first countries to institute a regular census was the added pride in the breadth of the inquiry and the quality of the published reports. The sixth schedule, dealing with "social statistics," was also part of this effort, in that it presented a portrait of the quality of local American institutions, whose progress was indicated by their increasing number.[6] It was not a question of statistics bearing directly upon the residents themselves, but of data indicating the density of social and cultural institutions per resident, whether schools, churches, or public institutions such as libraries or prisons.

Until 1850, each census resulted in a single volume of tables without commentary.[7] From 1850 on, the Census Office launched into a vast publishing enterprise that reached its limits only when Congress refused to pay the bills. DeBow laid claim to this new arrangement, which in his eyes was all for the glory of the nation:

> In the magnificent progress of the country within the past sixty years, so elaborately shown in this volume, in territory, in population, in industry, and in wealth—beyond all precedent in history, beyond all the dreams of enthusiasts— how much room is there for gratitude and pride in every American heart. With free institutions; with just and equitable laws, meted out with the same hand to the low and to the high, with virtue and intelligence, and energy and industry, co-working harmoniously together—the many constituting one; with power at home and character abroad,—who shall question the future which is before us ? The balance-sheet of the past has been made up. The record is presented here.[8]

Noting with equal pride that 45 marshals and 3,251 assistant marshals had been employed to produce 640,000 manuscript pages, DeBow bragged about the rapidity of the process that allowed results to be published without delay, comparing it favorably to the delays in publication of the British and French censuses of 1851.[9] Although DeBow did not mention it, it was Kennedy who had wanted the published volumes to do honor to the work that had been done and to be widely distributed. He used a simple argument to convince Congress, which had to vote on the budget for the undertaking: the United States could not afford to publish volumes of lesser quality than what was becoming the standard for national statistics in Europe. The first progress report Kennedy presented to Congress emphasized how a poor-quality publication would give a poor image of the country. In this, he showed the influence of those energetic statisticians in charge of the European censuses, whom he had met with when he took up his position:

> for the purpose of examining into the methods adopted for the procuring and classification of such facts as are enumerated by those governments in their statistical investigations, in order that our own Census might, when published, prove of the greatest value to ourselves, and not to seem inferior to those of countries which have the credit of having paid more attention to statistical science, although they may not have made greater advances in what we esteem rational forms of government.

Kennedy added that drawing inspiration from the best of the recent European developments in statistics, in terms of calculation and data presentation, would allow what he called "our great national work" to complete the analysis of American society and to "be able to institute comparisons with the advancement of other people."[10]

The superintendent of the census felt it would be an insult to the American republic to lag behind monarchies, whether or not they were constitutional. He equated the technical quality of the census with the advancement of peoples and progress on the path toward "rational forms of government." In fact, the census, through the mechanism of apportionment, contributed to a very rational form of government, in which numbers were the arbiter of power. From this patriotic point of view, the census was at one and the same time the indicator of the demographic and economic progress of the nation and the paper embodiment of American modernity. It allied quantitative progress, by the numbers that it produced, to qualitative progress, by the development of the census itself that bore witness to the technical and intellectual qualities of Americans. From then on, it would no longer be just a matter of documenting the unique pattern of growth of the American population, but one of showing the rest of the world the progress of the nation on all levels.

Kennedy concluded his report to Congress with this boastful statement:

> These explanations are deemed necessary only for information relating to the view of contemporaneous nations, and not as an apology for what is deemed correct and proper in the preparation of our own Census.
>
> Our materials are more varied and of better character than any nation has ever possessed; and shall it be said that, insensible of their value, we have not known how to render them useful?[11]

DeBow, who had taken up in midstream Kennedy's work in progress, followed his lead. Not only were the volumes published in a quarto format that was eas-ier to handle than the earlier, much larger folios, in spite of the much larger number of pages (about a thousand), but also the print runs were significantly increased.[12] Thanks to his better political relations, DeBow was able to win sup-port for a condensed edition in 1854, as well as for a volume entirely devoted to mortality statistics edited by Edward Jarvis. The *Compendium*, in handy octavo format, enjoyed a print run of 320,000 copies, an extraordinary number for the period and more than one copy per hundred people.[13]

The comparison with European practices, put forth by Kennedy and DeBow, showed itself by significant borrowings. Thus, the nomenclature of causes of death in the volume on mortality closely followed that of the British census. Edward Jarvis, who carried out the work published in 1855 as well as the correspond-ing volume of the eighth census published in 1866, was quite familiar with the European publications. His personal collection of books on statistics in general, and mortality statistics in particular, was so comprehensive that he refused to go to Washington to do the work, on the grounds that the task could only be done at his home in Concord, Massachusetts.[14] With regard to the nomenclature for causes of death, Jarvis acknowledged his debt in the introduction to the 1866 volume.[15]

At this time, statistical works were still rare in the United States, and the experts who had received training in the field were necessarily oriented toward England. This was especially true in the domain of mortality statistics and actu-arial tables, which were still lacking for the American population. Nonetheless, a specifically American character was revealed in the use of distinctions based on color, as well as in some homegrown causes of death, such as lynching, and the numerical importance of homicide.

Of course, the strength and variety of international influences varied depend-ing on the background of the individuals in question, but for Kennedy, Shattuck, and Jarvis, their reference point, in theory and in practice, was Great Britain. Jarvis, for one, noted several times during the preparations for the reform of 1870, in his correspondence with James Garfield, that "the British system is bet-ter than ours has been."[16] He also stated that in the volume on mortality for 1860 he was inspired by the work of Quételet and the reports of the international con-gresses of 1860 and 1863.[17]

To invoke international recognition by readers of the published work is not immaterial. Admittedly, it is difficult to determine the weight of this argument on those who held the purse strings for fieldwork and publications, each volume separately being the object of a fresh budgetary discussion in Congress. While the political and geographical stakes—between North and South—remained deci-sive, as shown by the replacement of Kennedy by DeBow, the first reports edited and published by the Census Office all position the government's statistical work within an international context, even to vie for first place. The 1854 publication of a compendium and the adoption of the quarto or octavo format clearly show that the Census sought to find its place in foreign libraries as well as those at home. However, even though Americans were eager to take the stage with their European counterparts, they continued to occupy a marginal position within the global community of specialists that was developing at the time. In fact, the American census is distinguished more by its scope, on the scale of a huge nation, than by technical innovations that could impress European statisticians.

Nonetheless, the desire of those in charge of the federal census to place their work within an international network is all the more remarkable in that the census remained a national enterprise, patriotic even in its commentaries. But this is equally true in other countries, and the contacts between the heads of governmental agencies took several decades before launching into a program of international statistics. Public statistics were above all national statistics, and whatever desire to establish a scientific plan emerges from the international congresses or Kennedy's correspondence with Quételet or Charles Babbage, the census projects remained an administrative statistical undertaking.[18]

These enthusiastic statements often came down to mere declarations of intent. Edward Jarvis's experience is very enlightening in this respect. In the introductions to official reports of the census, Jarvis did not restrain his criticism of the assistant marshals who gathered data in the field, and in private he admitted that he did not acknowledge any statistical competence on the part of the agents who compiled the data at the Census Office in Washington.[19] As early as 1850 Jarvis had indicated to Kennedy that, for the compilation of data, one ought not to engage "politicians" (that is, men chosen for their political connections), but rather serious people familiar with figures, such as accountants or teachers.[20] Jarvis told how he managed to avoid going to Washington to compile the volume and do his calculations. Using his personal library, he put together, for the documentation and calculations, a team of ten young women, high-school students in his home town of Concord, who could read French and German and who were mathematically gifted. This solution was not only frugal, but more importantly, it allowed him to obtain more accurate results. And the work went faster than if the tasks had been entrusted to "any of the old clerks in Washington," who, Jarvis was certain, were less competent than his team of high-schoolers hand-picked for their scholarly aptitude.[21] This anecdote says a great deal about the gap between intentions and practice, and about the skepticism with which an expert of Jarvis's standing viewed the federal government employees charged with compiling the results of the census. As early as 1853 DeBow had articulated the need to create a permanent bureau of the census, as the only way to train and deploy competent professionals.[22] The 1850 reform had transferred to Washington the work of compiling the schedules, which had formerly been done by marshals in each state, but Jarvis' critique marks the limits of this change.

Kennedy did not disagree with him; he advocated strongly for a permanent bureau and for the recruitment of more competent agents:

> In the preparation of this volume we have not hesitated to avail our-selves of the services of gentlemen unconnected with the public serv-ice, whose generous co-operation enhances its value and increases its claims to public confidence.[23]

Despite the declarations and the efforts to bring American statistics closer to the European publications, the American political context, with the Civil War and the increasingly important immigration question, would continue to limit the efforts and would affect the schedules as well as the reports. The reports themselves now took up a new aim: to propose, with all the optimism of future projections, solutions to the social questions that preoccupied Americans in the second half of the century, questions that especially concerned issues of population, such as the future of the black race, the arrival of non-European immigrants, and the new European immigration's links to pauperism and the "suicide of the race." If the organization of the census and its publications were the result of a compromise between the desires of experts and the expectations of Congress, the advantage rested with Congress, which in this period exerted two essential means of control, explicitly listing the topics for the schedule and funding the supplementary publications.

Garfield and the Abortive Reform of 1870

As the 1870 census approached, there was again a show of ambition to place the nation solidly among the modern nations, on the statistical level. And once again international statistical congresses were invoked with the aim of ensuring that schedules and reports should meet, if not surpass, their recommendations. According to Quételet, there were eight questions that were indispensable to any national census: name, sex, age, relation to the head of household, civil status or family situation, profession, place of birth, and blind, deaf, or dumb. Except for the question on relationship to the head of household and civil status, the American census since 1850 had met the current standards.[24] The inclusion of these last two questions was thus proposed for the 1870 census, along with new questions that the congresses judged desirable but not indispensable, such as language spoken and religion. In addition, the first plan for 1869 proposed asking whether one or both parents were of foreign birth, a question that was not among the recommendations, just like questions on race, which were absent in those terms from European censuses.[25] The context of the sectional crisis meant that the law framing the 1860 census renewed the text for 1850, and only minor modifications distinguished the 1860 schedules from those for 1850. In 1869, however, there was a renewed spirit of census reform among members of Congress.

To prepare for an eventual recasting of the legislation, the House of Representatives set up a Special Committee on the Ninth Census, under the direction of James A. Garfield, who brought in outside experts, in the first rank of whom were Edward Jarvis and Francis Amasa Walker, an eminent figure in the official pantheon of the history of statistics in the United States. The Special Committee also proposed adding a fourth choice in the list of possible options for filling in the column on "color": "Chinese."

> That relating to color has been made to include distinctively the Chinese, so as to throw some light on the grave questions which the arrival of the Celestials among us have raised.[26]

Chinese immigrants had begun to arrive on the West Coast of the United States in the 1840s, and the censuses of 1850 and 1860 counted persons as being of Chinese origin before this category was included in the printed list of choices on the schedules. The schedules for 1850 and 1860 had proposed three choices, printed in the column "Color," for free residents: "White, Black or Mulatto." For slaves, two possibilities were given in the instructions that accompanied schedule no. 2: "Black" or "Mulatto." The 1860 census enumerated 35,565 foreigners born in China (compared to 758 in 1850), but the published tables by county show that Chinese, like Indians in California, were frequently included in the total for the white race.[27] At this time, the term "Chinese" functioned as a nationality and not as a race. The addition of a specific racial category in 1870 thus responded to a need that arose in 1860, when this category had unexpectedly emerged from the responses.[28] Children born in the United States to Chinese parents were thus, for the census, Chinese in race without being Chinese in origin by birth, which explains why the numbers diverge.[29]

In spite of support from international statisticians and national experts,[30] the reformers were defeated in the Senate by conservatives claiming to keep the series identical so as to be able to conduct item-by-item comparisons across censuses.[31] This argument was all the more convincing to the senators since the 1850 law, renewed in 1860, claimed to be permanent.[32] The senators' hostility arose also from a political conflict based on patronage: Garfield's project proposed to remove responsibility for recruitment of marshals from senators so that they could be recruited according to the districts of representatives, and more generally so that their recruitment could be supervised by the Census Office.[33] This occurred in the context of a sectional conflict between the Northeast, the Midwest, and the South over the question of apportionment, which sparked strong opposition to a reform that would advance the transfer of seats to the

Midwest, the region that had gained the most inhabitants.[34] Francis A. Walker saw in this clientelist attitude the principal, and perhaps only, reason for the defeat of the Garfield Bill in the Senate.[35]

In the end, the 1850 law was renewed in 1870, with some changes that seemed insignificant to Congress and to officials, but which were nonetheless important in the evolution of racial and ethnic categories. These included the introduction of two new categories under "Color," "Chinese" and "Indian"; questions on the place of birth of parents, which created the statistical population of the second generation issuing from immigration; and the addition at the end of the schedule of two questions on the restriction of the right to vote of former slaves. If the hoped-for reforms of the Special Committee were postponed, they would be adopted in 1880, especially since Garfield's assistant, Francis A. Walker, was named superintendent in 1870 and his appointment was renewed in 1880. One of the unintended consequences of retaining the essence of the 1850 law was the recruitment in the South of census agents under the control of the political authorities of Reconstruction. In the view of Walker, who had ample cause to regret it, the census-taking was "thrown back into the hands of the Marshals of the United States Courts; officers thoroughly identified, at every point, with the party and race struggles that had convulsed society form 1865 to 1870."

In other words, in 1870 the clientelist system for recruitment of census agents passed, in the southern states, into the hands of Republicans, who hired blacks en masse, including many former slaves, to conduct the census in districts with a black majority, where the whites were traditionally Democrats. Walker deplored this practice in a tone typical of critics of Reconstruction:

> The power of appointment was exercised to the inexpressible injury of the census service. Negroes who could not write or read were selected for this difficult, delicate, and responsible duty. Accompanied, perhaps, by some poor white man, with such clerical accomplishments as might be expected, these officers of the law pushed their way into mansions where their intrusion was resented as an insult, or sought to traverse the bridle-paths of extensive districts—districts three or four or five times as large as could properly be assigned to single officers—to find the hundreds and thousands of log-houses in which the poorer part of the population, white or black, found shelter.[36]

Besides Walker's tendency to attribute to Reconstruction the shortcomings of the 1870 census in the South, it is generally admitted that the 1870 census data for that region were worse than they should have been, especially for the black population.[37] In addition to incompetence on the part of census workers, there were problems arising from the displacements of populations caused by the war. Moreover,

Walker opposed the recruitment of black or openly Republican agents in the South, arguing in favor of reform in the recruitment of marshals and assistant marshals. Recruiting agents from among professional ranks such as teachers, county or town clerks, or "other persons having familiarity with figures and facility in writing" immediately eliminated former slaves. The Republicans' use of black agents for the census of 1870, as described by Walker, became one of the standard arguments in calls for reform of recruitment of federal government agents.[38] Walker himself continued to blame black agents for the bad data in the 1870 census:

> When the appointments of enumerators were made in 1870 the entire lot was taken from the Republican party, and most of those in the South were negroes. Some of the negroes could not read or write, and the enumeration of the Southern population was done very badly. My judgment was that the census of 1870 erred as to the colored population between 350,000 and 400,000.[39]

A new period opened up with the end of the Civil War—one in which, alongside more numerous immigrants from more places, the American population counted roughly 4 million free men and women of African origin who were henceforth citizens. To say that American society was not prepared for this would be an understatement. During the war and even more in the following decades, statisticians, led by those of the census, went to great lengths to prove that this anomaly would be resolved naturally by the disappearance of this population.

From this time forward, the principal focus of the designers of the US census would be the political importance of population questions. The tradition established beginning in 1850 would become the practical and theoretical foundation on which later censuses would be based. The inferiority complex that we can sometimes read between the lines of American statisticians when they looked toward Europe would dissipate not only because the source of legitimacy would become more and more explicitly national, but also because, after 1870, the stakes would have less to do with the formulation of schedules than with the richness of statistical treatments. The Census Office would illustrate this with thousands of pages of figures, colored maps, and geographical, geological, and ethnological investigations that Walker would feature in the volumes published under his direction, and finally with the Hollerith machines and their perforated cards, used following the 1890 census. Census schedules remained under the tight control of Congress until 1930, since the list of questions appeared in the census law, giving additional emphasis to questions of national interest. The period from 1850 to 1870 thus appears as an exception in the long history of the US Census, and we must see the appeal to international scientific authority as one way for experts to give weight to their arguments, with mitigated success.

From Slavery to Freedom

The Future of the Black Race or Racial Mixing as Degeneration

The abolition of slavery consecrated by the Thirteenth Amendment in 1865 rendered null and void the Three-Fifths Compromise enshrined in the Constitution in 1787.[1] The Fourteenth Amendment, ratified in 1868, profoundly redefined American citizenship at the federal and state levels, in its Sections 1 and 2. Section 2 eliminated the Three-Fifths Compromise and tied states' representation to their recognition of the rights of all their male inhabitants, thereby rewriting the mechanism of apportionment of seats in the House of Representatives:

> Representatives shall be apportioned among the several states according to their respective numbers, counting the whole number of persons in each state, excluding Indians not taxed. But when the right to vote at any election for the choice of electors for President and Vice President of the United States, Representatives in Congress, the executive and judicial officers of a state, or the members of the legislature thereof, is denied to any of the male inhabitants of such state, being twenty-one years of age, and citizens of the United States, or in any way abridged, except for participation in rebellion, or other crime, the basis of representation therein shall be reduced in the proportion which the number of such male citizens shall bear to the whole number of male citizens twenty-one years of age in such state.

Finally, the Fifteenth Amendment, ratified in 1870, explicitly guaranteed black men the right to vote:

> The right of citizens of the United States to vote shall not be denied or abridged by the United States or by any state on account of race, color, or previous condition of servitude.

The changes introduced by the three Reconstruction-era amendments had two major consequences for the census: on the one hand, the end of the Three-Fifths Compromise; on the other, the development of the census itself into the instrument of control and sanction of the limitation of former slaves' right to vote. The 1870 census thus had to measure both the distribution of the population for the apportionment of seats in the House of Representatives and the enforcement of these amendments. States where the voting rights of blacks were denied would see their representation diminished accordingly. The task facing the census was a very difficult one, as we shall see. Even before the end of the Civil War, Kennedy had speculated on the future number of free black inhabitants. As the prospect of complete abolition drew near, a new situation had to be faced, and the census was no better prepared than other institutions to face it: what place would these new citizens occupy in American society? Although it published data on slaves until 1865, the census, through Kennedy's writings, had tried to clarify the future destiny of the former slaves, in the light of data gathered in 1860 on slaves and free blacks, both groups divided into black and mulatto. Kennedy's conclusion, expressed as early as 1862, was simple: American society would find a natural solution to the black question, that is to say, to the problem posed by the presence in the nation of 4 million free men and women of African descent. Because of the impossibility of returning all the blacks to Africa, and because the idea of integrating them permanently into the American population seemed inappropriate, even unnatural to some, the prospect of the gradual extinction of the black population offered a reassuring response, under the scientific guarantee of the publications of the federal statistical institution.

Belief in the Inevitable Extinction of the Black Race: Statistics as a Natural Solution to the Black Question after Emancipation

In the preliminary report of the Eighth Census, in 1862, when the general emancipation of slaves was becoming a real possibility, census superintendent J. C. G. Kennedy offered a scientific response to all those who were frightened by the prospect: the gradual extinction of the black race in the United States was a foreseeable fact.[2] He noted that between 1850 and 1860 the growth rate for the white population had been 32 percent, but only 22 percent for slaves and 12 percent for free blacks. Their combined share of the American population would shift from 13 percent in 1870 to 9 percent in 1900. Emancipation would thus lead to gradual extinction. In reality, the black population had gone from 700,000 to 4 million between 1790 and 1860, essentially without immigration.

This was an indication of significant natural growth, while the white population had benefited from large-scale immigration, which had sharply increased in the two preceding decades.

In the first volume on the population in 1860, published in 1864, before the end of the war, when emancipation was no longer in doubt, Kennedy detailed the reasons why biology and statistics combined to lead to the "unerring certainty" of the gradual extinction of the American black population "diffused among the dominant race":

> With the lights before us, it seems, therefore, quite rational to conclude that we need not look forward to centuries to develop the fact that the white race is no more favorable to the progress of the African race in its midst, than it has been to the perpetuity of the Indian on its borders, and that, as has been the case in all other countries on this continent where the blacks were once numerous, the colored population in America, wherever, either free or slave, it must in number and condition be greatly subordinate to the white race, is doomed to comparatively rapid absorption or extinction. How this result is to be averted, partially at least, we leave to the determination of others, feeling our duty accomplished in developing the facts, as the figures of the census reveal them respecting the past.[3]

In this passage Kennedy provided the arguments that would feed a tradition lasting at least to the beginning of the twentieth century: the black question would have a natural solution, not a political or social one, on the understanding that its members would never be able to be full members of American society. With the Indians pushed back by the advance of the Europeans, and the blacks assimilated or dying out, the future of the nation would be as a white man's country.

These arguments were not entirely new. The theme of degeneration had long been tied to the dominant discourse on mulattoes, in the context of polygenism. But the census report brought scientific weight to this reasoning, relying not only on a discussion of the physical and moral qualities of blacks and mulattoes, or of their congenital maladaptation to freedom, but also on projections on the basis of data from the censuses of 1850 and 1860. Since the 1860 census was the last to collect data on slaves, these analyses would often be tied to those figures for those who made use of them. From this point of view, it is meaningful that the reference data for all comparisons on the situation of blacks before and after Emancipation should have been produced in such a spirit.

Kennedy devoted the opening pages of the census report of 1860—several passages of which warrant quoting—to this question. Kennedy's intention in the long (over one hundred pages) introduction to volume 1 is clear: readers in 1864 needed to interpret the 1860 data in light of the wartime upheavals.

When the first volume on population appeared, it was essential to provide some context for the information. Kennedy had the data to produce a unique document on the living conditions of slaves and to provide some guidance on how to integrate these 4 million new free citizens into the American population. But the census superintendent made a different choice: to present data on the period immediately preceding the catastrophe, confident that it would hold true for the future, thanks to "the recuperative energies of our people, the accelerated flow of migration, and the natural fertility and redintegrating nature of our lands."[4] What mattered was the natural dynamism of populations of European origin; in listing the negative effects of the war, Kennedy foregrounded the interruption of immigration.

In extrapolating from the figures for mulattoes in 1850 and 1860, the report came to a conclusion about hybridization that seems improbable in retrospect, but that was acceptable at the time thanks to the ideological context and a high degree of tolerance for non-rigorous application of figures. Kennedy thus inaugurated a theme that would be taken up in the reports of the censuses of 1870 and 1880, especially because of the erroneous interpretation of data of poor quality on the blacks whose population was clearly underreported in the South in 1870.[5]

Comparing the growth rates for free blacks, mulattoes, and whites between 1850 and 1860, he sought to reassure those concerned with the specter of a threat to the white race, buried under the numbers:

> With regard to the future increase of the African race in this country, various extravagant speculations have been recently promulgated. An attentive survey of the statistics of the census will guide to a more satisfactory approximation.[6]

Kennedy showed that the growth rate for free blacks, between 1850 and 1860, was half that for slaves (12.32 percent vs. 22.07 percent), without mentioning that it depended in large part on the number of emancipations—that is, on a factor whose variations were unpredictable and tightly linked to the economic and political context—and without noting that, by reason of adult emancipations, this population could not possibly have the same structure by age. He could thus project the trend, observed over only ten years, and compare the growth of the slave population, which was due only to natural causes, with that of the population of free blacks, whose growth was due to more complex causes:

> Leaving the issue of the present civil war for time to determine, it should be observed, if large numbers of slaves shall be hereafter emancipated,

so many will be transferred from a faster to a slower rate of increase. In such case, nine millions of the colored, in the year 1900, would be a large estimate. Of these, a great portion will be of mixed descent, since in 1850 one-ninth part of the whole colored class were returned as mulattoes, while in 1860 it is more than one eighth of the whole, and 36 percent of the free.[7]

The table 9.1 accompanying the passage showed exactly that:

Table 9.1. **Blacks and mulattoes in free and slave states, 1850 and 1860**

Color	In the northern or free states				In the southern or slaveholding states			
	Numbers		Proportion		Numbers		Proportion	
	1850	1860	1850	1860	1850	1860	1850	1860
Blacks	139,452	155,994	71.04	69.07	3,093,605	3,697,274	89.87	87.70
Mulattoes	56,856	69,855	28.96	30.93	348,895	518,360	10.13	12.30
Total colored	196,308	225,849	100.00	100.00	3,442,500	4,215,634	100.00	100.00

Source: Census, *Population of the United States in 1860*, 1:x.

On the basis of these figures, Kennedy showed why mulattoes were proportionately more numerous in the North. But, although they represented three-tenths of the blacks in this part of the country, Kennedy did not emphasize that the 69,855 mulattoes counted in the North in 1860 were only 13.4 percent of the total number of mulattoes enumerated in the United States at that date and that, moreover, 94 percent of blacks lived at that time in the southern states, which lessened the representativeness of the blacks of the North. There were two possible hypotheses: that freedom made them more prolific, or that a greater proportion of mulattoes than blacks were emancipated. Kennedy chose the second. Above all, he emphasized the moral decline of mulattoes, who until Emancipation embodied the symbol of free blacks. According to him, this moral decline, tied to their free condition, explained their demographic decline. Taking up a recurrent argument of slavery defenders, Kennedy used the counter-example of the condition of mulattoes as an indicator of the future of free blacks. From this point of view, it seemed that the biological handicap that characterized mulattoes (that they were hybrids) was less of a defect than the notion that they had had more experience of freedom. This enabled Kennedy to use their characteristics, as revealed through the statistics, as a predictive model for the fate of the 4 million blacks in line to gain their freedom, mechanically transferring the growth of the one group to the other.

For the writer of the report, the moral decline of freed blacks was explained by their proximity to slavery, ignoring the fact that, in certain regions, black families had been free for generations. Moral, psychological, and biological conditions came together to present a reassuring picture in which free blacks would be no threat to white workers. The emancipation of the black slaves raised a new issue, which concerned white workers in the North, and which had already been brewing during slavery: the opposition between free labor and slave labor. Free blacks would be competing economically with white workers, who would be the first to have their welfare threatened by the arrival in the labor market of these rivals who were suspected of being ready to accept any kind of working conditions. On this level, in the fantasies of the white working class, blacks were about to join recent immigrants such as the Irish and the Asian "coolies," who were all suspected of not being fully free. To varying degrees, they were also racialized, especially the Irish, who were considered racially different from Anglo-Saxons. The theme of the free worker thus came to be at the core of the laboring identity of native-born American workers, and racism became a powerful factor in the stratification of the working class.[8]

The introductory text of the volumes could thus elaborate on the theme of moral decline, the absence of "virtuous moral reserve," invisible in the figures, but which was the principal explanation of the data that, when extrapolated, predicted the physical disappearance of blacks, since as Kennedy understood it all blacks, once free, would conform to the data collected for free blacks in 1860. The cause was their proximity to the slave status of their forebears and their African origin:

> That a race forcibly transported to a state of slavery here, from a country without history, literature, or laws, whose people remain in barbarism, should not have been able to attain an equality in morals with their intellectual superiors is not surprising.

Kennedy went on to explain the "unfavorable moral situation" of free blacks, "notwithstanding the great number of excellent people included in that population," by their heredity which, even when they were of mixed race, pulled them downward. Even while referring to the significant proportion of mulattoes among free blacks as a somewhat positive element, he attributed this to what he called the maternal side:

> They are maternally descendants of the colored race, as it is well known that no appreciable amount of this admixture is the result of marriage

between white and black, or the progeny of white mothers—a fact
showing that whatever deterioration may be the consequence of this
alloyage, is incurred by the colored race.[9]

Kennedy's explanations were sometimes confused and contradictory. He noted
that it was among mulattoes that the most valuable elements of blacks were to
be found—a widespread belief at the time—but that such mixtures, while beneficial for individuals, posed a threat for the race as a whole. The paradoxical racist stereotypes about mulattoes current in the mid-nineteenth century are well
expressed in his writings: mulattoes benefit intellectually from their biological
proximity to whites, but to some extent they pay for this intellectual gain in physical, psychological, and moral weakness.

> The extinction of slavery, in widening the field for white labor and
> enterprise, will tend to reduce the rate of increase of the colored race,
> while its diffusion will lead to a more rapid admixture, the tendency
> of which, judging from the past, will be to impair it physically without
> improving it morally.[10]

On the other hand—and in this he resembles less reputable writers—Kennedy
tended to explain his data by commonplaces that were not based on established
fact. Thus, if it is true that marriages between whites and blacks were rare in the
first half of the century, they were not nonexistent, and some were noted by census agents. Yet Kennedy was unable, intellectually as well as politically, to draw
from the 1860 census data facts that would have countered such firmly established prejudices which he himself shared.[11] We must, therefore, read the introductory text of the census separately from the data, the two constituting in some
sense different documents, which relate to each other but also conflict. The written introduction served to place the data into perspective, so as to make the statistics for the final years of slavery cohere with the new context of Emancipation,
emphasizing a statistical determinism that was proclaimed all the more force-
fully because it relied upon only two series of data.

> These developments of the census, to a good degree, explain the slow
> progress of the free colored population in the northern States, and indi-
> cate, with unerring certainty, the gradual extinction of that people the
> more rapidly as, whether free or slave, they become diffused among
> the dominant race. There are, however, other causes, although in them-
> selves not sufficient to account for the great excess of deaths over births,
> as is found to occur in some northern cities, and these are such as are

incident to incongenial climate and a condition involving all the expo-
sures and hardships which accompany a people of lower caste.[12]

But all these themes of the volumes published in 1863 and 1864 remained con-
jectures, because it was a question of projections about the fate of free blacks,
compiled and published at a time when emancipation seemed more and more
certain, but dependent on the date when the data were gathered—1860. The
case of the 1870 census is very different, since it was adapted to an unprecedented situation: for the first time, there were no more slaves in the Union, and
the census was newly charged with verifying the application of the Fourteenth
and Fifteenth Amendments, which affirmed the equal rights of all inhabitants
and the right to vote of black citizens.

The Census of 1870 and the Fourteenth Amendment: The Passage from the Three-Fifths Compromise to the Protection of the Rights of Blacks

Emancipation made inapplicable the Three-Fifths Compromise, which
decreased the weight of slaves in the apportionment of representation and
taxes among the states, and Section 2 of the Fourteenth Amendment removed
it from the Constitution in 1868. Thenceforth there remained in the article of
the Constitution organizing the census only the distinction between Indians,
untaxed and excluded from the census, and all other residents, who henceforth
all had the same weight.

Although the distinction of status between free and slave had continually justified census discrimination of color between white and black, the abolition of
slavery and the disappearance of the status distinction in the census could not
lead to the suppression of discrimination of color—something that, by the eve of
the 1870 census, had acquired sufficient autonomy in society and in the census
to continue to exist on its own. At this date, no one had yet envisaged making the
census color-blind, because race and color had become transparent, naturalized
categories that seemed to arise out of plain common sense.[13] As for preceding
censuses, the debates concerned the limits and definitions of these categories,
but never the necessity of the presence of a distinction of race or color in the
schedules.

Two principal reasons explain this: first, since 1850, the census had documented the presence in the United States of inhabitants of non-European origin, mainly Chinese, who had immediately become the object of new racial

classifications, expressed as "color," while the Indians who lived in enumeration areas began to be taken into account and classed under a specific color, "Indian." Second, the interest taken by experts and the public in the black question had not died out with the abolition of slavery, and the census was about to become the object of renewed requests for information on the "progress" of the black population.

Sweeping reform proposals preceded the 1870 census, notably through pressure from James A. Garfield and Francis Amasa Walker. The crucial point of the reform was to put an end to the clientelism that reigned in the distribution of posts for censustakers. This is why the Senate prevented the reform from seeing the light of day, pushing back the reorganization to the 1880 census.[14] Despite the partial failure of the census administration's attempts at reform, and although, for lack of adoption of a new law, the 1870 census was still bound by the law of 1850 and 1860, the population census was still profoundly affected by the abolition of slavery. It was not just the end of the Three-Fifths Compromise, which marked the definitive passage from a distinction of status to race- or color-based distinctions, but also the fact that the census, charged with establishing the apportionment that followed on the inclusion of 4 million new citizens with full rights of citizenship, now had a political function that was more important than ever.

Since 1865, the Republicans had begun to consider the question of the weight of the former slaves in the calculation for the apportionment of seats. The paradox was that, with the vast majority of blacks living in the former Confederate states, preliminary calculations showed that the Democrats were well positioned to regain the majority in the House of Representatives, and even the presidency, once these states were readmitted into the Union. Four solutions were suggested: (1) that Congress itself should give freed slaves the right to vote; (2) that the readmission of the Confederate states should be postponed until northern hegemony was firmly established; (3) that the basis for calculating apportionment should be changed by replacing the total population by the total number of voters; or (4) that states that did not give freed slaves the right to vote should have their representation reduced. With the exception of changing the basis for calculation, all these solutions were tried out. The census found itself at the heart of Reconstruction, and these options affected the fundamental balance of power.[15]

It was also a turning point in the history of the census: while Kennedy buried himself in his projections on the extinction of the black population, which were of no use at all to the politicians, a new generation of statisticians was preparing to take the lead and adapt the census to the new context of Reconstruction. In the same way that the political leaders had abolished slavery in order to win the war and not out of conviction, they were quick to recognize that, in order for Reconstruction to succeed, they needed the political weight of blacks in the South, where they were weakly established, while at the same time blacks were generally deprived of the right to vote in northern states. But there again, it was with eyes fixed on the number of seats coming out of the new calculation that the decision was made to find a mechanism that would guarantee the political dominance of Republicans. The demographic data offered no alternative to relying on black suffrage.

This mix of principles and pragmatism was expressed by Garfield—at the time a member of the House of Representatives—before an assembly in Ohio on the Fourth of July, 1865. He made it clear that if blacks did not have the right to vote, there would be fifteen additional representatives from states that had been in rebellion, without the addition of a single citizen, and fifteen seats less in the "loyal states":

> This will not only give six members of Congress to South Carolina, four sevenths of whose people are negroes, but it will place the power of the State, as well as the destiny of 412,000 black men, in the hands of the 20,000 white men (less than the number of voters in our own Congressional district) who, under the restricted suffrage of that undemocratic State, exercise the franchise.[16]

The threat was obvious: the move from three-fifths to five-fifths for blacks, without any further modification, would automatically entail a gain for the states having a large black population and a clear loss for the others—in other words, politically, a gain for the Democratic South and a loss for the Republican North. The solution was less obvious, to the extent that in the North, the feminist movement, which supported black suffrage, was demanding woman suffrage as well. Any calculation based on the number of voters and not on the total population was becoming extremely risky because it was the state legislatures that determined the composition of the electoral body. The possibility of the shift to voting population risked leading some states to engage in a kind of bidding war to extend the right to vote to foreigners or to women in order to increase their representation. Here again demography played an important role: the representatives from New England were quick to oppose this solution, because their states numbered more women than men and also had a large number of non-naturalized immigrants, which meant so many residents that would be excluded from the basis for representation.[17]

In the end, the solution adopted by the Committee on Reconstruction and drawn up in the Fourteenth Amendment in June 1866 provided for penalties to be imposed on states that restricted suffrage, without imposing black suffrage on the states. The device aimed to reduce proportionally the representation of states that did not grant former slaves the right to vote. The measure applied to the North as well, where not all blacks had the right to vote, but the proportion of blacks in the northern states meant that the penalties had no effect on their representation. For the South, the situation was altogether different. The wording of the amendment, referring only to adult male persons, left aside the woman question, which gave rise to disappointment and divisions among feminist organizations, which had seen it as a unique opportunity to win universal suffrage, while radical Republicans, partisans of universal male suffrage, accepted the compromise in the name of upholding Republican dominance. Certain feminist circles opposed the extension of suffrage to black men, while respectable white women remained deprived of the right to vote.

Even before the census, projections were made on all sides, on the basis of the 1860 data, by redoing the calculation with the new rules adopted in 1868.[18] But in 1870—the time of the census and of the calculation of the new apportionment—the United States ratified the Fifteenth Amendment, which explicitly affirmed black male suffrage, in the North and in the South. This rendered superfluous the application of Section 2 of the Fourteenth Amendment. Nevertheless, following the report prepared in 1869 by Garfield for the House of Representatives, the 1870 census called for a way to quantify restrictions on the right to vote.[19] Garfield had explained to the House the way he expected to use the census to serve the Fourteenth Amendment, without concealing the flaws that had already been pointed out. After having prepared a list of restrictions current in the different states, he proposed to use in the schedule for the 1870 census the precise formulation of the Fourteenth Amendment: male citizens of the United States twenty-one years or older, whose right to vote is denied or in any way abridged, except for participation in rebellion, or other crime.[20]

Due to senatorial opposition, Garfield's proposed bill, though adopted in a vote of 86–40 by the House, failed in the Senate, and thus was not passed by Congress.[21] Ironically, the mechanism for applying Section 2 of the Fourteenth Amendment, which Garfield had separated from the rest of the proposed law in view of possible conflicts with the Fifteenth Amendment, was actually adopted. The 1870 schedule thus included two questions concerning "constitutional relations," which would furnish data for fixing penalties.[22] This addition was the most direct political intervention in the schedule in the history of the census, developed in the instructions to census agents.

At the end of the schedule, under the heading "Constitutional Relations," appeared questions 19 ("Male citizens of U.S. of 21 years and upwards") and 20 ("Male citizens of U.S. of 21 years and upwards, whose right to vote is denied or abridged on other grounds than rebellion or other crime"). Question 19 made it possible to establish the potential number of voters, which would have permitted an apportionment based on that population. The responses to be filled in, in these columns, amounted to simply checking the box as applicable. But the instructions to census agents, generally quite concise, in this case included a long discussion, amounting to justification as much as instruction:

> Upon the answers to the questions under this head will depend the distribution of representative power in the General Government. It is therefore imperative that this part of the enumeration should be performed with absolute accuracy. Every male person born within the United States, who has attained the age of twenty-one years, is a citizen of the United States by the force of the Fourteenth Amendment to the Constitution; also, all persons born out of the limits and jurisdiction of the United States, whose fathers at the time of their birth were citizens of the United States (act of February 10, 1855); also, all persons born out of the limits and jurisdiction of the United States, who have been declared by judgment of Court to have been duly Naturalized, having taken out both "papers."[23]

The task was at once quite ambitious, because it meant asking the assistant marshals to supervise the application of amendments to the Constitution, and quite difficult to execute. Census agents had to be capable of making distinctions, including distinctions among inhabitants who had the right to vote but did not exercise it, those who fell strictly into the Fourteenth Amendment category of being denied their right to vote by virtue of electoral codes superseded by the Fifteenth Amendment, and those who would not be counted in this column. The legal complexity added to the ignorance of US inhabitants was the first difficulty. The adverse conditions of the rolling out of the 1870 census, especially in the South, did the rest. To these factors, which affected the census generally and especially the count of the southern population, in particular blacks, one could add the ill will of Francis Amasa Walker, the new director of the census. An economist and young Republican general, Walker was only twenty-nine years old upon his nomination in 1869. In his initial report as in many later writings, Walker opposed the recruitment of black census workers in districts where Reconstruction had transferred political responsibility to the Republicans. Walker clearly considered that the census was not a political instrument, still less part of the justice system, and that to include legal and political questions such as numbers 19 and 20 could only harm the census overall. Moreover, he was more than dubious about the political expediency of this survey, in a context that was difficult for the census, involving a disorganized and politically unstable South, eastern cities swollen by the influx of immigrants, and the West in full expansion mode and with a population difficult to enumerate because of its mobility.[24] Regarding questions on "constitutional relations," he very explicitly repeated in volume 1 of the 1870 census: "The census is not the proper agency for such an inquiry."[25]

The result of this political intervention in the very form of the schedule was extremely disappointing in quantitative terms, confirming a posteriori the arguments of those who viewed it as illegitimate. In his report to the House of Representatives, Walker stated that only forty thousand men had been deprived of their right to vote according to the terms of the Fourteenth Amendment, out of a potential electoral body of more than 8 million. He also made it known to the secretary of the interior that in his capacity as census superintendent he gave very little credit to the data collected by the assistant marshals concerning the right to vote.[26]

However, as Garfield had noted, these numbers, even if low, would have affected the apportionment of seats; Arkansas and Rhode Island each would have lost one seat if the penalties had been applied. But in 1872, Congress proceeded to the calculation of apportionment without applying the clauses of the Fourteenth Amendment. In the end, the former rebel states did not obtain greater representation in the House of Representatives, despite the growth of their representative population—that is, the number serving to determine the number of seats in the calculation of the apportionment—a growth highlighted in volume 1 of the census:

Assuming that the free colored population in 1870 would have borne the same ratio to the colored population as in 1860, . . . the total effect of this cause is to add 13.92 per cent. to the otherwise representative population of the Southern States, and 4.60 per cent. to the otherwise representative population of the United States.[27]

Counting former slaves as whole persons undoubtedly provided a bonus for the former slaveholding states, but the demographic growth of the past decade had been concentrated in the West, while the war had taken a heavy toll on the population of the South, as much in human losses as in the slowing of demographic growth. Finally, the level of disorganization had meant that the population of the South had been undercounted, probably by 1.26 million, or 3 percent of the population. This was according to Walker's calculations after the 1880 census, which gave the appearance of strong localized growth in the South, a likely indication of undercounts in those areas in 1870.[28] A certain number of demographic factors, independent of the methods of calculation discussed with so much effort, thus explained this result.

The report on the 1870 census contained several series of figures for correcting the size of poorly counted populations, including a "Table of True Population" giving estimates for populations that were either imperfectly enumerated or else lay outside the field of the census, such as Alaska at this time.[29] While from its beginning the census had been recognized as the barometer of demographic growth, Walker had the unwelcome task of presenting to the Senate a picture of weaker demographic growth than in previous decades. In the face of these disappointing results, it is understandable that Walker would have preferred to emphasize the weaknesses of the census rather than those of the population itself, and would have added populations occupying a marginal position with respect to the officially enumerated population. Nonetheless, it is astonishing that along with hundreds of pages of tables of the official census, the census superintendent would have presented an entirely different table as being that of the "true population."

Section 2 of the Fourteenth Amendment was never applied, as the political will to impose penalties on states refusing blacks the right to vote was lacking. But since the provision was never abrogated, periodically there were voices calling for its application, even in the next century, whose traces can be seen in the committees on the census in the House of Representatives.

Thus, a joint resolution of the two chambers was proposed in 1906 to abrogate Section 2, since it had never been applied, but without success.[30] A resolution of Representative Bennet of New York State in 1905 proposed a law strongly penalizing the southern states, to the extent of depriving some of half of their representation, since blacks had been prevented from participating in elections.[31] This proposal was presented again, in 1906, in an even stronger form, by Representative Keifer, then again in 1907 and 1908, but without any consequence on the calculation.[32] The committee similarly received a petition in favor of application of the Fourteenth Amendment, which shows that the proposal introduced in the House by Bennet had been presented in collaboration with the Equal Suffrage League.[33] These demands would be renewed each time the question of apportionment was debated, especially in the 1920s, when Congress, for the only time in its history, failed to reach agreement on a method of apportionment and kept the House as it was up until the 1930 census, in direct violation of the Constitution.[34]

Several protest letters and petitions were addressed to representatives against the apportionment anticipated after the 1920 census, since it did not reduce the representation of southern states that limited blacks' right to vote.[35] This demand was also tied to demands for an inquiry on lynching, which were submitted to the Committee on the Census.[36]

At the end of 1920 and the beginning of 1921, the committee heard Joseph A. Hill, an official of the Census Bureau who handled the development of methods of calculation on apportionment. Members of the committee asked him several questions about taking blacks into account in the calculation.[37]

We can see that Hill, although one of the Census Bureau's most competent statisticians and one of those most familiar with these questions, had only a vague notion of the origin of these clauses in the Constitution. These hearings gave rise to various proposals for decoupling the enumerated population from that taken into account for the calculation on the apportionment of seats but, in the end, the search for a compromise, after an entire decade without apportionment, brought about the continuation of the tradition of including all the inhabitants, citizens and non-citizens, voters or not, in the calculation. The Fourteenth Amendment would be regularly cited in congressional discussions on apportionment, but the section concerning the census would never be applied. Still, it is remarkable that, over a period of more than fifty years, the terms of the debate remained so constant.

The census of 1870 thus consecrated the disappearance of slaves from the US census, but it did not mark any retreat in distinctions of race or color—rather the contrary.[38]

10

From "Mulatto" to the "One Drop Rule" (1870–1900)

From 1850 onward censustakers had to note for each inhabitant a color or race by selecting an abbreviation: W (white), B (black), or M (mulatto). To these the Census Office later added Indians and Chinese, then Japanese, following the initiative of agents that had inscribed them on the schedules.

At the time of the 1870 census, the schedules offered five choices of "color": white (W), black (B), mulatto (M), Chinese (C), and Indian (I).[1] The instructions for censustakers emphasized the importance of the "mulatto" category, which from that time on explicitly included quadroons and octoroons, and went all the way down the line to the "one drop rule," which here made its debut in the official census instructions:

> Color.—It must not be assumed that, where nothing is written in this column, "White" is to be understood. The column is always to be filled. Be particularly careful in reporting the class *Mulatto*. The word is here generic, and includes quadroons, octoroons, and all persons having any perceptible trace of African blood. Important scientific results depend upon the correct determination of this class in schedules 1 and 2.[2]

There were no instructions for how to determine the "color" of Chinese, or of blacks or whites. (The case of Indians was treated separately, as the instructions distinguished those who were to be included in the census from the others.) Each inhabitant of the United States had a color, which, along with age and sex, formed part of his or her "personal description." The instructions for 1870 and 1880 stated that no census form would be accepted if one of those three boxes were left blank.[3] In contrast to Walker's attempts to impose a strict discipline on censustakers, to make up for the inability to recruit them on the basis of selective examination, this measure stood out because it put the responsibility for the precise accuracy of results into the hands of local officials and residents themselves: data were to be sent first to a local authority, and a list of the name, age, sex, and color of all those counted in a district was to be posted so that anyone who suspected an error could come and correct their form, in the presence of the censustaker, who was duly paid for these verification sessions. We can imagine how people whose posted color did not conform to how they were perceived in their community—that is to say, their immediate neighborhood—would be pressured by their acquaintances to go and correct their schedules. Thus, the very publicity of the information exercised a type of collective control on the basic descriptions of individuals (age, sex, and color).[4]

The invocation of science is noteworthy here, especially because the rule adopted had its origins in law.[5] We can see how the desire to know the composition of the black population kept being mixed up with the desire to use the census to prevent interracial mixing, since every individual who appeared to have an African origin was counted as black, whether categorized as "black" or as "mulatto." The census could not strictly apply the "one drop rule," which was rooted in genealogy. Censustakers—in this case, the assistant marshals—had neither the means nor the authority to investigate the origins of the people they enumerated. The mention of the "perceptible trace of African blood" thus represents an adaptation of the rule to actual field conditions, in which censustakers relied on observation or, in case of doubt, on interrogation, often in the absence of the entire group of individuals concerned, as had been the case in 1850 and 1860.

The black population thus remained divided into two categories, black and mulatto, and from this point of view the Civil War and Emancipation did not break with the past. The context differed, however, and even though the terms remained the same until 1920, the meaning of the categories would evolve. The polygenism of mid-century would give way to scientific racism, based on Darwinism. In terms of scientific racism, even if blacks and whites were no longer separated by a species barrier, they remained different races, at different evolutionary stages, and mixing of the two was still to be avoided. More precisely, some of the principles of polygenism as applied to the US population would remain, but would be placed into the larger context of Darwinism—even though Darwinism's founding principle, the unique origin of man, was in direct contradiction to polygenism. This American form of Darwinism was not incompatible with the central axiom of polygenism: that blacks and whites were fundamentally different, and that blacks constituted a permanently inferior race even if they were not a different species. This explains the survival of these distinctions even as Darwinism became the dominant paradigm, attributing a unique origin to all of humankind.[6] Thus, we can reexamine from this angle the statisticians' discussions of the "progress" of the black race. Statistics would be able to show the progress achieved by blacks, to quantify at once their advancement and the distance that still separated them from the norm of civilization based on statistics for the white population, but with the idea that they would never catch up with whites. As far as racial science was concerned the census could no longer prove the existence of an insuperable barrier between species, even though the theme of the "tragic mulatto" still persisted, but it could show that, on the scale of development of the races, the gap between blacks and whites was not going to narrow. Thus, in the new paradigm, the barrier of time replaced the species barrier, even if the quantitative elements of the proof remained the same.

Clearly, when both the theorists of racial separation and the courts made use of this theory to state that racial mixing was "prejudicial to both parties," in reality they were protecting the purity of the white race. With the disappearance of the Slave Schedule, on which the only two choices were black or mulatto, it might have been theoretically possible for "mulatto" to function as a third color, but this interpretation, illogical in the context, was rendered impossible. The instructions for censustakers and the ensuing treatment of the data, as well as the mindset of the agents and of the American people, inevitably linked these two categories to form what the census would henceforth call the "colored population" or the "colored race." The hierarchy of the categories and their interrelations did not appear directly in the proposed list for the 1870 schedules, but the instructions and the way they were interpreted, as well as the aggregated and published data, show that the preexisting configuration remained valid: whites constitute the normal population, while blacks and mulattoes were two complementary types of descendants of African slaves. Indians were included in the census only marginally and under certain conditions, and nothing was said about the Chinese. When, in reference to mulattoes, mention is made of the "dominant race," it was clear at the time to census agents that it was a question of blacks or "pure Negroes." The new scientific theories made it possible to predict that mulattoes were going to evolve toward their black racial origin, so that without further infusion of white blood, the entire black population would once again become purely black.[7]

The forms and instructions of 1880 were identical on this point to those of 1870, but in the extremely ambitious published volumes for the 1880 census, the data on the colored population did not distinguish between black and mulatto, even though there was the same invocation of "important scientific results" and even though public interest in the question remained strong. Neither reports nor archives offer an explanation for this, but it seems that at the time of tabulation and publication of the data, still under Walker's direction, the distinction did not seem particularly important to census officials. An examination of the responses given by agents on the manuscript schedules shows how strongly the determination of nuances of color, when a person was considered to be black, depended on the context of the inquiry. In 1880, censustakers were instructed not to accept responses that they believed were obviously incorrect, but the examples given in the instructions did not concern color. Color was not seen as a subject susceptible of an incorrect response, nor as one able to escape the observation of the censustakers themselves.[8] The instructions were general, and thus in practice could perfectly well apply to classification by color, especially because the agents could by no means have direct interactions with all the persons enumerated on the forms.[9]

In a statistical study on mulattoes in the 1880 census, Mary Lynn Washington showed the importance of higher social position and gender as factors favoring attribution of a person to the category of mulatto rather than black.[10] She noted that the instruction, which told censustakers to place more weight on their own perception or on an individual's reputation and self-presentation than on the person's responses, meant that the agents had to apply not only the letter but the spirit of color classification then current in American society.[11]

The form of racial classification that emerged from the new system, forged in mid-century around an original conception of racial mixing, served as a base for less strict rules that would be applied to other inhabitants from then on included in the census. The fundamental principle, the basis of the racial doctrine that characterized the census as well as the law in the second half of the nineteenth century, was that there existed only one pure race, the white race. All instances of racial mixing belonged to other races, for which mixing was only an accident. The category of mulatto, and its elaboration into quadroon and octoroon (included in the mulatto category in 1870 and 1880, but listed separately in 1890), served as a laboratory for development of the rules that would be applied to Indians and to other races—including, for the rest of the nineteenth century, the Chinese and Japanese. The principle applied by the census was derived from laws forbidding interracial marriages (but not interracial sexual relations), put in place in the South soon after the Civil War.[12] Called *hypodescent*, this principle held that in the case of a person who was the issue of a mixture of two different races, that person could only be attached to the inferior race—that is, he or she could never be considered white. In its extreme form, the "one drop rule," a black origin, however tenuous, was literally "a drop of black blood," which made an individual legally and socially black. In 1870 and 1880, the census did not address the question of unions between members of subordinate groups, but this was a secondary concern since the point of the system was to make it impossible for any person of mixed origin to claim membership in the white race. Only from 1900 onward was the question of racial mixing between non-whites formalized by the census. Up until then, census instructions and procedures for attribution of categories bore only on mulattoes, who always had to be distinguished from blacks, but never from whites, because that part of them was never named. The instructions and procedures also affected the case of Indians and the mixed-race persons of Indian ancestry called half-breeds. The ramifications of this system extended to all categories of the census, since the 1870 census also saw the appearance of inhabitants of mixed foreign origin ("mixed foreign parentage"), who had one parent born in a foreign country and the other a native-born American. In conformity with the logic of hypodescent, these individuals were attached to the group of inhabitants of foreign origin ("foreign parentage").

In the context of the legal and social segregation that took hold in the South after the end of Reconstruction, and that culminated in the Supreme Court's 1896 decision in *Plessy v. Ferguson* (recall that, in the terms of the era, Homer Plessy was an "octoroon," and that his lawyer stated that his black blood was indiscernible), the racial classifications applied to blacks by the 1890 census seemed to follow the direction of the scientific racism of the day, and the federal agency thus continued to align its categories on the most racist legislation of the South. The law empowering the 1890 census specified that it should distinguish as so many colors or races not only whites, Indians, Chinese, Japanese, and blacks, but also mulattoes, quadroons, and octoroons.

The reasons behind such a refinement of categories concerning blacks, when the 1880 data on mulattoes had not yet been compiled or published, were the same as in 1850: to distinguish the different products of racial mixtures in order to compare their characteristics and especially their life expectancy, which were expected to be different, and to prove the harmful nature of racial mixing. On 30 July 1888, Rep. Joseph Wheeler, a Democrat from Alabama, had introduced proposed legislation that would lead the 1890 census to a situation in which, out of eight possible "colors," blacks would represent four. The superintendent had to

> take such steps as may be necessary to ascertain, report, and publish the birth rate and death rate among pure whites, and among negroes, Chinamen, Indians, and half-breeds or hybrids of any description or character of the human race who are found in the United States, as well as of mulattoes, quadroons, and octoroons.[13]

It emerges clearly from this proposal that the census should make it possible to determine the destiny of individuals born of racial mixing ("amalgamation"), even as in Wheeler's mind it seemed to apply to species issuing from these mixtures. We may note that, in his list, mulattoes, quadroons, and octoroons seem to constitute a distinct group, separated from blacks by the enumeration of all the other categories. It is equally noteworthy that they are distinguished from "half-breeds or hybrids of any description or character," which clearly shows that in racial mixing blacks, like whites, occupy a separate place in the system of colors or races: on the one hand, whites always lose their whiteness as soon as they are mixed; on the other hand, blacks always keep their blackness no matter what the mixture.

The census law adopted on 1 March 1889 did not keep the exact wording of Wheeler's proposal, and mixtures of all species, including half-breeds, disappeared, but the distinction between mulatto, quadroon, and octoroon was retained. Carroll D. Wright, commissioner of labor and an important statistician, also discussed the importance of this distinction, in a letter to the Senate committee on the census.[14] Emphasizing how easy it would be to add these columns to the form, and while asking that mixtures of other races be included, Wright stated in the section "Statistics relating to the Negro Race" that:

> Whether the mulattoes, quadroons, and octoroons are disappearing and the race becoming more purely Negro, is a question which can not be settled by observation. It must be settled by statistics, and the sooner the statistics are collected, the better.[15]

We may note that Wright's distinction between observation and statistics is altogether typical of his time. Observation meant partisan or subjective inquiry, while statistics were scientific by virtue of their exhaustiveness, and not by the method of collection and construction of the data, since it was only a matter of gathering up the preexisting elements. The fact that censustakers proceeded concretely by visual observation of the color of persons had little importance here. If the criterion was applied to the population as a whole, Wright implicitly supposed that it was applied uniformly and that, according to a belief widespread even among the experts of that day, individual variations, or errors, offset each other. His optimism over the possibility of settling the question by statistics, or at least by those of the census, would quickly be disappointed.

We see here that the question of racial mixing remained for observers principally the issue of miscegenation between whites and blacks, the only mixture that counted numerically and politically. Congress followed these recommendations because the census law took up the four categories of the black population. The population schedule asked this question for each individual, "whether white, black, mulatto, quadroon, octoroon, Chinese, Japanese, or Indian." The instructions to censustakers for the first time indicated that these categories concerned "color or race" (two interchangeable terms), even if we might note that the term *race*, already at this time, was tending to replace *color*.[16]

The instructions accompanying the 1890 census had to explain these new categories, which divided the black population into four sub-populations and which might be perceived and interpreted differently in different regions. They were distinguished by their attempt to construct a rigorous tool, with arithmetical divisions, based on the genealogy of individuals, in order to determine the category to which the individual belonged:

> Write *white, black, mulatto, quadroon, octoroon, Chinese, Japanese,* or *Indian,* according to the color or race of the person enumerated. Be particularly careful to distinguish between blacks, mulattoes, quadroons, and octoroons. The word "black" should be used to describe those persons who have three-fourths or more black blood; "mulatto," those persons who have from three-eighths to five-eighths black blood; "quadroon," those persons who have one-fourth black blood; and "octoroon," those persons who have one-eighth or any trace of black blood.[17]

At first glance, these instructions fit perfectly into the period discourse of scientific racism, emphasizing genealogy in the form of fractions, as we find in the segregationist laws that defined the persons to whom segregation applied. The fractions correspond to the possible combinations over four generations—that is, eight great-grandparents, constituting so many potential eighths of black blood. They are approximately continuous, with "blacks" being persons who have three black grandparents or six black great-grandparents, and "quadroons" being those with one black grandparent or two black great-grandparents. "Mulattoes" are no longer those who are part black and part white, but those who are of mixed origin on both sides, and for whom the boundary is the most fluid. The case of "octoroons" is different, since the term traditionally designated persons with one black great-grandparent, that is to say, those who were affected by laws referring to blacks up to the fourth generation, such as certain laws forbidding interracial marriages, but the formula in use went further since it took up the principle of the "one drop rule," in the form of a trace, leaving it to be understood that it was possible to have a dash of black blood that was indiscernible in terms of the census. The limits of such a classification are clear, since there were mixtures going back further than the third generation.

The imperfection of these categories would be shown up by the report on the black population published in 1918. The formula used left gaps between the fractions, for example, in the case of persons having more than five-eighths of black blood but less than three-quarters. The report stated that, "by implication," censustakers would have rounded up, so that such persons would have been classed among those having three-quarters or more of black blood, but the hypothesis was unverifiable.[18] These fractions appeared rigorous, but in fact corresponded to discrete quantities.

The important thing was for the maximum number of persons having black origins, however tenuous, to be pigeonholed in these categories. The idea was to divide the black population into sub-categories, partly in order to be able to conduct an eventual comparison of the characteristics of the different types of mixtures, but mainly to make "passing" impossible.

In the view of statisticians like Walker, the American population was so sensitive to this question that they were accustomed to distinguish persons having one-eighth black blood, and that fact alone justified this distinction in the census, as opposed to mixtures between Europeans.

> A man or a woman who is one quarter French or German, or even one half English, Irish, or Scotch, may not be known as such except by family friends; but a man or a woman who has a quarter, perhaps even only an eighth, of negro blood is still recognized as belonging to that race, and is so classed, not only in popular speech, but in the enumerations of the census.[19]

In any case, the fate of these inquiries in the 1890 census was insignificant with respect to the goals of those who had pressured Congress to include these distinctions: census officials judged the results useless and the questions themselves misplaced, to the point that these data would have been completely omitted from census publications, if their inclusion in the text of the law had not obligated the census to minimal publicity of these results.

Under the direction of Robert Porter, the 1890 census published altogether only two series of figures dividing the black population into these four categories, and repeatedly emphasized their uselessness. In the introduction to the first volume of the 1890 census, we find the following figures accompanied by a commentary whose tone clearly expresses distance, in an unusual way, from the requirement set by Congress:

> The Eleventh Census shows that out of a total population of 62,622,250 the persons of negro descent numbered 7,470,040. In addition, there were enumerated 107,475 Chinese, 2,039 Japanese and 58,806 Indians competent to be enrolled among the general population, making the total colored element of the country 7,638,360 as compared with a total white population in 1890 of 54,983,890.
>
> The persons of negro descent are further classified, under the law, as follows: negroes, 6,337,980; mulattoes, 956,989; quadroons, 105,135, and octoroons, 69,936. These figures are of little value. Indeed, as an indication of the extent to which the races have mingled, they are misleading.[20]

The author of the introduction was extremely negative and reduced almost to nothing the efforts of Wheeler, Wright, and others outside the census, who were awaiting these data in order to confirm their theories on racial mixing. Following this unqualified rejection, all the tables that gave data by color, whether general tables of the introduction or those for different states, presented data on blacks combined into a single category. The text spoke of the "Negro population, [which] includes all persons of Negro descent," and the tables similarly gave only one column for all blacks under the heading "Negro," with a note at the bottom stating "includes all persons of black descent." Over the nearly 1,200 pages of the volume on the general population, only one table presented data for the four sub-categories of the black population, limiting itself to giving details by major regions and by states.[21] No processing was done of these data.[22] The only information we can take away from these figures, which is valid at the national scale as well as in different regions, is that the vast majority of blacks were classed as "black" (84.8 percent), followed by "mulattoes" in comparable proportion to those of previous censuses (12.8 percent), while the two new categories contained very few individuals: "quadroons" were 1.4 percent of the total and "octoroons" were 0.93 percent. Noteworthy here is that, while each category decreases as it gets further from "black," the figures for "quadroons" and "octoroons" are very close—as if there were no difference between them in the eyes of the enumerators. "Mulattoes" were a minority within a minority, and this is true for these two new categories with respect to "mulattoes," even without any actual hierarchy between the two, which shows that perception appears to have counted for more than arithmetic. The West was an exception to this rule, since its 2,195 "octoroons" outnumbered the 1,789 "quadroons," mainly because California counted 1,264 "octoroons" and 868 "quadroons," as compared to 2,648 "mulattoes" and 6,542 "blacks." California prohibited interracial marriages. We may hypothesize, then, that the higher number of these "octoroons" corresponds either to persons of mixed Mexican and black or Indian origins, or else to those of Mexican descent without black admixture. This hypothesis could be partly verified by finding possibly Hispanic family names, and the parents of each individual so categorized.[23] Since the report does not provide any level of detail below state, it would have been necessary to examine all the manuscript reports for California, which were not preserved, to support the hypothesis. An alternative hypothesis is that censustakers in the West had a different perception of race from those in other parts of the country. Here again one would have had to compare enumeration districts, agent by agent, to see if any significant variations showed up.[24] The experience of the early twentieth century would indicate that the color of the censustaker himself was the determining factor in the variability of these classifications.

Volume 2 presented statistics on disabilities and handicaps, one of the areas for which results were most eagerly awaited. Here, we find only one page where blacks are divided into "black" and "mixed blood," the latter an expression that had not previously been used by the census to describe people of mixed black blood, but which can be explained by the fusion of the categories "mulatto," "quadroon," and "octoroon" into a single category.[25]

Enshrining these minute scientific categories in the 1890 law resulted in the absence of any distinction of color and genealogy within the black population in the official statistics of the population of the United States in 1900—and for the first time since 1850, since with the exception of the two instances already mentioned, even the category of "mulatto" was missing. It is more than probable that the complete failure of the 1890 effort to apply in the field the categories of "quadroon" and "octoroon" was behind the omission of the "mulatto" category from the 1900 schedule. It made its last appearance in the censuses of 1910 and 1920 and was permanently dropped after 1920.

Despite multiple possible sources for the introduction of these categories in the 1890 law, their suppression in the publications of the 1890 census received little notice either at the time or subsequently. It seems, for lack of a direct explanation, that Superintendent Porter believed the results were inconclusive and possibly also that the ground for the inquiry was uncertain; moreover, he treated these questions as beyond the scope of the census, and in several places he criticized the fact that they had been imposed by the law, that is, by Congress.[26]

In a communication to the Royal Statistical Society in London, after his resignation, Robert Porter did not skimp in his criticism of the 1890 census, going so far as to propose an ideal schedule, whose categories for color would be white, black, Chinese, Japanese, or Indian. With regard to immigration, he proposed to record the place of birth of the person and of the two parents, but not their naturalization, a question that Walker had eliminated in 1880.

The manuscript schedules for the 1890 census were lost in a fire in the building where they had been archived after the end of the census. It is thus impossible to verify the quality (or the volatility) of the responses against the original results.[27] We can guess that the responses varied widely from one district to another, and between North and South, suggesting a highly problematic perception of these distinctions, which was one of the reasons for the elimination of the "mulatto" category after 1920. However, in the absence of the documents themselves, this must remain only a hypothesis.

We come away from this episode, often cited as an example of the American government's obsession with race and of the integration of the most racist norms of the South, with the recognition that the Census Office used the categories of quadroon and octoroon only because it was constrained to do so by the law passed by Congress. Its unwillingness was motivated by practical considerations rather than ideological concerns, but was nonetheless real and strong. Further, the experiment had no future and produced no more than the data required by the law. We should read this as an expression of the ideology and fears of certain members of Congress rather than as a dominant element of the classification practice of the US census. In the 1900 census, it would be the Census Office and not Congress that would push for the abandonment of any distinction among blacks.[28]

11

The Slow Integration of Indians into US Population Statistics in the Nineteenth Century

Since its creation, the census had separated the inhabitants of the territory controlled by the United States into three broad categories: free (presumed white, citizens, and taxpayers); slaves (property, reduced by the calculation of apportionment); and Indians, pushed back to the margin of the territory and excluded from the census because they did not participate in any of the mechanisms on which it was based: not citizens, not taxpayers, and not property.

As early as 1820 and 1830, it had been possible to enumerate Indians among "all other free persons," but without being able to determine their exact number. The Constitution, the laws, and the instructions for each census constantly repeated that untaxed Indians were never to be enumerated. But gradually, as the frontier advanced toward the west, and as more and more Indian tribes were subjected to domination by the Americans, growing numbers of individuals identified as Indians found themselves living within the borders of one of the American states, and thus under the jurisdiction of the federal census. From 1850 on, even while maintaining the exclusion of untaxed Indians, the census published statistics on those who had appeared in the responses indirectly, through the category of color.[1] Just as the presence of first Chinese, then Japanese, in the census had not been anticipated by census officials, Indians appeared thanks to the change in the questionnaire in 1850. If common sense saw "Indian" as an entirely separate color, the case of Indians of mixed birth was much more problematic for the census, which prompted census officials quickly to formalize empirical rules for taking them into account. Since the exclusion of untaxed Indians was maintained up until the extension of US citizenship to them as a group in 1924, the definition of belonging to the Indian community depended, for the census, more on the instructions specifying who was or was not to be enumerated than on the classification by color.

The 1850 *Instructions to Marshals*, in the list of persons to be entered on questionnaire number 1, stated clearly that "Indians not taxed are not to be enumerated in this or any other schedule."[2]

In the 1850 census, while the questionnaires offered only three color choices—white, black, and mulatto—the report noted the presence, in the heart of the "constitutional" population,[3] of a small number of Indians, "domesticated or taxed," included in the tables for whites.[4]

Their number in 1850 cannot be precisely determined. A special, separate census of all American Indians had been made by virtue of the Indian Appropriation Act of 1846, by authority of the secretary of war. Their number had been repeated in the publications of the 1850 census, but they did not form part of the official population of the United States and appeared in the census only as an item of information.[5] The inclusion of new territories in the Southwest also brought significant indigenous populations into census statistics. This can be seen in the census figures for the young state of California, which were then aggregated into those of the 1850 federal census. In 1860, the number of Indians living in zones subject to US law was greater, and the federal government's grasp on the regions where Indian nations lived had tightened to the point that government agencies could envision enumeration of the untaxed Indian population.

In 1860, the 1850 law was renewed, and the questionnaires still included only three colors, but this time the instructions, which for the most part were identical to those of 1850, stated the conditions under which Indians were to be included in the census and classed as such:

> 5. Indians. Indians *not taxed* are not to be enumerated. The families of Indians who have renounced tribal rule, and who under State or Territorial laws exercise the rights of citizens, are to be enumerated. In all such cases write "Ind." opposite their names, in column 6, under heading "Color."

The instructions for the column "Color" repeated the 1850 instructions while including the new category "Ind.":

> 9. Color.—Under heading 6, entitled "Color," in all cases where the person is white leave the space blank; in all cases where the person is black without admixture insert the letter "B"; if a mulatto, or of mixed blood, write "M"; if an Indian, write "Ind." It is very desirable to have these directions carefully observed.[6]

In the 1860 census tables of population by state, Indians, when few in number, were grouped with whites, as in the general table of US population by color. They were grouped separately only when present in larger numbers. Thus, in the table showing the population of California in 1860, the inhabitants were divided into whites (323,177), free people of color (4,086), Asians ("Asiatics"; 34,993), and Indians (17,798).[7] The enumeration of the new races by the assistant marshals was as yet quite spotty: in thirty-six counties of California, one of the states with a large number of enumerated Indians, both Indians (2,666) and Asians (11,352) were grouped among the white population, while the categories used in the other counties were white, free persons of color (divided into "black" and "mulatto"), Indian, "half-breed," and Asiatic.[8] In all, according to this report, California numbered 10,446 male and 7,111 female Indians, 141 male and 100 female half-breeds, and 33,149 male and 1,784 female Asiatics, all included in the white population in the general table for the state.[9]

If Indians were separated out from whites and blacks at the local level, in the national population total they were included in the white population. The system remained fundamentally binary, based on the opposition between "white" and "colored," that is to say, white and black. Indians and Asians were considered too marginal to constitute a separate color, but also too different to be included among "colored." Here we see a major peculiarity of the American system: a double exception, with whites and blacks both constituting separate populations. Other races, when their presence was still new and their numbers small on the national scale, were preferably grouped with whites. Clearly, census officials took care to avoid actions that would increase the proportion of "colored" in the population. For example, if in California Asians and Indians had been grouped with blacks, the result would have been a "colored" population of 56,877, nearly 15 percent of the total, instead of 1 percent for blacks alone. "Half-breeds" were Indians of mixed origin, and were represented only (with one exception) in subdivisions that also included Indians, and almost always those in which Indians were numerous—that is, where chances of contact with whites were higher. The subdivision for Los Angeles numbered 446 Indians, 10 half-breeds, 9 Asiatics, and 3,854 whites, for a total of 4,385 inhabitants.[10] We can hypothesize that if half-breeds were present in areas where Indians had plenty of contact with whites, those of mixed birth likely had one white parent, rather than being the result of an earlier mixture of blood, as would likely be the case for mulattoes. This would mean that the term *half-breed* was to be taken literally. Still, what seems likely for California is not necessarily true for other parts of the country, where Anglo-Europeans had had contact with Indians for a much longer time. It is interesting that this category of half-breed, which appeared spontaneously on the questionnaires, made its way into the report, given the small numbers in question; the compilers processing the manuscript questionnaires could easily have corrected these responses to "Indian" or "white." As we shall see, unlike mulattoes, who were indisputably black, half-breeds were still seen as genuine mixtures, that is, as having a white part that changed their racial category.

Even when they fit into the criteria that made them part of the national community, Indians were imperfectly enumerated in 1860, as were the Asians, to whom we shall return later. In 1870, Walker clearly made adjustments to ensure a better enumeration of Indians. The printed questionnaires now included "I." among the acceptable responses to the color question, while the assistant marshals were specifically instructed to enumerate the largest possible number of Indians:

> Although no provision is made for the enumeration of "Indians not taxed," it is highly desirable, for statistical purposes, that the number of such persons not living upon reservations should be known. Assistant marshals are therefore requested, where such persons are found within their subdivisions, to make a separate memorandum of names, with sex and age, and embody the same in a special report to the census office.[11]

This rather flexible interpretation of the law by Walker resulted in a census report listing a total of 383,712 Indians in American territory, of whom only 25,731 were separated from tribal affiliations, the others thus being untaxed Indians excluded by law from the count. Of this total, only 111,185 resided in the states, and 272,527 in the US territories and Alaska.[12] The territories (US possessions that had not achieved statehood but would do so gradually) had been included in the scope of the US census since the law of 1850, but their figures were presented separately. The census published, on the one hand, the constitutional population (that of the states), which was enumerated for purposes of apportionment, and, on the other hand, the total population living under American jurisdiction, which was enumerated at the same time and with similar questionnaires. Walker justified the inclusion of Indians in the census by emphasizing the fact that they physically formed part of the population and maintaining that the census was not limited to producing only the data required by the Constitution. He regretted that untaxed Indians had not been enumerated in the territories since 1850, noting that they should have been counted separately, but that in any case they should have been counted. In making this argument he relied on science more than on law, while also, in a more original fashion, expressing a benevolent view of Indians:

> An Indian not taxed should, to put it upon the lowest possible ground, be reported in the census just as truly as the vagabond or pauper of the white or the colored race. The fact that he sustains a vague political

relation is no reason why he should not be recognized as a human being, by a census which counts even the cattle and horses of the country.[13]

Similarly, Representative Niblack of Indiana submitted an amendment, ulti-mately rejected, stating that the clause excluding untaxed Indians from the cen-sus should be eliminated by virtue of the Fourteenth Amendment, which made all native-born inhabitants of the United States citizens.[14]

The census relied on Indian Office agents in 1870 to collect data constituting the most precise approximation ever obtained of the Indian population, in the words of the report. Census workers, in this case the assistant marshals, could not conduct an enumeration on the reservations, outside the jurisdiction of the marshals, so it was up to officials of the federal unit in charge of the Indian pop-ulation to perform the task. The figures given by Walker, 272,527 Indians in the territories, are comparable to the 278,000 enumerated by the Indian Office at the same date,[15] but the 111,185 Indians living in the states do not appear in any other source and are an original contribution by the Census Office. Francis Amasa Walker was even better positioned to integrate long discussions and sta-tistics on Indians living on reservations because in 1871, while retaining his position as superintendent of the census, he had been named commissioner of Indian affairs by President Grant. He remained in both posts before beginning a brilliant university career in 1872.[16]

The 1870 census report also lingered over the question of mixed-race Indians, strongly emphasizing the fact that the rules developed for the racial classification of slaves could not be applied to Indians and that half-breeds were not analo-gous to mulattoes, even if the half-breeds had black blood. The relevant passage reveals both the census officials' concept of what an Indian was and the way that census agents should identify individuals corresponding to a category that was as much social as racial.

> Where persons reported as "Half-breeds" are found residing with whites, adopting their habits of life and methods of industry, such per-sons are to be treated as belonging to the white population. Where, on the other hand, they are found in communities composed wholly or mainly of Indians, the opposite construction is taken. In a word, in the equilibrium produced by the equal division of blood, the habits, tastes, and associations of the half-breed are allowed to determine his gravita-tion to the one class or the other. It is believed that this is at once the most logical and the least cumbersome treatment of the subject, in the manifest inexpediency of attempting to trace and record all the varieties of this race, especially considering the small and fast-decreasing num-bers in which it is found within the States of the Union.[17]

The parallel with mulattoes existed on another level as well: the report foresaw the decline or even disappearance of the Indian race in the states of the Union, which reflected the reality of the time, but viewed the possibility with sympathy perhaps tinged with regret. There were no mentions of problems posed by the presence of Indians in the heart of the white population, although the presence of former slaves was, as we have said, a major problem in the view of census officials and one that called for a solution. If we reread the data on half-breeds in the light of this explanation, we might expect that those classified as such would later be categorized as Indian, while other mixed-race groups were invisible and classed as white. But we must not forget that this explanatory report came after the taking of the census and that the instructions to field agents were far from being so detailed. It is plausible that in practice things were much more fluid, and it is difficult to imagine census agents considering a person having Indian blood or black blood as making up part of the white population. In any case it is noteworthy that, on the theoretical level, the rules that had been in place since 1850 to prevent persons of mixed white and black birth from being enumerated as white were not transposed—as if at this time, when white domination over Indians was firmly established, Indians offered no threat to the purity of the white race. The principles set out by Walker would be valid only for a time, since later on the Indian race would be integrated into the wider system of hypodescent, which he here explicitly rejected for half-breeds.

The Census Office's interest in Indians became stronger in following years as territories became states, Indian Territory shrank, more and more Indians lived either on reservations under federal administration or among the constitutional population of the Union, and the need to document the characteristics of a population on the path to extinction took on increasing urgency.

The 1880 census, again under Walker's management, retained the same categories, maintaining the exclusion of untaxed Indians and specifying the treatment of those living in American society:

> By the phrase "Indians not taxed" is meant Indians living on reservations under the care of Government agents, or roaming individually, or in bands, over unsettled tracts of country.
>
> Indians not in tribal relations, whether full-bloods or halfbreeds, who are found mingled with the white population, residing in white families, engaged as servants or laborers, or living in huts or wigwams on the outskirts of towns or settlements are to be regarded as a part of the ordinary population of the country for the constitutional purpose of the apportionment of Representatives among the states, and are to be embraced in the enumeration.[18]

Indians living among the ordinary population would henceforth be integrated
into the national community. The criterion would be their way of life, their
degree of assimilation, rather than color. But of course, once they were enumerated as Indians, the color "Indian" was attributed to them.

Census officials' drive to know the Indian population grew to the point
that, within the framework of the 1880 census, the Census Office organized a special census of Indians living on reservations, under the direction
of Major Powell, special agent, US Census, Indian Division.[19] The questions on this special form were adapted to this particular population. Those
on civil status not only included as possible responses "bachelor, married,
widowed or divorced," but also asked: "Is this person a chief?" and "Is this
person a war chief?" For the person's name, census agents were to transcribe
the Indian name, according to a transcription manual that was provided to
them; they were also to give the English translation of the Indian name, and
the person's common name, whether English, Spanish, French, or other.
The questions on color, under the heading of "Personal Description," were
also adapted:

> 10. If this person is of full-blood of this tribe, enter "/." For mixture with
> another tribe, enter name of latter. For mixture with white, enter "W.,"
> with black, "B.," with mulatto, "Mu."
> 11. If this is a white person adopted into the tribe, enter "W. A.," if a
> negro or mulatto, enter "B. A."[20]

For lack of funding by Congress, the special census was broken off and never
resumed.[21]

In 1890, the census once again entrusted to a special agent the task of collecting data on Indians outside the zones of the general census, which were
published in a bulletin devoted to taxed and untaxed Indians.[22] In his report,
Thomas Donaldson, a specialist on the subject of Indian civilization, furnished
valuable information on the conditions of the census on the reservations, which
show that the special agents hired by the Census Office had interests and concerns that led them more in the direction of ethnology than statistics. For example, he suggested using a phonograph to record the languages of centenarian
Indians, before their disappearance. Donaldson reported that the census agents
were mainly Indians, which did not prevent some degree of resistance to the
enumeration.[23] Indians reacted to the census in different ways, sometimes by
opposition but sometimes also by insistence on being enumerated, as was the
case for the Cherokees of the town of Qualla, North Carolina, who as early as
1850 had demanded to be enumerated in order to strengthen their claims to
American citizenship.[24]

In the 1890 general census of the population, the instructions, after repeating verbatim the passage on Indians from the 1880 census, added that the regional officials and agents of the census should never become involved in the special census of reservation Indians, but on the other hand they were obligated to enumerate those who did not live on reservations, a smaller population, by entering them both on the general census and on a special questionnaire.[25]

In 1890 the general instructions on color or race did not include recommendations except for the classification of blacks, and said nothing about color or race for Indians, Chinese, Japanese, or whites. Indians living among the rest of the population were to be included on the general questionnaire especially because, since the Dawes Act of 1887, federal policy aimed to get Indians out of the tribal system and off the reservations, and to make them landowners of individual property. The idea was that Indians—unlike, say, the Chinese—were assimilable and capable of progress. By extending the coverage of Indians in the general census, their numbers were increased, although this did not mean growth in their population but rather an increase in the portion of the Indian population included in the general census. This trend continued over the next ten years, as shown in table 11.1.

Table 11.1 **Indian Population (1870–1910), according to the US Census and to the Bureau of Indian Affairs**

Years	*Indian Population*		
	United States		*Alaska (census returns)*
	Census returns	*Reports of the Commissioner of Indian Affairs*	
1910	265,683	279,023	25,331
1900	237,196	250,000	29,536
1890	148,253	228,000	25,354
1880		244,000	32,996
1870		278,000	

Source: US Bureau of the Census, *Indian Population in the United States and Alaska, 1910*, 10.

Two other special censuses were conducted by the Census Bureau in 1900 and in 1910, and to the extent that they were linked to the general census of the population, they will be discussed in chapter 16.

The significant increase in the figures for the Indian population included in the census between 1890 and 1900, unrelated to that observed by the commissioner of Indian affairs, clearly shows the extent to which it was the conditions of the inquiry and changes in the residential behavior of Indians that determined the number enumerated, much more than their own demographic evolution. In 1891, while the census extended over the entire United States, the Census Office announced the official end of the frontier, an event that the historian Frederick Jackson Turner saw as a turning point in American history.[26] The Indian population had never been so small. The year 1890, the year of Wounded Knee, also marked the end of the Indian wars. After this time, the Indian population would see a slow but continuous increase. The geographical distance would lessen and all Indians would be enumerated, but henceforth it would be poverty that would keep them on the fringes of the American population.

The First American Censuses of Alaska: Appropriation of the Territory and Assignation of Natives by Statistics

The first American census of Alaska in this period gave considerable attention to the question of the classification of natives, whether Indian, Eskimo, or Aleut. The 1880 and 1890 censuses of Alaska were special cases in that they were not required by law, and formed part of the investigations Walker wanted to conduct to broaden the scope of the census and count the "true population" of the United States. Beginning in 1900, Alaska would be enumerated as part of the general census, with several months' head start due to the constraints of the climate. The population of Alaska was very different from that of the rest of the United States, and was poorly known. The aim of the census was both to prepare an account of the human presence in Alaska and to furnish the elements for a description of the populations of the territory. One man, Ivan Petroff,[27] a Russian colonist turned American, conducted the 1880 census by himself and supervised the 1890 census, for which he obtained reinforcements in the form of agents sent from Washington.[28] Petroff posed for a photograph during the 1889 Alaska census, showing the picturesque but also difficult nature of his work (see figure 5).

Ivan Petroff, like the agents who had enumerated the Indians of the continental United States, showed a penchant for ethnology and the study of indigenous languages. In Alaska as in the continental United States, linguistics groups formed the basis for the classification of natives. The 1880 census was in fact a mixed bag of investigation of all the accessible locations and compilation of data for the areas that Ivan Petroff had not been able to reach.[29] His task had been all the more complex because Alaska attracted many seasonal workers, often Asians, whom the census did not hope to include. Moreover, the local population seemed so distinctive that Petroff created original categories to classify the natives and especially those of mixed birth, whom he counted as "Creoles" in 1880. He so designated the children born of unions between Russians and natives; the term would be replaced by "mixed" in 1890, more or less equivalent to the term "half-breed" applied to continental Indians of mixed birth. By his use of the term "creole," Petroff placed himself in the line of Russian censuses of Alaska, which took place in 1819, 1839, and 1860. He stands apart from the American norm developed in the nineteenth century, by unambiguously attaching his creoles to whites and not Indians. For each region of Alaska, he created a ratio of civilized to indigenous, and he included the creoles in the "civilized" population, a distinction reiterated in the qualitative section of the report.[30] (See table 11.2.)

The second American census of Alaska approached the current norm on the continent, since the categories used to classify non-Indian inhabitants were the

Table 11.2. **Alaska Population according to US Censuses (1880–1940)**

Year	Total Population	Whites	"Indians" (a)	Creoles and Mixed (b)	Others (c)	Aleut	Eskimo	Indians	Indians (1910 figures) (d)
1880	33,426	430	31,240	1,747	9	2,145	17,617	11,478	32,996
1889	32,052	4,298	23,251	1,823	2,400				25,354
1899	63,592	30,493	29,536						
1909	64,356	36,400	25,331	3,527					
1919	55,036	27,883	26,558		595				
1929	59,278	28,640	29,983	7,828	655				
1939	72,524	39,170	32,458		896	5,559	15,576	11,283	

Note: (a) In 1880 and 1940, Indians were counted separately from Aleuts and Eskimos. In the other censuses, the term "Indians" includes all these groups. No attempt was made here to reconstitute those groups from tribes or linguistic groups when they were presented as Indians. The total for 1880 and 1940 was obtained by adding these groups. Alaska censuses were taken a year earlier than the mainland census, but published as part of the decennial census taken in the years ending in 0.

(b) In 1880, the Creoles were a separate category, which was not a subdivision of the Indian population. This is why they are not included in the Indians column. At the following censuses they were included in the total for "Indians." In 1910 the "mixed" were 3,842 of Indian and white blood, 43 of Indian and Asian blood, and 1 of "unknown mixture" (*Thirteenth Census*, 3:1136).

(c) In 1890, the 2,400 Others included 2,282 Mongolian (Asians) and 112 "others," among whom was 1 woman.

(d) The volume *Indian Population in the United States and Alaska, 1910* (p. 10) gives revised higher figures for the years 1880 and 1890. It states that the 1880 figures are an estimate and that in 1890 the territory was only partly enumerated.

same, with the same rules for attribution. The "others" were described as followed by the report of the 1890 census:

> The last named class comprises negroes, mulattoes, Hawaiians, Malays and Portuguese mulattoes from the Cape Verde islands. Further distinction of these people was considered inadvisable, partly on account of their small number, but chiefly because they all belong to the class of temporary and transient residents of Alaska, being nearly all engaged in the whaling industry.
>
> The Mongolians are chiefly Chinese, also temporary residents, with a few Japanese among them.[31]

The same report gave especially interesting information on the "mixed," who were henceforth always counted as Indians:

> A few words must be said concerning the term "mixed Indian," which is applied to the descendants of intermarriage of Russians with native women in former times. They were a privileged class under the Russian régime, vested with certain rights denied even to natives of Russia. In numbers this mixed race is rapidly decreasing, and they were enumerated separately by the Tenth and Eleventh Censuses chiefly because they are the only people now remaining of the original inhabitants of the country to whom the clause of the treaty with Russia conferring the rights of citizenship could at that time apply, a point which may be of some importance when Congress sees fit to settle the political status of the people of Alaska.[32]

This decrease seems not actually to have happened, as the American censuses continued to enumerate "mixed." Moreover, the instructions told workers to count as "mixed" the children of a "mixed" person and an Indian, which increased their complement.[33] It is clear that this advantageous status could find no place in the racial hierarchy the Americans had imposed in taking possession of the territory. The population classed as "mixed" did not decrease in proportion to that of "full-blooded Indians." The indigenous population, even if it was better enumerated in successive censuses, represented a smaller and smaller part until it stabilized at about half of the total population, which had been bolstered by waves of American or European immigrants.

The "mixed" population of Alaska constituted a peculiar category in the American statistical system. The "mixed" category did not appear in the volumes on the general census, except in the form of "mulatto," which, as we have seen, was not synonymous with "mixed."[34] Yet "mixed race" was an important category in the classification of certain populations, whether those of outlying territories or that of American Indians. In the census of Alaska at the beginning of the twentieth century, we find both a category for "mulattoes," who are counted as blacks, and for "mixed," who are always counted as Indians.

The instructions to census workers, the examples provided for them, and the published reports all maintain the rule: no matter what the mixture, mixed persons were always to be attached to a group, whether it be blacks or Indians. The 1909 instructions stated:

> For census purposes, the term "black" (B) includes all negroes of full blood, while the term "mulatto" (Mu) includes all negroes not of full blood but having any trace of negro blood, whether one-half, one-fourth, one-eighth, as the case may be. Similarly, for census purposes, the term "Indian" (In) includes all Alaska Indians of full blood, while the term "mixed" (Mxd) includes all Alaska Indians of mixed blood.[35]

In the "Illustrative Example" for the 1909 census, we see that neither "Mu" nor "Mxd" occurs in mixed families: these categories were not set up to measure current racial mixing, but rather to attach the persons born of such unions to a precise racial minority.[36] The lack of correspondence between the continental model and the situation in Alaska, where there were very few blacks and mulattoes, led the Census Bureau to reprogram the perforating and tabulating machines so that the perforation generally used for "Mu" on individual cards would be used for "Mxd" as well.[37]

However, unions between Indians and whites increased over the years of the first American censuses, even if the status of the children issuing from these unions changed radically.

If we believe the 1890 report, the children of indigenous women and Russian colonists enjoyed a favorable status during the period of Russian administration, yet the standard American rules concerning race relations placed them in an inferior status. Census classifications, which made "mixed" a sub-category of Indians, for whom the census determined the tribe as it did for pure Indians, reflected official American racial classifications, which left no other space for children of mixed couples than to be classed as a minority. In Alaska, as in other new American territories, the racial mixing that had once been permissible continued, but was now relegated to the indeterminacy of non-white races. We find the same contradiction as in the case of mulattoes in the United States, where the concern for detail, going back two or even three generations, intertwined with the whites' imperative for racial purity, which meant that whatever the proportion of the mixture, it was always cause for rejection from the category of whites.

The Census Bureau had another problem specific to Alaska, arising from the question of classification of Eskimos and Aleuts, two indigenous peoples whom experts back in the Russian period already knew to be separate from Indians or, to use the language of that era, to belong to another race. This question became the subject of discussions between census officials and anthropologists up through the 1940s, as we shall see in chapter 16.

This example shows that when the census was less constrained by the law—since the population of Alaska at this time was not part of the constitutional population, and it differed in its characteristics from the American norm—local officials took a more qualitative approach to their work and invented original categories. The place given in Alaska to the "Mixed" forms a contrast to the rigidity of the rules developed in the United States. In the continental states, the census showed itself to be responsive to the existence of groups such as Asians, but still incorporated them into the general framework of preexisting categories.

The Chinese and Japanese in the Census

Nationalities That Are Also Races

Beginning in 1870, the American census added a new race to its question-naires: "Chinese." This was followed in 1890 by the addition of "Japanese." The remarkable thing is that what was a nationality immediately became a race as well. The same would be true, as of 1920, for "Filipino," "Hindu," and "Korean." Since 1850, the place of birth of all inhabitants had been recorded, whether or not they were immigrants, and in the case of non-European immigrants, two categories of origin were involved: on the one hand, foreign birth, and on the other hand, race, which was transmitted to the following generations. Examining the classification of these immigrants who were neither white nor black reveals how, in the general structure of population categories, national origin and race were related and how, in a weakened form, the rule of hypodescent that had been developed to separate blacks from whites would determine the attribution of these categories to the children of mixed couples.

In spite of their small numbers (see table 12.1), Asian immigrants were the object of disproportionate attention in the US census, to the point that in 1920, out of nine possible racial categories, five were Asian.[1]

Between the California Gold Rush of 1849 and the brutal termination imposed by the Chinese Exclusion Act of 1882, nearly 300,000 Chinese were counted as having entered the United States, of whom more than 90 percent were grown men.[2] The 758 Chinese in the United States recorded by the 1850 census was no doubt an underestimate. It designated persons born in China, side by side with another 377 persons born elsewhere in Asia without further pre-cision.[3] We may question the validity of this number—758 persons in 1850—because some of the results for California, the state that still included 78 percent of the Chinese in the whole country in 1870, were destroyed before reaching

Table 12.1. **Chinese Population, by Sex, Citizenship, Sex Ratio, and Proportion of Total US Population, 1860–1900**

Year	Men	Women	Total	Sex ratio	% of total	Total US population
1850			758			
1860			35,565	18.6: 1	0.11%	31,443,321
1870	58,633	4,566	63,199	12.8: 1	0.16%	39,818,449
1880	100,686	4,779	105,465	21.1: 1	0.21%	50,155,783
1890	103,620	3,868	107,488	26.8: 1	0.17%	62,947,714
1900 Total	85,341	4,522	89,863	18.9: 1	0.12%	75,994,575
Aliens	78,684	2,169	80,853	36.3: 1		
Citizens	6,657	2,353	9,010	2.8: 1		

Note: Daniels gives 34,933 for 1860, of whom 33,149 were men and 1,784 were women. Actually, this figure corresponds to California alone after the census of 1860. The total for the country was 35,565.

Source: Adapted from US Bureau of the Census; and Daniels, *Asian America*, 69.

Washington.[4] The Census Bureau used the figures from the California census of 1852 to fill in for the missing results, but clearly not for the Chinese.[5]

It appears that by April 1852, there were nearly 10,000 Chinese in California.[6] Already by that time, anti-Chinese sentiment had been translated politically to the highest level of the government in California, in the form of propositions for discrimination and segregation, on the one hand, and demands for control of immigration, on the other.[7] The question quickly became one of Chinese workers, commonly called "coolie labor," even if not all of the Chinese immigrants were miners or farmworkers. Labeled "coolies"—that is, unfree workers—Chinese immigrants fell victim to xenophobia as well as to the racism that identified free labor with the white race.

It was in this context of continuing Chinese immigration and growing hostility, at first centered in California, that the census recorded the presence of a larger number of Chinese in 1860.[8]

At this time, the census did not yet have a category of color or race to characterize the Chinese. The 35,565 Chinese in the United States were persons born in China, but the ambiguity of the term "Chinese," as a race and a nationality, did not seem problematic. The nuance of vocabulary, and also of concept, between "race" and "nationality" was still very fluid, and the compiler of this part of the census was not exempt from what appears to us as a lack of rigor but which was widespread at the time, even among specialists in questions of race. The discourse on race, opposing whites to others, in no way prevented a broader usage of the term "race," which may explain the wording "color or race" in the census, beginning in 1890, to specify in what sense "race" was to be understood. The unambiguous term was "color," while the term "race," even as it became more and more common under the influence of scientific racism, remained polysemous, as we shall see with regard to the "races or nations" of Europe. The text introducing the table that presented these figures is revealing: "The different *races* and *nations* in the United States are presented as follows: Nativities of foreign residents."[9]

In the table we find Chinese nationals, alongside French or Irish immigrants. Inversely, using the same data from the questionnaires, the Census Office drew up tables for the population of California by color, which gave the following numbers: white, 323,177; free colored,[10] 4,086; Asiatics, 34,933; Indians, 17,798.

These two presentations of the same figures use the same logic, making use of a category of race or color. But in fact, Asiatic is here synonymous with Chinese, and vice versa, while among them were at least 346 persons born elsewhere in Asia. From the summaries for California, which are the most detailed and which represent 98 percent of the Asians enumerated in the country at this date, it seems that the figures were obtained in part by place of birth and in part by questionnaires where the agents filled in—without specific instructions from the Census Office—"Chinese" or "Asiatic" as a color. The report notes that in California, out of 34,933 Asiatics, 11,352 were counted among the white population.[11] Thus, this sub-group would have been identified only by their country of birth, which would mean that the 23,581 remaining were identified by color as well. At this stage, with Chinese immigration representing virtually all of Asian immigration, the equivalence of the two terms is understandable if not rigorous.

In the next census, by which time this population represented 9.2 percent of the population of California, the questionnaire included a category of color or race, "C." for "Chinese," with no explanation in the instructions for census agents.[12] Reflecting the spread of this population beyond the West, the general tables by race of the report for the 1870 census included a column headed "Chinese," with this explanation in the introduction to the volume:

> Chinese.—Twenty-three of the States were found to contain "Chinese," which description for census purposes was held to embrace Japanese (who are, however, distinguished in the tables of population), but to exclude Hawaiians. The number reported in each State was as follows: Arkansas, 98; California, 49,310; Connecticut, 2; Georgia, 1; Illinois, 1; Iowa, 3; Kentucky, 1: Louisiana, 71; Maine, 1: Maryland,

2; Massachusetts, 97; Michigan, 2; Mississippi, 16; Missouri, 3; Nevada, 3,152; New Jersey, 15; New York, 29; Ohio, 1; Oregon, 3,330; Pennsylvania, 14; South Carolina, 1; Texas, 25; Virginia, 4.[13]

The category of color thus remained "Chinese" rather than "Asiatic," likely by reason of their predominance, and also because they served as the focus for the hostility of anti-Asian movements, to the point that the presence of other Asian immigrants was obscured. The numerical preponderance of the Chinese was indisputable, since in the 1870 census we find "63,254 Chinese, [which] includes 55 Japanese."[14]

From the moment of their appearance on the questionnaires, the Chinese belonged to a separate category. The statistical consequence of the fact that "Chinese" was not only a national origin but also a race was that this designation became permanent across generations. It was independent of citizenship, which meant that the few Chinese immigrants who became naturalized were not distinguished from others, and it was also independent of place of birth. Because of the composition of this body of immigrants, made up of grown men, births in the United States were rare, though not nonexistent. The census counted 518 Chinese born in the United States, "include[ing] one Japanese."[15] The figure of 63,254 comes close (within about seven persons) to the total of Chinese born in China (among the persons born in China, the census distinguished 352 whites, 16 "colored," and 62,674 "Chinese") and Chinese born in the United States, who were presumably US citizens, with the addition of 55 Japanese. The slight difference between the two figures (63,254 and 63,247) could arise from other persons born in Asia and counted as "Chinese" by their color. In 1860, the census enumerated 1,231 persons born elsewhere in Asia, and in 1870, 586 persons born in India and 864 born elsewhere in Asia.[16] The amalgamation of color between Chinese and Japanese is interesting because it did not involve all Asians. We might guess that the reason why persons born in India were not grouped among Asians might be that they constituted another phenotype, or even that they were viewed as Caucasians or Aryans. But to invoke a racial proximity between Europeans and South Asian Indians, as one might do at the beginning of the twentieth century, seems unlikely at this earlier date because it involves an argument too scientific for the census, which tended to create categories of convenience. Also, public opinion was not yet conscious of the presence of Indians, while white Californians were getting ready to broadcast the theme of the "yellow peril" to the rest of the country. The puzzle is rather that Japanese were distinguished from Chinese in the text and tables, while they appear to have been the only other Asians to be included in this color category in 1870.

If it was the Chinese who served as a focus for political attacks, and especially for proposed legislation to keep them from achieving naturalization, the same principle held for all those who were not considered as whites, by virtue of the US Naturalization Law of 1790, which reserved naturalization for "free white persons." Courts in the East had agreed to naturalize Chinese, but as early as 1854 the Supreme Court of California had excluded Chinese from access to citizenship, a decision based both on theoretical arguments and "on grounds of public policy."[17]

This remained the rule in California until the Civil Rights Act of 1870, which, by extending the protection of the laws to African Americans, could also include other populations of color. In the 1850s and 1860s, the California legislature passed several laws prohibiting Chinese immigration into the state—laws that were regularly struck down by the state Supreme Court, just like other unconstitutional forms of discrimination. The election campaign of 1871 in California was marked by competitive anti-Asian rhetoric, and from this time on, the debate became national in scope. Over the following decade, Congress continued to debate the Chinese question, which became a question of Chinese immigration and how to control it. Congress would pass legislation that was then blocked by presidential veto, the executive branch believing that the question should continue to be handled by diplomacy and not by law.

It was in this context that the 1880 census recorded a tripling over twenty years of the Chinese population in the United States, which by then surpassed 100,000 individuals. Chinese immigration continued to be made up of adult workers, with men outnumbering women by 21 to 1. This could show that the Chinese had no intention of remaining, but the hostility toward them came precisely from the world of labor, which complained of unfair competition from the "coolies."

In 1880 as in 1870, only one color—"Chinese"—on the questionnaire corresponded to Asians. However, the report of the 1880 census presented the US population as divided by color into *white, colored, Chinese, Japanese,* and *Indian.* Altogether, the 1880 census had enumerated 105,465 Chinese, of whom three-quarters resided in California, and only 148 Japanese, of whom 86 lived in California. But with only 148 individuals of the Japanese race, according to the census, a new color appeared in the report on the tenth census. Regardless of the table titles, the population was presented as "Chinese," with a note for each line indicating the number of "Japanese" included in the category. We can thus see that in 1880, out of 104,427 "foreign born Chinese," there were 145 Japanese, and that the 1,186 "native" among the "Chinese" included 3 "Japanese" (one man and two women).[18] The association of Japanese with Chinese in the census followed from the links that joined them in anti-Asiatic discourse. It is noteworthy that the 1880 census report, which distinguished Chinese and Japanese by color, was published at the time when the United States for the first time adopted measures explicitly excluding a certain category of persons from the possibility of immigrating to or becoming citizens of the United States. The Chinese Exclusion Act of 6 May 1882 suspended Chinese immigration for ten years. Those Chinese already present in the United States were exempted and could leave and return to the country, in the name of freedom of movement, but that clause would soon be abrogated. In 1892 the Geary Act renewed the exclusion for ten years with even more restrictive provisions; the law was made permanent in 1902. The year 1882 constituted a major turning point in the history of immigration to the United States, since it marked the end of the nation's Open Door policy. It was no accident that it was the Chinese who first paid the price in the movement for immigration control that had spread through the country since mid-century, since they were a nationality that was also racially distinct. European immigrants were also the victims of discrimination and acts of violence, but even if the xenophobic movements were permeated with racism, the basis of the discourse was different. Nativism, as the movement favoring native-born Americans over immigrants is called, did not possess a comparable arsenal of legislative and judicial measures. From this point of view, the fact that the census treated "Chinese" as a color or a race, arising from its experience with the racial distinction of blacks, was completely consistent with the codes forbidding marriage between whites and Asians. Laws that used race were themselves derived from the codes that legalized segregation with regard to former slaves. In law as in the census, non-white immigrants were racially distinct before being immigrants. For the census, the fundamental difference between a category of color or race and a category of national origin was the permanence of the racial category, which was transmitted to all future generations. In 1880, as in 1890, the instructions for census agents said nothing about the racial classification of Asians, nor about the children of mixed couples. In the twentieth century, however, the procedures that governed the racial assignment of children of interracial couples in which one of the parents was Asian would pick up, in a slightly different form, the rules of hypodescent that applied to persons having black ancestors.

The application of the Chinese Exclusion Act was translated quite spectacularly in the census figures. By referring to table 12.1, we see that the population enumerated as Chinese experienced almost no increase between 1880 and 1890, growing from 105,465 to 107,488 persons, while up until that time it had grown quite rapidly, and it decreased between 1890 and 1900, before stabilizing at about 75,000 persons in the 1920s, a trend that would reverse itself only progressively after the end of Chinese exclusion in 1943.[19]

Even before the passage of federal legislation, the census had racialized Chinese immigrants and their descendants. Just as, in principle, they would never be naturalized after 1882, they would always be Chinese for the census. Their children and grandchildren and later generations would always be classed as racially different, although children born in the United States (few in number because of the imbalance of sexes) would be citizens.

Another direct consequence of Chinese exclusion was the increase from that time in the rate of Japanese immigration. From 184 Japanese in the United States in 1880, numbers grew to 2,039 in 1890 and then to 24,326 in 1900. At the start Japanese emigration was different from Chinese, in that it was a much more recent phenomenon for the Japanese. But from the American point of view, from the mid-1880s on, it was a matter of labor immigration, in which the Japanese were equivalent to the Chinese. The xenophobic press spotted the similarity from the beginning. For its part, the census was already prepared to apply the same treatment to the Japanese as to the Chinese. In the volume of the 1880 census published in 1883, the Japanese were an entirely separate color, in spite of their extremely small numbers. In 1890, the Japanese, like the Chinese in 1870, had become a "color or race" in the questionnaires, which meant that, given the four racial classifications for blacks, "white" was now one color among eight.[20] We can see that in 1890 racial categories multiplied, but they did so artificially, since a more logical system would have had four categories instead of eight. In this the census proceeded by accumulation, transposing part of the experience of statistical segregation from blacks to Chinese, then reproducing for Japanese the procedure developed for Chinese. The ground was prepared, and we see the weight of racial ideology in the fact that the Japanese were a race all to themselves in the US census, even though their numbers remained insignificant.[21] If we compare the census and immigration law, we see that here again the census anticipated the unique treatment of Asians: in 1907 controls would be placed on Japanese immigration, not by law this time but by the so-called Gentlemen's Agreement between President Theodore Roosevelt and the emperor of Japan. The racial difference between these immigrants and the rest, southern or eastern Europeans, was continually repeated in the newspapers, which had transferred the "yellow peril" theme to the Japanese. But the Gentlemen's Agreement was not as far-reaching as the exclusion applied to the Chinese, as it permitted marriage between male immigrants and women whom they brought over from Japan— the famous "picture brides," who reversed the composition of Japanese immigration so that after 1907 women became a majority of the entering immigrants.[22]

While the discriminatory measures against Chinese and Japanese were taken largely in response to demands from the white population, there were some Americans who protested against them and even criticized the treatment of Chinese in the census after passage of the Chinese Exclusion Act. On 1 October 1888 Congress passed the Scott Exclusion Act, annulling the residency certificates that permitted Chinese who were legally present in the United States to reenter the country after a temporary absence.[23] Later an amendment was proposed in the House of Representatives seeking to modify the census law of 1

March 1890 so that it could distinguish those Chinese who possessed a residency certificate from the rest.[24] The bill, passed by the House and approved by the Select Committee on the Eleventh Census, sought to remedy the weak point of the Scott Exclusion Act, which was the lack of a way to put into effect the registration of all the Chinese present in the country. The report of M. McKenna, a member of the House committee, explained that in addition to the legal Chinese immigrants, there were illegal immigrants coming via Canada or Mexico, and that it was necessary to distinguish between them.[25] The report and the bill are of interest because they aimed to make use of a federal agency to identify illegal immigrants, a totally unprecedented step.[26] Once again, the difference between Chinese and European immigration is striking. The proposed system would require the superintendent of the census to

> enumerate the Chinese population in such manner and with such particulars as to enable him to make a complete and accurate descriptive list of all Chinese persons of either sex who may be found in the United States at the time of the taking of the census, and that the said Superintendent of the census be, and he is, further authorized and required to give to each Chinese person so enumerated in the census an engraved certificate, to be duly numbered and registered in the Census Office, which shall contain all the particulars necessary to fully and accurately identify the Chinese person to whom such certificate shall be issued, and such certificate, when produced by any Chinese person and found to appertain and belong to the holder thereof, shall be the sole evidence of the right of such Chinese person to be and remain in the United States.[27]

The bill also envisioned a series of penalties, including expulsion, to be applied in cases of absence of the certificate or adoption of a false identity. The bill thus aimed to make the census an auxiliary in the service of customs, which had jurisdiction over the entry and exit of persons on the ground. The accompanying report quoted in this context the secretary of the treasury, who likewise deplored the lack of means to control the borders.[28]

At a time when the idea of an identity card would have appeared to Americans as a total violation of individual liberty, this proposal for official registration by means of the census was far less shocking in the case of the Chinese. The discussion of this bill in the House of Representatives gave rise to protests on the part of the business sector, as represented especially by the New York State Chamber of Commerce and those of several cities following its lead. Thus, the business sector sought to protect the Chinese, as coming from a friendly nation, while the fiercest enemies of Chinese immigration were found among the labor movement.

It appears that business waged a campaign on this issue, since the House of Representatives received virtually identical petitions from the Chamber of Commerce of Duluth, the Philadelphia Board of Trade, the Minneapolis Board of Trade, and the Pittsburgh Chamber of Commerce.[29] The Pittsburgh Chamber went so far as to write:

> We heartily favor the adoption of wise, even stringent measures for the regulation of immigration from every quarter of the Globe, but we should protest against the absolute exclusion of the Natives of Any Country and upon this ground alone, if no other, the Exclusive Act of 1888 should be promptly repealed.[30]

The resolution adopted nearly unanimously, with only a single dissent, by the New York State Chamber of Commerce extensively criticized this congressional initiative, which posed a threat to business and to international relations. It ended on a warning note, stating that the day would come when this rapidly growing empire of 300 million inhabitants would demand an accounting from the United States and describing the bill as "absurd, barbarous, unchristian and cowardly."[31]

The transcription of the committee debates mentions the receipt of these letters, but notes that no remarks were made and no action was taken following receipt of the petitions.[32] The Senate failed to pass the bill, and meanwhile the starting date of the census was approaching and the questionnaires had to be printed.[33] Regardless of the hundred-thousand-dollar budget provided for by the bill—the Treasury had allowed $50,000 and then $30,000 for implementation of the Scott Act—the administrative task seemed a difficult one for the Census Office to carry out, given its working conditions and the fact that it was still a temporary agency. If it seems surprising that the committee on the census should have given this proposal the nod, its approval may be interpreted as evidence of the strength of anti-Chinese sentiment in Congress in 1890.

It is notable that the Chinese and then the Japanese should have been distinguished so early in the census, while they foreshadowed the discriminatory measures that would strike European ethnic groups. Their situation was different from that of blacks, who already had a long history of experiencing discrimination, but it also differed from that of white immigrants. The Chinese felt the combined effects of two types of bias—racial prejudice and xenophobia. The census followed this path, by isolating first the Chinese and then the Japanese, and thus contributed in its way to the irrevocable distinction of Asian from European immigration. Unlike the immigration restrictions applied in the twentieth century to the "new immigration" from eastern and southern Europe, the racial stigma imposed in the census on Chinese and Japanese remained specific to Asian immigration. The development by the census of categories devoted to these populations is linked to the development of categories taking account of origin, in a direct reaction to the "new immigration" of the second half of the nineteenth century. However, the racial classifications had an autonomous logic, which only emphasized the differences between the treatment of Asian and European immigrants, in statistics and in the law.

13

Immigration, Nativism, and Statistics (1850–1900)

By recording for the first time the place of birth of US residents, the 1850 census produced the bedrock of data and founded a statistical tradition that has served as the point of departure for studies on immigration to the country ever since. The preceding censuses had partly calculated the foreign or immigrant population, but no breakdown by country of origin was available before 1850, given that censuses until 1840 did not give individual data and were quite summary, as we saw in chapter 3.

The Slow Emergence of the Question of National Origins (1790–1860)

As opposed to color, which was already present in the first census, the distinction between Americans and foreigners was not introduced until the 1820 census.[1] The distinction between blacks and whites, initially based on the distinction between slave and free, was not fundamentally civic or political, since already in the first census, in 1790, free blacks (enumerated as "All other free persons") were counted separately. In other words, if the political function of the census made it necessary to count slaves separately for the calculation of apportionment, the census also included categories whose social dimension was more important than the legal or political dimensions.

The same thing was true of questions on citizenship. The 1820 census distinguished "foreigners not naturalized" from the rest of the population. The next census, in 1830, repeated the question but used a different term, *aliens*, referring to foreigners in the legal sense of the word—non-citizens, people from another country. We recall that the distinctions introduced by Congress, which fixed by law the headings of the questions to be asked, had no effect on the calculation of political representation. While slaves were counted at three-fifths of a free person, non-naturalized immigrants formed an integral part of the legal population. The US census has never been either truly de facto or truly de jure, since certain categories of people physically present in the United States were not enumerated, but it included more than the strictly legal population, even for purposes of calculation of the "constitutional population."[2] Enumerating foreigners offered more in information value than in practical use—all the more so because at that time there was no federal legislation concerning immigration, entry to and exit from the country being free up until 1875. The responses to this question did not make it possible to measure the proportion of immigrants in the population, since naturalized immigrants were not distinguished from the rest of the population. And given the state of the art of tabulation techniques, it also did not help to establish the number of citizens, since this would have required cross-checking these responses with those for sex and age. In any case this would not have helped in reckoning the number of potential voters, or of active citizens, since many American men older than twenty-one did not have the right to vote in 1820.

The 1840 lawmakers seem to have viewed the question as sufficiently unimportant for it to disappear from the 1840 questionnaire. Only with the 1850 census did immigration become a subject for official statistics. The very detailed questionnaires for 1850 included numerous social and economic questions, such as occupation, education, or property, and they tackled the immigration issue from a different angle than in 1820 or 1830. The questionnaires for 1850, followed by those of 1860, for the first time asked about the place of birth of each resident.

The wording was: "Place of birth. Naming the state, the territory, or the country." This factual question was asked of all residents. It was not a matter of a category specific to a sub-population, such as non-naturalized foreigners, who themselves formed only a portion of the immigrant population. Rather, it was a question whose answers would make it possible, after the information was processed, to distinguish the native-born American population from the foreign-born population.[3] It would also help to measure internal migration, at least wherever a state or territorial border was crossed. The question of interest to the census was to identify all immigrants, that is, the foreign-born, whether naturalized or not. This was the great novelty of this census, responding to a growing demand, at the same time that the xenophobic movement known as nativism (literally, the defense of the native-born) was developing. The importance of this information can be seen in the questionnaire for 1860: at the bottom of the page, which had forty lines for forty individuals, the enumerator was to summarize the total number of white men, white women, colored men and women, immigrants, blind, deaf-mutes, insane, idiots, the poor, and prisoners.[4]

This page-by-page recapitulation would make it possible to rapidly count the national total of immigrants.

This factual information in response to the question, "Where was this person born?" became the norm for all following censuses, and is the precise counterpart of the question asked in 1820 and 1830. Only the demographic or social aspect[5] was taken into account, and not the legal or political aspect of citizenship and nationality, because the censuses of 1850 and 1860, in spite of their broader scope and greater number of questions, did not address the distinction between naturalized immigrants and foreigners. It was the national or regional origin of residents that was sought.

For a long time, the question of origins did not appear to be central; it was introduced late and in a choppy fashion in the federal census. On the other hand, the questions concerning origin and foreign nationality clearly appear as two separate questions, concerning two different populations and responding to two separate demands.

In 1850, the question on place of birth was placed into a new context, that of investigation of the composition of the American population. This was to some extent a racial investigation, in that the meanings of race and nation often overlapped.

This emerges clearly in Kennedy's second annual report, which laid out the origin of immigrants, who represented the sizeable and unprecedented figure of 11.06 percent of the free population in 1850:

> The great mass of the white population of this country is of Teutonic origin, with a considerable admixture of Celtic. . . .
>
> One of the most interesting results of the Census is the classification of inhabitants according to the countries of their birth presented in an authentic shape in No. 5 of the accompanying table. We are thus enabled to discover, for the first time, of what our nation is composed.

This first description of the contribution of immigration to the US population was already accompanied by negative comments on the influence of countries of origin:

> While our country cannot boast the princely residences of European countries, the occupancy of which is limited to comparatively few persons, we think there is a general sufficiency and comfort in the house accommodations of the American people, and that, in the most remote regions of our country, where their accommodations are most limited, they exhibit a very satisfactory degree of comfort and cleanliness. The fact is notorious, that where wretchedness is at all general, there will

be found a population which formed habits and imbibed tastes in a foreign land.[6]

With the 1850 census, the United States found out that it was an immigrant nation. It was also able to measure the size of the most recent arrivals: among the places of birth of immigrants present in 1850, Ireland alone accounted for 43.5 percent. The United States had always been a country of immigrants, but as far as can be determined from the partial statistics for the earlier period, the proportion of the population born abroad had never been so large.[7] Also, 84 percent of immigration was to non-slave states, a fact the report did not neglect to point out. This fostered sectional opposition, as the Northeast was becoming increasingly urban, industrial, and immigrant, rapidly growing away from the model of a nation of small towns (as envisioned by Jefferson), a model that survived mainly in the rural South. Kennedy grouped the immigrant population with the free population since, with the slave trade prohibited since 1808, there were essentially no more foreign-born slaves. After Emancipation, the census generally compared the white immigrant population to the native white population, black immigration being quite small and Asian immigration, which was treated separately, being insignificant on the national scale. If we consider the immigrant population in relation to the total population over a century and a half, we see that the level reached in 1850 was already significant, being followed by a sixty-year plateau during which it remained between 13.2 percent and 14.7 percent, until the restrictions of the 1920s through 1960s (see table 13.1).

Table 13.1. **Proportion of the Foreign-born Population in Total US Population (1850–2000)**

Year	Total	Foreign-born	% foreign-born	Year	Total	Foreign-born	% foreign-born
1850	23,191,876	2,244,602	9.7	1930	122,775,046	14,204,149	11.6
1860	31,443,321	4,138,697	13.2	1940	131,669,275	22,594,896	8.8
1870	39,818,449	5,567,229	14.0	1950	150,697,361	10,347,395	6.9
1880	50,155,783	6,679,943	13.3	1960	179,323,175	9,738,091	5.4
1890	62,947,714	9,249,560	14.7	1970	203,302,031	9,619,312	4.7
1900	75,994,575	10,341,276	13.6	1980	226,545,805	14,079,906	6.2
1910	91,972,266	13,515,886	14.7	1990	248,709,873	19,767,316	7.9
1920	105,710,620	13,920,692	13.2	2000	281,422,000	31,108,000	11.1

Source: Anderson, *Encyclopedia of the US Census.* The figures for 1850 differ slightly from those published in 1850, due to later corrections. Total includes slaves in 1850 and 1860.

The immigration figures, whether for immigrants present at the time of the census or for annual entries into American territory, caught the public imagination. The year 1850 saw a record number of immigrants entering the United States: 369,980, a significant number with respect to the population at that time.[8] A certain number of these entries were of persons who would leave again or who were returning to the United States after an absence. Along with mortality, this explains why the number of immigrants enumerated in 1850 was less than the total number of entries for the preceding decade. Between 1840 and 1870, 6.6 million European immigrants entered the United States. The introduction of the question on place of birth was thus very relevant, and it brought out a different image of the American population: until this time, the dynamic revealed by the figures had been that of population growth and westward expansion. From this time on, another dynamic would be the focus of attention—that of the internal balance of the population, between whites born in the United States, free or enslaved blacks, and white immigrants, each with a different rate of growth. The perception of a profound change occurring in the identity of the American people would be nourished by comparisons between countries of origin as well as, in the following decades, by the association that would be made between urbanization and immigration. Natural growth would remain the principal factor in the dynamic, but the debates on the future of the population and of American society would focus on immigration.

The published volume of the 1850 census could thus present statistics on disabilities by country of birth, like those for different regions.[9] Just as the comparison of statistics on insanity among blacks in 1840 had given rise to a long debate between advocates and opponents of slavery, the data on immigrants would undergo the same treatment on the part of sincere but scarcely rigorous commentators. As in 1840, the different rates for disease and insanity for different populations would feed public fear, this time at the expense of the Irish, who appeared to be more susceptible to these problems. In other words, as soon as the technical modifications of the census made it possible to construct and publish tables on disease by nationality, the issue became a topic of public debate. It appears that the higher rates of insanity among recent immigrants, especially the Irish, was due to the fact that in the United States the wealthier families cared for their invalids at home or placed them in private institutions, while the poorer families entrusted them to public institutions where they were statistically more visible as invalids, unlike those in private homes or private institutions. This statistical bias, consciously or unconsciously, escaped those who sought to portray recent, poor immigrants as carriers of dreaded disease.[10]

The 1860 census used the same questionnaire as the 1850 census, but the place-of-birth question gained added importance in the published commentaries, and emphasis was put on the differences among the new arrivals, which were

presented as so many races. The introductory text gave the keys lacking in the
statistical tables, and provided a theoretical context for the type of ethnology the
Census Office aimed to contribute to with its data:

> From France, it should be remarked that a large number are natives of
> the provinces of Alsace and Loraine [*sic*], who are really Germans by
> descent, and speak the German language, although they have been enu-
> merated indiscriminately with the other natives of France. . . .
>
> Similar statements [to ethnological observations made in England
> and Wales showing that the fusion of races did not erase the persistence
> of distinct racial types after several centuries] will, evidently, apply to
> this country, where the vast collection from all the races and kindreds
> of earth opens a most extensive field of research. Undoubtedly, future
> observers will find in particular valleys and districts many individual
> traits of the original settlers distinctly preserved, but for the most part,
> the next and following generations are Americanized in a new national-
> ity, and become a part and portion of their adopted country.[11]

The emphasis on cultural differences, insufficiently distinguished by place of
birth—such as people of Alsace and Lorraine, who were French by citizenship
but in reality ethnic Germans for the author of the report—and on origin rather
than on nationality opened up with the 1860 census the new field of what I shall
call *ethnic statistics*. The 1860 report could only speculate on the "fusion of races,"
but we see here a trait that would strengthen over the following censuses: the
need to take account of individual heritage, cultural as well as biological. The
shift from immigration statistics to ethnic statistics was gradual and unforeseen,
following the course of events. We can see the change as early as the 1860 census, which was conceptually identical to that of 1850, but with a change in the
treatment of the data.

The 1860 census generally used the same instructions and questions as that
of 1850, which recommended that enumerators should record for place of birth,
in cases of foreign birth, the name of the country, but for 1860 the instructions
were expanded to make the answers more precise to the level of the state:

> If born out of the United States, insert the country of birth. To insert
> simply Germany would not be deemed a sufficiently specific location
> of birth place, unless no better can be had. The particular German State
> should be given—as Baden, Bavaria, Hanover. Where the birth place
> cannot be ascertained, write "unknown" in the proper column; but it
> must be of rare occurrence that the place of birth may not be under-
> stood. You should ascertain the exact birth place of children as well as

of parents, and not infer because parents were born in Baden that so also were the children.[12]

From 1860, a special case was permitted in the responses: that of Poles, who no longer had either a country or a state. It was not specified in the instructions, but this answer was accepted and compiled as a country of birth.[13] From 1860 to 1890, the US census enumerated as "born in the former kingdom of Poland" those US residents who had been born in regions that corresponded to the former Polish borders.[14] In practice, those who were enumerated as Polish were the residents who considered themselves as Polish. Here we see the introduction of a genuinely ethnic category, in the divergence between recording the country of birth—nation-states recognized by other governments including the US government—and US residents' perceptions of their own identity. The divergence was not yet significant, but it is very revealing. It might be the result of a demand made by Poles in the United States rather than an initiative by the US government, although the archives are silent on this point.[15] To enumerate persons "born in the former kingdom of Poland" as Polish offered the advantage of documenting differences perceived as important among immigrants themselves, something that would not have been possible by restricting responses to nationality.[16] To some extent, it represents a concession to American social reality on the part of a system based on legal categories. One might say that it was an adaptation, a translation of the categories of international law into a peculiarly American idiom. Of course, these differences were not ignored in Europe, where state statistics also recorded the existence of national or cultural minorities.[17] Still, we may interpret this evolution as a way of transforming past foreign origins to actual local identities.

The exception made for the Poles was upheld until 1900. In that year, the instructions to census workers clearly stated that only persons born in Polish territory and whose mother tongue was Polish should be enumerated as born in Poland. Here the ethnic criterion had clearly gained ground on geographic origin, since Jews and other Polish minorities, even if they had in fact been born in Polish territory, were not enumerated as "born in Poland" but in the countries whose governments held sovereignty over the different parts of Poland.[18] To be statistically "born in Poland" in the US census, it was no longer enough to have been actually born in Polish territory. Instead, one had to conform to what the census and, more broadly, American society, considered as Polish identity. Others who came from that part of the world, people who on American soil were not attached to Polish communities but to others, were not to be enumerated as "born in Poland." The aim was to know not the places of birth of people who had come to the United States, but their ethnic identity.[19] Thus it was in

1870, under the direction of Garfield and Walker, that the census was to become the barometer of change in the composition of the American population.

From Foreign Birth to "Foreign Stock": "New Immigration," "Race Suicide," and Statistics (1870–1900)

The results of the 1870 census would sharply accelerate the evolution that had been evident since 1850: in 1870, 28 percent of the population were blacks or immigrants while 26 percent lived in urban areas. The census documented at one and the same time the rapid transformation of post–Civil War America into a great industrial power and the transformation of its population, which was experiencing two mutually reinforcing anxieties. A major development was the introduction in 1870 of the question of foreign birth of each parent; Garfield clearly explained the reason for it in Congress in 1869:

> It has been strongly urged, and with good reason, that to the inquiry of birth-place there should be added the birth-places of the father and mother of each person. This would enable us to ascertain the relative fecundity of our American and foreign-born populations. It has lately been asserted that the old ratio of increase among our native population is rapidly diminishing. If this be true the vitally important fact should be ascertained and its full extent and significance determined.[20]

The theme of a decrease in fertility, especially in the rural areas that had been the earliest settled, in contrast with the higher fertility rate of immigrants had appeared in print starting in the 1860s.[21] Garfield was only partly heard on this point in 1870. The country of birth of the parents was not recorded in the 1870 census but only in 1880. But in 1870 the census had asked, in addition to the place of birth of each individual, if their father or mother were of foreign birth, thereby producing a second-generation immigrant sub-population, which the census was to call "foreign stock." It included persons born abroad ("foreign born"), those who were themselves born in the United States but both of whose parents were foreign born ("foreign parentage"), and persons born in the United States who had one foreign-born parent ("mixed parentage"). In the report on the 1870 census Walker had deplored this lack of precision, pointing out that the enumeration of immigrants was desirable but not sufficient. It was necessary, he said, to also measure the contribution of each European nation to the native population.[22]

The creation of a first- and second-generation immigrant population was nonetheless an important development. The inclusion in "foreign stock" of persons who had only one foreign-born parent followed the hypodescent principle, in that children of partly foreign origin were attached to the population of the immigrant parent rather than to the native population. In 1870 this population was nearly double the immigrant population, or 10,892,015 persons versus 5,567,229.[23]

Among the many improvements he made to the volumes published by the census, Walker created a *Statistical Atlas*, which displayed on large, colored maps data that otherwise would have been daunting for nonspecialist readers or would have held little meaning for them, such as the concept of population center, which was popularized by this means.[24] Several maps of the *Statistical Atlas* of the population in 1870 were devoted to the immigrant population, of the first or second generation. The advantage of cartographic representation was that it could easily show the relative distribution of different populations. Thus, plate 21 showed the density of the colored population east of the 100th meridian. It differed dramatically from the map in plate 22, which showed the density of persons having one or two foreign-born parents, the regions where the density of colored persons was important (the South) being those where the density of second-generation immigrants was weak and vice versa. We can see clearly on the map the concentration of persons of "foreign parentage" in the Northeast and the Midwest, which we can also see, with regard to the distribution of immigrants, in plate 25. Other, more detailed maps show the distribution in density and in percentage terms of the total population of the principal categories of European immigration: Irish, German, "British American" or Canadian, English, Welsh, Swedish, and Norwegian.

In the brief comments that accompanied the maps, Walker took care to highlight the complementarity of these two populations: "Speaking broadly, where the blacks are found in the United States, the foreigners are not."[25]

On this point as on others, Walker obtained satisfaction with the law that reformed the census operation from 1880 on. The law was also a posthumous success for Garfield. The parents of foreigners were distinguished by country of birth, just like enumerated individuals.[26]

This count was done for twenty-eight states, seven territories, and the District of Columbia. We can find 4,529,523 children of an Irish father and 4,448,421 children of an Irish mother. Thus, per each thousand US residents who had been born in Ireland, there were 2,442 residents who had an Irish father and 2,387 residents who had an Irish mother. This calculation was also made for certain important places, such as the city of New York, for which the table by "foreign parentage" made it possible to cross-tabulate the place of birth of the father and that of the mother.[27] In spite of the growing interest shown by Congress and public opinion in the immigration question, which also involved that of the assimilation of new arrivals, Walker successfully opposed the proposal that the 1880 questionnaire should include a question on the naturalization of foreign-born persons. He based his argument on the difficulty posed by the fact that census workers generally obtained their responses from women, who according to him would not understand such a subject.[28]

In a letter to the House Committee on the Census, read in Congress, Walker formulated what would become the basic principle of the census with regard to adding new questions:

> A question which has to be asked by 30,000 officers respecting 50,000,000 of people should not be one that makes any great demand upon the intelligence of the person asking or of the person answering.[29]

In Walker's view, census agents should ask simple, factual questions, leaving it to the census to correct or amalgamate later the responses that it wanted to group.

In the volumes of the 1880 census, the population could be viewed by country of birth of the individual or by country of birth of each of the parents, in the form of cross-tabulation. In his brief comments, the editor pointed out, for example, the unexpectedly small number of Irish men married to German women. The text also stated that it was not improper to use the term "German" for someone born in the United States, if they had been brought up in a German family, but it noted that this was not the point of view of the census law. We have already noted that the census used "foreigners" to designate those of foreign birth, as in: "The statistics of the second generation of foreigners will be found in a still later series of tables (Foreign Parentage)."[30] The census thus bowed to the rigor of legal vocabulary, but the object it constructed corresponded to categories in the public mind. The cross-tabulations, even if they did not concern all those whose parents were foreign born, nonetheless gave an idea of the endogamy or exogamy of second-generation immigrants, an indication of their degree of assimilation.

This practice was further perfected in the 1890 census, when the electric tabulation machines developed for the Census Office by Hollerith made it possible henceforth to do cross-tabulations rapidly and at lower cost.[31]

The first pass of the punch cards through the machines divided the population into "a primary classification of native white of native parentage, native white of foreign parentage, foreign white, native colored and foreign colored."[32] These basic populations were then subjected to further passes through the Hollerith machines, which divided them first by gender and age groups.

For all adult males of foreign birth a classification is also made as regards the number who have been naturalized, have taken out naturalization papers, or are aliens, together with a separate classification as to the number of aliens who cannot speak the English language. In the same way for the native and foreign colored a separate classification is made as regards the number of blacks, mulattoes, quadroons, octoroons, Chinese, Japanese and Indians.[33]

Ten years on, Porter could return to the tabulation Walker had judged "very complicated," in order to demonstrate the progress that had occurred between the lists compiled by hand in 1880 by workers who only had adding machines at their disposal and those done by workers using electrical tabulating machines in 1890. Walker had only managed to tabulate half the population according to these criteria: native-born or foreign-born person and father born in one of the seven following places: United States, Ireland, Germany, Great Britain, Scandinavia, British America (Canada), and other countries. This information was cross-tabulated with the same seven possibilities for birth of the mother, which was said to make ninety-eight possible combinations for foreign birth in 1880.

For foreign parentage, however, it will be possible in 1890 to show as regards each of these primary subdivisions a classification of birthplace of father in combination with the birthplace of mother for the following countries: United States, Ireland, Germany, England, Scotland, Wales, Canada (distinguished as to French and English Canadians), Sweden, Norway, Denmark, Bohemia, France, Hungary, Italy, Russia, with a grouping of other countries, and unknown.... Measured by possible combinations of facts, this means a total of 1620 points in 1890 as against a total of 98 points in 1880.[34]

The Hollerith machine was not designed solely to compare different subpopulations, but the tabulations for which it was used, as well as the order of the runs through the machine, give clues to the hierarchy of categories by importance. We see here, then, that color or race and foreign birth came before more classical demographic categories, such as sex or age, since they came in the first run.

This technical progress served to fuel the immigration debates, but it also provided other information. Electrical tabulation made it possible to see early on the migration of blacks to northern states: their state of birth was part of the basic data, and it was easy for one state to show the number of blacks born in another state, although the importance of this phenomenon aroused little interest at the time.[35]

The geographical distribution of second-generation immigrants, compared to that of first-generation immigrants, received less comment than practices of intermarriage, which could be deduced from the global data. This suggests that the object of interest to the census was the ethnic composition of the population, the biological patrimony, rather than the localization of these residents in American society.[36]

Moreover, the multiplication of possibilities of treatment made it possible to record responses in previously unknown variations. From this time on, it was necessary to establish rules for codifying all these responses, given that one perforation in the card corresponded to each birth country, and that in certain cases multiple foreign regions corresponded to one code.

What had happened with regard to Poland in the 1860 census was later extended to other groups: from 1870 to 1900, Bohemia was a birth country, although it was no longer an independent nation-state.[37] More generally, from 1870 on, the census asked as country of birth, in the case of multinational states, the name of the country or of the regional state, even if it was only after 1890 that this type of data could be processed separately.[38] Persons born in Canada were divided, beginning in 1890, into Canada-English and Canada-French. This division was not strictly geographical, but also partly ethnic and linguistic, being based on "French or English extraction."[39]

This new classification by descent was clearly a response to the nativist movement of the day. Walker, beyond his remarkable work in modernizing the methods of the census, became known as one of the principal experts on the economic and demographic policies of the country, especially on immigration. On the basis of his experience with the census and his knowledge of figures, he became a propagandist for what was later known as "race suicide."[40] This concept, which came to be attached to the name of Walker, was based on the idea—supported by statistics (which was a novelty)—that new immigrants, who would work for lower pay, caused Americans of old stock (that is, at least second-generation, the authentic "native Americans") to have fewer children, because the economic prospects of their descendants were reduced by the presence of these cheap workers. This thesis, which was very popular at the turn of the twentieth century, claimed to be a scientific exploitation of census data, showing that the native-born birth rate was lower than that of the foreign-born. From this came the idea of "race suicide"—the gradual disappearance of Americans of Anglo-Saxon stock due to the number of new immigrants from central and southern Europe, whose birth rate was always higher.[41] From then on, the census was appealed to by the federal government, by representatives of immigrant communities who wanted to be better enumerated, and by advocates of immigration restrictions who wanted to use census results to bring about legislative change. Walker exerted great influence on the advocates of immigration restriction, who frequently quoted him. One might say that he contributed, even after his death, to the passage of restrictive measures, since his ideas still held sway at the time.[42]

In the 1880s and 1890s, in his capacity as president of the American Statistical Association and the American Economic Association, Walker published a number of articles, intended for a specialist audience and also for the general public, in which he set forth his theory of racial competition between new immigrants and the descendants of the old families who had come to America before 1830. Walker himself called for immigration restrictions, making use of census data to establish the demographic and social differences that characterized the new immigrants, in a work that summed up the theory of "race suicide," as a kind of transposition of Darwinism to the economic competition between immigrants and native-born Americans. The core of his argument was the lowering of the American birth rate compared to the competition, whether voluntary or caused by a shock to the "population principle." Claiming that Americans had less "vital force" than the European immigrants, Walker wrote in 1891 that the cause of this decrease in the birth rate was due *"perhaps to the appearance of the foreigners themselves."*[43]

Walker's argument was that between 1790 and 1820, the population was growing by more than 30 percent per decade, while immigration remained weak. Extending the trend, in 1840, with immigration increasing, the population still had the same growth rate. According to Walker, the immigrants had simply replaced the births that would have taken place in their absence, and they had done so not only in time but in space, with a larger decrease in native birth rate in the regions where immigrants were most numerous.

> Our people had to look upon houses that were mere shells for human habitations, the gate unhung, the shutters flapping or falling, green pools in the yard, babes and young children rolling about half naked or worse, neglected, dirty, unkempt. Was there not in this a sentimental reason strong enough to give a shock to the principle of population? But there was, besides, an economic reason for the check to the native increase. The American shrank from the industrial competition thus thrust upon him. He was unwilling himself to engage in the lowest kind of day-labor with these new elements of the population; he was even more unwilling to bring sons and daughters into the world to enter into that competition. For the first time in our history, the people of the free States became divided into classes. Those classes were natives and foreigners. . . .
>
> No! Whatever the causes which checked the growth of the native population, they were neither physiological nor climatic. They were mainly social and economic; and chief among them was the access of

vast hordes of foreign immigrants, bringing with them a standard of living at which our own people revolted.[44]

This mixture of statistical analysis and mass psychology is fairly representative of the way in which the debate over immigration restriction would dominate the next three decades.[45]

The 1890 census provided immigration restriction advocates with other arguments, as the questions on naturalization that had been rejected by Walker in 1880 were asked in 1890, as well as a question on the language spoken. Three new questions were to be asked only of "adult *males* of foreign birth twenty-one years old or older": length of residence in the United States, naturalization, and whether a request for naturalization had been made ("First papers"). To these was added question 21, on language spoken, which completed those already in place concerning reading and writing, whether in English or another language:

> 21. *Able to speak English. If not, the language or dialect spoken.*
>   *This inquiry should also be made of or concerning every person 10 years of age or over.* If the person is able to speak English so as to be understood in ordinary conversation, write "English"; otherwise, write the name of the language or dialect in which he usually expresses himself, as *"German," "Portuguese," "Canadian French," "Pennsylvania Dutch,"* etc. For all persons *under* 10 years of age use the symbol "X."[46]

The choice of examples for proposed responses shows that the census sought to obtain information that would indirectly indicate ethnicity, such as "Canada French," which would allow French Canadians to be distinguished from other French speakers. The mention of the "Pennsylvania Dutch" language is also interesting, since it serves as a reminder that this question was posed not only to immigrants and their children but to all residents, who might retain, generations after the arrival of their ancestors, the particular language of their group. From this point of view, a question that had been intended to provide information on the assimilation of new immigrants could also help reveal longer-lasting kinds of cultural diversity that were not tied to recent immigration, such as speaking German: German speakers were still a majority in certain parts of Wisconsin, for example.[47] Porter explained his aims clearly with regard to questions on naturalization, spoken language, and fertility, showing the importance of the immigration question and immigration restrictions in census planning:

> The inquiries concerning foreign-born male adults as to the length of residence in this country, and whether they are naturalized or not, will furnish data in regard to the problem of unrestricted immigration. For

all persons ten years of age and over, either of foreign birth or foreign extraction, an inquiry was made as to whether they were able to speak the English language. The results of these inquiries, particularly as regards the alien element of our population, will determine the number who have not yet learned to speak our language. Concerning all married women, also, a new inquiry has been introduced into the census calling for the number of children born to them since marriage and the number of these children now living. This will aid in solving the question as to the relative fecundity of women of various nationalities.[48]

The questions whose presence was justified by the debates over restriction of the "new immigration" in turn provided matter for studies on immigration that, especially after 1890, could make use of statistical data to establish the differences between the "new immigrants" and the descendants of earlier immigrants. One example is Richmond Mayo-Smith, author of one of the earliest American statistical manuals and an influential expert on questions of population and immigration. Mayo-Smith wrote that the census, thanks to its figures on foreign birth and foreign parentage, should be "in a position to analyze to better advantage than ever before the effect of race character upon institutions and of races upon each other."[49] For him as for other writers of the period, the "assimilation of races" applied only to different European nationalities, and not to persons of different color. But it is no coincidence that it was the language of race that was used to describe the competition between the new arrivals ("foreign") and the older arrivals ("natives"). Mayo-Smith's language for speaking of intermarriage is the same that had been used earlier in speaking of mulattoes: a mixing of blood. Here, however, it was also a question of a common way of life. The question that statistics was going to help resolve was which element would predominate in mixed marriages, the foreign or the "native." Statistics on the naturalization of immigrants would make it possible to measure, beginning with the 1890 census, the electoral strength of immigrants, whether of the first or second generation. Mayo-Smith reached rather moderate conclusions on the question of the vote, which he felt was diverse and fragmented, and on that of the differential fertility of immigrants (more children but also higher child mortality). He also noted in passing that statistics confirmed a higher level of criminality among immigrants and their descendants, but did not permit the conclusion that immigration nourished crime. This reasoned analysis was not shared by all, but it shows the range of areas, such as political science, demography, criminality, and poverty, for which the census would go on to furnish ever-richer data, which would feed into American sociology.

The fact that parents could both be foreign-born but from different countries meant that the census had to establish rules for assigning the children to one or the other of the nationalities. To do this, it adapted in a less rigid manner the principle of hypodescent that had formed the racial barrier between blacks and whites. In the first half of the twentieth century, this principle in part inspired the rules for attribution of categories of origin to children of mixed couples, but without going so far as to reproduce the absolute hypodescent that character-ized the African American population. Immigration would become more than ever the main business of the census, until the Great Depression and the imposi-tion of immigration quotas brought economic statistics to the forefront.

PART IV

APOGEE AND DECLINE
OF ETHNIC STATISTICS
(1900–1940)

In 1902 the Census Office, which since 1850 had been a temporary organization that was dissolved after each census, became the Bureau of the Census, a permanent agency under the Department of Commerce. The change came more than half a century after census officials had first proposed it. The administrative change, which actually included the 1900 census, was a very important development in the history of the census—in effect, its third founding, after 1790 and 1850. Having become a permanent agency hiring and training its civil service employees, the Bureau of the Census was organized into divisions tasked with different duties. In relation to the American population, this division of work would have significant consequences in the first decades of the new century. Its most spectacular manifestation would be the creation of a section on Negro Statistics, under the direction of a black employee, Charles E. Hall, "Specialist, Negro Statistics," something the bureau would often publicize. More generally, various population sectors would have different spokesmen within the bureau, which also shows the increasing autonomy of the Census Bureau with respect to Congress. The lawmakers were in part short-circuited by lobbying groups, while the executive branch gained increased authority over the census.[1] The period, from the end of the nineteenth century to US entry into World War II, was characterized by a new phase of modernization of the census, with the administrative reorganization facilitating statistical progress. The period was also marked by the hiring of a new generation of census officials after World War I. The increasingly advanced training of senior workers, more and more of whom had university degrees in statistics, would have an effect on the institutional culture of the bureau. Technical considerations and economic statistics began to overshadow the traditional demographic investigations into the nature of the American people.[2] This orientation, which revealed itself in the bureau's internal decisions on research credits, publication, or the number of columns on the questionnaires, became more obvious with the 1930 census: on the one hand, according to census officials, the immigration laws passed in the preceding decade had stabilized the composition of the American population; on the other hand, the economic crisis that began in 1929 brought to the fore economic statistics and the men who had charge of them.

This period of four decades and five censuses was marked by several significant developments that transformed the Bureau of the Census: the transformation of racial categories and the apogee and decline of the immigration question; the increasing involvement of representatives of the population in the definition of categories; and the increasingly complex work of the census, confronted with a multiplicity of actors.

The Disappearance of the "Mulatto" as the End of Inquiry into the Composition of the Black Population of the United States

In 1900, for the first time since blacks had been individually enumerated, the entire black population was combined into a single category, "Black," that included all persons who were "negro or of negro descent." It is often said that this had already been the case in 1880, but that is not quite true. In 1880, the black population had been divided into two categories, "Black" and "Mulatto," as it had been from 1850 to 1870, but the published volumes did not reproduce that distinction and presented the black population under a single "color." Nonetheless, both the law and the instructions caused individuals to be so distinguished on the manuscript schedules.[1] The instructions for the 1900 census simply indicated, under the heading "Color or race":

> Column 5. Color or race. Write "W" for white; "B" for black (negro or negro descent); "Ch" for Chinese; "Jp" for Japanese, and "In" for Indian, as the case may be.[2]

The absence of the "mulatto" category in 1900 basically resulted from the failure of the census' attempt to break down the black population into four categories (black, mulatto, quadroon, and octoroon) as specified by the census law of 1890. Instructions were minimal: "negro or of negro descent" could be interpreted as including persons of partly black origin, according to custom. A supplementary volume of the 1900 census stated with regret that for the first time in sixty years, the racial categories applicable to blacks had been simplified. The author reckoned that in the case of black and white mixtures—which he referred to, unusually, as "half-breeds"—censustakers probably followed local opinion in classing as black all those persons who, though primarily white, had a perceptible trace of black blood.[3]

Even noted experts in the study of race seemed disappointed. One such was W. Z. Ripley, who pointed out the shortcomings of the 1900 census with regard to identifying the racial composition of the American population, while approving of the abandonment of the 1890 distinctions, which would leave room for other questions "of vital importance and of a more practical nature."

Ripley is best known as the author of the *Dictionary of Races and Peoples*, which would serve as the basis for the racial and racist nomenclature used by the immigration service. He seems surprisingly progressive, however, on the question of the condition of black Americans: he believed that the Census Bureau needed to keep the "average southerner" at arm's length from this study, contrary to the notions of census officials, who felt (in keeping with the racist discourse of the period) that southern whites had the best knowledge and understanding of blacks. Ripley went so far as to confess his "lamentable mental obscurity in the matter of what constitutes a quadroon or an octoroon."[4]

Giving up the distinctions did not mean abandoning the principle of hypo-descent and its underlying racial hierarchy. The definition of blacks was vaguer but also broader. For the first time, the census applied, implicitly, the "one drop rule," putting all persons of black origin, of whatever degree, into a single category, identified as "black"—a term that the census had previously reserved for "pure" blacks.[5] Given the public interest in mulattoes and the haunting fear of passing—a perennial fantasy of undetectable blacks hiding themselves among whites—this absence of distinction between blacks and mulattoes appears to be an anomaly. It seems that the experience of the 1890 census weighed more heavily this time than did the general context. In any case, even if publications on the figure of the "tragic mulatto" reached their peak in the first decades of the twentieth century, there was still concern over the possibility of measuring the phenomenon.[6] The mulatto problem was no longer so much about the degeneration and future of the black race, as it was about passing and the disturbing possibility that a growing number of individuals might be impossible to identify. The census, in its own way, echoed this diffuse but vivid worry. Passing is inseparable from the principle of the "one drop rule": in order for a black to pass as white, that person must have some slight degree of black ancestry, undetectable, but which nonetheless suffices to make him or her as much a black as a person of purely African ancestry, according to the most racist laws, with which the census put itself in line.

And in fact, the census did document passing, almost in spite of itself, one might say. But it did so in a way that entirely escaped the notice of the readers of the reports, since only a longitudinal study based on the manuscript schedules and following individuals or families from one census to another would be able to reveal it. Such an inquiry is well within the power of genealogists, but inconceivable at the national level. An interesting case from this point of view is that of the family of Shirley Taylor Haizlipp, author of a family memoir. Several members of her family were categorized successively as mulatto in 1880, black in 1900, and mulatto again in 1910, before becoming white in 1920. Haizlipp herself notes that the classification of some family members as black while others were mulatto is due to the fact that they were "the working poor of mixed race" and lived in a part of Washington where "many many poor mulattoes and obviously black people lived." This example is all the more interesting because it concerns a family that included, even according to the census, blacks as well as whites. Thus, Haizlipp's great-grandfather Edward Morris was listed as mulatto in 1880 and black in 1900. His wife, who was listed as white in 1880, was still white in 1900, but their children were black.[7] One reason for this was certainly the fact that the mulatto category did not exist in 1900. This example clearly shows the kind of movement between categories that could be experienced by the same individuals. Some members of this family (those with the lightest skin) passed, abandoning the author's grandmother (whose skin was too dark and risked endangering the undertaking) to the care of the "black" members of the family. The census schedules kept the traces of this passing, by means of which people who were black in 1900 were mulatto in 1910 and then, after a process of rising social mobility that distanced them from segregated neighborhoods, became white in 1920. In 1920 this dynamic, in a family composed of the descendants of slaves, prominent white Americans, and Irish immigrants, appeared to the many experts on racial issues who took an interest in statistics as proof of the shortcomings of the census and not as a response to the economic and social limitations imposed by segregation.

The question was no longer that of mixing of blacks with mulattoes, but of the hidden contribution of black blood to the population as a whole. The theme of the extinction of the black population was transformed, to reappear in the form of mixing of blacks with whites, made possible by invisibility, as outlined in 1931 by the sociologist Caleb Johnson:

> This theory (that the Negro race will eventually die out from infertility because of the increasing white mixture) seems to be based on a false analogy between the human white-Negro hybrid, the mulatto, and the ass-horse hybrid, the mule, notoriously sterile, and it has been cherished by many who believed that by such a dying-out process alone will the Negro problem be solved.
>
> The results of this scientific investigation indicate that the Negro race is not dying out from infertility but is bleaching out through admixture with the white race.[8]

By the start of the twentieth century the "Negro question" had become one of the mixing of blacks and whites (called amalgamation), henceforth by action of blacks and no longer by the choice of the whites using these theories. At the same time, the new theme of the superiority of mulattoes over "true blacks" had emerged, supposedly thanks to their white ancestry, which was credited for the social and intellectual success of men such as Booker T. Washington and W. E. B. Du Bois.[9]

From this point of view, the reappearance of the mulatto category in 1910 seems to link up with tradition, but in the new context of a difference in ability rather than a biological difference between blacks and mulattoes. The census showed itself to be especially poorly adapted to respond to this new question. The initiative came, as had been the case in 1890, from a belated amendment introduced in Congress. The concern of Congress was to obtain data from the census that would allow for measurement of interracial marriages. In December 1908, Rep. James Slayden of Texas wanted the schedule to include an inquiry on "intermarriage of persons of the white race with negroes and Asiatics, usually known as the black and yellow races, and with the descendants of such races." In the Senate version, the Asians had disappeared, which indicates that racial mixing between blacks and whites was the main concern.

This proposition, enthusiastically supported by certain southern representatives, was debated, unlike the 1890 amendment that divided the black population into four groups according to the proportion of black blood. For Slayden, this information was not primarily demographic but rather pertained to "the social and economic problems of the country."[10] To the objections regarding the difficulties of implementing this query—which would lead, according to Representative Crumpacker of Indiana, to censustakers asking women, who might be alone at the time of the visit, the embarrassing question whether their husband was black or Asian—another Texas representative, Choice B. Randell, responded that the need to know the extent of racial mixing outweighed any awkwardness caused by this indiscretion:

> If there are no such marriages, then we want the satisfaction of knowing that in this great Republic, under our system of government, and under our present conditions and environments, we are moving on in the progressive march of humanity, keeping the races separate and the blood pure.

Although Randell's response received applause, the amendment was rejected. However, shortly afterward the Senate adopted another, equivalent measure, which included the additional question of whether it was the husband or wife who was of black descent.[11] Two weeks later, the debate was altered by the presentation to the Senate of a letter from census director S. N. D. North, who opposed the amendment. His reason was that, since the census classified each individual by race, the data on mixed marriages were already being collected by censustakers; if the data had not been compiled or published up to that time, it was because there appeared to be no urgent demand for it. North expressed doubts on the validity of compiling data concerning interracial marriages as a measure of racial mixing, noting that fewer than 10 percent of blacks lived in states where such marriages were legal. He proposed instead reestablishing the distinction between black and mulatto, noting that it had been used in all cen-suses since 1850, except that of 1900. In his view, this would give the best approx-imation of racial mixing and would show whether the rate was increasing or decreasing. He concluded his letter with the statement that he would reestablish the mulatto category whether or not Congress adopted the proposed amend-ment, "under the discretionary authority vested in the Director as to the form and subdivision of the inquiries."[12] This last argument is interesting for two rea-sons: first of all because it reveals that North was demanding reestablishment of the lapsed category of mulatto, and second because it involves a very direct claim regarding the autonomy of the agency, with North putting to good use the new status of the Census Bureau. In fact, 1909 was the first time that Congress was faced with the director of a permanent Census Bureau. Both chambers followed his lead, but it is not certain that this demonstration of authority was the decisive argument. Congress continued to require that certain questions be placed on the schedules, whether the Bureau wanted them or not. Only after 1930 would the director genuinely have the right to modify the schedules in such a way that the questions would not be precisely identical to the terms in the census law passed by Congress. North achieved a limited victory, but we cannot conclude from this that he had significantly changed the balance of authority between the Census Bureau and Congress. However, his position explicitly affirms the bureau's desire to free itself from congressional oversight by appealing to the prerogatives of the executive branch. North himself was a confirmed advocate of immigration restrictions who believed in the impossibility of assimilating non-European immigrants, as well as blacks, into the white population:

> But anything like an amalgamation of the white and black races has been proved, by this fifty years of experience, to be impossible. While about 16 per cent of the American negroes are reported by the enu-merators as having some degree of white blood in their veins, it is a fact well known within our knowledge that practically none of those mulat-toes, or hybrids, are the offspring of marriage. Miscegenation remains the one impossible outcome of the close association and juxtaposition

of the two races in the southern states, according to the invariable opinion of the southern whites.

North also noted that the law obligated the census to use the term *nationality*,
instead of *race*, to distinguish the origin of immigrants:

> The citizenship of the United States is the best concrete example of
> racial amalgamation which exists anywhere in the world today. It is in
> fact the only example where the possibilities of racial amalgamation can
> be statistically studied, and the definite results partially measured. . . .
> For the word "race," we are compelled, by the existing methods to
> substitute the word "nationality." The word "race" is too general and
> vague in meaning, as applied in existing censuses, to permit of much
> intense analysis of census results. . . . In the census reports it is ordinar-
> ily used interchangeably with "nationality as indicated by the country
> of birth."

We can see in this statement the extent of the fluidity of the terminology. The
census generally used the term *nativity* for country of birth, showing no interest
in nationality as a legal tie to a foreign country, but North ignores this distinction
between the precise legal sense of the word *nationality* and its common but inac-
curate meaning of "national origin." North also shows the limits of the census
when it came to taking account of groups poorly defined in terms of race:

> Intermingled and intermediate is the great group of people, popularly
> described as "half-breeds," of whom the census takes no cognizance,
> chiefly consisting in the United States of persons living contiguous to
> the Mexican border, speaking the Spanish language but very largely of
> Indian blood.[13]

The return of the mulatto category in the 1910 census, even if for North it signified a renewal of the continuing series interrupted by the 1899 law, came in a
different context from that of 1890. In fact, this category would reveal new limits,
such as the increasingly widespread perception that the results obtained did not
correspond to reality and were less and less relevant.

The races or colors listed on the schedule thus constituted an original combination, returning overall to the choices proposed in 1880, with the addition
of "Jp," which had been present since 1890.[14] For the first time, the instructions
specified that the meaning of the terms *black* and *mulatto* as used in the census
did not necessarily correspond to common usage. They introduced the option
of writing *other* for persons who did not fit any of the proposed categories, while

noting in the margin the response given. It was no longer a question of important scientific results, as in 1870 and 1880, nor of fractions as in 1890, but of a
flexible definition of *mulatto* in the context of the census:

> For census purposes, the term "black" (B) includes all persons who are
> evidently fullblooded negroes, while the term "mulatto" (Mu) includes
> all other persons having some proportion or perceptible trace of negro
> blood.[15]

This broad definition of mulattoes, which covered all blacks except for those of
pure blood, could be understood as being more inclusive than the three categories (mulatto, quadroon, and octoroon) of 1890, which went as far as five-eighths
or 62.5 percent of black blood. This may explain the higher proportion of mulattoes in relation to the entire black population observed in 1910 than in 1890.
However, a new interpretation would be formulated in the 1910s and would be
used after the 1920 census to justify the elimination—definitive, this time—of
the mulatto category.

Looking at the figures for 1910, one might think that the significant increase
of mulattoes with respect to 1890 resulted from, among other things, the change
in the definition given in the instructions.[16] This interpretation was still current
in 1932, when assistant director Joseph A. Hill, who had personally been tasked
with the bulletin on the black population published in 1915, wrote:

> Thus a person who was seven-eighths Negro and one-eighth white
> would, according to the instructions, have been reported as black in
> 1890 and as mulatto in 1910.[17]

This explanation was plausible in 1915, but not in 1932, when it had been
acknowledged, as Hill notes further on, that visual observation did not permit
coherent, let alone precise, distinctions between "black" and "mulatto." The special volume on the black population published in 1918 devoted an entire chapter
to the color of blacks and commented at length on the problem of definitions.[18]
Pointing out that the 1890 categories permitted finer distinction of persons having the smallest proportion of black blood (one-eighth) than of those with larger
proportions, the report noted that the color perceived by the censustaker did
not necessarily correspond to the racial mixture, and that the results depended
on the agent's judgment in matters of "some proportion or any perceptible trace
of black blood."

> Under a condition of complete segregation of the races this proportion
> not "evidently full-blooded Negro" must inevitably increase, unless

the fact that the children of mixed black and mulatto marriages are not "full-blooded Negroes" becomes imperceptible in the case of at least one-half of such children, assuming a uniform natural increase for the black and mulatto elements of the Negro population.

The perceptibility of a trace of Negro or of white blood probably does not correspond uniformly to the physiological proportion of Negro and white blood in the individuals enumerated. Moreover, perceptibility is dependent upon the ability of the enumerator to perceive, and this ability varies from enumerator to enumerator.

There are undoubtedly many individuals in the United States in whom the trace of white blood has become absolutely imperceptible, and many other individuals in whom the trace, although perceptible is not in fact perceived by the enumerator. Similarly the trace of Negro blood may have become imperceptible, or be unperceived in individual cases.

The census classification is necessarily based upon perceptibility, qualified by the ability of the enumerator to perceive.[19]

The report stated further that even in cases where the agent correctly identified the mixture, the 1890 categories did not allow for correct reporting of all the possible cases, such as three-sixteenths. This caution is quite interesting, because it emphasizes the impossibility for the census of perceiving the invisible—which is what was asked of it by including in the black population anyone with one drop of black blood. While acknowledging that it had taken the "one drop rule" into account in its principles of classification, the Bureau noted that the results from the field could not properly do so, admitting that agents failed to perceive the trace even though it was perceptible (but without specifying to whom). Here the report omitted a fact that would weaken its position: censustakers, whose "capacity for perception" was so important in this regard, did not personally see all the persons whom they enumerated, but they still had to assign a race to all inhabitants.

This concrete limit had already been pointed out in 1904 in a census publication compiled by the Progressive white sociologist Walter F. Willcox and the black sociologist W. E. B. Du Bois:

Nature and accuracy of returns.

Definition. For census purposes a negro is a person who is classed so in the community in which he resides. The enumerator is supposed to know this fact or to ascertain it by observation or inquiry.

The censuses of mulattoes, as distinguished from full-blooded negroes, taken in 1850, 1860, 1870, and 1890, though subject to a far greater and wholly indeterminate probable error, have shown a general agreement of results.

They indicate that between 11 and 16 per cent of the negro population have, or are believed by the enumerators to have, some degree of white blood. . . .

Local opinion probably classes as a negro any one known or believed to have any trace of negro blood, even if it be less than one-eighth, and the definition of the census, if accurately followed, would probably class more persons as negroes than the prevalent definition of the statutes.[20]

The two sociologists went significantly further than earlier or later reports, noting, as no other source did, that to some extent blackness—like Indianness, for which this truth had already been admitted—depended on the social and residential context rather than on heredity alone; moreover, they stated that visual observation was not the unique criterion for determination of color—something that was known but had never been admitted so clearly in an official census publication. The reports drawn up by censustakers would not go so far as the admission that color depended, at least in part, on context and that it was not as visible and stable as the categories specified by law would have people believe.

The collection of photographs that Du Bois arranged and presented for the Paris Exposition of 1900 shows the diversity of what he called the "types" of American blacks (see figure 13).[21] Clearly Du Bois's intention was to give an image of American blacks that would counter the stereotypes of the day, whether of social position or of color. By including among the chosen portraits some "American Negroes" whose skin was white and whose hair was blond, Du Bois questioned, or implicitly criticized, categories of color. Moreover, his collection, though it also showed the way of life of poor southern blacks, emphasized instead representations that brought to mind the European or white American bourgeoisie.[22] In some images it was the décor, professional or domestic, in others clothing and posture, as in the child portrait shown in figure 13 or in the image of Milton M. Holland, a Civil War veteran born into slavery in Texas in 1844 who became the first black American to be awarded the Medal of Honor.[23] As a whole, the collection showed the extent to which "race" was a performance, as it might have been viewed in the lawsuits of white slaves from the 1850s. But at the turn of the century, Du Bois presented a different situation, apparently using the codes associated with the white stereotype, not in order to say that these individuals were not black or should not be perceived as black, but in order to challenge the relevance of these distinctions and the basis of the discrimination of which black Americans were the object.

The Census Bureau did not seek to call into question the relevance of these racial categories, but rather the weakness of the data, which it attributed to the conditions of the inquiry. The implicit conclusion of the introduction of the Census Bureau's 1918 special report on the black population was that the number of mulattoes was underreported, losing some from both ends of the spectrum, with "imperceptible" mulattoes being classed among whites and those with only a small proportion of white blood being classed as blacks. Unintentionally, this text seems to pull the interpretation of the term *mulatto* toward what was current at the time in the Virgin Islands, and what had led US census officials to judge that the data on color there were worthless. In these islands of the Caribbean purchased by the United States in 1917, censustakers had classified the majority of the colored population as being of mixed blood, and reserved the category of black for a minority, the reverse of the United States tradition.

According to this report, the "true" proportion of mulattoes was certainly larger than the 20.9 percent enumerated in the census. Anticipating genetic estimates made at the end of the twentieth century, the report concluded logically that the mixing of pure blacks and mixed-race individuals within the black population would in time lead to the entire black population having some degree of white blood. This development would necessarily bring about a revision of the definitions themselves, in the case where "pure blacks" disappeared. The census believed it likely that the "the proportion more or less affected by the dissemination" would increase to three-quarters of "blacks," and that if the 1910 census had counted only 20.9 percent, it was because of "the imperceptibility being probably due in part to a modification of the standard of discrimination." That is, the dilution of white blood among the majority of blacks must have progressed quite far, and censustakers must have lost the ability to see its traces. The report even suggested an inversion of the color reference used to define *mulatto*:

> As this gradual modification of the racial character progresses the black element in the population must decrease, and tend to disappear. Under these conditions, the standard of classification as black and mulatto may change, the term mulatto being defined with reference not to a pure-blooded Negro, but with reference to a Negro somewhat affected by the general diffusion of white blood.[24]

This document bears witness to another important turn in the census's use of the mulatto category: Here it is no longer a question of distinct racial types, but of porous categories dependent upon context. The entire analysis is oriented toward the idea that the number of mulattoes would constantly increase, the decrease of 1870 being explained by the wretched quality of the enumeration of blacks at that time.[25]

From this point of view, the marked decrease in the proportion of mulattoes in the 1920 census, only two years after the publication of this report, was problematic. In a fairly consistent fashion, the Census Bureau had concluded that it was not the proportion of mulattoes that had decreased, but rather the ability of the censustakers to identify them—especially the inability of white agents to use this distinction as effectively as the black censustakers did. This was explicitly stated in the report of the 1920 census, thereby managing to remove all credibility from the inquiry. In November 1921, the Census Advisory Committee, a scientific council composed of three members of the American Statistical Association, three from the American Economic Association, and Census Bureau officials, adopted a resolution stating that the decrease came from the greater use of black census agents in 1910 than in 1920, and asking that this explanation should feature in the report.[26] The resolution of the Census Advisory Committee, an influential body created in 1919, was followed by the Census Bureau, as was generally the case.[27] The report for the 1920 census thus provided this explanation:

> Considerable uncertainty necessarily attaches to the classification of Negroes as black and mulatto, since the accuracy of the distinction made depends largely upon the judgment and care employed by the enumerators. Moreover, the fact that the definition of the term "mulatto" adopted at different censuses has not been entirely uniform doubtless affects the comparability of the figures in some degree. At the census of 1920 the instructions were to report as "black" all full-blooded Negroes and as "mulatto" all negroes having some proportion of white blood.[28]

In addition, the Census Bureau emphasized the wide variation of figures in certain counties between 1910, when blacks were employed, and in 1920 when all the censustakers there were white. It then conducted a special tabulation of these data for twenty-six states in which districts had been enumerated by black agents in 1910. The Census Bureau thus determined that the decrease was greater in the counties where at least three black agents had been employed in 1910 (from 21.8 percent to 16.1 percent in 1920), but that in those where only white agents had been employed, the decrease was from 19.6 to 15.9 percent, or roughly two-thirds of the decrease observed in the counties where black agents had been employed. However, in certain counties where only whites had been appointed, the decrease was still greater. The Census Bureau concluded from this that the more frequent use of black agents in 1910 than in 1920 had had as a consequence a decrease in the proportion of mulattoes in the same period, but that this was neither the only nor the principal cause of the decrease.[29] The argument based on the hiring of black agents, which would become commonplace later, cannot fully explain the decrease observed in 1920.

This appeal to the influence of the recruitment of black workers on responses is interesting because, now that it had become a permanent federal agency, the Census Bureau became the object of demands on the part of representatives from the black community for such hiring, especially in its Washington offices.[30] One of the arguments that would be made later, in 1930, in favor of the recruitment of black censustakers was their greater ability to identify light-skinned blacks. For representatives of the black community, this would allow them to include the largest number possible, and for the census, to claim greater accuracy.[31] Whether it was a question of recruiting field workers or Washington statisticians, the idea was that to entrust responsibility for statistics on blacks to black workers was at once a way to promote the condition of blacks and a way to guarantee the quality of the results by counting on racial pride. The Census Bureau, although it partly satisfied these demands, did not make it a rule and generally made effective use of black workers as links to the black community, while remaining attentive to the protestations of whites offended by the presence of these agents in white neighborhoods. Each time that black workers were hired, the Census Bureau made a point of letting this be known, which earned it congratulatory letters from representatives of black institutions.[32]

Reinforced by the experience of the 1920 census, the recurrent argument during the 1920s for the elimination, pure and simple, of the mulatto category was the volatility of the data and the marked difference of perception between black census agents, to whom the census could not systematically deny their place in the field, at least in black neighborhoods, and white census agents.[33] In this new context, where the perception of nuances of color within the black population appeared more and more fluid, the 1920 figure of 15.9 percent (close to that of 1890) could not be interpreted as a simple return to the past. The results of the 1890 census had been criticized for the poor fit of the finely divided categories, but after 1920, it was the interest in a distinction between "pure" and "mixed" blacks that disappeared.

Another argument, which was not mentioned in the published reports but appeared in the internal discussions of census officials, was that the reason for the use of this category at the beginning of the century—to prevent "passing"— had lost its urgency. This comes through most clearly in the document transmitted by Hill to the Census Advisory Committee in 1932, after the 1930 census in which a single category, "Negro," had been applied to the black population:

> The Negro.—The term "Negro" as defined in recent censuses includes all persons having any proportion of Negro blood. In the actual enumeration a certain number of persons who according to this definition strictly applied should be classified as Negroes are probably returned as white because they are not distinguishable in appearance from the white

and pass as whites in the community in which they live. Of course, it is not known how many such persons there were in any census, but the number is doubtless relatively small. . . .

The very nature of things makes it impossible in a census to distinguish accurately between black and mulatto. The enumerator must either judge by appearances—which are often deceitful, and he does not by any means meet or see all the persons whom he enumerates—or he must accept the answer he gets to the question if he takes the trouble to ask it. In most cases the question probably is not asked at all, and, if it is asked and answered, it is not at all certain that the informant knows or will give the correct answer. This inquiry has been thoroughly tried out at six decennial censuses, and the consensus of opinion appears it should be omitted from the future schedules.[34]

Hill, who was at that time the assistant director of the Census Bureau and one of the most important census officials of the period, expressed in this document an opinion that seems to represent a broad consensus: passing was no longer a cause for concern. In a 1938 communication to the American Statistical Association, Calvert Dedrick, who was then acting chief statistician, even placed the children of immigrants who "passed" for native-born on the same level as blacks who passed as white. He noted further that they often did so unconsciously, in a desire to raise themselves to a higher or more respectable status, much like sickroom attendants who passed for nurses and abandoned women who passed as widows.[35] With the 1930 census translating the "one drop rule" in its instructions, the distinctions within the black population that had been used in varying contexts between 1850 and 1920, and which had been the object of so much speculation and commentary, would disappear definitively from the census of the US population. From the moment when the difference between "mulatto" and "black" became a matter of secondary importance and no longer a factor in the stratification of the black population, the mulatto category lost its place in the census, which could conform to the "one drop rule" in its simplest form. Even if the mulatto category had still constituted a group strictly contained within the black population (the percentages or numbers of mulattoes per 1,000 inhabitants had never referred to the entire population or to the white population, but always to the subtotal of the black population), its presence in the census revealed the possibility of a mixing of the races. Once it had been asserted that racial mixtures were no more than different shades of black, after 1910, the logical result was the elimination of the distinction from the census. A double, contradictory development took place: the "one drop rule" was affirmed, while at the same time the census acknowledged more and more openly that its categories were as much cultural and social as biological. But the paradoxical advantage of the "one drop of negro blood" rule was that it was compatible with a fluid definition of blacks: it had the merit of simplicity and made it possible to abandon the scientific claims translated into fractions, while remaining compatible with the most racist legislation of the period, such as Virginia's 1924 "racial integrity act."[36] At the same time, the census could respect the strictest principles in its definitions and acknowledge that in the field, blacks were those who were known as such, downplaying the quantitative impact of this fact by deciding that the "one drop rule" had been internalized by American blacks, by endogamy and by identification with the group. The relation of the Census Bureau to the black population during the last prewar decade was characterized by the priority given to economic statistics. In fact, *Negro Statistics*, which Charles E. Hall had overseen, could just as well have been called *Negro Social and Economic Statistics*. The Census Bureau was far from admitting the equality of races, as shown by the permanence of a system of categories organized around the opposition between white and black, based on the fundamental inequality of the two races, but thenceforth it had to give up devoting its resources, whether intellectual or material, to defending this principle of racial inferiority by forcing all persons with some black ancestry into the black statistical category.[37]

The Question of Racial Mixing in the American Possessions

National Norms and Local Resistance

The retention in certain US territories of a "mixed" racial category highlights the national norm that made mulattoes into simply lighter-skinned blacks. In the various territories acquired by the United States since 1898 the rigid imposition of the categories of the US census was difficult because they were the product of a national history that had not been shared. Whether in the US Virgin Islands or Puerto Rico, the perception of what made a person black, white, or mulatto was so different from North American usage that in 1930, when the category "mixed" (which, in the Virgin Islands, corresponded to the "mulatto" category of the mainland with some differences) should have been eliminated, local protests ensured that it was kept.[1]

The Virgin Islands

The US Virgin Islands are a small Caribbean archipelago purchased by the United States in 1917 from Denmark. The Danish authorities had carried out nine censuses of the colony between 1835 and 1911, but had never made use of racial classifications. Instead the Danish censuses of 1901 and 1911 had asked inhabitants about their religion.[2] Denmark had projected onto the colony categories that reflected its own practices; so did the United States upon taking possession of the territory. As early as November 1917, it applied the same racial categories used in the continental United States in 1910. Even before the 1917 census, American officials were concerned that the color line, so important in their work, was blurred to the point that there were "comparatively few whites of unmixed blood, probably not more than 10 percent of the total population," and that "the color line is not at all strictly drawn, mixed marriages being very common, and the major portion of the people are mulattoes."[3]

In spite of the notion that the majority of the population was composed of mulattoes or other racial mixtures, the US census found a majority of blacks: 75 percent, with 17.5 percent "mixed" and 7.4 percent whites. The report that presented these figures carefully emphasized that the number of persons classified as black (rather than "mixed") had been overestimated, and the same was no doubt true for the number of whites.[4] What made this territory different, in the eyes of census officials, was that racial mixing was recent and ongoing. In addition, color in the American sense did not have the same significance in the Virgin Islands as it did in the United States, to the extent that "some of those enumerated are ignorant of the facts as to their race, while others may desire to conceal the facts."[5] In the Virgin Islands, as on the US mainland, racial categories were attributed on the basis of observation, but officials expressed strong doubts about the effectiveness of this method:

> If the race mixture usually is shown by a difference in color, it is quite probable the enumerator frequently will neglect to ask the race of the person being enumerated, and will enter the apparent race on the schedule according with the person's shade of color.

Here we see all the ambiguity of American racial categories, which were intended to be simple in practice but which varied between physical appearance and genealogy.

With respect to the compiled results, the report concluded that the wide variation of the division between blacks and mixed could only be explained by carelessness on the part of censustakers, who had ignored the instructions provided them. This 1918 report gives an explanation quite close to the one in the general report of the 1920 census, in favor of eliminating the "mulatto" category. Even if the census recognized that racial terminology and the relations of the inhabitants to racial categories differed between the United States and this territory that had only been American for a few months, the reports drew similar conclusions. Census officials made the logical decision that in 1930, in the Virgin Islands as elsewhere, there would no longer be a category applying to persons who were partly white and partly black. The reaction of the local population to this decision, however, was atypical. Even though racial categories had only been used in the censuses since 1917, apparently there were protests and demonstrations in favor of retaining the "mixed" category—so much so that the governor of the Virgin Islands requested and received permission to depart from the new rule.[6] The original 1930 instructions required that mulattoes would be counted as blacks (Negro) if the person in question had the slightest percentage of black blood. After the protests, the modified instructions used in 1930 and kept in 1940 explicitly rejected the American "one drop rule" in favor of a category labeled not "mulatto" but "mixed." The latter term emphasized the mixture:

> The population of the Virgin Islands is classified according to race as (1) White, (2) Negro, (3) Mixed and (4) Other. The classification "White" is used for full-blooded white persons; "Negro" for full-blooded Negroes and for persons whose fathers were Negroes and whose mothers were nonwhites other than Negroes; "Mixed" for persons of mixed white and Negro blood; and "Other" for Chinese, Hindus and other persons of nonwhite races other than Negro, including those whose mothers were Negroes and whose fathers were nonwhites other than Negroes.[7]

In the published report, "mixed" were systematically distinguished from blacks and included among "other races."[8] The particularities of the census in these new US possessions meant that if the rules were strictly applied, a person who would be categorized as "mixed race" (or even "white" in some cases) in 1930 in the Virgin Islands would be counted as "black" in New York at the same date. In 1940, the same person would be classed in Panama as "Negro-Mixed" and would appear in US census publications as simply "black." The same supervisor had authority in Panama as in the Virgin Islands: the supervisor for Puerto Rico, who had responsibility for three territories where racial categories had been adapted to local situations.[9]

We should emphasize here the exceptional character of the protest in the US Virgin Islands over the elimination of the mixed category. As far as we know, this was the only such demand in the history of the census, before the demands that led to the option of claiming affiliation with more than one race in 2000. We should also note the limits of the exception obtained in 1930 for an underpopulated territory whose inhabitants did not form part of the constitutional population for which the census was obligatory. Although in the census volume on the Virgin Islands the mixed were distinguished from blacks and whites, and were treated as a third race, in the tables of the general volume for the 1940 census, they were combined with the colored population. Even as they adapted schedules to local conditions, census officials in their reports tended to minimize the differences, which were sometimes significant, and to affirm the rigid principle of hypodescent, as in this report on the 1930 fieldwork in the territories:

> Race or Color.—The object of the race question was to determine the racial extraction of the population. The racial designation varied on the

different schedules in accordance with the known composition of the population. Any mixture of white and nonwhite was invariably reported according to the nonwhite parent, while mixtures of colored races were reported in accordance with the race of the father.[10]

Puerto Rico

In Puerto Rico (or Porto Rico, as it was often spelled at the time), which was a Spanish colony before it became a US possession in 1898, racial affiliations were also perceived differently. Ignoring the tradition established by the several colonial censuses, the Census Bureau, after a simplified census in 1899, applied in 1910 the methods and the schedule used in the mainland United States, translated into Spanish.[11] The Census Bureau's intention was to export its practices, not treating the possessions as colonies with a special status, which is what they were, but rather producing unified results—which we can interpret as the construction of an imagined national community.[12] In the 1899 census the division of the population into three groups—whites, blacks, and mixed—as found in the Spanish census of 1887 was used, but in 1910 the Census Bureau wanted to fit Puerto Rico into the US norm.[13] However, in its details, the practice was different. While up until 1910 the American definition of "mulatto" as someone having black blood without being entirely black was applied, the 1920 instructions modified the principle, in the continental United States as well as in Puerto Rico, but with different results: there, blacks with white blood were classed as mulatto. No longer was it black blood that prevented an individual from being white, but henceforth white blood that prevented him or her from being black.[14] This difference is illustrated in the printed sample for 1920 distributed to census-takers, in which the first family given as an example is a mixed family whose head of household is white, the wife and children mulatto (Mu.). Here is an example of mixing within the family, which would not be found in the printed samples for the mainland United States. This same family of four children also furnished an example of consensual marriage (CC: *contrato consensual*, cohabiting outside of wedlock), while results showed that consensual marriages were just as common among whites.[15] In practice, censustakers in Puerto Rico went much further in 1910 and 1920, classifying first 20 percent and then 35 percent of the children of mixed couples as white. They were running counter to the entire American tradition of hypodescent, a practice partially corrected by local officials who reclassified as "mulatto" a large number of "whites."[16]

This change of definition, imposed by local practices, was much more significant for the overall results than the simple fact of counting mulattoes separately as they did for the mixed-race category in the Virgin Islands. Some of the persons whose origins were mixed were counted among whites, if whiteness predominated. While between 1850 and 1910 mulattoes had oscillated between 11 percent and 16 percent of the black population of the continental United States,[17] in Puerto Rico the proportions were reversed, and mulattoes were much more numerous than blacks (Table 15.1).

The elimination of the distinction between mulatto and black, although it took place in Puerto Rico as it did in the continental United States in 1930 and for the purpose of bringing the island's racial categories into conformity, did not have the same consequences, since it actually contributed to increasing the number of whites.[18] In Puerto Rico it meant melding two populations of different size into a single category, called not "black" but "colored" in the census.[19] In fact, in view of the past significance of mulattoes in the population figures for Puerto Rico, the official in charge of territorial statistics in the Bureau of the Census explicitly stated in 1939 that the classification rule used on the island was the opposite of that used in the continental United States. At a time when the Census Bureau had eliminated the distinction between blacks and mulattoes in the continental United States in order to make this population black, in Puerto Rico, those of mixed race had for the most part statistically become white:

> It is understood that the term "white" is applied in Puerto Rico to any person having any perceptible amount of white blood, even though Negro blood might predominate.[20]

In other words, a mulatto in Puerto Rico would have been considered white if he had been enumerated on the island in 1940; he would have been classed as black at the same date in New York, and in Hawaii his race would no doubt have been listed as Puerto Rican (PR).

Table 15.1. **Distribution of the Population of Puerto Rico by Race, 1900–1930**

	Black		Mulatto		White		Other		Total	
	Number	%	Number	%	Number	%	Number	%	Number	%
1900	59,390	6.2	304,352	31.9	589,426	61.8	75	0.0	953,243	100
1910	50,245	4.5	335,192	30.0	732,555	65.5	20	0.0	1,118,012	100
1920	49,246	3.8	301,816	23.2	948,709	73.0	38	0.0	1,299,809	100
1930			397,156	25.7	1,146,719	74	38	0	1,543,913	100

Source: Census, *Fifteenth Census of the United States : 1930. Outlying Territories and Possessions.*

The drift of a certain number of individuals toward the category of white began with the earliest American censuses of Puerto Rico. A statistical analysis of the variation in the number of whites in Puerto Rico between 1910 and 1920 by Maria Loveman and Jeronimo O. Muniz showed a "surplus" of 100,000 whites, or about 9 percent, which the authors attributed in part to the change in the definition and the racial reclassification of a large number of blacks into whites carried out in Puerto Rico by censustakers. Their convincing analysis confirms that the largest category-crossing happened between 1910 and 1920, while the mulatto category continued to exist, and that only one-fifth of the changes can be explained by the acquisition of new characteristics by the individuals concerned, especially their social mobility; more could be explained by a difference in the practice of ascription by censustakers on the island.[21]

While in the American context mulattoes constituted a sub-group of blacks, in Puerto Rico, as in the rest of the Caribbean, this distinction was all the more important because the censustakers were recruited from the local population, which had clearly shown some degree of resistance to the norms of the American racial hierarchy, something that did not escape notice among American officials:

> Another point which I found was particularly pleasing to the Porto Ricans and commented on frequently in the press was the fact that the work was done almost entirely by the native Porto Ricans and we did not use to any great extent Americans who are in the island temporarily and do not always treat the natives with quite the consideration that they expect.[22]

Figure 8, showing an agent on horseback enumerating an inhabitant whom he towers over, holding his large portfolio on his lap with one hand, illustrates how the Census Bureau in its publicity campaigns tried to show the local, even exotic, nature of census-taking in Puerto Rico. Perhaps this was an unconscious way to indicate that down there the same words signified something different. The arrangement of the two men is obviously contrived: it would scarcely be feasible for the agent to fill out the schedule without dismounting, and the interview was to take place in people's homes, not in the street. This image can be viewed as a representation of the relations between the census and the population of Puerto Rico: the agent is better dressed than the man standing, and his clothes, like his skin, are lighter. The two men's respective body language also speaks of the unequal conditions that we find in other photos of Puerto Rico that show, from 1899 on, censustakers as belonging to the upper classes of the island.[23]

The American Censuses in Hawaii
(1900–1940): Resistance to the American Binary Model

In Hawaii, even more than in the Virgin Islands or Puerto Rico, the imposition of the US system of racial classification, based on the opposition between whites and blacks, revealed the extent to which it was specific. The Hawaiian population was characterized by the absence of a majority group and by its long tradition of racial mixing, already attested to by the censuses of the independent kingdom of Hawaii. Since 1853, the Hawaiian censuses had established a mixed category, translated into English as "half-caste," but which in Hawaiian meant "half-foreign" (*hapahaole*).[24] Based on this category, which opposed natives and immigrants and whose definition referred to whether or not the person spoke Hawaiian, the Census Bureau produced a racialized distinction, replacing a distinction of national or cultural origin by hereditary physical characteristics—"Part-Hawaiian."

Virginia Domínguez, in an illuminating article, has shown that the Hawaiians were aware of and took note of differences in origin, but that the concept of "race," which they knew to be important for Americans, remained largely unthinkable for them because they saw no point in it. Commenting upon the abrupt shift brought about by the American census of 1900, two years after the annexation of 1898, she wrote:

> The change is striking and immediate, and revealing of both Hawaiian life without "race" and U.S. life with "race."[25]

The application of American racial categories to Hawaii presents, beyond doubt, the most interesting case for studying the problems posed by the imposition of norms that were seen as objective and technical by those who conceived of them. The constant negotiation of these categories shows the extent to which statistical apparatuses depend upon the social conditions of their production.[26]

The value of the racial hierarchy adopted by the US Census was repeatedly challenged in Hawaii. The principal stumbling block was the question of the status of Hawaiians of mixed race and of "pure" Hawaiians, which had not previously existed in the American classifications. More generally the criticisms emanating from Hawaii were directed at the rigidity of the racial classification system. Moreover, the census would find itself competing with a body of classifications and administrative statistics that went into far more detail on genealogies. The reductive nature of the census's racial categories became a recurrent theme of criticism.

The fact that the Hawaiian race had no place in the categorization system of the 1900 census, as well as the obsession with the black-white dichotomy, are strikingly illustrated in the first report that included Hawaiians. Unlike Asians, who had already been racialized in the continental United States, Hawaiians were included among the white population, while Asians (Chinese and Japanese) were presented as homologous to blacks in the mainland, in an explicit comparison with the most dualistic of the American states, South Carolina and Mississippi.[27]

The figures led whites to think that Hawaiians, like blacks or Indians of the same era, were a population en route to extinction. Over the first half of the twentieth century, it was the presence of mixed-race individuals—more numerous than "pure Hawaiians" from 1930 on—that circumvented a statistical decline. Upon their publication, Romanzo Adams, a sociologist at the university in Honolulu, examined these data and found them very poorly adapted to the local situation. He emphatically criticized the census's tendency to count as Asiatic-Hawaiians rather than as European-Hawaiians children who had all three origins. In Hawaii, some of these children were considered to be European-Hawaiians, the local custom in cases of multiple mixtures being to follow the mother's race.[28] However, his criticisms ran up against a firm response from the director of the census, for whom the federal census could not take account of, far less align itself with, local practices, and indeed established its own norms.[29] It was an atypical case in census history, usually prone to respect local usages when racial mixing was at issue. But when pushed to modify its rules for the treatment of the data to allow finer nuances in racial distinctions, the Census Bureau dismissed the authority of other administrative agencies.

Adams undertook to produce his own data and sociological studies on racial mixing in Hawaii, which emphasized the rigidity of the American categories and their inability to account for what he, like other American sociologists who were equally fascinated, saw as a model of coexistence and a unique racial mixture. He worked with the Census Bureau and several times met with territorial statistical officials.[30] In his writings, however, he often drew attention to the fact that continental racial categories in general, and those of the census in particular, could not explain the situation in Hawaii, whether it was a question of Hawaiians of mixed blood or of the peculiar racial categories "Puerto Rican" or "Portuguese," which the census applied solely to Hawaii.[31] His successors in the sociology department of the University of Hawaii in Honolulu, such as Andrew Lind,[32] a disciple of Robert E. Park, or the collaborators on the review *Social Process in Hawaii*, pursued this critique, expressing ideas that were current in Hawaii but rare in the continental United States. For example, in a 1948 article B. L. Hormann, unusually for an American sociologist, placed quotation marks around the term "race" and concluded by saying:

> The main difference between racial statistics and sex and age statistics is that race is not a permanent and clearly definable entity.[33]

The delegate representing the Hawaiian Islands in Congress also appealed to the special nature of Hawaii, before the 1930 census, in an attempt to ensure that the term "colored" would not be applied to non-white populations other than blacks in census publications,[34] and that Pacific Islanders would be distinguished from American blacks, in the name of scientific accuracy and to avoid offending the populations concerned.[35] Besides these political appeals, we find in Hawaii, as in the continental United States, requests from the business sector, which was heavily involved in census work through the Chamber of Commerce of Honolulu. The Committee of Users of Census Data of Hawaii, advised on this issue by the sociologists Adams and Lind, made some suggestions, which in general were followed for the 1930 and 1940 censuses, asking especially that the multiracial character of the islands should be made more visible. In the 1940s, the Chamber of Commerce, which absorbed the committee in 1939, would debate the elimination of all racial categories. This was an advanced position, even for Hawaii, and was rejected by Lind, who believed the census should take race into account, if only to grasp the reality of the melting-pot in Hawaii.[36] The Census Bureau, for its part, relied on local authorities to justify the special racial categories found in Hawaii up until 1940: Hawaiians, part-Hawaiians (who were more than three times as numerous as "Hawaiians" in 1940), Portuguese, and Puerto Rican, alongside "Caucasian" and other categories that conformed to the continental schedules.[37]

There was thus a broad consensus in Hawaii that the census categories were inadequate to measure the extent of racial mixing taking place in Hawaii. An unsatisfied demand for categories that could have better represented the characteristic mix of this American territory was expressed, which claimed that Hawaii had very different racial relations from those of the continent. The real issue was how to obtain useful statistics from the census—that is, statistics that corresponded to population categories as they were perceived in Hawaii. This is why there was collaboration with the Census Bureau more than challenge, and collaboration to a very high degree, since the Bureau sent its proposals for review to Romanzo Adams, the governor of Hawaii, or the Hawaiian delegate to Congress. The Census Bureau had to reconcile two contradictory requirements: to produce statistics that were comparable to those for the continental United States, and to respond to demands coming from Hawaii, some of which appeared to have more legitimacy because they were institutional. Here we see the permanent problem of the Census Bureau, condemned to reinforce its weak authority by availing itself of other authorities, scientific or institutional, only to find itself torn between contradictory goals, in this case, the comparability and representativeness of its statistics.

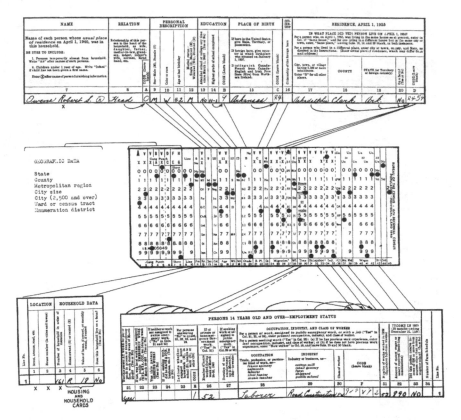

Figure 1. Population punch card and corresponding line of the population schedule, 1940. Source: National Archives, no. 29-C-1B-34.

Figure 2. Census Bureau operators, 1941. Source: National Archives, no. 29-C-1B-38.

SIXTEENTH DECENNIAL CENSUS

By the President of the United States of America

A Proclamation

WHEREAS, pursuant to the act of Congress approved June 18, 1929, 46 Stat. 21, the Sixteenth Decennial Census of the United States will be taken beginning April first, nineteen hundred and forty; and

WHEREAS, this Census, which will mark the one hundred and fiftieth anniversary of the first United States Census, is required by the Constitution of the United States to determine the apportionment among the several States of seats in the House of Representatives; and

WHEREAS, the information obtained from the Census inquiries this year must present a complete and current factual picture of the Nation's people, homes, farms, factories, and other resources to measure the effects of the difficult decade now closing and to guide us intelligently in the future:

NOW, THEREFORE, I, Franklin D. Roosevelt, President of the United States of America, do hereby declare and make known that, under the aforesaid act of Congress, it is the duty of every person over eighteen years of age to answer all questions on the Census schedules applying to him and the family to which he belongs, and to the farm or home occupied by him or his family, and all other Census schedules as required by law, and that any person refusing to do so is subject to penalty.

The sole purpose of the Census is to secure general statistical information regarding the population, business activities, and resources of the country, and replies are required from individuals only to enable the compilation of such general statistics. No person can be harmed in any way by furnishing the information required. The Census has nothing to do with taxation, with military or jury service, with the compulsion of school attendance, with the regulation of immigration, or with the enforcement of any national, state, or local law, or ordinance. There need be no fear that any disclosure will be made regarding any individual person or his affairs. For the due protection of the rights and interests of the persons furnishing information, every employee of the Census Bureau is prohibited, under heavy penalty, from disclosing any information which may thus come to his knowledge.

Life and liberty in a free democracy entail a variety of cooperative actions for the common good. The prompt, complete, and accurate answering of all official inquiries addressed to each person by Census officials should be regarded by him as one of the requirements of good citizenship.

IN WITNESS WHEREOF, I have hereunto set my hand and caused the seal of the United States of America to be affixed.

DONE at the City of Washington this 9th day of February in the year of our Lord, nineteen hundred and forty, and of the Independence of the United States of America the one hundred and sixty-fourth.

Franklin D Roosevelt

By the President:
CORDELL HULL
    Secretary of State.

Figure 3. 1940 Census Proclamation. English text surrounded by its translation in twenty-three languages. Source: National Archives, RG29/E. 238/Scrapbooks, vol. 4, p. 2.

ΕΛΛΗΝΙΚΟΝ GREEK

Παρατίθεται ἡ προήγουμενος προκήρυξις τοῦ Προέδρου Ρόζβελτ, σχετικῶς μὲ τὴν Δεκάτην Ἔκτην κατὰ Δεκαετίαν Ἀπογραφήν, ἥτις θὰ ἀρχίσῃ τὴν 1ην Ἀπριλίου. Δι' αὐτῆς ἔρχεται, ὅτι, ἡ ταύτη Ἀπογραφὴ ἔγινε πρὸ 150 ἐτῶν καὶ ὅτι γίνεται ἀποκλειστικῶς διὰ τὰ συγκεντρωθῇ τὰ βασικὰ τρέχοντα γεγονότα περὶ τοῦ λαοῦ καὶ τῶν πόρων τοῦ Ἀμερικανικοῦ Ἔθνους. Λέγει, ὅτι εἶναι τὸ νομικὸν καθῆκον ἑκάστου προσώπου, ὅλιγον ἀπὸ τῶν ἰδίων αὐτοῦ ἐτῶν, νὰ ἀπαντήσῃ εἰς τὰς ἐρωτήσεις τῆς Ἀπογραφῆς, τὰς ἁπωμένας αὐτῷ καὶ τὴν σίιατύνεσθ τοι. Λέγει περαιτέρω:

"Οὐδεμία ζημία εἶναι δυνατὸν νὰ προσέλθῃ εἰς οἱεῖον, ὅστις θὰ μεταδώσῃ τὰς ἀπαιτουμένας πληροφορίας. Ἡ Ἀπογραφὴ δὲν ἔχει καμμίαν σχέσιν μὲ τὴν φορολογίαν, μὲ τὰ στρατιωτικὰ ἢ μὲ τὴν ὑποχρέωσιν ἐνόρκων, μὲ τὴν ἀναγκαστικὴν σχολικὴν φοίτησιν, μὲ τοὺς μεταναστευτικοὺς κανονισμοὺς ἢ μὲ τὴν ἐφαρμογὴν οἱασδήποτε ἐθνικῆς, πολιτειακῆς καὶ τοπικῆς νόμων ἢ διατάξεων. Δὲν χρεία νὰ ὑπάρξῃ κανεὶς φόβος, ὅτι δὲ ἀποκαλυφθῇ μυστικά. Ἀρνεῖται πρόσωπον τι ἡ τὰς ἐνοθείσας τοι. Διὰ τὴν δικαίαν προστασίαν τῶν δικαιωμάτων καὶ συμφερόντων τῶν προσώπων, τὰ ὁποῖα θὰ δίδουν τὰς πληροφορίας, ἀπηγορεύθη εἰς πάντα ὑπάλληλον τοῦ Γραφείου Ἀπογραφῆς ὑπὸ ποινίας νὰ καὶ εἰς κανεὶς Ἀπογραφεὺς οιανδήποτε ἐγκαταληφθὲν εἰς τρίτον πρόσωπον, ἥτις ταῦτα παρεδόθη εἰς γνῶσίν τοι."

Independence of the United States of America the one hundred and sixty-fourth.

[signature] Franklin D. Roosevelt

By the President:
CORDELL HULL
Secretary of State.

LIETUVIŠKAI LITHUANIAN

Čia yra Prezidento Roosevelto neseniai išleista proklamacija kaslink Šešiolikto Dešimtmetinio Cenzo, kuris bus imtas prasidedant su balandžio mėnesio 1d. Jis pasiūkina, kad Cenzas yra 150 metų senas, ir kad imtas su vienatiniu tikslu surinkti pamatinius, bėgančius faktus apie Tautos žmones ir jos turtą. Jis sako, kad yra kiekvieno žmogaus, virš aštuoniolikos metų senumo, legalė pareiga duoti atsakymus į klausimus, kuric liečia jį ir jo šeimą. Jis toliaus sako: "Žmogus, teikdamas reikalingas informacijas, jokios skriaudos sau nedarys. Cenzas neturi nieko bendro su takasvimu, su militariška ar "jurės" tarnyste, su priverstinu lankymu mokyklų, su immigracijos sutvarkymu, ar užlaikymu kokio tautiško, valstiško ar vietinio įstatymo ar tvarkos. Nei mažiausios informacijos bus išdoutos kaslink atskiro žmogaus ar jo reikalų. Apsaugojimui teisių ir interesų žmonių, kurie duoda informacijas, kiekvienas Cenzo Biuro darbininkas yra draudžiamas, po sunkia bausme, nuo išdavimo kokių nors informaciju, kurios jo žinioms papuola."

HOLLANDSCH DUTCH

Hier is de jongste proclamatie van President Roosevelt, betreffende de Zestiende Tienjaarlijksche Census, die gehouden zal worden te beginnen op 1 April. Hij richt er den aandacht op, dat de Census 150 jaar oud is en dat deze volkstelling uitsluitend gehouden wordt voor het verzamelen van belangrijke, hedendaagsche gegevens betreffende de bevolking en de hulpbronnen van het land.

Hij verklaart verder: "Geen persoon kan ooit eenig nadeel ondervinden van het geven van de vereischte inlichtingen. De Census heeft niets uit te staan met belasting, militaire of jury dienst, verplichting om naar school te gaan, immigratie voorschriften of met de toepassing van de nationale, staats of gemeente wetten of verordeningen. Niemand behoeft te vreezen, dat de verstrekte inlichtingen verder zullen worden doorgegeven. Ten einde de rechten en de belangen van alle personen, die de gevraagde inlichtingen verschaffen, te beschermen, is iedere geëmployeerde van het Census Bureau op straffe verboden om eenige inlichting, die hun ter oore is gekomen verder te geven."

SUOMEKSI FINNISH

Tässä on Presidentti Rooseveltin äskeinen julistus Kuudennestatoista Kymmenvuotisesta Sensuksesta, joka toimitetaan huhtikuun 1 päivästä alkaen. Hän selittää, että Sensus on 150 vuoden vanha ja että se toimitetaan yksinomaan Kansakunnan kansaa ja sen varoja koskevien perustiedollisten, nykyhetken tosiasioiden talteen kokoamista varten. Hän sanoo, että jokaisen kahdeksantoista täyttäneen henkilön velvollisuus on vastata häntä ja perhettään koskeviin sensuskysymyksiin. Lisäksi hän selittää: "Ketään henkilöä ei millään tavalla vahingoita tietojen antaminen. Sensuksella ei ole mitään tekemistä verotuksen, sotilas- tai jurypalveluksen, ei pakollisen koulunkäynnin, ei siirtolaisuusasetuksien eikä minkään maan, valtiota tai paikallista lakia tai säädöstä koskevan toimenpiteen kanssa. Ei ole syytä pelkoon, että tohtisiin mitään ilmaisuja yksityisestä henkilöstä tai hänen asioistaan. Kaikkien tietoja antavien henkilöiden oikeuksien ja etujen turvaamiseksi on jokainen Sensusvirastossa palveleva kovan rangaistuksen uhalla kielletty ilmaisemasta niitä asioita, jotka siten joutuvat hänen tietoonsa."

Figure 4. 1940 Census Proclamation (detail).

Figure 5. Ivan Petrov taking the census of an Alaskan family, 1889. Courtesy of The Bancroft Library. Source: University of California, Berkeley. Petroff Papers, Bancroft Library, University of California, Berkeley, Mss C-B 989.

Figure 6. Census of a family living in a trailer, 1940. Source: National Archives, no. 29-C-1B-18. [P 5.]

Figure 7. Farmer enumerated in 1940. Source: National Archives, RG29/E. 215/Box 234/Alice Short folder.

Figure 8. Census of Puerto Rico, 1940. Source: National Archives, no. 29-C-1B-49 [P 6.].

Figure 9a (day) and 9b (night). Advertisement billboards by a local electricity company, Seattle, 1930. Source: National Archives, RG29/E.215/Box 213/E2.

Figure 10. Census employee with the electric tabulator used to compile data from individual punch cards, 1941. Source: National Archives, RG29/E.215/Box 234.

Figure 11. Enumerators. First American census of Puerto Rico, 1899. Source: National Archives RG 350-PR Records of the Bureau of Insular Affairs. Prints: General Photographs of Puerto Rico, 1899–1928, Box 5, no. 350-PR-44C-21.

Figure 12. Census Advisory Committee, 1941. Source: National Archives, no. 29-C-1A-42.

Figure 13. Negro child, Georgia. Photo from W. E. B. DuBois' Exhibit, "American Negro," for the 1900 Paris Exposition Universelle. Source: Types of American Negroes, compiled and prepared by W. E. B. Du Bois, v. 1, no. 59, Library of Congress, Prints & Photographs Division. Reproduction number: LC-USZ62-121108.

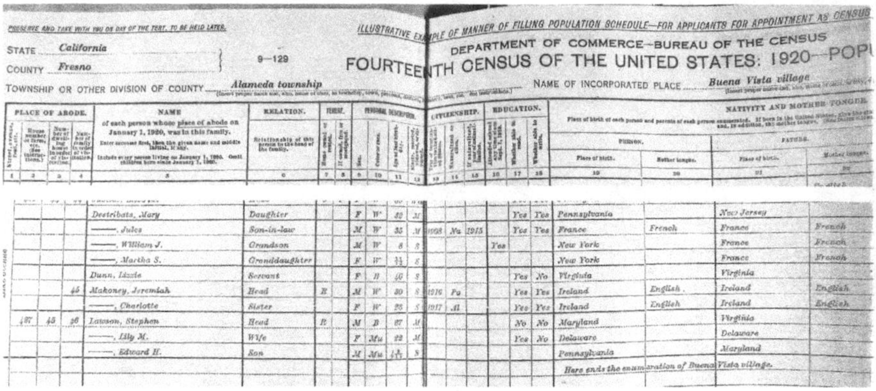

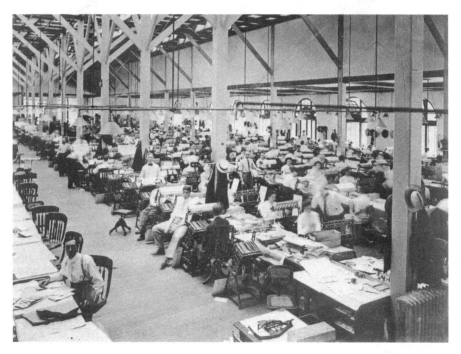

PRESERVE AND TAKE WITH YOU ON DAY OF THE TEST, TO BE HELD LATER.

ILLUSTRATIVE EXAMPLE OF MANNER OF FILLING POPULATION SCHEDULE—FOR APPLICANTS FOR APPOINTMENT AS CENSUS

DEPARTMENT OF COMMERCE—BUREAU OF THE CENSUS

FOURTEENTH CENSUS OF THE UNITED STATES: 1920—POP

STATE California

COUNTY Fresno

9—129

TOWNSHIP OR OTHER DIVISION OF COUNTY Alameda township

NAME OF INCORPORATED PLACE Buena Vista village

1	2	3	4	5 NAME	6 RELATION	7	8	9	10	11	12	13	14	15	16	17	18	19 Person: Place of birth	20 Mother tongue	21 Father: Place of birth	22 Mother tongue
				Destribats, Mary	Daughter			F	W	32	M					Yes	Yes	Pennsylvania		New Jersey	
				——, Jules	Son-in-law			M	W	35	M	1908	Na	1915		Yes	Yes	France	French	France	French
				——, William J.	Grandson			M	W	8	S				Yes			New York		France	French
				——, Martha S.	Granddaughter			F	W	11/12	S							New York		France	French
				Dunn, Lizzie	Servant			F	B	40	S					Yes	No	Virginia		Virginia	
			45	Makoney, Jeremiah	Head	R		M	W	30	S	1916	Pa			Yes	Yes	Ireland	English	Ireland	English
				——, Charlotte	Sister			F	W	25	S	1917	Al			Yes	Yes	Ireland	English	Ireland	English
	487	45	46	Lawson, Stephen	Head	R		M	B	67	M					No	No	Maryland		Virginia	
				——, Lily M.	Wife			F	Mu	22	M					Yes	No	Delaware		Delaware	
				——, Edward H.	Son			M	Mu	1 4/12	S							Pennsylvania		Maryland	

Here ends the enumeration of Buena Vista village.

Figure 14. "Pre-completed example of the 1920 questionnaire, for the purpose of training census workers." Source: RG 29/238/Scrapbooks, vol. 1, p. 26.

Figure 15. Census Bureau employees in Washington, 1910. Division of mechanical tabulation for the 1910 census. Source: National Archives, no. 29-C-1B-42.

Figure 16. Census Bureau employees in Washington, 1941. Source: National Archives, no. 29-C-1A-7.

Figure 17. Employee recording data on a punch card, 1910 census. Source: National Archives, no. 29-C-1B-43.

Figure 18. Machine using punch cards for coding geographical information, 1941. Source: National Archives, no. 29-C-1B-48.

Figure 19. Electric verification of errors on punch cards, 1941. Source: RG 29/215/box 234, Envelope "Alice Short. Pictures 1940 Census."

Figure 20. Shipping cartons for questionnaires, 1941. Source: RG 29/215/box 234, Envelope "Alice Short. Pictures 1940 Census."

Figure 21. Archiving old questionnaires at the Census Bureau, 1941. Source: RG 29/215/ box 234, Envelope "Alice Short. Pictures 1940 Census."

Figure 22. Census Bureau employees, 1941. Division of mechanical tabulation. Source: RG 29/215/234.

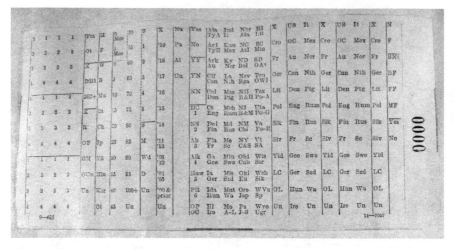

Figure 23. Sample of an individual punch card, 1930. Source: RG 29/238/Scrapbook 1, p. 124.

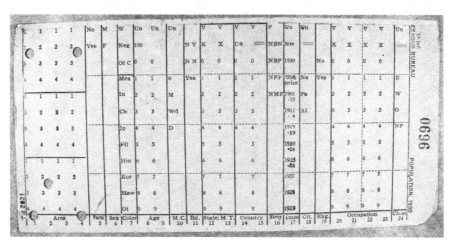

Figure 24. Punch card, 1930, encoding the person's place of origin and citizenship. Source: RG 29/238/Scrapbooks, vol. 2, p. 83.

FAMILY SCHEDULE—1 TO 10 PERSONS.

[7—556 b.]

Eleventh Census of the United States.

SCHEDULE No. 1.

POPULATION AND SOCIAL STATISTICS.

Supervisor's District No.

Enumeration District No.

Name of city, town, township, precinct, district, bead, or other minor civil division.) ; County : ; State :

Street and No.: ; Ward : ; Name of Institution :

Enumerated by me on the _____ day of June, 1890.

Enumerator.

A.—Number of Dwelling-house in the order of visitation.	B.—Number of families in this dwelling-house.	C.—Number of persons in this dwelling-house.	D.—Number of Family in the order of visitation.	E.—No. of Persons in this family.
INQUIRIES.	1	2	3	4	5
1	Christian name in full, and initial of middle name.				
	Surname.				
2	Whether a soldier, sailor, or marine during the civil war (U. S. or Conf.), or widow of such person.				
3	Relationship to head of family.				
4	Whether white, black, mulatto, quadroon, octoroon, Chinese, Japanese, or Indian.				
5	Sex.				
6	Age at nearest birthday. If under one year, give age in months.				
7	Whether single, married, widowed, or divorced.				
8	Whether married during the census year (June 1, 1889, to May 31, 1890).				
9	Mother of how many children, and number of these children living.				
10	Place of birth.				
11	Place of birth of Father.				
12	Place of birth of Mother.				
13	Number of years in the United States.				
14	Whether naturalized.				
15	Whether naturalization papers have been taken out.				
16	Profession, trade, or occupation.				
17	Months unemployed during the census year (June 1, 1889, to May 31, 1890).				
18	Attendance at school (in months) during the census year (June 1, 1889, to May 31, 1890).				
19	Able to Read.				
20	Able to Write.				
21	Able to speak English. If not, the language or dialect spoken.				
22	Whether suffering from acute or chronic disease, with name of disease and length of time affected.				
23	Whether defective in mind, sight, hearing, or speech, or whether crippled, maimed, or deformed, with name of defect.				
24	Whether a prisoner, convict, homeless child, or pauper.				
25	Supplemental schedule and page.				

TO ENUMERATORS.—See inquiries numbered 26 to 30, inclusive, on the second page of this schedule. These inquiries must be made concerning each family and each farm visited.

[10278—1,750,000.] L b   34

Figure 25. Family schedule, 1890 census. Source: RG 29 UD75 (NC 3-29-81-4).

Figure 26. Census worker enumerating a large family, 1940. Source: National Archives, no. 29C-1B-14.

Figure 27. Census worker enumerating the family of a railroad worker, test-census for Indiana, 1939. Source: National Archives, ser. 29-C-1B.

Figure 28. Example of interaction with a census worker, 1940. Source: National Archives, no. 29C-1B-14.

Figure 29. Census of the population, 1940. Source: National Archives, ser. 29-C-1B.

FOREIGN-BORN ARE COUNTED IN CENSUS

DEPARTMENT OF LABOR
BUREAU OF NATURALIZATION
IN COOPERATION WITH THE
DEPARTMENT OF COMMERCE—BUREAU OF THE CENSUS

FIFTEENTH CENSUS OF THE UNITED STATES

In 1790, when George Washington was President of the United States, the Government counted the number of people in this country. It has been done every ten years since that time, as required by the Constitution. The next time for this to be done is in April, 1930. This is called "TAKING THE CENSUS" of the United States.

The Government will appoint men and women to go from house to house in every city and on all of the farms, all over the United States to learn the number of people in the United States. These men and women are called "Census Enumerators." Each one of them will have a sheet of paper with printed questions, and these questions will be answered by all the people of the United States. Everybody who lives in the United States, whether a citizen or not, will be called on to answer the questions.

The following are some of the things the Government wants to know about each person in the United States:

Your name.
Your age on your last birthday.
The name of the country in which you were born.
The name of the country in which your father was born.
The name of the country in which your mother was born.
If you were born in a foreign country, you will be asked to give the year in which you first came to the United States, and the language which you spoke in your home in the country from which you came.
There will be other questions to answer, telling whether you are a citizen, and whether a native or naturalized citizen.
You will be asked to tell the kind of work you do; whether you own the house in which you live; the value of your home if you own it, or the amount of the rent if it is rented.

Talk these census questions over with your home folks, so that if you are not at home when the census-taker calls he can get correct answers.

Do not be afraid to answer all of the questions, for the President has promised that the census-taker will be the only person who will know what your answers are. The census has nothing to do with taxation, or military service, or school attendance, or the regulation of immigration, or the enforcement of any law. It will never be used to harm you or your family, or to get you into trouble of any kind.

The census-taker will have a certificate of appointment from the Government. Any person not having this certificate was not sent by the Government. Tell your friends about the census, and that the census man is coming, so that you can help Uncle Sam in this work.

RAYMOND F. CRIST,
Commissioner of Naturalization.

15—268

UNCLE SAM EXPECTS YOU TO HELP HIM

U. S. GOVERNMENT PRINTING OFFICE: 1930   11—7027

Figure 30. Appeal from the Bureau of Naturalization urging immigrants to have themselves counted, 1930. Source: RG 29/215/F2.

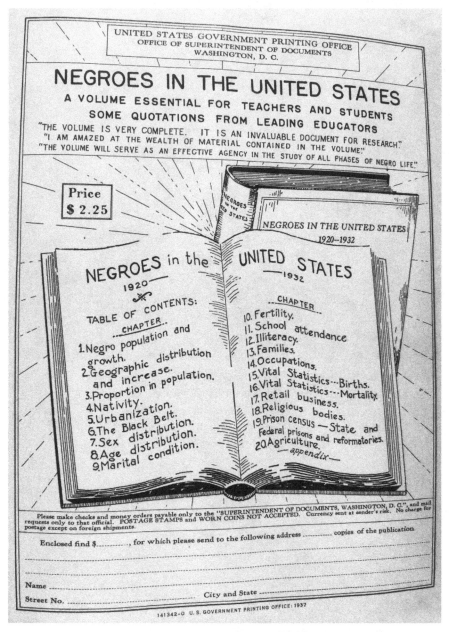

Figure 31. Publicity for the book *Negroes in the United States, 1920–1932,*
1935. Source: RG 29/238/Scrapbook 4.

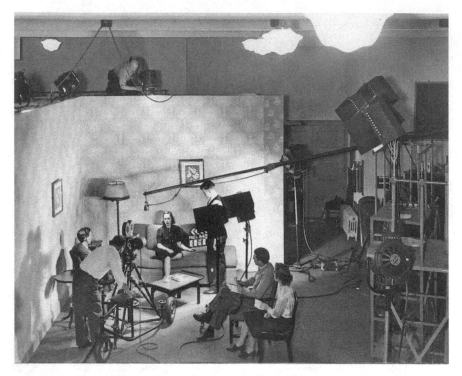

Figure 32. Photo of the making of a training film for agents for the 1940
census. Source: RG 29/215/234/Folder "Motion Picture Personnel, March 12, 1940."

16

New Asian Races, New Mixtures, and the "Mexican" Race

Interest in "Minor Races"

Whenever there was a question of racial classification of new populations, whether in the continental United States or in the territories acquired since 1867, the census always relied on the principles and techniques developed since 1850 to distinguish blacks from whites. Chief among these was the principle of hypodescent, in more or less rigid forms. The early twentieth century saw change occurring in two directions: on the one hand, the racialization of a growing number of non-European immigrants and their descendants; on the other, the weakening of the distinctions between the descendants of European immigrants.

Accompanying the 1900 census, the Census Bureau published, for the first time, a detailed commentary on definitions and usage of terms used to distinguish the population by race. In so doing, it differentiated its own practices from those of European countries, and also distinguished its use of terms from other, current or specialized uses. Lamenting the loose use of the word "race" in popular speech, the Bureau in a 1906 volume spoke of the conceptual fluidity that affected even the most recent census:

> In the third volume of the Twelfth Census "race" is thus used to include "nationality as indicated by country of birth" [*Twelfth Census*, vol. 3, p. lxix, col. 1].[1]

For the first time, the Bureau contrasted physical and linguistic criteria, skin color and ethnic group ("ethnical stock"). In so doing, it established the basis for a distinction that would actually emphasize the differential treatment of whites and other groups. It presented the problem as a practical one, skin color being the easiest criterion for agents to observe, provided these physical features were sufficiently obvious:

The oldest and most familiar physical test by which races are distinguished is that of skin color. Whether or not it is the most important to the ethnologist, it is certainly the one which the enumerator finds easiest to apply. This test in a country like the United States, which contains many members of the white race, the black race, the red race, and the yellow race, with obvious race characteristics not effaced or completely obscured by race intermixtures, gives fairly accurate results even in the hands of more than 50,000 untrained enumerators.

In the absence of a definition of racial terms in the instructions for the 1900 census, census workers were left to their own interpretation and physical features were interpreted in various ways according to region and social context:

Their answers reflect local opinion, and that opinion probably is based more upon social position and manner of life than upon the relative amounts of blood. In the application of race terms local usage and judgment vary, and accordingly there is no definition applicable throughout the United States of the words employed by enumerators. Perhaps "negro" may be interpreted in the light of statutes against miscegenation in many Southern states whereby intermarriage is prohibited between white persons and persons having one-eighth or more of negro blood. At least this seems the only available means of interpreting the word precisely.[2]

To alleviate the vagueness of these terms, the report proposed a summary guide for future censuses, defining as white "a person at least seven-eighths of white or Caucasian blood and regarded in the community as belonging to the white race." Conversely, black was defined as "a person at least one-eighth of negro, or African, blood, more negro than Indian or Mongolian and regarded in the community as a negro." The same rule was applied to Indian and Mongolian[3] races. In none of these three latter definitions was the "white race" mentioned. We might see this as one of the last attempts to establish a priori definitions of racial categories. But this urge to codify by fractions, inspired by the unfortunate experience of 1890, had no future.

By 1930, after the "mulatto" category had been abandoned for the continental United States, the issue of persons of mixed black and white descent no longer mattered to the census. However, since the beginning of the century, the treatment of responses had become more and more complex, by reason of the multiplication of racial categories and the possibilities for racial mixing. Another factor was the rapid progress being made in the electronic processing of data, thanks to ongoing improvements in the Hollerith machines.[4]

The instructions for 1930 thus set out new rules, which organized racial categories by a double, but asymmetric, "one drop rule," according to whether the mixture involved black and white or other races:

151. Negroes.—A person of mixed white and Negro blood should be returned as a Negro, no matter how small the percentage of Negro blood. Both black and mulatto persons are to be returned as Negroes without distinction. A person of mixed Indian and Negro blood should be returned as Negro, unless the Indian blood predominates and the status as Indian is generally accepted in the community.

152. Indians.—A person of mixed white and Indian blood should be returned as Indian, except where the percentage of Indian blood is very small, or where he is regarded as a white person by those in the community where he lives. (See par. 151 for mixed Indian and Negro.)

153. For a person reported as Indian in column 12, report is to be made in column 19 as to whether "full blood" or "mixed blood," and in column 20 the name of the tribe is to be reported. For Indians, columns 19 and 20 are thus to be used to indicate the degree of Indian blood and the tribe, instead of the birthplace of father and mother.

154. Mexicans.—Practically all Mexican laborers are of a racial mixture difficult to classify, though usually well recognized in the localities where they are found. In order to obtain separated figures for this racial group, it has been decided that all persons born in Mexico, or having parents born in Mexico, who are definitely not white, Negro, Indian, Chinese, or Japanese, should be returned as Mexican ("Mex").

155. Other mixed races.—Any mixture of white and nonwhite should be reported according to the nonwhite parent. Mixtures of colored races should be reported according to the race of the father, except Negro-Indian (see par. 151).[5]

The instructions to regional census officials drew their attention to the difficulty of determining race in certain cases, and reminded them to alert their agents on this point. This was something new, since race or color had never been presented as something difficult to record in the continental United States. Acknowledging the difficulty "in some districts," the instructions also noted that the census did not establish the legal status of an individual with regard to color. "That is not the purpose of the census." They made the same recommendation that Du Bois had done at the beginning of the century: in cases of uncertainty over those of mixed race, a determination could generally be made by the way the person was perceived in the community where he or she lived.[6]

The 1930 census brings us to the end of a long evolution, which saw the triumph of the "one drop rule" in the classification of persons of black and white ancestry. This rule was less strict in other instances, the white and black races remaining special cases. Absolute hypodescent characterized mixtures between blacks and whites, and all mixtures between whites and non-whites, with the exception of mixed-blood Indians, when they were accepted socially as whites.[7] For other races and more recent mixtures, census workers were to use the father's race, following the rule that had long been in use in the case of two parents of different foreign birth. In fact, attributing a racial category to children whose parents were of different races could pose difficulties for census workers, since these cases were so far out of the norm. For the 1930 census, the instructions for coding individual cards stated that, within a single family, the races had to be consistent; this did not mean that the race had to be the same, but rather that the rules had to be strictly applied. Thanks to the permanent status of the Census Bureau since 1900, for this period we have available rules for the treatment and correction of data, which allows us to paint a more detailed picture than was possible when limited to schedules and census publications. The coding instructions placed each individual in his or her household, making parents and children consistent whenever there was what the Census Bureau called an absolute inconsistency.[8]

Coding punched cards was the first stage of correcting handwritten data. Since 1890, the census no longer simply compiled responses, but corrected inconsistencies according to precise rules. These rules often went further than the instructions for agents in the field. Thus, the rules for 1920 stated that children of a black parent and a mulatto parent were to be listed as "Mu," something that did not appear in the instructions given to the census workers who recorded responses in 1920.[9] This confirms the intent of census officials of the day to maximize the chances of black individuals being classified as mulatto—though this did not prevent their numbers from decreasing, as we have seen. The next step was programming the machines and verifying the cards that were rejected by the machines for inconsistency. The cards made a first run through the machine so they could be verified, before proceeding to further treatment. Cards were rejected either because of a faulty perforation or because of suspect values. Rejected cards were then verified manually. In the case of race, the machines were programmed to reject cards punched as W (white) if in the column for place of birth there occurred "Chi" or "Jp" and "F" (Foreign-Birth); cards where the race was "Chi" or "Jp" and the place of birth was not in agreement; cards for nonimmigrant populations of color (B, Mu, and In) if the place of birth was foreign (F); and finally, all cards punched for "minor races," "Fil" (Filipino), "Hin" (Hindu), "Kor" (Korean), and "Ot" (Other). For "Other," the race had to be spelled out on the card as given on the schedule.[10]

Although not every verification entailed changes, they are still of interest, as is the order of passage through the machine, to which we shall return shortly. In each census, there were a few cases of whites born in Asia, but since Asian origins meant not only country of birth but also race, the rule was that persons of Asian origin should be of the corresponding race. The coding instructions for mortality statistics for the 1940 census showed the same tendency, the selected examples all featuring people classified as white by mistake. In doubtful cases, employees were to refer to all the indicators on the card, in order to establish a race consistent with the other available information.

> If White, Negro (or Black), Indian, Chinese or Japanese is clearly stated, this item is not coded unless the racial designation is inconsistent with other facts on the transcript. For example, if the name is given as "Charley Sing" with the race as "White", and if the country of birth of the decedent or his parents is given as "China", the nativity determines the code. In such cases, "Ch" is written over "White" in item 4. If the race is stated as "Colored," "Malay," "Brown," "Yellow" etc., the nativity determines the code.[11]

These internal rules for coding and correction were generally more restrictive than the instructions to agents, applying the "one drop rule" more strictly. Still, there was a growing proportion of persons of Asian race born in the United States, since the prohibition of Chinese immigration in 1882 and the restriction of Japanese immigration in 1907; these cases also had to be verified, with the rule—implicit at the time of census-taking and explicit at the point when the punched cards were coded—being that persons of Chinese race should be born in China, unless there was clear evidence of the opposite.

Following the tradition established by the consolidation of Chinese national origin into a race, three new Asiatic races appeared on the schedules for the 1920 census: Filipino, Korean, and Hindu.

In fact, these categories were already in existence at the time of a special census conducted in Oklahoma in 1918, which tends to show that this was not a decision by Congress but an adaptation of the schedules to the presence of these groups, similar to the cases of the Chinese in 1870 and the Japanese in 1890.[12] The "Hindu" category (that is, Indians from India) is especially interesting, since according to the racial theories of the day, Indians could be Caucasian or Aryan, but they were not white. This was established by the Supreme Court in the well-known ruling *United States v. Thind* (1923), recognizing the legal authority of popular beliefs in matters of race.[13] The census followed along by making "Hindu" a race or color, according to the beliefs of the man in the street. After this ruling, and especially at the time of the

1930 census, the "Hindu" category followed the path taken by the law, but we have seen repeatedly that when the law did not explicitly call for terms to be used rigorously, the census tended to veer toward the popular meaning of categories. According to census officials, this was a way of ensuring equivalence between the questions and people's answers. The census welcomed confirmation through law, but did not seek it; and recourse to poorly defined racial categories offered advantages as well as disadvantages. Since the end of the nineteenth century, the census had given up invoking scientific or legal authority, preferring to follow its own practices. When its racial definitions might lead to confusion, the census consistently had recourse to the same phrase, whether in the instructions to agents or in census reports: "for census purposes." This was considered sufficient justification.

The numbers of Koreans, Indians from India, and Filipinos were quite small in the 1920s, to the point that in the 1920 census report they were relegated to the category "All other," which in that year totaled only 9,488 persons, less than 0.01 percent of the total population, divided into 5,603 Filipinos, 2,507 "Hindus," 1,224 Koreans, 110 Hawaiians, 19 Malays, 17 Thai (Siamese), 6 Samoans, and 2 Maori.[14] In contrast to what we shall see in the case of Mexicans, numbers were not the justification for a separate racial class. Rather, we see here the continuation of the tradition begun in 1860, according to which each Asian country of origin had a corresponding race—a tradition that continued all the way through the 2010 census, regardless of the small number of persons enumerated in each.[15] All other Asian immigrants became subject to the same procedures that had been developed in the nineteenth century to radically separate the Chinese and Japanese from the rest of the population. After 1924, the census would be reinforced in this path by the prohibition on immigration and naturalization of persons originating from Asia.[16]

During this period, Native Americans continued to be a separate case. They were divided into two groups: reservation Indians, for whom the Bureau of Indian Affairs provided statistics; and Indians, or those considered to be such, living among the rest of the population, who were enumerated by the Census Bureau. One last separate census of Indian tribes took place along with the 1910 general census; the instructions announced that there was no longer a need for a separate census, so this would be the last one, and hence it would involve extra investigative effort, going further than the questions for the general census.[17]

In fact, although the 1910 special census of Indians was indeed the last, detailed information on Native Americans would continue to be collected, within the scope of the general census. For the 1920 census, on the grounds that few Indians were of immigrant origin, the columns for father's and mother's place of birth were to be used respectively to record the father's and mother's tribe, when the race of the individual was "Indian."[18] This practice of recording

Indian tribes in place of nationality of origin continued throughout the twentieth century.

With the abandonment of the mulatto category after 1920, the Census Bureau developed a renewed system of racial classification, in which the black race was to some extent neutralized, as autonomous and separate from other less numerous racial minorities. With the bureaucratization that characterized the history of the Census Bureau between the two world wars, procedures were formalized and the training of field workers was improved, especially by written tests. The reports for the 1910 and 1920 censuses had already appended filled-out fictional schedules for the use of readers. In these we can glimpse rules that were not always explicit in the instructions, such as the fact that the children of a black ("B") man and a mulatto ("Mu") woman were "Mu," visible in certain coding instructions. In order to illustrate the maximum number of examples, the same sheet contained individuals of all races and many origins, a diversity that was more than unlikely in a real neighborhood but served a pedagogical purpose.[19]

The tests for recruiting census agents that were used systematically from 1930 on were narratives of family histories that candidates for such posts had to transcribe correctly on the schedules. The cases were deliberately selected to be complex, involving atypical families. A 1940 test gave the case of a family made up of John, a Mexican; his wife Ruth, half Indian and half Mexican; their daughter Marion, who is married to a man, George, whose father is mulatto (although in 1940 mulatto was no longer a census category) and whose mother was born in Mexico and spoke an Indian language as a child.[20] This fictitious example is interesting because it tests the limits of the hypodescent rules and also mixes racial categories that were in use in 1940 and others that had been dropped (mulatto and Mexican, as we shall see). The applicants had to choose between the following choices: Mexican, Indian, White, Negro, Other. The answers were to be drawn from the instructions for 1940, which agents had to study carefully in order to make determinations in ambiguous cases.[21]

In spite of this trend toward greater complexity, the system of racial categories, so important in American public statistics, still relied on the primordial opposition between whites and blacks. In fact, the relationship by this time had been solidified by locking the definition of the black population, so that it was finally stable, while the definition and limits of the "white race" were called into question by the importance of the immigration issue, which was also a racial issue even if not a question of color, and by the creation, with the 1930 census, of a Mexican race. The classification of blacks, though acknowledged as somewhat arbitrary by the head of the population division, was justified henceforth as a way of measuring the economic spread between whites and blacks, especially in the South, while skin color came to serve as a marker of a difference that was increasingly viewed as social (as a Census Bureau statistician noted at the time).[22]

The Strange Career of the "Mexican Race"

The 1930 census introduced a new race, the Mexican race, which was the first to mark a distinction within the white population. Though it appeared simple, this category was actually complex, since, while it was a race just like white, black, Indian, or the various Asiatic races, it was tied to Mexican national origin.[23]

There were early indications of the Census Bureau's desire to racially distinguish Mexicans, especially because in the early years of the century the Bureau considered Mexicans to be a hybrid racial group. An analysis of the 1900 census reveals people of mixed race who did not fit into census categories (for the first time since 1850 the Census Office had not enumerated mulattoes).[24] The paragraph on "half-breeds" (a generic term here including mulattoes and mixed-race Indians) shows the statistical invisibility of Mexicans, despite their different "blood":

> Many persons living along the Mexican boundary, speaking the Spanish language and wearing European clothes, but largely, perhaps predominantly, of Indian blood, have probably been returned by the enumerators as whites, the word Indian being reserved by local usage for descendants of the wild hunting and nomadic Indians.[25]

The plan to create a racial category specifically for this poorly defined population did not appear so early, and the problem was later reformulated. Still, the idea of a localized population that was of part-Indian origin and was Spanish-speaking, and the difficulty in identifying them for the census, was already present. For the census, these people were not only on the frontier of the nation but also on the frontier of existing categories. In fact, until the 1920s the census recognized "Mexican blood" only in connection with Indians. The 1910 special volume on the Indian population made a distinction within "half-breeds" according to whether the responses had indicated a mixture with white or Mexican blood. The authors of the report had decided to retain the distinction, as shown in table 16.1.

The report also admitted that "while a 'Mexican' is presumably white, or a mixture of white and Indian, there is no way of telling what proportion, if any, of his blood, is Indian."[26]

The concerns aroused by the lack of a way to get a grip on Mexicans changed after 1910, when Mexicans were no longer viewed as a small part of the Indian

Table 16.1. **Degree of Mixture within the Indian Population of the United States (1910)**

Degree of mixture	Number	Proportion
Total	88,030	100.0
Less than half white	18,169	20.6
Half white, half Indian	24,353	27.7
More than half white	43,937	49.9
Unknown proportions	1,571	1.8
Part Mexican	1,072	1.2
Other unknown	499	0.6

Source: Census, *Indian Population in the United States and Alaska. 1910.*

population but rather as new arrivals and laborers. The transformation of the public image of "Mexicans," from a small regional group that aroused curiosity to a significant number of immigrant workers, is probably what prompted the Census Bureau to make them a race in the 1930 census.[27]

The justification after the fact was the growth of this population, which had mostly been counted as white previously.

> The instructions given to enumerators for making this classification were to the effect that "all persons born in Mexico, who are not definitely white, Negro, Indian, Chinese or Japanese, should be returned as *Mexican*." Under these instructions 1,422,533 persons were returned as Mexican in 1930, and 65,958 persons of Mexican birth or parentage were returned as white.[28]

Historical studies based on the manuscript responses to the 1920 census in the Southwest show that in these states, a very large number of people who were classified as mulatto had Spanish surnames and did not live among the black population.[29] In the 1910 census, a large number of persons of Mexican origin were classified as "M" or "Mx" by census agents.[30] Since the instructions stated that "mulatto" was to be noted as "Mu," it is likely that this category was corrected when the punched cards were coded. Thus, for the census, there were two motivations for the 1930 racialization: on one hand, following the model of the racial classification imposed on Asian immigrants, it offered a mechanism for demarcating this immigrant population concentrated within a specific region; on the other, it responded to a practice of differentiation by race or color, which was already current locally and was apparent in the responses, whether on the initiative of census workers or of certain inhabitants.[31]

As a result of the new race category, the census was able to produce two sets of figures in 1930: on the one hand, the 641,462 immigrants who had been born in Mexico; on the other, the 1,422,533 inhabitants belonging to the Mexican race.[32] The new category was unique in being based on national origin yet conditional upon color and appearance. The instructions aimed to distinguish—exclusively among first- and second-generation Mexican immigrants—those who were neither white nor members of other racial categories used by the census; these persons would constitute the Mexican race. The problem for the census was more complex than in the case of Asian immigrants, because it was understood that some persons of Mexican origin were white, and it was necessary to remove them from the Mexican racial category. The descendants of Mexicans annexed in 1848 were all white, by the terms of the treaty, even if they were the target of racially based segregation and discrimination.[33]

The application of this category, though in principle limited to only two generations, actually overflowed these bounds: among the persons of Mexican race were 264,338 "Mexicans" whose parents were born in the United States—that is, persons who did not fit into the definition but whom the Census Bureau had not reclassified as white, limiting itself to stating this fact in its report. That the Census Bureau should publish data that contradicted its own definitions gives a sense of this plan for racial classification of Mexicans: to respond to current immigration but at the same time to incorporate all those of "Mexican race." This is why, although the instructions at first made it an ethnic category, tied to foreign birth, it was actually a racial category. Unlike categories of origin of that era, it was not conceived of as limited to the two first generations. Applying the "Mexican" category was a very clear case of racialization of a minority group.

This plan unambiguously showed the extent to which this "race" had been defined by social status, as the instructions stated clearly that the object was to capture laborers—a highly unusual qualification for a racial category:

> Practically all Mexican laborers are of a racial mixture difficult to classify, though usually well recognized in the localities where they are found.[34]

Clearly, census officials viewed the persons who were the object of this category as passive subjects, to whom they applied a statistical method of separation. This fact can be linked to the parallel development that made Mexicans into people whose presence on American soil was increasingly seen as illegitimate. The census was a participant in this attempt to delegitimize Mexican immigration, which had deportation as a consequence.[35] The reports as well as press releases on the 1930 census simply stated that this new category appeared on the population schedule, without further explanation except for mention of the new numerical importance of this population.[36] At first, neither the announcement of this classification nor the publication of the results seemed to arouse any reaction. Not until 1935 did a broader movement put pressure simultaneously on the Census Bureau, the Department of Commerce, the State Department, and the White House. Supported by the Mexican government, the Mexican ambassador to Washington, and the Mexican consul general in New York, the campaign to reclassify Mexicans as whites was driven by organizations of Mexican-Americans in the southwestern states, who emphasized the fact that they were US citizens. These organizations, federated within the League of United Latin-American Citizens (LULAC, founded in 1929), were generally made up of members of the middle class who were rather ambivalent about their connection with Mexican immigrants. The LULAC manifesto spoke of their attachment to the United States and to the "racial origin" of Mexican-Americans. The organization did not accept Mexican nationals as members, but rather saw itself as an instrument for the integration of American citizens wishing to maintain their culture.[37] The reason for their individual and collective opposition to the classification of Mexicans as a race or color was an analysis of the risks that loss of the quality of whiteness would pose for their status in southwestern society. The problem was not seeing their origin distinguished, even in terms of race, which they themselves did in their newspapers and their organizations. Rather, it was the risk of being treated as "colored" and, especially in Texas, seeing their children assigned to segregated schools.

To fully understand the timing of the campaign for reclassification, we need to recognize that the problem was not the census classification per se, but the authority it gave courts and other administrative entities to view Mexicans as non-white and hence to discriminate against them, not just in fact (as was already the case), but in law, which was intolerable. In fact, the movement leaders intervened when various courts in Texas and New Mexico considered persons of Mexican origin as non-white—a position also held by a number of state and federal social service agencies.

Several events in 1935 marked the development of this trend, notably the decision of the newly established Social Security Administration to classify Mexicans as non-white, and the ruling by federal judge John Knight in Buffalo, New York (First Federal Circuit Court, 12 December 1935), denying a request for naturalization made by Timoteo Andrade, on the basis of his Indian ancestry. These and other similar events sparked the mobilization of Mexican-American organizations with support from the Mexican embassy. The Social Security Administration, as a federal agency, and Alex Powell, head of the (state level) Texas civil service in El Paso, had done no more than follow the census. But the historian F. Arturo Rosales, who has studied this episode in the greatest depth, notes that when city officials in El Paso excluded Mexicans from the white population, they were also motivated by the desire to lower the figures on infant mortality among whites.[38]

The Census Bureau had hoped to make use of Mexicans' feelings of ethnic pride to convince them to participate enthusiastically in the 1930 census. This is apparent from a letter of Acting Director Hill to Alonso Perales, a Texas lawyer who later represented LULAC in the 1940 reclassification of Mexicans as whites. In his letter, Hill asked Perales to write positive pieces about the census for the Spanish-language press:

> If the Mexicans in this country could be convinced of the value of the census work and of the impossibility of the information they give being used against them, I believe we could secure their hearty cooperation. The census will furnish most valuable material regarding the number, growth, and economic advancement of the Mexican population in the United States. This is the first census in which Mexicans will be given a separate classification.[39]

Prominent people of Mexican origin had cooperated with the Bureau in this process. However, as we shall see for other groups, acts of cooperation with the census, such as publishing census announcements in the ethnic press, did not necessarily mean the persons involved shared the goals of the Census Bureau. The bureau's correspondence shows no trace of comment or protest on the part of Mexicans at this time. In March 1931, as proposed by census director Steuart, the Census Advisory Committee recommended a study on Mexicans as a race, either as a single publication or to be accompanied by similar studies on other "minor races"—that is, in the language of the census at that time, all those races that were neither black nor white.[40]

In April 1934 the Census Bureau decided that Mexicans should be classed as non-white in its reports on vital statistics (based on data provided by state agencies), to avoid using different classifications in different reports. If those at the top were still in favor of this classification, they had nonetheless begun to take account of objections from some Mexicans, supporting the view the Bureau had expressed about Mexican workers. This comes out of the minutes of a meeting of the Census Advisory Committee, which Leon Truesdell, chief statistician for population, attended in order to assist Joseph A. Hill on the subject of the classification of Mexicans. This was an important topic on the agenda—even though the introduction of the category had left no trace of discussion. It is the most extensive justification of the "Mexican" race found in the census archives.

> Dr. Hill explained that at the 1930 Census for the first time Mexicans were classified separately from the white population because of the feeling that they were not strictly white. . . . Dr. Truesdell said the

term "colored" is ambiguous, in the South, the term being synonymous with Negro, and in other sections of the country, it is a hodge-
podge of Chinese, Japanese and Negroes in varying portions. He said
in the case of Vital Statistics, it is not easy to segregate Mexicans as the
Mexicans have a prejudice against returning themselves as other than
white, and seventy-five percent of the local registrars in New Mexico
and lower California are Mexicans who credit themselves with being
white. Mr. Austin [director] saw the same objection in the case of the
population census, as in the same sections a large percentage of enumerators and supervisors are Mexicans. He was of the opinion that
the wealthy class of Mexicans called themselves white, while the peon
class will return itself as Mexican. Dr. Truesdell suggested including
on the death certificate an inquiry in regard to national origin.[41]

In the case of death certificates, it was generally family members who stated the
race of the person, in effect a form of self-assignment. But it appears from the
discussion at this meeting that even assignment by observation, as practiced by
the census, was problematic—an issue, as in Puerto Rico, involving disagreement between the perception of field workers and that of census officials in
Washington. The traditional policy of local recruitment was intended to ensure
better cooperation of populations, but it came with this cost. Moreover—and
this could come as much from later protests as from census experience in the
field—the Census Bureau placed responsibility for this rejection on a minority
of prominent, "wealthy," Mexicans, who wanted to be white, while the majority
"peons" would not object to their racial classification as Mexican. This conversa-
tion is remarkable for the clarity with which the Census director articulates race
and class, opposing the "wealthy class of Mexicans" and the "peon class" as to the
different racial self-identification he believes them to practice.

Already at this date, the Census Bureau seems to have taken the claim seriously: Truesdell had already estimated the cost (two to three thousand dollars)
of a recount of Mexicans as white between 1930 and 1940, assuming that the
punched cards would be available for comparison with the 1940 figures, if the
Mexican racial classification was not continued. Truesdell estimated that the
Bureau would be tasked with undertaking a new enumeration in this case. As
we have seen, the Census Bureau had already, in 1931, performed the reverse,
and more uncertain, procedure of reclassifying as Mexican a portion of people
classified as white in 1920.

Another argument was invoked to justify a separate racial category for
Mexicans, which recalls that of the insurance companies on the subject of the
vital statistics of blacks at the end of the nineteenth century: that of the value of
government statistics for actuarial tables and insurance companies.[42]

At the same time, the Census Bureau's efforts to get the states to use a "Mexican race" in their birth and death certificates brought uneven results, once again attributed to resistance on the part of agents of Mexican origin. Commenting on the progress made in this direction by California and Colorado, the head of vital statistics regretted the failure of these efforts in New Mexico:

> New Mexico, however, still continues to report all Mexicans as white on the birth and death certificates, undoubtedly for the reason originally assigned by the state registrar, namely that most of her local registrars are themselves Mexican and can not be expected to classify their own people as Mexican knowing that they will be shown in our reports in the column for colored.[43]

Mobilization against this classification was crowned with success when the Census Bureau was ordered not to pursue it in 1940, and it reluctantly admitted that the decision had come from the State Department. Some branches of the Bureau continued to have recourse to the classification, while others were tempted, but the internal memos of the director contained sharp reminders that Mexicans were white, at the same time forbidding use of the contested term "colored" for all populations of the continental United States and the territories. The tone of these documents testifies to the Bureau's awareness that it was under political surveillance, as shown in a memorandum from the director to the chief of the statistical division, 15 October 1936:

> One of the most serious situations the Bureau has had to face recently was your classification of Mexicans as "Colored." The classification by race or color of individuals, or even entire populations, is not only very difficult, but is a very delicate matter to the United States Government, and our classification must always be in accordance with the policy of the Federal Government.
>
> Please observe to the letter the following instructions, which cannot be disregarded, changed or modified at any time except upon the written order of the director of the Census:
>
> (1) No classification is to be made in your tabulations, general or otherwise, which contains the word "Colored." The word "colored" must be eliminated both in text and tables in referring to classifications by race or color.
>
> (2) The classifications by color or race must be as follows:
> White
> Negro
> All other

> Mexicans are Whites and must be classified as "White."
>
> This order does not admit any further discussion, and must be fol-
> lowed to the letter.
>
> Please acknowledge in writing receipt of the memorandum.[44]

A second memorandum, on 3 December 1936, extended these instructions to
the entirety of the Bureau's work:

> In further reference to my order of October 15, 1936, concerning the
> Census classifications by color or race, please note definitely the follow-
> ing instructions:
>
> (1) Mexicans are to be classified as "white" and are to be included
> with the white population.
>
> (2) The term "colored" used by the Bureau must hereafter be elimi-
> nated entirely from all Census classification and publication.
>
> There must be no deviation from these instructions.
>
> Please acknowledge in writing receipt of the memorandum.[45]

These two documents are unusual for two reasons: first, they show the director
of the census shifting the responsibility for the Bureau's political problems onto
one of its division heads and clearly angry with his subordinates; second, they
show, for the first time, that the classification by color or by race fell into the
political domain. The victory of the movement against the racial classification
of Mexicans was thus complete, especially because over the course of 1936, by
virtue of the change imposed on the Census Bureau, other federal agencies also
had to cease distinguishing Mexicans as a race.

One important consequence of this decision was that the federal immigration service likewise had to accept that Mexicans were white—this, at a time
when the law restricted immigration and naturalization to whites.

A letter from the chargé d'affaires of the Mexican embassy to the US secretary
of state, dated 29 July 1937, shows the real stakes of this classification. At this
time, the federal government required all agencies to use the same definitions,
which had not been the case for the Census Bureau and the Immigration and
Naturalization Service earlier in the century. The letter invoked the authority of
the new census policy, calling for it to be imposed on the immigration services
of the port of San Francisco, which had continued to classify Mexican nationals
as being of the Mexican race.[46]

The precedent established by the reversal of the Census Bureau's decision
made it possible to demand the application of the same rule to other federal agencies. However, the rule about systematically classifying Mexicans
as white, though confirmed by agency heads, was not always consistently

applied at the local level. This is the gist of a memorandum of the Immigration and Naturalization Service, dated 18 May 1937, which emphasized the concern for uniformity. What the memorandum did not say was that the decision made for the Census Bureau was political, and that the Immigration and Naturalization Service could scarcely implement a policy contrary to that which had been openly adopted by the federal government.[47] This decision made people of Mexican origin eligible for naturalization, with the exception of those who remained "racially ineligible," meaning not white.[48] The archives of the Immigration and Naturalization Service show that, although the agency repeatedly confirmed that Mexicans were white, up to the early 1940s it continued to receive letters of complaint from Mexicans informing the agency that the rule had been broken.[49] Nonetheless, organizations that knew how to mobilize significant resources, had a good understanding of the political world and the judicial system, and perhaps also had support from the diplomatic service of a foreign state, had been able to compel the Census Bureau, in its racial classifications, to take into account the feelings of the populations being enumerated.

Advocates of the suppression of the Mexican racial category were able to efficiently mobilize diverse resources toward its reversal. Their tactics included individual refusals to apply the rule, press campaigns, lawsuits, and appeals to elected officials and to the government. The movement made savvy use of the administrative rules concerning uniformity, at the very moment when the Central Statistical Board was established and tasked with reconciling the statistics of the various federal agencies.[50] Still, it seems that the most important factor was the influence of the Mexican government. This becomes apparent through the regrets of census officials, who in 1940 attempted to reestablish this classification in a different form.

The summary of a meeting of the Census Advisory Committee of 5 January 1940 indicates that the Census Bureau tried unsuccessfully to win reestablishment of the Mexican racial category through the State Department.[51] This shows the nature of the decision to abolish the category, since the Bureau came under the Department of Commerce and ordinarily had very little contact with the State Department. Truesdell regretted the decision of the State Department, and emphasized the Bureau's hope that the question on maternal language, which was to be posed to a sample of 5 percent of the population, would furnish a substitute for the abandoned racial category.[52] This was the position followed by the Bureau, which tried to link the Mexican race of 1930 with the Spanish-speakers of 1940, then with persons having a Spanish surname, with all the limitations this entailed.[53]

The Central Statistical Board also issued a recommendation in 1939 requesting that information on Mexicans be preserved, in one form or another, and noting the value of the 1930 data:

> It is urged, therefore, that steps be taken in some way to meet this need, perhaps by two subheads under the category "white" in column 13, namely "white except Mexican" and "Mexican."[54]

This 1939 proposal is extremely interesting, even though it was without result, because it anticipated the configuration adopted in 1980 with the creation of the Hispanic "ethnic group," which was not a race but a way to divide the white population into "non Hispanic white" and "Hispanic white."[55] This proposal would have made it possible to maintain the distinction of 1930, without the stigma of race and color, and while attempting to protect the census from having its classifications linked with discrimination. In the end, the question posed by this proposal is twofold: Why, in the 1930s, did Mexican-American associations successfully mobilize against a separate classification of Mexicans in the census and other government agencies? And why, in the 1970s, did Hispanic associations join together, with equal success, in favor of a separate classification of Hispanics or Latinos?[56]

The disappearance of the "mulatto" category, followed by the introduction and forcible elimination of the "Mexican" category, shows that over the first decades of the twentieth century, the system of racial classification was modified, primarily to take into account the cooperation, or lack thereof, of the population. Although gradual, this development was significant, and it moved more rapidly in the last decade of the period.[57] In the nineteenth century statistics on national origin began gradually to take into account the perceptions of inhabitants. The first three decades of the twentieth century were a time when immigration was a national obsession and the Census Bureau was central to immigration regulation.

From Statistics by Country of Birth to the System of National Origins

In the second half of the nineteenth century, the question on place of birth had gradually been transformed into an ethnic question, the central element in an ever-growing list of questions aimed at measuring the immigrant population of the first and second generations: country of birth (1850), foreign birth of parents (1870), place of birth of parents (1880), naturalization (1890). Some of the questions that generated social statistics served the desire to take the measure of the "new immigration": questions on insanity and especially those on illiteracy, with their corollary, the ability or inability to speak English, which in 1890 became the means to collect information on the mother tongue of non-English-speaking inhabitants of the United States. The case of the "former kingdom of Poland"—a state no longer in existence but which had appeared in the census since 1860 as the place of origin of a certain number of inhabitants of the United States—as well as those of Bohemia and of a Canada divided into English-speaking and French-speaking groups, showed that what mattered most was not information on countries of origin, but information that would give some inkling of the place occupied by such and such category of immigrants in the host society. From this point of view, the absolute indifference of the census with respect to nationality of origin only served to privilege ethnicity—that is, identities reconstructed in American society—over legal categories that only appear rather later under the secondary distinction between foreign and naturalized immigrants.[1]

The period from the beginning of the twentieth century to the 1930s is a crucial period for the US Census, in which statistics on immigration and ethnicity take first place in the schedules, in the published reports, and, of course, in public policy. Not only did census figures establish immigration quotas, but also census statisticians, with their methods and their culture, constructed the mechanism for exclusion by national origin. After 1928, and the definitive adoption of the system of national origins developed by Joseph A. Hill, perpetual assistant director, the retreat from measuring ethnicity was clear. It showed itself in the 1930 and 1940 censuses by a marked lack of interest in questions of origin, of mother tongue, and of degree of assimilation, as measured, for example, by year of naturalization—even if a certain number of these aspects were retained despite the Census Bureau's desire to reduce them to a strict minimum in the schedules.

The history of the categories that made it possible to measure ethnicity, one way or another, is a complex one, involving three main groups of actors: advocates of immigration restriction, representatives of immigrant populations, and Census Bureau statisticians, with each group attempting to respond to contradictory demands and to defend their own interests.

From Country of Birth to Mother Tongue: A Stage on the Road to Self-Identification

The gradual introduction of ethnic criteria, by means of mother tongue, had contributed to the shift in significance of place of birth in the years from 1860 to 1900. There can be no doubt that the desire of the Census Bureau, and the state more generally, to measure the immigrant population or the population of immigrant origin coincided with the desire of the groups themselves to be better distinguished by the statistical apparatus. The case of Poland, already mentioned, had come even closer to this step in 1900, when census instructions specified that only persons born in Poland and whose mother tongue was Polish should be enumerated as being of Polish birth. In parallel, the census had tried since 1890 to produce statistics on the Jewish population in the United States. An early bulletin of the 1890 census provided figures, but it was based on a sampling of data provided by religious organizations that had not been combined with those produced by the census.[2] Superintendent Porter had opted for this solution on the recommendation of Billings, the statistical specialist responsible for the investigation. He stated in a letter to a leader of the Jewish community that Jews should be treated as a race and not as a religion. Since they did not have data on Jews as a race, the figures had to be derived from numbers provided by community leaders.[3] Through the question on mother tongue, the census could make its closest approach to this population, since the separation of church and state prevented it from enumerating inhabitants by religion. The heads of the census had stated several times that investigations of the Jewish population concerned not religion but race, not on religious practice but on family ties to the community. They deplored opposition to their efforts on the grounds that membership in this population was based on private criteria. But the Census Bureau's efforts did not bear fruit; in particular, it failed to gain the sought-for political sanction of Congress.[4]

In 1909 W. W. Husband, secretary of the Immigration Commission, had asked Congress to amend the census law so that Jews would be classified as a separate race,[5] as was already the case for the Bureau of Immigration, which accounted for "Hebrews" on their point of entry. Jews were classified as members of the "Hebrew Race" by Immigration from 1898 to 1943. The definition of Jews used by the congressional Immigration Commission appeared in the *Dictionary of Races or Peoples* that it published in 1911: "HEBREW, JEWISH, or ISRAELITE. The race or people that originally spoke the Hebrew language: primarily of Semitic origin."[6] Senator Guggenheim of Colorado not only opposed Husband's proposal but demanded that Jews should not be classified as either a race or a nation in the census.[7] The reaction of various notable members of the Jewish community of Chicago, to take only one example, echoed that of Guggenheim: emphasizing that Russian Jews were Russian, just as those of Germany or France were German or French.[8]

Others added that only Zionists were in favor of such a measure. We can guess that the *Chicago Record Herald* reported the position of liberal Jews, for whom religion was a private matter, while the Yiddish press criticized such a position as leading to loss of identity. The split seems to have been between liberal and Orthodox Jews, generally reflecting the opposition between Jews of German origin and Russian or Polish Jews.[9] There was not just one attitude among the Jews of Chicago regarding the publication of data on Jews, but rather several, depending on their social status.

The issue of the identification of Jews by the census was transformed by the unexpected introduction of the question on the mother tongue of immigrants in the 1910 census. This development was well received by the Yiddish press, which suggested that accounting for Jews in the census would no longer be a subject for debate on the part of Jewish organizations.[10] Here we can see the difference between the Census Bureau, which sought to rely as much as possible on consensus, and the Immigration and Naturalization Service, which retained its category of a Jewish race regardless of criticism. This would continue during the 1930s and 1940s as shown by the opinion of the INS's attorney in response to criticism from the American Jewish Committee in 1930.[11] The introduction of a question on religion in the population schedule for 1940 was considered in 1938, and this would have made it possible to eliminate the Census of Religious Bodies, a census of religious institutions that provided the number of their adherents. The idea was rejected by the Census Advisory Committee because of the parallel that might be drawn with the Nazi regime.[12]

The addition of a question on the mother tongue of immigrants came via a last-minute amendment introduced in Congress when the forms and instructions for the 1910 census had already been printed. It was the result of a lobbying campaign in Congress, whose Committees on the Census, in the House and in the Senate, controlled not only the budget for the census but also the questions to be asked on its schedules. The successful campaign was led by representatives of several ethnic communities, consisting of immigrants or the children of immigrants from Central Europe supporting the national movements in the Old World. The Czech organizations of large, northern industrial cities used their links to Congress to win the adoption of this amendment to the census law. The explicit aim was that mother tongue would serve to distinguish the Slavs from German-speaking immigrants from the empires of Central Europe. This goal is also apparent in the speeches of congressional orators,[13] as well as in the ethnic press or in petitions addressed to legislators, such as that of "2,735 Slovak citizens of the city of Cleveland" (protesting their classification as Hungarian in the coming census).[14] This mobilization was by no means limited to Slovaks from Cleveland, as can be seen in the minutes of a meeting in Pittsburgh on 7 March 1910 of the Slovak League of the United States of America.[15]

This proposal met with the approval of the census director and the House and Senate committees on the census, who saw it as a way to learn more about the population of foreign origin. Once again, political and scientific interests converged. Once the amendment had been adopted, the ethnic press urged their readers to make use of the census in order to increase their official numbers. The usual theme was what we might call ethnic patriotism, which pushed representatives of the communities to encourage their members to respond enthusiastically to the census in order to "show the world how numerous we are." The Census Bureau recognized and exploited this feeling, since it had always been concerned that the official aspect of the census might scare away populations uncertain of their status and supposedly suspicious of anything that smacked of government. This is why the Bureau had a list drawn up of the principal ethnic leaders of the country, to whom the director wrote a letter asking them to make the Bureau's efforts known.[16] While the letters emphasized civic duty, they were often reinterpreted in ethnic newspapers according to the overt interests of the group. This is clear in the case of a very free "translation" of the census director's letter, done by a Chicago lawyer of Norwegian origin. Mentioning the opportunity of marking the centennial "of the beginning of systematic and continuing Norse immigration which has contributed as much if not more to the development of our common country," his version of the letter ends as follows:

> The circumstances that possibly there may be many who do not agree with the policy of the political party that elected the present administration or with the personal policy of its head, should not stand in the

way of aiding it to secure for all the people as great success if not greater
in taking this census than any of the 13 preceding ones.

The census director thanked him for his assistance and remarked that he was
sending this text to Norwegian-language newspapers.[17] Similarly, since 1920
the Census Bureau had had foreign-language translations made of the presidential proclamations announcing the census, which were then distributed to
local officials in areas where the 1910 census had identified concentrations of
residents speaking these various languages.[18] In this, the Census Bureau took
its traditional position: Avoid becoming involved in political conflict, but make
use of all possible good will, no matter what the motivation or ulterior motives,
in order to maximize the effectiveness of the census. The census had never
balked at being made use of, as long as this would help it gain the support of
some additional part of the population and as long as there was no corresponding cost for the administration. Its course was always to seek the support of the
greatest number of actors, while remaining unconcerned by their contradictory
aims, and this helped reinforce its legitimacy as an agency. Placed under the
control of Congress, it had every incentive to avoid provoking frequent or public protest.

A study of the ethnic press of Chicago reveals the competition among interest
groups that launched a war of numbers, after the 1910 figures were published by
the Census Bureau, challenging the attribution of thousands of individuals to
another group, on the grounds that the criterion of mother tongue was prefera-
ble to that of country of birth. Thus, a Czech-language newspaper criticized not
only the Census Bureau's methods, which presented totals by country of birth,
but also a local German-language newspaper, the *Abendpost*, which counted
the majority of immigrants born in Austria as German.[19] Here we can see two
conceptions of ethnic identity, one based on language, the other on a geogra-
phy whereby persons born in Austria were culturally German, and thus could
be viewed in the United States as "ethnic Germans" or of German origin. The
instrumentalization of the theories is obvious here, but still we cannot conclude
from this that the figures are valueless. In a broader view, all the figures relating to
populations of immigrant origin were produced in response to social demands,
and this is precisely what constitutes their worth.[20]

The satisfaction felt by the ethnic communities was shared by Congress and
by census officials, each for their own reasons. An appeal such as the one that
appeared in *The Courier*, a Yiddish-language newspaper in Chicago, on 8 April
1910, just a week before the start of the census, must have pleased the Census
Bureau, which was always concerned at the thought of failing to reach wary
inhabitants:

They will also ask you of your nationality and your mother tongue. Our plea is, do not deny that you are Jews. This information goes only to the government and cannot be used against you by any anti-semitic groups. Denying your Jewish heritage would, in this instance, be a cowardly act. A census is taken only every ten years, and this is one opportunity for Jews to be proud of themselves. The insertion of this question into the census was a victory for the recognition of the existence of national minority groups.[21]

In taking account of mother tongue, the census was responding to a demand for information on Central European immigrants, who at that time were an object of attention for lawmakers. Through a historical irony of the sort that statistical tools tend to favor, data on mother tongue were considered in the development of immigration quotas (laws of 1921 and 1924) that sharply reduced immigration from Central Europe. Ultimately, only the criterion of country of origin was used to establish the quotas. However, census officials such as Joseph A. Hill, who were responsible for the technical aspect of the project, made use of these data, which were available thanks to the mobilization of Slavic communities in the United States.[22] On the eve of the 1920 census, Hill was an enthusiastic advocate for data on mother tongue, thinking it would provide a more accurate picture of the ethnic makeup of the population. He even asked the Census Advisory Committee to think about the future adoption of "a racial classification based partly on mother tongue and partly on country of birth, and adopt it in place of the country of birth classification in presenting sex, age, illiteracy, occupation, and other data for the foreign born population."[23]

The use of ethnic or cultural data, such as mother tongue, posed a technical problem in that quotas were assigned in the form of visas to nationalities and not to ethnic groups, a problem that was made more difficult by post-1918 border changes. Thus, in the case of Poles coming from Russia, the State Department geographer, working for the congressional commission on quotas, proposed in 1928 that a large number of the births in Russia should be converted into a quota for Poland, as quotas were attributed based on the number of people born in a given country and already present in the United States.[24] Contrary to the majority of the Census Advisory Committee, he held that the data on mother tongue were more precise than those by country of birth, and agreed better with foreign statistics on country of departure.[25]

The categories used by the Immigration and Naturalization Service to classify immigrants were not exclusively national: aside from classification by nationality of origin or passport, arrivals were classified by race or people, according to anthropological criteria laid out in the official manual, the *Dictionary of Races or Peoples*. The use of different classifications or statistical systems across agencies was still the norm, in spite of efforts to unify official statistics.[26] In the inter-war period, despite efforts to harmonize categories, the Census Bureau and the Immigration and Naturalization Service still used different categories to distinguish immigrants—more racial for the INS, more cultural or sociological for the census, reflecting the difference in their respective missions.[27] Not until 1977, with Directive 15 of the Office of Management and Budget (OMB), were the racial and ethnic categories unified across all government agencies.[28]

Mother tongue, used in 1920 and 1930, continued to serve as an indicator of the ethnic stratification of the American population. But with the adoption of quota laws, census officials decided that the composition of the population had been stabilized, since the quotas were intended to maintain the balance between Anglo-Saxons and other Europeans at the levels of 1920. By 1930, the Census Bureau tried to eliminate the mother tongue question, as a way to make room on the schedule for questions relating to unemployment. This fit into a general tendency on the part of the census to give priority to economic statistics as the most dynamic area of its field of investigation. However, thanks once again to activism by representatives of electorally significant minorities, the question was retained for the 1930 census. This comparative lack of interest in questions relating to immigration can be seen in a meeting of the Advisory Committee on the Census of Population for the 1930 census.[29] Deciding that the minorities that had called for this question in 1910 had since become part of independent states corresponding to their regions of origin, the committee recommended the elimination of the question. It also voted to omit the question on year of naturalization, a point it won with the lawmakers. Opposing arguments came from representatives of the minorities, who sometimes also had an economic interest, such as publishers of foreign-language publications. Some government agents supported the suppression, claiming that country of birth was information used by the government, especially with regard to immigration policy, while mother tongue was not. The census director also noted that the Census Bureau received numerous requests for information concerning the size of groups by country of origin, but not for groups by mother tongue. Other issues, such as cost, were also raised.[30]

The Census Bureau also had to deal with more extreme demands, such as those seeking to determine the racial origins of the white population. An example was H. H. Laughlin, a major figure in the American eugenics movement, who wanted the census to ask white inhabitants about the origins of their ancestors and then calculate the fraction of blood from each origin in the total white population. The director responded politely but firmly that the census was not an appropriate tool for this type of inquiry and that in any case he doubted the ability of the white population in the category "native of native parentage" to declare their ancestry by fractions. Steuart ended by stating that many questions had been removed from the schedule by the Commerce Department's Advisory Committee on the Census of Population, and that "if the members of the Eugenics Research Association fully understood the conditions under which a census is taken and the difficulties of the task, they would not urge the inclusion of these questions in regard to racial origin."[31]

In spite of the Census Bureau's desire to lessen the number of questions and publications devoted to immigration, mother tongue was retained on the 1930 schedule, though only for persons of foreign birth. They were asked to state the language spoken in their home before coming to the United States.[32]

The mother tongue question was still present in the 1940 census, and it is noteworthy that even if it was only one of the supplemental questions that were posed to only one person out of twenty—in other words, a 5 percent sample—it was no longer limited to immigrants but was asked independently of place of birth, in these words: "Language spoken in home in earliest childhood."[33] This indicated a new stage in the autonomy of ethnicity from immigrant origin, since this question implied that a person could, in theory, come from a family that had been in the United States for several generations and still belong to a linguistic minority. Thus, it could also, as we have seen, extend the range of the population of Mexican origin, assimilated to the Spanish-speaking population, because it would no longer be possible to classify them racially according to the new rules. More generally, questions on native tongue, introduced and retained at the request of representatives of ethnic minorities, laid the groundwork for overt questions on ethnic origin that were asked starting with the 1980 census, such as "what is this person's ancestry?"—a different question from place of birth.[34]

Through these examples of negotiations over the categories used to define and enumerate immigrants and their descendants, we can see that even while staying in the realm of factual questions, the US census was an instrument for strategies of construction of collective identities. Far from weakening its legitimacy, its way of coopting questions and sources conferred legitimacy on the federal census, the place of a form of democracy by numbers. Such a development was certainly neither designed nor imagined by the authors of the Constitution, who made the census the arbiter of democratic balances, but it was not a perversion of the original plan. The American democratic project placed population statistics at the heart of the federal apparatus, making it an eminently political tool. The appropriation of their number by different ethnic groups was, in its way, a form of Americanization, of adaptation to the rhetoric of representative democracy, proportionate to the number of inhabitants.

Until the 1960s and the adoption of affirmative action, these statistics were the object of essentially symbolic rather than material stakes. The strategies of construction of identity through figures and the categories seem quite similar, whether or not there were concrete individual or collective advantages in prospect.

At the same time, for the Census Bureau, the 1920s were marked by mechanisms of immigration restriction that, from 1921 to 1928, occupied a significant amount of the agency's time and resources. The measurements of populations of immigrant origin served two opposite goals at the same time, as they were done simultaneously in response to a social demand for statistical visibility and on the instructions of Congress. The Census Bureau provided Congress the technical solutions it needed to accomplish its political objective of severe restriction of immigration with the avowed goal of stabilizing the ethnic composition of the US population.

The Census Bureau and Quotas by National Origin (1921–1928)

The political and intellectual history of the immigration restriction movement is well known.[35] Rather than retell that history in detail here, I aim to shed light on the manner in which the Census Bureau accomplished this task, which transformed the census into a mechanism for apportionment not only of seats in the House of Representatives but also of the number of immigrants admitted to the United States annually by country of origin. Since 1882 and the Chinese Exclusion Act, as well as the adoption of the first qualitative restrictions, Congress had affirmed its authority over immigration as a federal domain. Various mechanisms for a policy of selective immigration were proposed between 1882 and 1920; some were adopted and others rejected, often by presidential veto. They included interdiction of prostitutes, of contagious sick people, or of paupers, as well as literacy tests, but none of these tools of selection managed to significantly modify the flow of immigration or to restrict its size.[36] The peak number of immigrant entries (1,285,349) was reached in 1907, and nearly reached again in 1914, before dropping abruptly as a result of the war in Europe.[37] Three methods of restriction, qualitative and quantitative, were adopted by the United States between 1921 and 1928, all three based on census data. The 1920s were a major turning point, perhaps the most important, in the history of the politics of population, since Congress wanted not only to control the immigration policy of the day but also plan the composition of the future population by national origin and by race.

Long viewed by advocates of restriction as the best barrier against the "new immigration," the literacy test adopted in 1917 disappointed them by its ineffectiveness since the number of entries surged again after the war. Congress then turned toward the quota system that had been considered by the Dillingham Commission along with the literacy test but had been rejected at that time.[38]

The trend toward restriction that had been building for the last two decades of the nineteenth century ultimately led to a quota system based on the national origin of immigrants, which in 1921 limited the number of immigrants by nationality in proportion to the number of US inhabitants who shared the same origin. For the first time, the census, which had often served as a reference in the discussion, became directly and explicitly the instrument of immigration laws. The 1921 law reduced the number of persons authorized to enter the United States as immigrants to 3 percent of the immigrant residents enumerated in 1910, allotted to their countries of origin.[39] The reference point was the group of persons, whether or not they were naturalized, who in 1910 had given a country as their place of birth, or whose place of birth had been coded by the Census Bureau as corresponding to countries existing in 1920. Non-European countries were excluded from the quotas, either because their emigrants, African or Asian, had been entirely blocked from immigration and naturalization, or else because, like inhabitants of the Western Hemisphere, their entry was not subject to restriction. Each European country was assigned a quota corresponding to 3 percent of the immigrants present in 1920 and born on its soil, with adjustments for the movement of borders.

The criterion used in the 1921 law was place of birth, affecting the "foreign born," who had been the focus of attention of census officials in the second half of the nineteenth century. The opposition between "natives" and "foreign born" was still alive; the quota system can be seen as the triumph of the nativist movement of the previous century, but it had taken a more racial direction: immigration had been accepted within limits, provided that the new arrivals looked like the old.

The system of national origins, as embodied in the 1921 law, necessarily had to be based on census data; the population in the statistics of the Immigration and Naturalization Service, collected since 1889, had been categorized as "races or peoples" and not strictly by nation-states, which did not support the allocation of quotas to specific countries.[40]

The 1921 law was extended beyond its initial terminus of mid-1922 to 1924, but for the strong movement that opposed immigration, it still seemed too weak. The 1924 law, rightly seen as the most restrictive, was in fact doubly so. First, it established a temporary mechanism—awaiting the implementation of the definitive system in 1928, one year after the planned date—that reduced quotas to 2 percent and adopted the 1890 census as a reference point. In 1890, the immigrants of the "new immigration"—a concept the census had helped construct—were already numerous, but they were far from forming the majority of inhabitants of foreign origin present in the country at that date. The change in the law had direct consequences for the composition of immigration, since the new quotas did not correspond to current flows of migration. Certain countries of northern Europe did not fully use their quotas, while the countries of the most recent migration saw their flow to the United States rendered largely illegal. The goal of the Immigration Restriction League had been achieved: not only was the total number of immigrants decreased, but also this second law was quite selective. The shift to the 1890 census rather than the 1910 census as a reference point and the drop from 3 percent to 2 percent meant a reduction in the annual quota for Italy from 42,000 to about 4,000; for Poland, a drop from 31,000 to about 6,000; and for Greece, a decrease from 3,000 to 100, the minimum number specified for a country by this law.[41] Between 1900 and 1910, on average 200,000 Italians entered the United States each year. Their quota for 1924 reduced that number by 98 percent. The racist hierarchies underlying the program, which had formed the basis for the concept of the "new immigration," reached fulfillment in these eloquent figures. Those who pushed the bill through made no attempt to disguise their agenda; one year after the 1924 law took effect, the commissioner of immigration stated that virtually all immigrants "looked exactly like Americans" now.[42]

Second, the 1924 law established quotas only for three years, with the expectation that on 1 July 1927 another system would go into effect. That system would set an overall quota of 150,000 immigrants each year, based on the national origins of all the inhabitants of the United States, immigrant or non-immigrant, in 1920. This constituted a major conceptual change. It would no longer be a matter of defining the composition of immigration with respect to past patterns, but rather of ensuring that new immigration would have a composition identical to that of the American population as a whole. In fact, this law did not take effect until 1929, once its complex mechanism had been developed and approved by Congress; it remained in place until quotas were eliminated in 1965. The historian Mae M. Ngai sees the most enduring result of the quota system for American society as the transformation of a large part of the country's inhabitants into illegitimate or illegal residents, a change that had enormous consequences for society at large and for the labor market.[43]

The system of national origins was more complex to implement than the two preceding systems. The total number of immigrants was fixed, but the method of calculating and allocating the quotas was more vague. The law envisioned assigning each inhabitant of the United States in 1920 a birth or ancestry in a foreign country—not by means of genealogy, but based upon "statistics of immigration and emigration, together with rates of increase of population as shown by successive decennial United States censuses, and such other data as may be found to be reliable."[44]

The precise scope of "national origins" was undefined, but clearly it included more than just the simple place of birth used in 1921 and 1924. Since the law states "origin by birth or ancestry," second-generation immigrants could be counted, which would increase the proportion of the older immigration. Yet the law did not make census data the only reference point. As we have seen, the statistics of the Immigration Bureau were based on a much more racial concept of differences. In fact, the census categories were used, because the data were more solid. In spite of several proposals for a quota for Jews, no such quota was ever established. This was due in part to the application of the legislation in international law. If people could claim origins that did not correspond to a nation-state to make up a quota, then they were assigned to states recognized by international law, where they could request an immigration visa from the US legation.[45]

The law extended the prohibition on immigration of persons ineligible for naturalization—that is, Chinese and Japanese.[46]

The Quota Board, the congressional committee charged with setting quotas, had its own interpretation of the concepts developed by the census in the nineteenth century, which varied from ordinary usage. Where the census had defined "native stock" as persons born in the United States of parents who themselves had been born in the United States, and "foreign stock" as first- and second-generation immigrants, the Quota Board defined "native stock" as descendants of the white population of the United States in 1790, and "foreign stock" as the descendants of whites who had immigrated to the United States since 1790. The documents Hill prepared for the Quota Board sometimes referred to "original white stock," that is, present in 1790.[47] The descendants of slaves, blacks, and mulattoes had been subtracted from the basis for calculation of quotas, which avoided the issue of assigning quotas to African countries and made it possible not to take away 13,000 visas for Europeans. The inhabitants of US territories (Alaska, Hawaii, and Puerto Rico) were also excluded from the calculation, as were Asians, whether immigrants or born in the United States and thus citizens by birth.[48]

Between 1924 and 1928 Hill, working on behalf of the Quota Board but within his position at the Census Bureau, devoted intensive effort to attempting to establish the racial composition of the white population of the United States, to borrow the title of one of his reports. He was trying to establish, by combining different methodologies, the origin of all white Americans, by determining the geographical and ethnic origins of all immigrants, including for the colonial period. Thus, methods were developed for evaluating the proportion of surnames drawn from the 1790 census that were Anglicized, in order to reattribute them to other nationalities (especially Scotland and Ireland). There is also a contribution establishing, on the basis of family names, the proportion of Irish among the first colonists.[49]

In a table combining census data and estimates of immigrant entries since 1790, Hill attempted to synthesize the composition of the American population in 1920. He came up with a distribution of 45 percent of the population coming from "foreign stock," a figure obtained from census statistics from 1890 to 1920, adding up immigrants, their children, and half of the grandchildren; 10 percent assigned to quota countries following immigration statistics for 1790 to 1870; and 45 percent "native stock," descendants of the population of 1790, corrected for the Anglicization of surnames.

The shift from the quotas in effect from 1924 to 1928 to the system of national origins of 1928 on this basis resulted in a new reduction of quotas for all countries except Great Britain. The quota for Great Britain increased from 34,007 to 65,894, while Germany's decreased from 51,227 to 24,908.[50] This revision drew protests addressed to Congress and passed on to the Census Bureau, such as a manifesto by the American Irish Historical Society entitled "Strike Out the 'National Origins' Clauses from the Immigration Act!"[51] In the final version, the quotas were slightly modified, but remained about the same size.[52]

At the same time, Census Bureau statisticians responsible for producing the quotas, while performing their tasks, privately or between the lines, expressed their concern about methodological rigor, admitting that things were largely cobbled together. Once the system of national origins was adopted in 1928 and implemented starting in 1929, the Census Bureau no longer concerned itself with the question of national origins.

Following the recommendation of the Census Advisory Committee, the Census Bureau wanted to eliminate the question of mother tongue from the 1930 census, on the grounds that thanks to the new immigration legislation and especially the quotas by national origin or even the prohibition of non-European immigration, the racial composition of the American population had been fixed as it was in 1920, and that it no longer had any tendency to evolve. It was therefore appropriate to make room on the schedules for more important and more current subjects. The year 1928 thus represented both the extreme point of immigration restriction and the peak of the census's work on immigration. In the following decade, staff changes among the census teams helped speed up this trend.[53] Accordingly, the Division of Methods and Results became the Division of Statistical Research and occupied itself during the following decade with the development of statistical techniques for sampling and surveying, while research in the 1920s, under Hill's supervision, had mainly served to provide Congress with politically effective and understandable methods for apportionment and quotas, even if they were scientifically debatable.[54]

The Bureau's Lack of Interest in Immigration after 1928

By the end of the 1920s, the situation had entirely reversed: the Census Bureau, which had launched itself enthusiastically into the production of ever more complex data on immigrants and their descendants, made every attempt to play down as far as possible the importance of these questions in its work. Starting in 1927, the majority of division heads, Census Bureau directors, and members of the Census Advisory Committee constantly advocated the elimination of the mother tongue question.

Beginning with their collection, the data on mother tongue had posed certain problems for the Census Bureau: more work, cost overruns, and a larger number of errors in coding, to the point that the agency had to reorganize the distribution of punch cards so that those of immigrant families would be equally divided among all the employees. Some employees complained that their boss gave them only cards for immigrant families, while their coworkers had none. The young women who transcribed the schedules onto perforated cards were paid as piecework. The Census Bureau admitted that the cards bearing information on the mother tongue of individuals and their parents required more time to process, and that it was necessary to distribute them differently, or else move to hourly pay.[55]

Adoption of the national-origins system helped reinforce the decisive argument of cost with that of the uselessness of the question. As early as 1927, Leon Truesdell, head of the Population Division, recommended the elimination, pure and simple, of the question of mother tongue, stating that it required more work than any other to process the results. Further, with the new map of Europe, which would in principle ensure that borders agreed with nationalities (in the sense of peoples), it was no longer needed.[56] Truesdell's position was followed by the Census Advisory Committee, which in December 1928 passed a resolution that clearly set out the Census Bureau's new line on these questions: elimination of the questions for the person and his or her father and mother were approved. The main reason was that the new European borders corresponded to the distribution of "nationalities," and that place of birth would be the closest approximation.

> The Poles and the Lithuanians, for example, who were among the principal petitioners for the mother tongue inquiry in 1910, now have their own national boundaries. The point was made, also, that even with the omission of the mother tongue question, the Census devotes an almost unduly large percentage of its attention to the foreign stock

which promises to become of continually decreasing importance in the future.[57]

To make more room on the schedule, the proposal was also made to merge two questions into one: "Whether able to read" and "Whether able to write." Truesdell also noted that, while the Census Bureau received numerous requests for reports of data by country of birth, the classification by mother tongue at the level of ward or for cities of less than 25,000 inhabitants had never been done, due to cost, and that no one had ever requested these data.[58] This opinion was not unanimous on the Census Advisory Committee. Walter Willcox hoped to retain the question, but the majority of members and Census Bureau officials who were present favored its elimination. Similarly, the Census Bureau eliminated the question on year of naturalization, which had been intended to measure the rate of assimilation of immigrants by nationality, by relating it to the year of immigration.

In spite of this radical change in the hierarchy of interests on the part of the Census Bureau, the question of mother tongue, reduced to just the language of persons enumerated and not their parents, remained in the 1930 census for persons born abroad. According to the Census Bureau, this was a result of campaigns led by representatives of immigrant communities, and especially by Read Lewis, director of the Foreign Language Information Service, a New York–based organization that sold manuals and books in foreign languages to immigrant populations, and which had an obvious economic interest in knowing their distribution in the country.

Lewis, who closely followed the decisions of the Census Advisory Committee, engaged in correspondence with Steuart, the Census Bureau director. Unlike those who opposed the question on mother tongue, for whom the significance of the responses lay in Europe, Lewis emphasized the importance of this information for understanding American society. In his view, it was better all the way around to eliminate the question on country of birth, on the basis that mother tongue would be much more useful for social workers, sociologists, and businessmen who wanted to know the ethnic makeup of the country.[59] In a memorandum attached to the correspondence, "The 1930 Census and Our Foreign Born People," Lewis set out a view that privileged ethnicity over country of birth and political borders, and which is worth quoting here, as it seems to arise from another view of what America is, one opposed to the vision of Census Bureau and Immigration officials:

What every immigrant brings to his country is that multiform complex of cultural traits and traditions, customs and ideas, of which the native language is the tangible indication. Culture and nationality are, partially at least, inherited by the second generation, and they—not passports and birthplaces—go into the process of America's making. . . . Finally, the emotional attitude of countless immigrants toward the present political situation in Europe should not be disregarded. They refuse to accept the new boundaries and to recognize the new states. . . .

It is easy to argue that the American census has no bearing upon the political situation in Europe, but it will be difficult to persuade hundreds of thousands of immigrants to give information which will seem to increase the numerical strength of the "enemy" nationality of this country.

In order to secure accurate census returns this mass psychology must be taken into account and one way to do it will be to continue the inquiry in regard to mother tongue, that is, nationality.[60]

Steuart responded that a choice had to be made between mother tongue and country of birth:

Some consideration was given to the possibility of dropping the country of birth inquiry and retaining mother tongue. But it was the general opinion that if we can carry only one of these questions it should be the country of birth or country of origin, especially as that is the basis of the quotas in the present immigration restriction laws.[61]

Steuart also noted that the Census Bureau had received no requests for data by mother tongue, while numerous requests had been made for statistics by country of origin. He added that there was less room on the schedule for 1930 because Congress had ordered the addition of a question on unemployment.[62]

Ultimately, the question was retained in 1930, in spite of the opposition of the Census Bureau, which complained of pressure from such groups as the publishers of foreign-language publications and agitation on the part of Ukrainians in the United States. The internal report on the deployment of the census in the field stated that the question on mother tongue had been retained "to lessen dissatisfaction."[63]

The same debate took place all over again, with the same participants, as the 1940 census approached. Truesdell's position had evolved so that he was willing to retain the mother tongue question going forward, as an auxiliary to classification by country of birth. But from another perspective, he felt that the most important category was the distinction of the white population by the birth country of the parents, and that the distinction by country of birth of persons themselves could safely be abandoned. In his view, the distinction of foreign/ native parentage was henceforth the most important, while that of country of birth ("foreign birth") had lost its relevance with respect to earlier decades. With the restriction of immigration, the number of first-generation immigrants would decrease, while those of the second generation would have greater prominence.[64]

Following a new request by Read Lewis, the comment was made that the head of the Foreign Language Information Service was motivated more by publicity to strengthen his power with respect to other associations than by a real interest in the data. In the belief that he would not be swayed by Census Bureau arguments, the Census Advisory Committee intended, without voting on it, to test Lewis's commitment by asking him to pay for the tabulation of data by mother tongue. Truesdell proposed eliminating nine questions, modifying four, and adding eight. Among the questions he wanted to modify were those of father's and mother's place of birth, which would significantly reduce the work of correction and tabulation; year of immigration, a question that was no longer of interest and whose elimination would spark little opposition; the ability to speak English, for the same reasons; and mother tongue. Among the questions he proposed adding was place of residence in 1930, which would permit measuring internal migrations—an indication of the shift in areas of interest.

Truesdell noted that the question of mother tongue had been eliminated in 1930, then reinstated as a result of pressure from the Foreign Language Information Service, but that the competition would be more intense for placement on the schedule for 1940.[65] The committee also recommended that country of birth should be defined as the country where the place of birth was located on 1 January 1937, in order to avoid an "avalanche" of protest from organizations representing Czechs or Poles.

Ultimately, in the 1940 census, the questions of father's and mother's place of birth, as well as the person's own mother tongue, were asked of only one random person in twenty (line 14 and line 29), or a sample of 5 percent, a compromise made possible by technical developments.[66]

In the end, the fortunes of questions concerning immigration on the census population schedule show how the Census Bureau became more and more subject to contradictory pressures and had to take account of different users of statistics. The increasing involvement of external actors in general and of certain segments of the population in particular will be the subject of the final section of this book.

PART V

THE POPULATION AND THE CENSUS

Representation, Negotiation, and Segmentation (1900–1940)

Once it had been made a permanent agency in 1902, the Census Bureau was endowed with a building in Washington, a staff made up of civil service workers, some of whom made their entire career in the service of the census, and an institutional memory—something that had been lacking for most of the nineteenth century. The permanent Census Bureau was a large employer, and especially after 1933, aimed to become a center for statistical training and research. For all these reasons, in the twentieth century it became the recipient of numerous solicitations from members of the public, whether seeking employment, requesting statistical information, complaining or congratulating, or making suggestions on the part of individuals, enterprises, or economic interest groups, such as statistical specialists. As a permanent organ of the federal bureaucracy, it maintained for its own internal use a large number of archives of all kinds, some of which were eventually destroyed while some were sent to the National Archives. These archives, especially those of letters received as well as the very rich archives of the public relations department, allow us to see how the Census Bureau operated in the face of innumerable requests. As before, it remained subject to pressures from Congress, which continued to impose questions on it, as well as to its parent authority, the Department of Commerce. From 1919 on, the community of statistical experts was closely associated with the development of the censuses, through the Census Advisory Committee, so that one might say that the Census Bureau's relations with the statistical community were internal relations, which by no means implies that they were free of conflict. The question of sampling shows that the rift was not between the Census Bureau and its researchers, but rather within the community of experts, with the heads of the Census Bureau themselves being divided over the issue.

Unlike in earlier periods, the Census Bureau was henceforth directly accessible to external actors. This was a matter of choice, encouraged by the administration, but sometimes regretted. Thus, the census director, William Steuart, was pleased with the change introduced in the census law of 18 June 1929, which authorized the director to decide on his own precisely what questions would appear on the schedule. According to him, this would allow the experts to retain only the relevant questions, which Congress had not always done in the past. But Steuart failed to anticipate that the questions, suggestions, or calls for changes in the schedule would no longer be addressed to Congress by the various interests, whether private or scientific, but instead would be sent, directly and in unexpected numbers, to the head of the census himself.[1] As Diana Magnuson notes, the Census Bureau was responsible for this avalanche of letters, since in 1928 and again in 1929 it had solicited public input in developing the schedule for 1930, formed committees for sorting the requests, and organized a general conference on population around this theme.[2]

The Census Bureau's relations with the outside world—whether the general public, the expert community, or politicians—became over time the object of constant arbitration, which had not been the case before it became a permanent agency. What we know of the relations between the Census Office and the outside world in the previous century is that they revolved around three axes, with only three categories of actors. The first relationship was with Congress, and was characterized by a gradual process of emancipation, seen especially in the reforms of 1880 and 1890, which strengthened the Census Office's control over the recruitment of census workers. Second was the relationship with the public, which essentially involved claims by census workers who demanded extra pay due to the difficulty of the work and, more rarely, claims by local officials challenging the figures.[3] The lack of a permanent census agency meant that the schedules were largely compiled by the Senate and House committees on the census, and we have seen that these decisions were often made against the advice of the Census Office. Proposals or claims regarding the schedule were generally addressed to members of Congress, and rarely to the administration.[4] The third avenue of dialogue, if we can call it dialogue, was the press, which often led harsh campaigns, such as against the "fraudulent census" of Superintendent Porter in 1890.[5]

At the beginning of the century, things changed, and we begin to find many more traces of relations between the census and outside actors. The opening up of the census shows up on three different levels. The first is correspondence with actors outside of the Census Bureau, whether individuals or groups, especially on the subject of its actions. Second is the production and publication of data or reports concerning a particular population. The most important example of this is statistics on the black population, which had a noticeable public relations aspect, to which we could add targeted publicity campaigns conducted through a network of correspondents. Third is the opening of recruitment to new categories of the population, whether it was a question of employees of the Census Bureau in Washington or of its workers in the field. The Census Bureau very early on had recourse to women workers, in its offices and in the field. With equal rapidity, it grasped the advantage of recruiting census workers who shared the origins of the majority population in a given census district, both for reasons of cost, by limiting the need for paid interpreters, and also to make the census more popular with the public in question.

Rather than study these areas separately, I have chosen instead to look in succession at the three major categories of the population that were the focus of the Census Bureau's attention: the black population; women, especially middle-class white women; and ethnic communities. This approach takes into account the administrative development of the Census Bureau between 1900 and 1940; in other words, it recognizes that the modernization of the bureau's activity involved practices resembling those of large private enterprises benefiting from the development of marketing to adjust their activity to consumer demand. To take up an expression used by a director of the census, we shall see that the Census Bureau was not only a federal agency working for the government and Congress, but also an institution that saw the satisfaction and trust of "users of statistics" as the criteria of success for the population census and the best guarantee of "good statistics."

The Census and African Americans Within and Outside the Bureau

The history of the Census Bureau's relations with the black population in the first half of the twentieth century is that of an incomplete transformation. Historically, as we have seen across the last three chapters, the separate treatment of blacks in population statistics was the foundation of the entire system of classification of the population. For the census, blacks were the most objectified inhabitants, to the point that slaves were deprived of names to literally become numbers in the population statistics, and the ones least likely to be viewed as subjects. Even at the end of the nineteenth century, census speculations on the black population of the nation concerned their degree of hybridization and the possibility of their natural extinction.

At the same time, blacks as a category were always the object of particular attention in census reports. From this point of view, the studies on the black population—which from the 1900 census onward became more and more concerned with their economic condition and less and less with their anthropological characteristics—rested upon a tradition: for a long time, the census had devoted sections in its publications to the black population. In spite of the omnipresence of the color distinction in the US census, it was not until 1904 that the first major publication devoted exclusively to the American black population was published—a special bulletin entitled *Negroes in the United States*, a major statistical study of 336 pages, which we have already mentioned.[1] This bulletin has several claims to importance. It confirms that the vocation of the census was to be the main source of statistics on the black population, but it is essentially concerned with the economic status of blacks and was not compiled by statistical specialists on mortality or racial theories. In fact, it was conceived by two academics, the Progressive economist Walter F. Willcox[2] and the great black sociologist W. E. B. Du Bois. The fact that one of the two men, even though he was the second author, was African American is no coincidence. Rather, we can see here the first stage of the growing involvement of black authors and statisticians in Census Bureau publications devoted to the black population. The second major publication of the Census Bureau on this subject was the weighty monograph, *Negro Population 1790–1915*, which reviewed all the statistics on the black population collected and published by the census since 1790, constituting an unparalleled reference work.[3] Reviewing the nineteenth-century data, the commentary provided much more nuanced explanations.[4] The wording on the title page is significant:

> It is worthy to note that the tabulations of the report were made by a corps of Negro clerks working under the efficient direction of three men of their own race, namely, Robert A. Pelham, Charles E. Hall and William Jennifer.[5]

This information gives rise to two observations: First, the Census Bureau felt it was worthwhile to make it known that the report on the black population had been done by African Americans, some of whom were surely more than simple employees. Charles E. Hall would be the principal author of the following volume, published in 1935, *Negroes in the United States 1920–1932*, whose subtitle, perhaps chosen by him, was "A Publication of Negro Progress."[6]

The information was not gratuitous, because once the Census Bureau made it known that it employed staff of color for its publications on the black population, it received many congratulatory letters from black organizations.[7] (It was often stated that no one in the Census Bureau, until Hall became "Specialist, Negro Statistics," worked exclusively on statistics for the black population; the Census Bureau only mentioned its black employees in relation to these two publications.) One particular point that brought congratulations from black readers in the 1920s was the Census Bureau's capitalization of the word "Negro" in its publications.[8]

Members of the black community profited by this position on the part of the Census Bureau to seek employment whenever they knew that studies on their population were under way, but generally without much success. Hall and Jennifer appeared often, as the two names that were always mentioned. When Hall was named specialist in "Negro statistics" in May 1935, a press release from the Commerce Department stated:

> For the first time in the history of the Bureau of the Census of the United States Department of Commerce a Negro civil service "Career man" has been promoted to a position of responsibility, one that carries with it the full authority to disseminate all available statistical data relating to the Negro population, and to sign official correspondence.[9]

Another piece of information contained in the mention of recourse to black agents, intentionally or unintentionally, is that the agency employed blacks for bureaucratic tasks, but that the offices were segregated. The black statisticians had people under their supervision, but all were blacks. Hall himself protested in the name of his subordinates when the women's toilets at the Census Bureau were segregated, at the request of white employees who petitioned in August 1920.[10] A report on him in 1930 showed that ten years later, in spite of several promotions, he was still working in a segregated environment. Upon his return from a field trip, Hall was given responsibility for "a unit of colored employees editing farm schedules; an assignment which the Census bureau considers quite important."[11] He was the first African American to have such supervising responsibilities.

His career also had its reverses, though it was unquestionably brilliant, and in 1935 he could be presented in a newspaper article as an exception in the government's roster of federal employees.[12] However, internal documents of the Census Bureau show that if it was ready to recruit black agents as censustakers and to let the fact be known, it was still not inclined to send them out to represent it in the field in a higher position. A letter of 16 March 1907, from Director North to Senator Hopkins, Hall's political godfather and a Republican from Illinois, seems fairly representative of the Census Bureau's policy with respect to its black employees. Hopkins had recommended his protégé for a position as a special agent to collect judicial statistics in Illinois, in counties where there was a large colored population, there being "probably a hundred thousand colored people in the state." North gave assurances of his personal sympathy for the colored workers, but wrote that because of prejudice and segregation, as official representatives of the Census Bureau, they would be treated in a manner that would be humiliating to the agency, so it was not desirable to send them into the field.[13]

Hall's career with the census, from his debut in 1900 to his retirement in 1937, shows the gradual lowering of the barriers thrown up by segregation.[14] Other documents, in response to his many requests to be sent into the field, show that the Census Bureau agreed to send him to Chicago in 1904 because he was an excellent employee, but they emphasized that—according to Steuart, who at that time was chief statistician for industrial statistics—he was not to leave the regional bureau.[15] Hall repeatedly complained in writing that he was a victim of discrimination, in spite of the fact that North had told him that his request for assignment to field work would be considered on the basis of equal opportunity, which obviously was not the case. Nevertheless, in 1907, he conducted a field investigation in Philadelphia, which his superior noted with astonishment given his "peculiar status," asking that it not happen again:

> Upon completion of Mr. Hall's assignment in Philadelphia, I find that because of the peculiar status of his case it will be necessary to recall

him to the office. I know of no other city, in the East or elsewhere, where a colored man can be used to advantage.[16]

The fact that Hall occupied a relatively high-level position among the black employees created problems for personnel management, since white employees could not be placed under his supervision, which justified the reluctance to promote him, as expressed by the head of the special agents:

> Mr. Hall is one of the colored men I have in mind for assignment in the office of the chief special agents, if such arrangements be practicable. I doubt, however, whether it would be advisable to assign colored men for this work unless the entire force, with the exception of the chief special agent, is composed of the same race.[17]

Little by little, as Hall's career progressed, more employees were placed under his supervision, but all were black. In 1921, he was serving as a section chief in the Agriculture Division, and had under his supervision all the colored employees of the division, several dozen people. Hall denounced, several times but unsuccessfully, the Census Bureau's racism, but it is possible that his superiors, who saw him as very competent but difficult, may have thought, on the contrary, that the Census Bureau was generous with him.

Hall made internal complaints to the Department of Commerce, but with respect to the outer world, he defended the Census Bureau. An article published in the 8 May 1915 issue of the great black newspaper of Chicago, the *Chicago Defender*, gave a highly critical account of a visit to the Census Bureau by one of its journalists, who had found that Pelham, Jennifer, and Hall were segregated in the southeast corner of the room they occupied—"at a safe distance from the white clerks." The author, Ralph Tyler, was astonished that Hall and Pelham, both of whom were known as opponents of segregation, would put up with such treatment.[18] The three Census Bureau employees mentioned, Hall, Pelham, and Jennifer, were responsible for Bulletin no. 128 (1915), "Negroes in the United States," which Tyler saw as "the result of their segregation and their inwardly protested acceptance of segregation." They addressed a joint letter to the editor of the *Chicago Defender*, in which they said that what Tyler saw as segregation was merely an efficient working arrangement. In a spirited defense of their superiors, they gave their assurance that their superiors neither approved of nor practiced segregation with respect to their black employees:

> We are convinced that the officials of the Bureau, in assigning the work of compiling the statistics of the bulletin to Negro clerks have in every

respect sought to be fair and just, and have also sought in every honor-
able and reasonable way to accommodate the convenience of the clerks
engaged on this work and to meet the desires of the Negro as expressed
by one of its leading organizations and sponsored by some of its most
influential and capable men, who, under recent dates, have written
the highest commendation of the work and the policy pursued by the
Bureau with regard to the preparation, publication, and distribution of
this bulletin.[19]

This very accommodating position is interesting. On the one hand, it shows
that within the Census Bureau there was strong peer pressure against public
criticism of the agency. Of course, the three agents in question had also been
personally criticized for their passivity with regard to segregation. On the other
hand, the three letter writers seem to say that if the Census Bureau did indeed
have a policy of placing black employees together, separate from whites, to some
extent this worked for the black employees themselves. Finally, it confirms that
the Census Bureau's publications on the black population were closely followed
by black organizations, both in their preparation and in their distribution, since
these bulletins would be bought mainly by black institutions—whence the
Census Bureau's emphasis on the fact that they showed the economic and social
progress of that population group. This aspect underwent further development,
since a large part of the work of Charles E. Hall when he became "Specialist,
Negro Statistics," was to establish and maintain contacts with the Negro
Chambers of Commerce. The Chambers were seen as the main consumers of
census publications on the economic activity of blacks, as we shall see shortly.
    Although he was a recognized specialist in statistics on the black population
(even if that job did not yet exist), Hall was sent to Chicago for the 1930 census,
where he assisted a black supervisor. The Census Bureau had a long tradition of
using black workers for the population census as well as for agricultural censuses,
but with instructions to assign them only to black areas, which did not always
happen. In 1930, in a letter to a job candidate for the post of census worker or
supervisor in Alabama, the census director noted that Census Bureau policy
favored the recruitment of black workers in districts with black populations, at
the discretion of regional supervisors who recruited them and gave them their
assignments. Under this heading, the Census Bureau requested the "loyal cooperation" of colored persons, whether the census workers were black or white, on
the grounds that it was in the interest of the colored population itself that the
census should be correct. This was the response to a letter claiming that blacks
were best qualified to enumerate blacks, and that they ought to be hired in proportion to their share of the population, which in Alabama represented about
half of the state's inhabitants. This letter was part of a campaign, and several

others with identical content were sent to the Census Bureau, which issued the same noncommittal response to all.[20] The argument that blacks were best qualified to enumerate black areas had already been made in previous censuses, but with little success.

The best-documented episode was reported by Heidi Ardizzone with respect to the 1930 census. She cited the arguments made by black representatives to the supervisor in Galveston, Texas, which specifically upheld the idea that they alone could identify light-skinned blacks who did not live in black neighborhoods. She noted that this was a campaign organized mainly by Claude Barnett, an African American official of the NAACP and head of the Associated Negro Press, based in Chicago.[21] Earlier campaigns had aimed to allow the black population to benefit from the numerous census agent jobs afforded by the Census Bureau. One such campaign, in 1910, made the case for a more accurate enumeration, while demanding that blacks should enumerate whites exactly the same way that whites could enumerate blacks.[22]

The version given out unofficially by Census Bureau officials grew out of the legend of the hiring of incompetent blacks for political reasons going back to 1870 and to the use of black census workers in the South, whom Walker had blamed for the poor quality of results. In 1890, opponents of the Republicans blamed them for having used their influence to recruit black workers.[23] Walker's successors did not systematically deny the competence of black workers but in the first half of the twentieth century, the argument of suitability was the one that came up the most often. It occurs, for example, in the memoirs of E. Dana Durand, census director in 1910.[24] Earlier, the elimination of the "mulatto" category had been justified by the different perception of that distinction on the part of black workers hired in 1910, as opposed to that of white workers, who would have made less use of the category—which is debatable, as shown by detailed analysis of the figures.

The number of black census workers appears to have kept increasing, even if we do not have overall figures, since the recruitment of this type of employee was done at the local level by local supervisors. The idea of using African Americans, at least in black neighborhoods, was sufficiently important that the Census Bureau made a list of supervisors to whom it would send the names of persons known in the black community in order to help them with their work in 1930.[25] At this time, there were not only black field workers but also a small number of black supervisors.

A memo by Joseph A. Hill to the supervisors laid out the reasons for this development. He felt it "would be helpful if some competent representative of that race of good standing and reputation were given some recognition in connection with the census." This would be a volunteer position without authority over agents, in places with large numbers of African Americans.

What we want is an accurate and complete census of the Negroes; and in order to do that it is important that the Negroes should understand about the census and not be suspicious of it or antagonistic. We want to enumerate all the Negroes and enumerate them *as* Negroes.[26]

The rule was that in the South—but also in the rest of the country—blacks should only enumerate blacks, or if necessary, poor foreigners who, as one census worker put it, did not count. At the time of the 1930 census, the supervisor responsible for Chicago's South Side objected to the fact that his equivalent in the city's Eighth District was black. He preferred the use of assistants rather than the recruitment of black supervisors for areas where that community was heavily represented, and found the choice shocking for a wealthy white neighborhood:

A colored supervisor should under no conditions be placed in charge of white Enumeration Districts and above all, under no circumstance in charge of whole city wards that are occupied by white people. The 8th Supervisor's Districts, assigned to a colored supervisor, included Ward No. 1, which is not only inhabited largely by white people but it comprises the heart of Chicago's business area. Within this ward lies all of the large downtown hotels of Chicago. No colored supervisor should have had it. The 11th ward of Chicago, or the Hyde Park area should never have been assigned to a colored supervisor. The 11th ward is occupied almost solidly by white people. Along the lake, in wards 2, 3, and 4, race feeling is as tense as in Alabama or Mississippi. A colored supervisor, no matter how efficient, would be a liability to the Census bureau in these areas.[27]

The problem posed by the employment of black supervisors was different from that of agents, since they did not go into people's homes, but held a position of authority and publicly represented the census, and certain parts of the city had more prestige than others. In this letter, we can hear jealousy sprouting, while no incident is reported that could justify such a position on principle. On another level, we find the same prejudices among many census agents and supervisors who expected to encounter significant difficulties in enumerating "ignorant blacks" and foreigners who did not speak English. Many reports coming in from field workers mentioned pleasant surprises in neighborhoods with large concentrations of immigrants and, on the other hand, took note of the contempt and rudeness with which they were sometimes treated in wealthy neighborhoods.[28]

It would be impossible to obtain complete information on the tens of thousands of census workers employed in each census, since the Census Bureau kept no record of their names. One would have to pick up the census workers' names as they appear at the head of every one of the manuscript schedules, which are not made available until seventy-two years after the date of each census. One would then have to search the schedules themselves, line by line, to find out their color or race. Nonetheless, the Census Bureau archives contain some partial information, which allows us to see that the use of black workers was fairly widespread. Further, we know that in 1921, at the moment of peak recruitment for the processing of the 1920 census, the Census Bureau had 930 black and 5,371 white employees, which made for a fairly high proportion of colored personnel.[29]

The Census Bureau's relations with the African American business community developed from the time when Hall was appointed to head the Negro Statistics section, since his work largely consisted of convincing African American businessmen of the importance of statistics. This was in part an aggressive commercial policy on the part of the Census Bureau, which sent Hall on the road around the country to tout this theme, but it was also no doubt a sincere pedagogical effort on the part of the Bureau, which wanted to communicate the importance of its economic statistics as widely as possible, to African Americans as well as the rest of the population. Obtaining recognition from economic actors, wherever they came from, was an important element of the Census Bureau's legitimacy, especially in the difficult context of the 1930s, when the Bureau was forced to sharply economize. A speech by Charles Hall to the Cleveland Board of Trade in 1937 showed how one might use various economic statistics collected by the Census Bureau to reach a targeted public. Using census statistics, Hall illustrated the economic progress of African Americans in Cleveland over a ten-year period—for example, a 58.3 percent increase in the number of business owners—but juxtaposed this with supporting data showing that their support to their community through their spending was not strong enough.

> Although it is unnecessary for the businessmen of other racial groups to make such appeals, it would be advisable, in my opinion, for the Cleveland Board of Trade to conduct an Educational Campaign through the newspapers, churches and fraternal organizations before venturing too far. This conclusion is based on the Business Census of 1930 and the low sales per capita of Negro population in the retail stores operated in Cleveland by Negro proprietors. From these data it is not apparent that the Cleveland Negro population is as yet very much interested in business enterprises operated by members of their own racial group; not interested in creating employment for their own sons and daughters, or in the idea of bringing money from *without* for circulation *within* their racial group.
>
> I wish to repeat the statement the PURCHASING POWER of a minority group is a powerful lever and a great asset when properly organized and used.[30]

We can see from this example how the Census Bureau's activity with respect to the African American community—which culminated in the creation of the Negro Statistics Section in 1935, after decades of demand by black organizations since the 1910s—worked to the benefit of everyone involved: the African American business community and African American leadership, whose economic progress was highlighted; the Census Bureau, which consolidated its popularity with that community and maintained its contacts with the potential market for its statistics on the black population, generally a success in terms of sales; and finally Hall himself who, thanks to the Bureau, was presented to the outside world as the undeniable expert on the issue. Provided they were African Americans, Hall was able to engage in relations with business actors, local authorities, and elected officials, but the directors of the Census were ambivalent about an African American employee acting and behaving in a position of authority and competence.

This adaptation of the Census Bureau's work toward the consumers of statistics, who at the same time found themselves to also be the object of those statistics, is not unique, but it was with respect to the black population that this orientation became most solidly institutionalized and endowed with material and human resources. From this point of view, Hall's use of Census Bureau statistics to encourage blacks to develop their own economic circuits, and to help them find therein evidence for collective pride, was in no way opposed to the interests of the Bureau itself. When Hall spoke of "OUR business men," he might appear to be making an unwarranted appropriation of the figures, but we must remember that census data were produced precisely in order to be appropriated. This is clear from the example of the ethnic pride fed by census data. In both cases, what was said was not what the census director himself would have said, but it was surely in the interest of the Census Bureau to allow the greatest possible number of people to appropriate its data for themselves, whatever use they made of it. In the particular case of statistics on the black population, this appropriation was integrated upstream into the work of the Bureau, as shown by the targeted management of personnel by the chief clerk and as illustrated by publicity photos used by the census in 1941. The photos show black women entering data from schedules onto punched cards in the Negro Section (see cover photo) and, separately, white women doing the same work (see figure 2), but their physical separation was strict. Other photos in the same series suggest the absence of black workers in higher positions such as data verification or analysis: the work of analysis was done by groups of men and a very few women, all white, in working conditions much less evocative of industrial labor, if we keep in mind that the women who punched the cards were paid as piecework.[31]

Women as Census Workers and as Relays in the Field

Women are notably absent from this history, even though they were obviously present throughout the transformation of the census since 1790. They get short shrift in studies published by the census, and they appear here first as respondents to the inquiry and then as census agents themselves. For the taking of the census they constituted more a category of agents than a population category, to the extent that the latter only rarely was the subject of debates or the object of specific procedures. In the early censuses, only the names of the heads of household were reported on the schedules. If it was assumed that these were generally free white men, it was nonetheless specified that heads of household could also be women or free blacks. Before 1820, blacks, whether free or slave, were not distinguished by sex, but it was the evolution of the census from 1850 onward that opened up a gap between men and women in the quality of information obtained. The questions were the same, even if some items (on the right to vote, the age for bearing arms, on what concerned citizens generally) were reserved for men while others were reserved for women, in terms of the functions that defined them, such as the number of children, living or dead, they had borne. Similarly, the shift from imprecise statistics of "foreign parentage" to data giving the place of birth of each of the parents allowed the Census Bureau to comment on the choice of spouses made by men and women beginning in 1880. Recall that in the case of two parents of different foreign birth, the birth country of the father defined the national origin of the child. Here the principle of inequality between men and women won out over that of hypodescent. In the case of only one immigrant parent, the 1910 report justified counting the children as being of foreign ancestry because they typically resembled immigrants and the foreign parent was more often the father, whose origin strongly influenced the social and economic status of the children.[1] It has been shown that women's work was greatly and systematically underrated by the censuses of the second half of the nineteenth century. Likewise, their role as census workers, though documented for the late nineteenth century, was overlooked by census documents in the twentieth century, which ordinarily represented the recruitment of women as census workers as a twentieth-century innovation.[2]

What changed was that, beginning with the 1920 census, and with women gaining the right to vote that same year, the Census Bureau would now devote considerable effort to women, in two distinct directions: first, by making house-wives a focus of attention as the interviewees of census workers and the repos-itory of their husbands' information; second, more discreetly, by recruiting a growing number of women as census workers and supervisors. Documents for external use showed that women at work in the Census Bureau in Washington served several purposes: demonstrating to all that the Census Bureau was a great modern enterprise, but also, and more specifically, attracting more applicants. As was the case for blacks, the information furnished on the activity of women in the Census Bureau—photographs in particular—reveals sex segregation in jobs at the very heart of the agency.

As a consequence of women gaining the status of active citizens, their status with regard to the laws on naturalization changed: after 1922, married women no longer automatically followed the nationality of their husbands. The census was taking more account of personal information on women, even if this was at first a source of complications for the Census Bureau.[3]

Little by little, in both the internal and external communications of the Census Bureau, women ceased to be viewed merely as obstacles to questions that were too difficult, as they were in Walker's writings, and instead came to be seen as useful cogs in the census machinery.

The change seemed greatest with regard to recruitment into the offices in Washington, especially after 1920. For a long time the Census Bureau had employed largely female staff, but between the two world wars, its public rela-tions department worked to emphasize the importance of female staff, appar-ently in the effort to promote a modern image of the agency. To this end, it published brochures illustrated with photographs featuring women busy with workday tasks that became feminized in fact through this representation.[4]

A little booklet produced by the Census Bureau, entitled "What Census Bureau Does" and published in the *National Republic* on 5 November 1928, is significant in this regard. The three-page text, by Joseph A. Hill, the immova-ble assistant director of the census, features the activities of the Census Bureau between censuses. On the first page is a photo captioned "Some of the Federal Census Workers," in which one can see rows of desks in a large, well-lighted room without partitions, presumably a floor of the Census Building in Washington. Seated at each desk is a woman busily typing. At the back of the room stand several people who appear to be managers, among whom we can identify only one male individual. In a second photo, "Compiling American Statistics," which seems to be a view of the same room, the image is divided by a central aisle. On the right side we see a row of secretaries, all women, seated before large typewriters. On the left, near the windows, is a long row of Hollerith tabulating machines, also staffed entirely by women. The third page includes two small inset photos: census director William M. Steuart, posed in front of bookshelves, his hand resting on a folder; and Joseph A. Hill, assistant director and author of the article. Modernity (the premises, the organization of the workplace, the use of machines) and feminization of the work appear to be the twin foci of the image the Census Bureau wanted to present in this publication.[5]

At the same time, the director emphasized the responsibilities entrusted to women in the field: in 1920, the first census in which women were allowed to be employed as supervisors (that is, regional managers), only five supervisors were women. In a press release of 28 December 1929, Steuart announced that twenty-four women had already been recruited to this post, in which they would be charged with hiring about two hundred census workers each, and with managing the census in their district in 1930.[6] The release gave the name and city of each of the women. We can see here a parallel with the publicity treatment of black employees at the Census Bureau in Washington. Steuart stated that the census legislation had never prohibited the recruitment of women supervisors, and that the Census Bureau had never opposed their hiring, but that before the 1920 census, it seemed obvious that this was "a man's job."

According to this piece, women had been recruited as censustakers since the 1900 census, and possibly "in rare instances" even before that date. In fact, women had been hired in this sort of capacity since at least 1880, but evidently this fact had not been retained in the institutional memory of the Census Bureau, unlike the recruitment of black workers in the nineteenth century, which had given rise to the dark legend we have mentioned.[7]

The press frequently mentioned the use of women for the census, as in New York City in 1910, when 10 percent of the 1,700 census workers were female.[8]

It is not impossible that some of the women recruited as supervisors might have taken advantage of their position to make the development a reality—such as Mary B. Wood, of Ithaca, New York, who hired a majority of women for the urban districts (ten men out of twenty-eight enumerators in the county) in 1930.[9] For its part, the Census Bureau may have been encouraged in this path by the many favorable comments on its employment of women as census workers, which stand out in the reports on work in the field. Moreover, the widespread use of written tests made possible broader recruitment of women for these posts, since they were credited more often than men with the qualities that made a good census worker: conscientiousness, seriousness, and meticulousness in their handling of the schedules.[10] The census itself noted in 1930 that, in terms of required qualifications, there were more women available than men.[11] One notes also that the most effusive evaluations on the recruitment of women came from supervisors who had hired a significant proportion or even a majority of women, such as P. P. Boli of the 22nd District of Ohio or Mary B. Wood in Ithaca. The distribution of women within a supervisor's district seems to have taken into account the details of the area; women were assigned much more often to urban areas than rural, as far as it is possible to tell from the archives. Some reports stated that women were not the best choice for the agricultural census, which in rural areas took place along with the population census, because they would not understand the technical terms used.[12]

The recruitment of women peaked at the approach of the 1940 census, at all levels of the organization: Out of a total of 122,777 census workers, 68,734 were white men, 51,776 were white women, 839 were black men, 1,293 were black women, and there were 115 men and 20 women of other "colors."[13] The feminization of the job was quite obvious in 1940, since women, all categories combined, represented 43.24 percent of the total (against 49.8 percent of inhabitants), while African Americans made up only 1.7 percent of census workers, against 9.8 percent of inhabitants (in 1940), with black women being relatively better represented. Women could also be found at the higher levels of the hierarchy, though in much smaller proportions: for example, two women served on the Special Advisory Committee for the population census in 1940.

A memorandum from the director of the census intended for the secretary of commerce, linking the presence of two women on the committee to the possible inclusion of a black man, reveals the politics behind the public relations, since it seems that William Austin was responding to a demand from the secretary of commerce.[14] In publications, as in the accounts of field agents, the choice of whether or not to recruit women was often linked to the question of recruiting blacks. Generally, census agents who were hostile to the recruitment of women also opposed the recruitment of blacks, and the idea that women could only cover the streets in certain respectable neighborhoods often resurfaced in these accounts, as did the idea that if black agents were recruited, they would need to be assigned to black neighborhoods.[15]

If the census emphasized the growing presence of women among its personnel, its main publicity campaign with regard to women in the general population focused on those whom William Steuart saw as an essential element in the success of the census in the field—housewives, whom Walker had described half a century earlier as the chief limiting factor to the complexity of questions that could be posed. Starting from the observation that most of the enumerators' visits occurred during working hours, it was very often women who spoke for the whole family.

In a brochure sent by the Census Bureau to several Chambers of Commerce for wider distribution, Steuart explained why the census sought to gain women's trust. He distinguished those questions that a housewife might easily answer (her age, the ages of her husband and children, the date of her marriage, whether or not her children attended school) from those that were more difficult, such as the property value of the family home, if they were homeowners. One of the purposes of the brochure was to encourage wives to consult their husbands before the enumerator's arrival. What was needed was an estimate, not an exact value, "and that I believe every man, if not every woman, ought to be able to give." In the sex-segregated world where the census enumerator would have to operate, "husbands who gain such information in the source of their reading or business" should "tell the wife about it."

After mentioning the bully pulpits of the Chambers of Commerce, marketplaces, community associations, municipal authorities, and press outlets, the census director concluded:

> If the woman in the home and the census enumerator meet in a spirit of whole-hearted cooperation, the success of the 1930 census will be assured.[16]

Here we see a more traditional image of American women than that of the women seated before a typewriter, but we must view the return to stereotype (in quotes in the article) as an educational concern, arising from the search for accuracy by consensus that characterized the communications of the census directors. This also explains the recourse to familiar slogans that would stick in people's heads, such as the one found here: "Tell the wife about it."

This brochure was not the only such, and the census made other efforts to reach out to women: a similar article appeared in March 1930 in the popular magazine *Woman's Home Companion*. In a letter mentioning it, Steuart distinguished the wife, who responded to census questions, from the husband, who engaged in economic activity, a distinction that separated the feminine cogs in the production of the census from those who might have call to use its results.[17]

We frequently find in census literature the hope that the population would debate census questions ahead of time. This seems to have been more hope than reality, but many newspapers did agree to publish an advance list of the questions on the schedule.

As it did for ethnic communities, the Census Bureau would also reach out to women's organizations to spread its message. On 17 March 1930, Steuart sent a letter to the "officers and members" of the General Federation of Women's Clubs, asking them to talk about the census in their meetings.[18]

The publicity campaigns of 1940 that made use of photos and led to the shooting of publicity films also highlighted women, whether as census workers or as people being interviewed, the former shown as young middle-class women and the latter as housewives and mothers of families (see figures 6, 26, 27, 28, and 32).

Women's involvement with the census, at all levels, increased during the 1930s. After 1940, the new context of a wartime economy introduced significant changes for the census as for other government agencies, but on groundwork prepared over a long time. If we look at the recruitment of women by the census from 1880 on, we do not see evidence of a concerted policy, all the more because there were hundreds of supervisors with very different hiring policies for agents. Still, from 1920 on, while the number of women employed in the field increased and women gained greater access to mid-level positions in the hierarchy, the Census Bureau exploited this fact to project a modern image of the agency.

20

Ethnic Marketing
of Population Statistics

The Census Bureau greatly extended its external relations after becoming a permanent agency in 1902. With regard to populations of immigrant origin, the main focus of its concern with ethnic communities in urban environments was ensuring that populations thought to be suspicious of the census would nonetheless participate. We saw in chapter 17 how categories of origin were negotiated with representatives of ethnic communities. Another aspect of the Census Bureau's relations with these populations, which did not bear directly on the categories used, deserves to be mentioned here: publicity programs directed specifically toward ethnic groups.

The US Census from the beginning had made a point of official announcements to alert the population, but only from the beginning of the twentieth century did the Census Bureau engage in actual publicity campaigns, going far beyond the presidential proclamations sent out by the State Department, the text of which scarcely varied from one census to the next.[1]

Since the census did not become a permanent agency until 1902, the archives earlier than that date give no indication of earlier campaigns. The three censuses of 1910, 1920, and 1930 saw the development of a sustained program with the goal of preparing the population for the arrival of enumerators, but also with the aim to promote the work of a federal agency whose budget was subject to strict control by members of Congress. At the time of the 1940 census, methods changed significantly, and the Census Bureau's publicity made it possible to view its progress.

The originality of the work of the Census Bureau consists of the modernity of its methods: short radio broadcasts by the census director in 1930, recourse to sponsors, and use of marketing techniques to identify specific targets and outlets for particular messages.

In 1930, the Census Bureau clearly entered the modern era. Its machines were the most modern available: the 1930 census was in fact processed by new, specially designed IBM machines, which the company developed from the earlier Hollerith machines originally created for the census. Further, since the end of World War I, a new generation of statisticians, trained at university, had replaced the pioneers from the turn of the century. By their training, and in the context of the economic crisis of the Great Depression, these new men set increasing importance on economic data, at the expense of traditional demographic data. Steuart, former head of the industrial census, favored this development, even though he himself belonged to the older generation. From the point of view of the Census Bureau's external relations, this priority was revealed in the systematic adoption of modern methods. Even the conception of the American population by the census was influenced by the modern techniques of the consumer society.[2]

The targeted campaigns of the census made use of marketing techniques. The year 1930 was also when the Census Bureau made extensive use of photography, to spread the images of its machines, and also for posters that made the official proclamations in black and white seem obsolete—all the more because the posters were combined with publicity for businesses that made themselves sponsors of the census. Thus, in 1930, in a Seattle street, a large billboard, lit up at night, featured the slogan: "Census! Be sure you're counted" with the logo of the local electric utility, Puget Sound Power & Light. What made this billboard original, and what doubtless struck the passers-by as much as the publicity for the census, was how, the full length of the sign, electric letters spelled out the name "Puget Sound Power & Light Co."[3] (See figures 9a and 9b, day and night views of the billboard.)

In the 1940 census, after a decade of innovations, the Census Bureau, thanks to its new film team, made at least four film reels, showing enumerators engaging with members of the public. The films were intended for census training centers, as from this time on, census workers attended training schools to learn the methods of the census. At this time, the Census Bureau's new Division of Public Relations had passed its first anniversary. Figure 32 shows the making of one of these films, which portrayed a young woman, at first suspicious, but then reassured about the purpose of the census.[4] Most of the stage sets for the films were urban, and the census agents, like the residents, were shown as middle-class and white. Yet another series of photos, drawn from the test-census of the year before, shows a different America: more working-class, though picturesque, like the railroad workers who live with their families in train cars (figure 27) or a family living in a trailer camp (figure 6). In these, the socioeconomic contrast between the census worker and residents is much more noticeable than in the photos with actors acting out census interviews, or in other cases posed with Hollywood stars such as Tyrone Power or Cesar Romero.[5]

Another modern tool used by the census was radio. Ironically, just when the census began to use radio as a means of publicity, the introduction into the population census of 1930 of a question, "Do you own a radio set?" was one of the most debated items on the new schedule.[6]

The radio broadcasts took several forms, such as a dialogue between a supervisor and an actor playing the role of a "Mr. Brown," who was receiving a visit from a census enumerator.[7] On 24 March 1930, census director Steuart read a text over the radio in Boston. This text, presented as last-minute instructions to field agents, in fact largely repeated the wording of "The Woman in the Home." The use of radio had begun on 1 December 1929 with a broadcast by Robert P. Lamont, secretary of commerce (the department with oversight of the census). His style was more general and impressionistic than that of census officials—referring to the enumeration of Israel by King David and evoking the army of a hundred thousand men and women who would jump into action at the bidding of the government on 1 April 1930—but his subject matter was the same.[8]

A theme frequently found in these communications—one that comes up repeatedly in census publications for the general public—is that of the immensity of the task. The theme figures mainly in terms of the ever-growing numbers of Americans, but also in the quantity of punch cards, number of days of work, numbers of sheets of paper and of ever more modern electrical machines. From this point of view, census communications bowed to popular perceptions of the dryness of statistics by condensing figures into the form of record numbers, a familiar form of quantitative data that the American public encountered daily in the business section or sports pages of its newspapers.

In 1930 the Census Bureau even commissioned a theatrical work on the census,[9] and it had a piece on the census included in the radio program *Amos 'n' Andy*, which was especially popular among African Americans. This had good results for the Census Bureau, which saw it as a success story in public education.[10] The modernity of the Census Bureau also found expression in its relations with privileged consumers of statistics, including other statisticians working in universities or in the business sector.

Two main targets formed for census officials, in varying degrees, important cogs in the smooth operation of the Census Bureau's work. First off, among the US population, specific efforts were aimed at employers and at representatives of ethnic groups, who were expected to calm any fears raised among immigrants by the official inquiries. Also, and especially important for the 1930 census, women were identified as the main contacts of census enumerators. The methods used by the Census Bureau, both for public service messages and for explaining its work to those whom it had defined as consumers of statistics (universities, Chambers of Commerce, businesses, newspapers), bear witness to the agency's rapid modernization. (We shall leave aside relations with Congress, which were not really publicity, though the arguments used were often similar.) This list from 1930 shows the targets of the Bureau's publicity division:

> Dailies and Sunday newspapers; Weeklies; Magazines; Schools; Women's clubs; National Educational Association; Chambers of commerce; Announcements by the supervisors; Publishing the schedule questions in newspapers; Reaching the foreign born population; Reaching the Negro population; Cooperation that might be sought in enumerating the Chinese and Japanese particularly on the Pacific Coast; Circulars; Radio[11]

New techniques emerged in the forty years that separated the establishment of the Census Bureau as a permanent agency, at the beginning of the twentieth century, from the 1940 census, the first one to be prepared through test-censuses and polls. The new techniques were based on the idea that the participation of the population should be systematically encouraged, partly in order to assure a high-quality census, but also in order to solidify the legitimacy of an agency whose scope had broadened considerably during this period.

Presidential Proclamations: From the General Public to Ethnic Minorities

The widest public outreach was achieved by the presidential proclamations that announced the date of each census and recalled its origins in the Constitution. The text of the proclamations attested to the importance of the census, and to its obligatory nature, and emphasized the confidentiality of the data. The proclamation explicitly stated that the purpose of the census was strictly statistical, and that no individual would experience repercussions because of their responses, whether it was a matter of taxes, military obligations, jury duty, schooling, or immigration. The proclamation itself would warrant only limited attention, since it was an ongoing practice and an unvarying text, but its distribution offers a wealth of information. The means of distribution involved several other agencies and actors: the postal service, which was to display the proclamation in post offices;[12] the Immigration Service, which would relay the messages; schoolteachers, who would read aloud to their classes a text prepared by the Census Bureau; and more generally, prominent individuals. In the terms of a message of January 1920 from Samuel L. Rogers, director of the 1920 census, it was a question of soothing groundless fears and public concern, especially on the part of those who were of foreign birth or foreign origin, while acquainting the public in advance with the questions to be posed and the goals of the census. After explaining the census questions, the text of the message ended with this slogan, in capitals: "Uncle Sam needs the help of every loyal citizen in this gigantic task. He is counting on you."[13]

The size of the print run of the proclamation supports this impression of enormous scale: nearly 400,000 in 1920, but only a little more than 200,000 in 1930, issued in twenty-three languages.[14]

The total number was reduced by half, but the proportion of different languages remained stable from 1920 to 1930: one finds the same languages in 1920 and 1930, with almost the same respective proportions. There was no diminution of the ethnic factor, although in 1930 census officials believed that the immigration laws had put an end to the phenomenon of migration, but rather a more limited use of proclamations in favor of other methods. Early on, the Census Bureau expected to print for the 1930 census one proclamation for every fifty persons who had given a native language other than English on the 1920 census. This would have meant 212,500 proclamations in foreign languages, instead of the 196,500 in 1920, but the print runs were cut in half for the entirety.[15]

The biggest groups were Germans (2,267,000 speakers), Italians (1,624,000), Jews[16] (1,091,000), and Poles (1,077,000).[17] In 1920, the US government did not have proclamations distributed in German, while in 1930, the Census Bureau had 17,000 proclamations printed for this largest linguistic minority of the nation. This came about in the years following World War I, which had seen a notable decrease in German-language schools, and more generally a repression and self-censoring of public expressions of German culture.

Thus there was relative stability in the proportion of proclamations in foreign languages, to which should be added the Spanish-language proclamations used in Puerto Rico and Panama. That these translations should total as many as the English-language proclamations shows a real effort by the Census Bureau to reach ethnic groups. If in 1930 one proclamation was printed for roughly every hundred speakers of a foreign language, we can calculate that the 100,000 proclamations printed in English for an English-speaking population of more than 100 million inhabitants gives a figure of one proclamation per thousand inhabitants.[18] Clearly, the English-speaking population were exposed to publicity beyond the proclamations, especially in 1930, but this was also true for immigrant populations, which were the focus of particular concern.

This deliberate effort was justified repeatedly by census officials who, in public statements as well as in meetings or internal memos, shared their fear that the suspicions felt by immigrants might cause them to avoid taking part in the census.[19] Despite efforts by the Labor Department, of which the Immigration and

Naturalization Bureau formed part, the fear of coordinated efforts between the immigration services and census workers remained strong among the population.[20] Of course, these concerns were reinforced by an event such as the raid organized by Attorney General Palmer and the immigration service, which took place the evening of 2 January 1920: Police arrested several thousand presumed "radicals" and "communists," mostly foreigners. The purpose of the raids was to provide the Labor Department with evidence to expel undesirables, such as the activist Emma Goldman. The census had begun that very day, 2 January.[21] If it had been made known to the public, the cooperation of the census with the Federal Bureau of Investigation, and then, after the Japanese attack on Pearl Harbor, with the War Relocation Authority, in violation of the rules of confidentiality (which existed in spirit if not in letter), would surely have strengthened people's suspicions.

This was why census officials urged their local executives to organize meetings in foreign languages in immigrant neighborhoods, and why they themselves contacted the press and representatives of ethnic communities to promote the census.[22] Census employees in Washington drew up lists of prominent members of ethnic communities in major cities, to whom they sent the text of the presidential proclamation for distribution.[23] The ethnic press largely took up these appeals, most often not by faithfully translating the proclamation, but rather by adapting them to their own goal of ethnic patriotism. Census officials often encouraged this sort of attitude, which facilitated the work of census agents. An example is the appeal in Norwegian made by a lawyer of Norwegian origin, mentioned earlier, which was well received by the Census Bureau in spite of its overt opposition toward the government.[24]

Other actors also intervened, such as academics, who expected the census to provide a wealth of statistics on minorities. The introduction in 1930 of a new racial classification, "Mexican," grouping Mexican Americans and Mexican immigrants, led Paul S. Taylor, an economics professor at the University of California, leading expert on the Mexican labor migration (and the future husband of photographer Dorothea Lange), to write to the director of the census to recommend that he contact Alonso S. Perales, who was viewed as a promising link to the Mexican community.

We see that between 1910—when a Jewish organization in Chicago published in a Yiddish-language newspaper an appeal to readers to give Yiddish as their native tongue in order to increase the statistics for the size of the Jewish population—and 1930, the ethnic stakes of the census in no way diminished. We can even see greater involvement by representatives of ethnic communities in carefully planned publicity campaigns in advance of the census, while at the beginning of the century the ethnic press had generally limited itself to publication of the population figures for different communities.

The Census Bureau visually expressed this representation of society with a large poster published for the 1940 census, in which the English-language proclamation, signed by President Roosevelt, takes center place, bearing the seal of the United States, and surrounded by translations in twenty-two languages in smaller type (see figure 3).[25]

The Experience of Agents in the Field: A Perception of Immigrants Contrary to the Prejudices of Census Directors

While census officials emphasized the wariness of immigrant communities, the reports of census workers and supervisors tell a different story—of how frequently enumerators were surprised by the absence of any particular difficulties and by the warm welcome they received on their visits to the households of immigrant families. Pieces of this story show up in newspapers, often in picturesque form, as well as in reports from the field archived by the Census Bureau.[26]

In Chicago in 1910, a local daily related, among a number of anecdotes about the progress of the current census, an encounter between a well-intentioned enumerator and a woman of the German neighborhood of the city's South Side. The census agent spoke to her in bad German, asking her, "Hast du ein Mann?" The woman replied in perfect English, adding, "I was born in Germany, but that's no reason I'm not a good American now."[27]

The regional director of the census in Chicago was preoccupied with ethnic minorities, partly because of the practical problems they presented, and partly because of the attitude of the immigrants, to whom he attributed a different understanding of institutions and a different perception of anything official ("officialism"). The Census Bureau had the foresight in certain cases to provide its agents with the assistance of an interpreter, who was bound by the same rules of confidentiality.[28] Interpreters increased costs, so the Census Bureau as far as possible discouraged the supervisors from using them. The preferred solution was to recruit agents who spoke the language most commonly used in a given district; this solution also had the advantage of sending into those neighborhoods people who would tend to inspire confidence. Thus, in Chicago's Chinatown in 1920, census supervisor Gaynor hired two Chinese students from the University of Chicago as censustakers.[29] In the same city, in 1910, census supervisor Hotchkiss had reached out to people of foreign origin to conduct the census in predominantly ethnic neighborhoods. For example, in the Fourteenth and Fifteenth Wards, censustakers of Polish origin replaced colleagues unable to get results in this majority Polish area.[30]

The recruitment of agents who shared the origins of the majority group in a neighborhood was a well-established practice, but it was limited in 1930 by a ban on the hiring of census workers who were not US citizens. For the 1910 census, the Justice Department, responding to a request for clarification made by the Commerce Department, had explicitly stated that only those agents employed by the Census Bureau in Washington, in positions with a public function, were affected by the condition of nationality, and that it did not apply to census workers hired on a temporary basis by the supervisors and not by a federal office.[31] In 1920, non-naturalized immigrants had been used in certain areas, with the endorsement of the director. But the law for the 1930 census prohibited this practice, which had been in effect for supervisors since 1920.[32] In some parts of the Southwest, census agents were recruited from the Mexican American population, but this was a case of national origin, since most of them were US citizens.[33]

When censustakers did not belong to the communities they enumerated, they often shared the usual prejudices about the special difficulty of enumerating immigrants and their children. However, the archives abound in stories of experiences that contradicted those assumptions, of which we shall cite a few examples here.

In 1930, Anna Lee Puckett, who enumerated district 63-9 of Burgettstown, Pennsylvania, noted: "The foreign element, as a rule, in this district are good citizens and especially splendid to work with are the natives of Jugoslavia." Cathryne E. Foley handled the neighboring district 63-12, in Canonsburg: "I found a few adverse in answering the questions [on occupation and employment], this is to be confined to Americans only. I found to my own interest that a great many of the foreign and negro element of our community are interested in education, music, and are becoming very apt in their own line of work."

Some of the censustakers in Pennsylvania, when asked by their supervisor to provide a report on the progress of their work in the field, went so far as to paint a highly flattering portrait of foreigners in general.[34] This is also what appears in testimony from California:

> There were white folks unable to look another human being in the face; dark-skinned folks whose honor would make any enumerator proud to add their name to the government record of the population. . . .
>
> The Chinese were splendid. No enumerator could fail to note with pride the Americanization of many of our foreign born population. The Chinese live their lives isolated from their white neighbors—yet nowhere were more conspicuous examples found of their adaptation to the new country than among these.[35]

Yet other accounts were much more critical about foreigners, precisely on this same point, Americanization, with many faulting them for their high proportion of foreign nationals and their lack of interest in naturalization.

Some were neither hostile nor full of praise, but simply noted that the foreigners posed no particular problems. Some made use of the opportunity to issue good-conduct awards to the foreigners with whom they came in contact; one such was George H. Wolkinson, who enumerated district 63-20 of Carroll, Pennsylvania:

> The foreign element seem to be rather an intelligent class. I don't think there are any radicals among them, at least that is my opinion after talking to them and they are pretty near all citizens.[36]

Some census agents stated that they had received a better welcome in immigrant areas or black neighborhoods than in wealthy households, where they were often treated with disrespect and received little cooperation.[37] Still, it is hard to imagine a Census Bureau publicity campaign that would have substituted, for the traditional complaint about the difficulty of enumerating immigrants, a paragraph on the arrogance of respectable white middle- and upper-class society and how it needed to be prepared for the censustaker's arrival.

A report from the Field Division on the progress of the 1930 census, which occupies a middle position between the accounts of individual agents and official census communications, states:

> As concerned nationalities, the reports indicated that Jewish people generally were the most cooperative; Italians, Swedes, Chinese, American Negroes, and various foreign-born peoples, the most difficult. Servants, working people, and small business families apparently were the most cooperative; the wealthier classes of people cooperated very reluctantly. As concerned marital conditions, married people seemed to be more cooperative, than those unmarried. American people were reported as being both the easiest and the hardest to enumerate, as were also educated people. Of all classes of people, however, the Southern-born American Negro seemingly was the most difficult to enumerate.[38]

Accounts of willing cooperation with the census on the part of immigrants should not obscure another aspect of the Census Bureau's relations with the foreign population: the use of census agents and their work against foreign nationals suspected of dangerous activities.

The Census Bureau against Foreigners
and Bad Americans

All the census laws of the period, as well as the presidential proclamations and many Census Bureau communications, note that all census staff were required to maintain confidentiality, whether censustakers, the interpreters who sometimes accompanied them and who were also bound by oath, or workers in the Washington offices who handled personal data. The confidentiality clauses themselves became stricter between the turn of the century and 1940. However, Census Bureau archives contain numerous examples of personal information being provided to the FBI or to other government agencies, which testify to what was at best a flexible interpretation of the law.

In 1917 and 1918, the Census Bureau received numerous requests from individuals and institutions for information about the population of German origin of this or that place or region. Typically, the Census Bureau responded by providing statistics.[39] In the context of the war effort, the Census Bureau, like other government agencies, had been placed at the service of "War Work." Given its unique competence in the statistical domain, the Census Bureau was charged with compiling statistics toward the size ranking of groups for purposes of conscription. To the same end, it also issued registration cards, which included nationality and, for race, had a corner that was to be torn off if the person was of African origin: obviously, this would help in planning for the assignment of troops into segregated regiments.[40] But at the same time, in certain cases, the Census Bureau informed local authorities of the age shown in the 1910 census for individuals suspected of attempting to avoid conscription.[41] In 1917 and 1918, we find reports compiled by the Census Bureau on job candidates for the census who were suspected of pro-German sympathies. And when the Census Bureau received letters denouncing someone as a possible spy, it typically handed them over to the Justice Department for investigation.[42]

More serious was the Census Bureau's action in transmitting to the Bureau of Investigation (predecessor of the FBI) denunciations made by census agents themselves, who thus played a role as police informers. In particular, in 1920 the Census Bureau passed on names of "bolsheviki" and those of Wobblies, or members of the Industrial Workers of the World (IWW).[43]

In addition, on several occasions the Census Bureau received Justice Department approval to interpret the laws on the confidentiality of the census in directions that would have shocked the defenders of civil liberties as well as all those who had heard the repeated assurances of the census director on this subject.

For example, in 1917, on the subject of the communication by the director regarding the age of residents for purposes of identifying conscription status, the prohibition—which affected all census workers—on revealing such information without permission from higher up did not apply, precisely because it was the director of the census himself, and not an agent, who made the communication. For the Justice Department, there was no contradiction between the act of transmitting this information and the text of the presidential proclamation.[44] If various agencies turned to the Census Bureau for information on the age or nationality of certain inhabitants, it was because of the lack, at this date, of a complete registry of the population or of identity papers. The wartime context favored this porosity of personal data from the census, but the immediate postwar context and the Red Scare did so just as much, as shown by the decision of the attorney general in February 1920, just five weeks into the census, while the schedules were just beginning to be counted. This decision authorized the Census Bureau to provide the Bureau of Investigation with information from the manuscript schedules in order to ascertain the citizenship status of individuals against whom expulsion procedures were being instigated. The decision noted that the wording of the relevant clause of section 33 of the census law of 1919 did not prohibit the communication of information, except for prejudicial uses, thereby freeing the census director from any consequences of divulging information.[45]

The issue of keeping lists of foreigners, called alien registration, directly concerned the Census Bureau, since it was, in principle, the only institution that held information on the place of birth and citizenship status of all inhabitants. The bureau's activity in this area fell after this episode, only to become an issue once again on the eve of the 1940 census, with the bureau about to become involved in a war as it never had been before.

In June 1939, a request from the State Department suggested that in preparing the 1940 census, the censustakers should collect information on the foreign population potentially subject to expulsion. The Census Advisory Committee rejected the possibility, noting that confidentiality and public trust in complete discretion concerning the responses were the essential conditions for the success of the census, the principle that had been consistently enunciated by the Census Bureau since the turn of the century. We have already seen that public trust was a major goal of the Census Bureau's modernization since the 1930 census.[46] A resolution along these lines, charging censustakers with collecting information on the legality of the length of stay of foreigners, had been debated by the committee in May 1939. Dedrick, who had been looking for a precedent, noted that in 1870, when the census became involved in collecting data on persons deprived of the right to vote, the results had been of very poor quality.[47] The committee unanimously expressed its disapproval and moved that the secretary of commerce make every effort to block this proposal.[48] In the course of 1940, the Census Bureau, like other agencies, had begun investigations of, and in some cases had dismissed, census workers suspected of disloyalty to the United States, or of being communist or Nazi sympathizers.[49]

But the darkest episode of the Census Bureau's active participation in discrimination against and persecution of US residents was certainly the deportation of Americans of Japanese origin after the Japanese attack on Pearl Harbor. For a long time the Census Bureau tried to minimize its active role in the roundups and denied having seriously violated its rules of confidentiality. However, Margo Anderson and William Seltzer have shown that this official history was not based on evidence but rather on statements made by census officials following the war, repeated since in various reports, each using its predecessors as the source.[50] The facts have not yet been clearly established regarding the systematic communication of names of Japanese individuals to the military authorities,[51] but census director J. C. Capt was ready to jump on it as early as January 1942:

> We're by law required to keep confidential information by individuals. But in the end, if the defense authorities found 200 Japs missing and they wanted the names of the Japs in that area, I would give them further means of checking individuals.[52]

At this time, about a month after the attack on Pearl Harbor, the Census Bureau had already given the Army statistics at the most detailed level short of personal data, that of the finest geographical divisions, on the order of one or more census tracts of houses ("tract level"). Two days after the Japanese attack, on 9 December 1941, the Census Bureau had published its first report on the Japanese population in the United States, and had then provided the Army with more detailed data. The Army had no need to identify all the individuals precisely, but in the following month, Calvert Dedrick was detached by the Census Bureau to the Western Defense Command, at first to help with alien registration, and then to conduct detailed planning for the forcible evacuation of Japanese Americans.

Foreigners were targeted by the census not only collectively, when statistics fed the discourse of immigration restriction, but also individually, when, in times of crisis, the Census Bureau participated actively in the suppression of subversive activities and the expulsion of suspicious foreigners, even their forced relocation to internment camps, in the case of Americans of Japanese origin. Anderson and Seltzer believe that without the assistance and the skills of Census Bureau staff, the identification and detention of Americans of Japanese origin on the Pacific coast would have been much more difficult to set in motion, even if there remains some uncertainty over the exact degree of the bureau's active collaboration in the effort. It is henceforth clear that the Census Bureau supplied statistics that were used in planning the roundups; the question that remains is whether it also provided data that named individuals or were sufficiently exact, such as addresses, to identify them. Anderson and Seltzer have also shown the link between the detention of Japanese Americans and the Census Bureau's work in alien registration. Here there was a break with the immediate prewar years, when the census opposed alien registration, or when experts even in 1940 saw the dichotomy between the census in a democracy, confidential and worthy of public trust, and censuses in authoritarian regimes.[53] This event was an extreme manifestation of the close tie between population statistics and the political.

Epilogue

The Fortunes of Census Classifications (1940–2000)

At the end of this study, which has tracked the transformations of categories used in the US census from its creation in 1790 to 1940, it is of some interest to reread the period of the past half-century in the light of this history. During the 1930s, three factors combined to contribute to the decline in the importance of questions of population categories: the restriction of immigration, which weakened the polemical and political dimension of statistics of origin; the coming up of a new generation of statisticians whose research and interests were more technical; and the context of the Great Depression, which made economic statistics the ground where means, ideas, and policy demands converged.

Population statistics, once the top division of the federal agency, lost its luster, even within the Census Bureau itself. And yet, while the long period from the earliest censuses to 1940 still required clarification in many respects, the activity of the census during the second half of the twentieth century is better known. On the one hand, the Bureau of the Census itself published for every census an administrative history (called *Procedural History*) of the census; on the other hand, sociology and political science adopted the goal and, since the 1960s, have focused considerable attention on categories of race and ethnicity, especially the so-called "ethnoracial pentagon"—the five major categories defined by the federal administration in 1977 as those which government agencies should utilize.[1] The 1965 immigration law, putting an end to the system of national origins and authorizing immigration from regions that had been excluded since 1924, profoundly affected the discourse on, and studies of, immigration, whose share of the population reached once again, at the end of the twentieth century, its historical levels of the 1900s. This law marked a turning point in the history of immigration, as well as in the history of the census, because immigration and the racial and ethnic composition of the US population would once again become an important preoccupation of the census. That immigration in recent decades has become majority non-European, originating from Asia and the Americas, has brought about a redirection of the discourse on race and immigration, different from that at the beginning of the twentieth century. Scholarly language in the United States since the 1970s has effectively tended to reserve the term *ethnicity* for descendants of European immigrants, and that of *race* for groups constituted as racial minorities. For its part, however, the census in 1970 chose to take a new and much discussed route, consisting of defining one unique "ethnic group," Hispanic or Latino, while immigrant origins were defined as ancestry. Before returning to this point in more detail, we need to explain how the census's renewed interest in immigrants developed.

The shifts of the questions on the birth of parents and native language between 1910 and 1940 continued into the postwar period. In 1950, the census eliminated the question on native language, only to reintroduce it in 1960. At that time it was one of the questions posed to a 25 percent sample, along with the birth country of the parents, but the question on language was only to be asked of immigrants, who were asked what language they spoke before coming to the United States. Implicitly, persons born in the United States were assumed to have English as their native language, and asking the question in this way automatically produced this impression: the 1940 census had asked one person in fifteen about the language spoken in their early childhood, whether they were immigrants or American-born, which made it possible to recognize speakers of other languages who had been born in the United States; in 1960, however, they became invisible.

Racial categories had not changed much, as witness the repeated instruction to classify Puerto Ricans, Mexicans, and other people of Latin ancestry as white, unless they were "definitely Indian, or of some other race." It was specified that these terms were not racial categories, just as it was for Europeans, especially southern Europeans, and nationalities of the Near East ("*Italians, Portuguese, Poles, Syrians, Lebanese, and other European and Near Eastern nationalities*—These are not racial descriptions; mark 'White' for such persons.").[2] Asian Indians were to be classified as "Other," and "Hindu" was to be noted opposite. We can see how the conceptual fluidity between nationality and race or color perpetuated itself, while the successful mobilization of Mexican American associations in 1936–37 continued to bear on the census classification, and the term *Hindu*, referring to the religion of Hinduism, continued to be used as a racial category. In distinction from other Asian "races," *Hindu* was "Other," although the census still printed on the schedules, under the heading "Color or Race," "Japanese, Chinese, Filipino, Hawaiian, Part-Hawaiian, Aleut, Eskimo, etc." Nonetheless, the census showed a growing level of interest in those whom it called "of Latin descent": thus a supplementary question on place of birth was to be asked of all the inhabitants of the state of New York. There were three possible responses: United States, Puerto Rico, or elsewhere.[3] Two important changes would be introduced in the

1970 census: self-identification, and the creation of a question on "Spanish" origin, posed to 20 percent of households, which would later be consolidated into the question on Hispanic ethnicity.

It is clear that, symbolically, the passage from observation to self-identification is significant, from the moment when people began to fill out the schedules themselves. Nonetheless, the consequences were limited. On the one hand, it was specified in 1970 that the enumerator was to complete blanks by observation when necessary, and the census assumed that all the members of the same family living under the same roof were of the same race, except when the enumerator had information to the contrary. On the other hand, analysis of the division of the American population by race in the decades that followed the changeover shows that few Americans used the choice that was offered to them. We conclude from this that nearly two centuries of imposition of official racial norms had produced a great deal of inertia, especially since inhabitants of the United States had many other opportunities to identify themselves or to be identified racially on official forms. Finally, the most important change affecting racial categories would be the possibility, offered in 2000, of identifying oneself with more than one race.

The 1970 schedules proposed the classical choices under the heading "Color or Race," but the possibility of choosing "Other" and of writing out the response led the census to specify in its instructions to agents the manner of reclassifying the responses to this question, which was posed to all inhabitants: responses of "Chicano," "La Raza," "Mexican American," "Moslem," or "Brown" were to be corrected to "White," while "Brown (Negro)" was to be changed to "Negro or Black."[4] A 5 percent sample were asked, when birth was foreign, whether the person was naturalized or not, and the year of arrival in the United States, and then a sample of 15 percent were asked if a language other than English was spoken in their childhood home (the suggested choices were Spanish, French, German, and Other—To be completed). The greatest upheaval, however, was the introduction of a question addressed to the 5 percent sample:

> Is this person's origin or descent—*(Fill one circle)* Mexican. Puerto Rican. Cuban. Central or South American. Other Spanish. None of these.[5]

While the census persisted in considering that Mexican origin was not a race, the ancestry that was called "Spanish or Hispanic" in the 1980 census and was a question posed to all inhabitants was the object of a separate category, somewhat parallel to racial categories, since each inhabitant was supposed to say if they belonged to the group or not. The invention of the "Hispanic" category has been the subject of a number of studies, which have frequently emphasized the complexity of this device and the inadequacy felt by many people when faced with a question supposedly separate from the question on race but in fact closely linked to it: there is a strong positive correlation between a response of "Other" on the question on race, and a "Yes" response to the question on Hispanic ancestry.[6] This new category created in 1970 has been extended to all federal government statistics. While Mexican American organizations actively opposed their group's classification as a separate race in the 1930s, in the context of the 1970s, this new visibility was generally well received by associations representing the "Hispanic" population of the United States. The lifting of this resistance can be explained by the fact that this category was not a "race" in the census, and that the civil rights legislation of 1964 had made segregation illegal and had brought about mechanisms for affirmative action, some of which were indexed to the group sizes identified by the census. Nonetheless, it seems that political interest was not the principal motive, but rather, as for other groups in the past, a form of symbolic recognition that would peak at the beginning of the twenty-first century when census figures would make the Hispanic minority—a term encompassing great heterogeneity—the largest in the country, ahead of African Americans.[7]

Self-identification became the norm for the Hispanic category following a congressional resolution of 1976, and for racial categories starting in 1980. Instructions explicitly excluded observation and specified that the enumerator record the race with which the persons most identified themselves. If several answers were given, the race of the mother was to be retained, or failing that, the first term given.[8] One might see this as the first step away from the "one drop rule," but one that did not necessarily reflect itself in the results, with this norm having been so thoroughly internalized both by census agents and by inhabitants, as would be seen in 2000.

The evolution toward more open questions, giving more room for the perceptions that people had of themselves, can be seen also in the creation in 1980 of an "Ancestry" category. This question, posed to a sample of 50 percent in cities and 17 percent in rural areas, is interesting in that it does not relate specifically to immigrants, but rather to all inhabitants, who were asked to affiliate themselves with a group of origin. The schedule suggested nationalities, but also "Afro-American," which led to categories of ethnicity, in the sense of an ancestral community. It was possible to give multiple answers to this question, as opposed to the question on race. The question that preceded this one on the schedule concerned mastery of English. It thus appears that the census, at the end of the twentieth century, in a context where immigration had greatly increased and where ethnicity had once again become a significant concern, was repeating its inquiries from the end of the previous century—with the important difference that self-identification had replaced information on place of birth and the language spoken by parents, which had in turn brought about a great variability of responses.

The 1990 census barely shifted this equilibrium, while the following census in 2000, after long negotiations, put its blessing on recognition of multiracial families by offering, for the first time, the possibility of checking off more than one race on the schedule.[9] This was an unprecedented break with the American tradition of racial classification, the full effect of which has not yet been felt.

The choice that was eventually adopted, of making it possible to check off more than one race, was preferred over the option of creating a multiracial category, because it allowed persons who checked off "White" and another race to be reallocated to the minority group in order to produce reference groups for public policy that would not be reduced in size. The argument was thus reformulated by opposing majority and minorities, but it also appears as a last avatar of the "one drop rule," in reverse, since henceforth it would be organizations representing minorities who would demand that their visibility be maximized by the statistical device. In the case where a person checked off the box "White" and a box corresponding to another race, he or she would be added to the total of persons who had checked off only that other race—which in theory would ensure the size stability of minorities. There was considerable inertia in the way Americans used this new possibility that had been given them, especially African Americans. Just 2.3 percent of the total population of the United States chose to check two boxes, and if we add those who checked off three or more, the total is still less than 2.6 percent.[10]

Portrayed as the most important break in the history of racial categories in the census, this option can nonetheless be tied into the long history of the US census's attempts to take special account of racial mixing. To the extent that the question makes it possible to account for the growing number of mixed marriages, it is indeed something new. However, given that the African American population—although it had a long experience with mixing—is the one that made least use of this option, sometimes seen as a danger for the group, the new question might also be interpreted as another addition, whose function is to document a newly widespread phenomenon, rather than an upheaval in the entire system of categories. Stated differently, it seems that this change affects mainly new entrants (immigrants or young people) more than the population with a longer experience of American racial classifications, whether imposed or arising from self-identification. In any case, we can reasonably expect that the number of those who identify with more than one race, like the number of those who do not see themselves reflected in the official races of the census, will continue to increase.

Conclusion

What does the study of the racial and ethnic categories of the US census mean from the perspective of the *longue durée*? At a time when it has become trite to state that race and its categories are social constructs, it seemed that there was a need for a close examination of the construction and use of these categories. In order to reject the simplistic opposition that would see the categories of the past as univocal and rigid and as a transparent reflection of the system of racial domination, this historical depth is useful, as we ourselves are living in a period where the porosity of categories seems to be the dominant paradigm for the present, but not for the past. If one wanted to base this shift between the distant past and the more recent past on the mobilization of actors—characteristic of the period that one could define schematically as following upon the postwar Civil Rights movement—the distinction would not be relevant because, although rare, these mobilizations can be observed, or their traces discerned, as early as the second half of the nineteenth century. While viewing these categories as fundamentally political, in that they organize society and are the object of conflict and negotiation, this study has tried to emphasize the wheels of the machinery of the census rather than the intentionality of the policy decisions that tightly bound it from its origins in the Constitution until today.[1]

Shifting the emphasis from the intentionality of policy to the broad spectrum of actors in this history, allows us to show how these categories of race and origin bear upon a distinctively American national history. The concepts of race, ethnicity, and national origin need to be contextualized and translated, as the comparison with classification practices in other areas of policy demonstrates.[2] The strong national specificity of the US census categories is especially visible when we include the territories that eventually became American: Hawaii, Puerto Rico, the US Virgin Islands. These are the only regions for which census archives retain traces of the challenging of racial categories, of the very principle of racial statistics, but these territories were never integrated into the story of the construction of the nation through population statistics. American public debates before World War II on the mainland show no challenge to the principles of classification by race, and it is noteworthy that the only case where a group obtained modification of its classification— Mexicans in 1936—happened outside the place where the classifications were promulgated, that is, Congress. It is possible that Mexicans in the United States, beyond the risk that accompanied their classification as other than white, were able to take up their position so effectively to the extent that they were not all of American culture—that is, because they knew that other racial classifications were possible, for example, in Mexico, and that those who waged this campaign saw the place occupied by each category in the general economy of racial classifications and in the particular context created by the United States, *a fortiori* the southern states. This distance with respect to the naturalism and essentialism of the categories is much more visible from without than within. The forms of resistance that we have seen expressed in the new possessions to the imposition of American racial categories shows how entirely these were the product of a time and a place. This is an important dimension of any comparative study, and helps explain why, in the final years of the twentieth century, it was generally political conservatives who called for eliminating race in the census, while the spokespersons for minorities and more broadly the partisans of redistributive public policy wanted the categories maintained, both as a tool for measuring social inequalities and as the criterion for allocation of certain resources.[3]

This study takes up the last half century only marginally, but it should be read as an implicit comparison with the present,[4] since reflection on categories is so much a historical focus of today. Unlike authors such as Matthew Frye Jacobson, who holds that the census, in producing statistics that make it possible today to make up for past discrimination, has partly redeemed the racism of its former classifications, it can be argued that this opposition between past and present obscures more than illuminates the history of the census.[5] In showing that a certain number of attributes of modernity can be traced back through archival evidence, this study tried at once to historicize the categories of today and show the contribution of an approach that, if it takes concepts as the main object of analysis, assumes empiricism as its principle, staying as close as possible to the past meaning of the concepts, when they were clear as well as when they were muddled. Thus, as early as the debates surrounding the 1850 census, we can see, most often in the gaps, social resistance to census classifications. The attention devoted to the spread between the results expected by those who designed the inquiries and the difficulties encountered in the field allowed for a slight shift in point of view, but a useful shift, to highlight the practices of classification rather than writing their intellectual history. Far from wanting to play down the violence of the ideology that drove them, I have tried to show the role of improvisation, chance, and circumstances and also the incoherence and contradictions inherent in the machinery of the US census, torn between the desires and constraints of experts, of agents, of politicians, and of the population itself.

A number of works have taken up the 1890 racial classifications, which distinguished, within the black population, mulattoes, quadroons, and octoroons, but these works paid no further attention to the fact that the census explicitly rejected these categories in the report that contained them, and only applied them to the extent that it was constrained to do so by law. This 1890 episode is illuminating because it shows how lawmakers were obsessed with race, but it seems equally important to highlight the census reports that spoke of the practical impossibility of applying such categories to the American population of that day, using the methods of the census. The practical reasons that led officials to decide on eliminating the mulatto category after the 1920 census strengthen the assertion that racist prejudices were shared by the successive directors but were not sufficient to explain the variations in time and space of the application of racial categories. In the same way, the opposition between observation and self-identification can be reread in the light of a long history of subtle, discreet, and often invisible negotiations over which historians are often reduced to making hypotheses on the basis of faint indications. Their traces must be followed in the archives, and statistical studies can sometimes corroborate them, as we have shown in the case of the racial statistics for Puerto Rico.

The other aim of this book was to treat the population census as a whole, and to reunite in a single study the categories of both race and ethnicity, following the approach of Brubaker, Loveman, and Stamatov, who convincingly critiqued this dichotomy and made the case for treating race, ethnicity, and nation as one.[6] To break through the rather solid walls that separate racial studies from studies of immigration and ethnicity, it helps to show how the "one drop rule" not only determined the operation of the categories of white and black, but also affected other racial categories (those the census called "minor races") and even, in a weaker form, the treatment of foreign origin. It is clear that the "one drop rule" played a much more important role in American history than the creation by the census of a category like "mixed parentage" for persons with one parent of foreign birth; however, it relates largely to factors outside of the census.

At the conclusion of this study, there is reason to question the importance of the census in the history of American racial and ethnic categories. For individuals, the census may have played only a minor, even insignificant role in the constitution of their identity. The brief visit of a censustaker every ten years, who generally (and at best) met with only one member of each household, was not of a nature to strongly affect the representation of the self, whether racial, ethnic, or other, that individuals made for themselves. It was only one moment among many others when Americans were defined by their race or their origin. From birth to death, and passing through schools, hospitals, and so on, there

were many times in the life of Americans when they had to state their race, and
the material stakes in those other cases were often clearer than with the census.

If one thinks that it was only in 1967, with the Supreme Court ruling *Loving
v. Virginia*, that the last US states had to allow interracial marriages, a prohibition
that rested on birth certificates where race figured prominently, we see on the
contrary the strength of registry documents, with legal status, in people's lives.
From this point of view, the census appears more as the expression of one aspect
of complex situations, as illustrated in the variations in responses or racial iden-
tifications across the life of a single individual, possibly even in the course of a
single day, than as a privileged space for the construction of individual identity.
On the other hand, if I have chosen to emphasize questions of race, ethnicity,
and national origin, we must recall that for census officials, if not for the publicity that prepared the public for the censustaker's visit, the expected difficulties
lay elsewhere—especially in the proverbial reluctance of women to reveal their
age, and in questions concerning inheritance or income. I have remarked how
such questions occupied the attention of commentators, even though in the case
of women's ages, what we know from field reports systematically contradicts
the stereotype: this problem was entirely invented, but the theme still enjoyed
a certain degree of popularity. This public discourse also expresses a particular
attitude, and the fact that classifications of origin were generally presented as
non-problematic can likewise be read as a construct.

The main function of the census was not to assign characteristics to individuals, but to assign individuals to groups, and this is why we should take an interest
in the study of categories, which were precisely the means used for the purpose.
This is even more true because individuals themselves were largely ignorant of
the way they were classified; it was mainly a practice of observation or of later
corrections of which people were unaware. Few of them tried, even when they
had the right to do so, to find out what the census had recorded about them.
Those who did, based on archival evidence, contacted the Census Bureau for
proof of age or veteran status, for lack of other sources. But nowhere do we find
evidence of people asking the census about their race or their country of birth,
questions which we may imagine would have seemed equally absurd to them,
given the widespread belief that except for occasional errors, the census faithfully reflected what inhabitants reported. The mistrust of inhabitants with regard
to the census, though real, did not affect personal identification.

The mobilization of organizations to get the census to modify the classification of groups is evidence *a contrario* of the importance of collective classifications. We can also interpret these mobilizations as an expression of confidence
in the possibility of an adequate classification of everybody, provided the census heard the demands. What these mobilizations show, though there was
often no tangible benefit at stake, is the symbolic importance of the place of

groups in the classification system, which sometimes went in the direction of an established hierarchy, as when Mexicans refused to be classed as a separate race, which would have caused them to lose the real benefits of belonging to the white race. Sometimes mobilization went in the opposite direction, like the Slavic immigrants who in 1910 got themselves distinguished by the language of the nationalities that they identified with their oppressors in Europe. To belong to a particular census category gave no rights, with the notable exception of Mexicans, for whom the racialization projected by the census was tied to other administrative practices. This case is exceptional in several respects, because it is the only US example in a century of a group challenging their racial classification. That said, the stakes were not the treatment of an individual—to know whether such and such a person was white or Mexican—but the logic behind it, that of segregation.

The different collective mobilizations underline the political role of the census. It was not a matter of indifference for the spokesperson of a given group to bill their group as the second or even the first minority in terms of numbers, a stake that for a long time remained local, but carried weight at the local level. Covert manifestations of resistance to the symbolic order of categories, such as "passing" and more generally what the census too quickly dismissed as anomalies or errors, also spoke out in their own way.

Finally, the benefit of a long-view history of the census is not only to restore the complexity of categories, but also to show how the census became a place where particular circumstances periodically intersect, which explains the addition or deletion of questions, and a site of institutional memory, visible as much in intervals and interstices as in the better-known moments of public redefinition of categories. Of necessity, statistical agencies are conservative organisms, since the comparability of data over time is their reason for being. What a historical study brings to light is the thickness of the categories that claim to be uniform. It is not so much a matter of claiming that their origin in a context of racial domination strictly determined or disqualified them, but of attempting to bring out the specific ways in which these categories carry a history that profoundly shapes them. Beyond questions of race and ethnicity, the history of the US census poses the questions of what a category is and how it is embodied in a given society.[7]

ABBREVIATIONS

Standard Abbreviations

ASA   American Statistical Association
CFLPS   The Chicago Foreign Language Press Survey
HR   House of Representatives
INS   Immigration and Naturalization Service
JAH   *Journal of American History*
NA   National Archives of the United States
NAACP   National Association for the Advancement of
          Colored People
RG   Record Group (archival series)

Abbreviations Used for Series in the National Archives of the United States

RG 29   Record Group 29, Administrative Records of the Bureau of
          the Census
RG 46   Record Group 46, Records of the U.S. Senate, Congress
RG 48   Record Group 48, Archives of the Department of the Interior
RG 85   Record Group 85, Records of the Immigration and
          Naturalization Service
RG 233   Record Group 233, Records of the US Congress, House of
          Representatives

Other Abbreviations

"Census" as author name in bibliographical citations refers to the federal agency called variously the Census Office, Census Bureau, or Bureau of the Census.

NOTES

Introduction

1. Here I am referring only to the history of demographic, economic, and social statistics, and not to the history of the mathematical developments in statistics, for which I refer readers to Gerd Gigerenzer et al., *The Empire of Chance: How Probability Changed Science and Everyday Life* (Cambridge: Cambridge University Press, 1989), and to Lorenz Kruger, Lorraine Daston, and Michael Heidelberger, eds., *The Probabilistic Revolution* (Cambridge, MA: MIT Press, 1987).

2. Cf. INSEE, *Pour une histoire de la statistique*, vol. 1: *Contributions* (1977) and vol. 2: *Matériaux*, ed. Joëlle Affichard (Paris: Economica, INSEE, 1987); Alain Desrosières, *La politique des grands nombres: Histoire de la raison statistique* (Paris: La Découverte, 1993); Theodore M. Porter, *The Rise of Statistical Thinking, 1820–1900* (Princeton, NJ: Princeton University Press, 1986); Theodore M. Porter, *Trust in Numbers: The Pursuit of Objectivity in Science and Public Life* (Princeton, NJ: Princeton University Press, 1995).

3. Cf. Benedict Anderson, *Imagined Communities: Reflections on the Origin and Spread of Nationalism*, 2nd ed. (New York: Verso, 1991), "Census, Map, Museum," 163–85.

4. Cf. Tamar Herzog, *Defining Nations: Immigrants and Citizens in Early Modern Spain and Spanish America* (New Haven, CT: Yale University Press, 2003); Emmanuelle Saada, *Les enfants de la colonie: Les métis de l'Empire français entre sujétion et citoyenneté* (Paris: La Découverte, 2007).

5. Cf. Alain Desrosières and Laurent Thévenot, *Les catégories socio-professionnelles* (Paris: La Découverte, 1988); Margo A. Conk, *The United States Census and Labor Force Change* (Ann Arbor, MI: UMI Research Press, 1980).

6. For a comparison between the racial categories of the US census and those of the Brazilian census, see Melissa Nobles, *Shades of Citizenship: Race and the Census in Modern Politics* (Stanford, CA: Stanford University Press, 2000).

7. Porter, *Trust in Numbers*, 77.

8. Cf. Peter Kolchin, "Whiteness Studies: The New History of Race in America," *Journal of American History* 89, no. 1 (June 2002): 154–73; Theodore Allen, *The Invention of the White Race*, vol. 1: *Racial Oppression and Social Control* (London: Verso, 1994); David Roediger, *The Wages of Whiteness: Race and the Making of the American Working Class* (London: Verso, 1991); Matthew Frye Jacobson, *Whiteness of a Different Color: European Immigrants and the Alchemy of Race* (Cambridge, MA: Harvard University Press, 1998); Noel Ignatiev, *How the Irish Became White* (New York: Routledge, 1995); Michael Omi and Howard Winant, *Racial Formation in the United States from the 1960s to the 1990s* (New York: Routledge, 1994; 1st ed., 1986); Virginia R. Domínguez, *White by Definition: Social Classification in Creole Louisiana* (New Brunswick, NJ: Rutgers University Press, 1986). For the legal construction of race, see Ian F. Haney López, *White by Law: The Legal Construction of Race* (New York: New York University Press, 1996); Ariela Gross, "Litigating Whiteness: Trials of Racial Determination in the Nineteenth-Century South," *Yale Law Journal* 108, no. 1 (1998): 109–88.

9. Scholars are divided over the question of whether race is a sub-category of ethnicity or vice versa. See Werner Sollors, ed., *Theories of Ethnicity: A Classical Reader* (New York: New York University Press, 1996), xxix–xxxv.

10. Mary Lynn Washington, "White, Black, or Mulatto: A Sociological Exploration of the Meaning of Racial Classification in the United States Census of 1880" (PhD diss., Johns Hopkins University, 1997); Melissa Nobles, *Shades of Citizenship: Race and the Census in Modern Politics* (Stanford, CA: Stanford University Press, 2000); Heidi Ardizzone, "Red Blooded Americans: Mulattoes and the Melting Pot in US Racialist and Nationalist Discourse, 1890–1930" (PhD diss., University of Michigan, 1997).

11. The remarkable work of Mae Ngai responds to this lack by strongly articulating the construction of race with the racialization of immigrants; see Mae M. Ngai, *Impossible Subjects: Illegal Aliens and the Making of Modern America* (Princeton, NJ: Princeton University Press, 2004).

12. "In all parts of the country, in the East and North with its host of nationalities no less than in the more homogeneous South, the Negroes stand out because of their 'visibility.' They are not the only 'visible minority,' but they are the most visible one. In this respect, they somewhat resemble new immigrants, who invariably constitute the most 'audible' of all minorities and therefore are always the most likely to arouse xenophobic sentiments. But while audibility is a temporary phenomenon, rarely persisting beyond one generation, the Negroes' visibility is unalterable and permanent." See Hannah Arendt, "Reflections on Little Rock," *Dissent* 6, no. 1 (Winter 1959): 47.

13. This is also the case for Patricia Cline Cohen (*A Calculating People: The Spread of Numeracy in Early America* [Chicago: University of Chicago Press, 1982]), who devotes a chapter to the question of statistics about blacks in the 1840 Census; for Diana Magnuson ("The Making of a Modern Census: The United States Census of Population, 1790–1940" [PhD diss., University of Minnesota, 1995]), who discusses the implication of the census under the direction of Francis A. Walker in debates on the "new immigration"; and for Margo Anderson (*The American Census: A Social History* [New Haven, CT: Yale University Press, 1988]), who has shown the political stakes in demographic questions and official population figures.

14. I have excluded the censuses of Cuba and the Philippines from my field of study, even when they were conducted by agents detached from the Census Bureau, because of the transitory character of American domination in those places.

15. A notable exception to this is the article of Virginia Domínguez, who studies the American censuses in Hawaii as an imposition of national racial norms; see "Exporting US Concepts of Race: Are There Limits to the US Model?" *Social Research* 65, no. 2 (1998): 369–99. Colonial censuses were the subject of a special issue of the journal *Histoire et Mesure*, "Compter l'autre," 13, nos. 1–2 (1998).

16. The passage from identification by others to self-identification for racial affiliation did not greatly modify the distribution of sizes, which the continuing weight of the norms developed during the period of our study suggests. In contrast, several studies have shown the great volatility of responses on ethnic affiliation: see Tom W. Smith, "Ethnic Measurement and Identification," *Ethnicity* 7, no. 1 (March 1980): 78–95.

Chapter 01

1. "The first census of the entire United States was taken in 1790, or nearly ten years before the first census in any European country, except Sweden." Census, *A Century of Population Growth* [1909], 2. The use of "Census" as an author refers to official publications of the US Census under its various names, which changed over the years. See the section "Official Census Publications in Chronological Order" in the Bibliography at the end of this book. The census referred to is that of Spain in 1798. France and England each had its first national census in 1801.

2. Anderson, *American Census*, 9–10.

3. The history of apportionment, in its political as well as technical and mathematical aspects, has been studied in detail by Michel Balinski and H. Peyton Young (*Fair Representation: Meeting the Ideal of One Man, One Vote* [New Haven, CT: Yale University Press, 1982]). These developments were taken up in a more general and less technical comparative study by Balinsky

(*Le suffrage universel inachevé* [Paris: Belin, 2004]). Seats were divided among the states once the figures were known, according to the method defined by law before the census. It was the state legislatures that proceeded to carve out the districts, which meant that Congress did not control all levels of the division. See also David McMillen, "Apportionment and Districting," in *Encyclopedia of the US Census*, ed. Margo J. Anderson (Washington, DC: CQ Press, 2000), 34–42.

4. Indentured servants were not free, but their servitude was temporary ("bound to Service for a Term of Years"), as opposed to that of slaves, which was permanent and hereditary. Of European origins, they were included by the census among the free population even though they did not enjoy all the rights of free persons.

5. The historian Howard Ohline saw in this compromise the alliance between the interests of slaveowners, partisans of the implicit recognition of slaves in the Constitution, and the partisans of a "popular republicanism" who wanted to inscribe in the Constitution an automatic mechanism that would prevent the formation of rotten boroughs, which, in their eyes, embodied in England the perversion of the representative principle. On this topic see Howard A. Ohline, "Republicanism and Slavery: Origins of the Three-Fifths Clause in the United States Constitution," *William and Mary Quarterly* 28 (October 1971): 563–84. On the place of slavery in the text of the Constitution, see Roger L. Ransom, *Conflict and Compromise: The Political Economy of Slavery, Emancipation, and the American Civil War* (Cambridge: Cambridge University Press, 1989), 27–33; and especially Robin L. Einhorn, "Slavery and the Politics of Taxation in the Early United States," *Studies in American Political Development* 14, no. 2 (October 2000): 156–83, and Einhorn, *American Taxation, American Slavery* (Chicago: University of Chicago Press, 2006).

6. Session of 26 December 1775, *Continental Congress*, 1775, 3, 458.

7. Session of 12 July 1776, *Continental Congress*, 1776, 5, 548.

8. Session of 25 June 1778, *Continental Congress*, 1778, 11, 650–52. Proposition of New Jersey on quotas for military service rejected by 6 nays, 3 yeas, and one divided vote. A divided vote means that the two delegates from the same colony did not vote on the same side. The proposition also envisioned conducting a census every five years to revise quotas for military service, by reason of the unequal growth of the states.

9. *Continental Congress*, 1783, 24, 191, 215. The terms crossed out in the text reveal the original formulation of the text, which was modified in the final redaction.

10. A note indicates that the corrections are in Madison's hand: ibid., 215n1.

11. Hamilton et al., *The Federalist* (New York: Modern Library, 2000), No. 54: 351. Madison commented on the first version of the text "Census," dated 25 and 26 January 1790; C. F. Hobson et al., eds., *The Papers of James Madison*, vol. 13 (Charlottesville: University Press of Virginia, 1981). See also Magnuson, "Making of a Modern Census," 12–23.

12. John Hope Franklin and Alfred A. Moss, Jr., *From Slavery to Freedom: A History of African Americans*, 8th ed. (New York: Knopf, 2003), 94. One must understand Morris and place this quote in the context of the geographic cleavage over taking slaves into account. Moreover, Morris was one of the few delegates who opposed Georgia and South Carolina on the question of slavery. Marie-Jeanne Rossignol, "La Révolution américaine et l'abolition de l'esclavage: d'une ambition des Lumières à l'échec constitutionnel fédéral (1765–1808)," in *Les empires atlantiques entre Lumières et libéralisme (1763–1865)*, ed. Federica Morelli, Clément Thibaud, and Geneviève Verdo (Rennes: Presses Universitaires de Rennes, 2009), 21–38.

13. As its name indicates, this law concerned only the first census. Each census afterward would give rise to a new law, which permits the historian, in the absence of administrative sources, to follow the evolution of the census through the debates and reports of Congress.

14. Census, *Century of Population Growth*, 43; Madison cited by Cohen, *Calculating People*, 160–61.

15. Census, *Century of Population Growth*, 50.

16. Marshals were the representatives of federal power in the states. Up to the reform of 1880, it was the marshals and their assistants, hired by senators on the basis of political patronage, who did the fieldwork. The assistants went door to door and completed the questionnaires.

17. On the procedure and legislative history of the First Census Act, see Margo J. Anderson and Stephen E. Fienberg, "The History of the First American Census and the Constitutional Language on Census-taking: Report of a Workshop," February 1999, http://lib.stat.cmu.edu/~fienberg/DonnerReports/.

18. Carroll D. Wright and William C. Hunt, *The History and Growth of the United States Census* (Washington, DC: Government Printing Office, 1900), 13–15; Anderson, *American Census*, 14.

19. Facsimiles or reconstructions of questionnaires for the censuses from 1790 to 1850 are reproduced in Census, *The Seventh Census of the United States: 1850* (Washington, DC: Robert Armstrong, 1853), xi–xiv; Census, *200 Years of US Census Taking: Population and Housing Questions, 1790–1990* (Washington, DC: Government Printing Office, 1989); and in part in Census, "Measuring America: The Decennial Censuses from 1790 to 2000" (2002); see http://www.census.gov/prod/2002pubs/pol02marv.pdf.

20. The year of the first federal census was also that of the adoption of the first law on naturalization, which reserved the possibility of acquiring US citizenship to "free white persons," a restriction that would encourage European immigrants to define themselves as whites in order to benefit from the advantages linked to the legal and social status. See Jacobson, *Whiteness of a Different Color*, 15–38.

21. Census, *Century of Population Growth*, 50.

Chapter 02

1. *Memorial of the Connecticut Academy of Arts and Sciences* and *The Memorial of the American Philosophical Society* (Philadelphia, 1800), both directed to the attention of the Senate (6th Congress, 1st session, 1799–1800). Reprinted in the volume devoted to the history of the census, US Congress, *House Reports, 41st Congress*, 2d session, Report 3, "Ninth Census," 18 January 1870, pp. 35–36, and cited in part by Wright and Hunt, *History and Growth*, 19–20. They note that the version of the memorials reprinted in the 1870 volume is somewhat different from that conserved in the archives of the State Department. Cohen, *Calculating People*, 161–64; Magnuson, "Making of a Modern Census," 15–16.

2. Census, *200 Years of US Census Taking*, 17.

3. Ibid., 18; Wright and Hunt, *History and Growth*, 20–25; Anderson, *American Census*, 18–19, 23, 25.

4. Census, *Occupations at the Twelfth Census*, 1904, xxix. See also Census, *Measuring America*, 6, for the inquiries about manufactures.

5. Cohen, *Calculating People*, 162.

6. "Ninth Census," 18 January 1870. The document reproduced in Census, *200 Years of US Census Taking*, 19, is the facsimile of a questionnaire used in Massachusetts, which differed from those used in the other states. The questionnaire does not include a place for slaves because this state no longer had any by 1790; the local census officials thus had recourse to questionnaires that did not include this category. As we have noted, not until 1830 did the federal government distribute uniform printed questionnaires throughout the country. On the rejection of slavery in the northern states, see Franklin and Moss, *From Slavery to Freedom*, 91–93.

7. The classes for 1830 were multiplied for the two groups, but without coherence. Archibald Russell, *Principles of Statistical Inquiry* (New York: D. Appleton, 1839), 46. Cited by Magnuson, "Making of a Modern Census," 26–27.

8. House of Representatives, 28 February 1839. *Congressional Globe*, 25th Congress, 3rd Session (1839), vol. 7, p. 219.

9. Clara E. Rodríguez, *Changing Race: Latinos, the Census, and the History of Ethnicity in the United States* (New York: New York University Press, 2000), 193–97.

10. Census, *Century of Population Growth*, table 17, p. 80; table 114, p. 276; and note 1, p. 276.

11. "Instructions to Marshals and Assistant Marshals. Census of 1850," in Census, *Measuring America*, 10.

12. Roediger, *Wages of Whiteness*, 55.

13. Tabulation, or the compilation of numerical results in the form of a table, was the fundamental statistical activity of these agents. For a long time it remained the only statistical activity of the Bureau of the Census. Not until 1850 were these operations removed from field agents and transferred to a Washington bureau, whose staff grew explosively. On this point, see Part II.

14. Anderson, *American Census*, 21. While in the first three censuses there was no employee in Washington charged with this task, in 1820, $925 went to pay an unknown number of workers. In 1830, their maximum number was 43, and in 1840, 28. Ibid., 242, table 2.

15. "Instructions to Marshals. Census of 1820," signed by John Quincy Adams, Secretary of State, 20 June 1820. Reproduced in part in Census, "Measuring America," 6.

16. Census, *200 Years of US Census Taking*, 20.

Chapter 03

1. Intervention in the House of Representatives, 3 March 1849, *Congressional Globe, 1848–1849*, Thirtieth Congress, 2d session, vol. 20, 638.

2. Cohen, *Calculating People*, 164–65. On the importance and the generally good quality of statistics published by journals and reviews, see Robert C. Davis, "Social Research in America Before the Civil War," *Journal of the History of Behavioral Sciences* 3 (January 1972): 73.

3. Anderson, *American Census*, 21.

4. Cohen, *Calculating People*, 168–69.

5. Robert C. Davis, "The Beginnings of American Social Research," in *Nineteenth-Century American Science: A Reappraisal*, ed. G. H. Daniels (Evanston, IL: Northwestern University Press, 1972), 157. Davis sees this as evidence that Congress considered this work superior to the official government publications. The fact that Seybert was a member of Congress surely facilitated the public financing of his work.

6. President Van Buren had personally supervised the census of 1830, as John Quincy Adams, President Monroe's secretary of state, had done for the 1820 census. It is not known why in 1839 the secretary of state decided to hire an official to take charge of the census. Cohen, *Calculating People*, 178.

7. "Skepticism about the reliability of numbers replaced the earlier naïve view that all numerical facts were sacrosanct." Ibid., 178.

8. Weaver later engaged a third assistant, one of his own sons. The account given here owes a great deal to Patricia Cline Cohen's chapter on the census of 1840 (ibid., 175–204).

9. Census, *200 Years of US Census Taking*, 21. Patricia Cline Cohen notes that among the seven categories of activity, five (mining, agriculture, commerce, manufacturing, and the learned professions) corresponded to the text of the law of 1839, while the last two, ocean navigators and navigators on rivers, can only be explained by reference to Weaver's experience in the navy. Cohen, *Calculating People*, 87.

10. The two editions are: *Compendium of the Enumeration of the Inhabitants and Statistics of the United States* (Washington, DC: T. Allen, 1841); and *Sixth Census or Enumeration of the Inhabitants of the United States, as Corrected at the Department of State, in 1840. Published, by authority of an Act of Congress, under the direction of the secretary of state* (Washington: Blair & Rives, 1841).

11. John Quincy Adams pointed out errors in the statistics on the black population of Massachusetts even before publication of the census, while reviewing the data prepared for the printed report. Davis, "Beginnings of American Social Research," 162.

12. See the 1840 questionnaire, in Census, *200 Years of US Census Taking*, 21.

13. Edward Jarvis, "Statistics of Insanity in the United States," *Boston Medical Journal* 27 (1842): 116–21.

14. Ibid., 281–82.

15. Examples drawn from pp. 5, 7, 9, and 11 of the Allen edition of 1841. The examples given here are the first ones I encountered when consulting the volume; it would have been possible to include many others for all of the northern states, like those noted by Jarvis. The Allen edition was published in 1842 and not in 1841, as printed; Thomas Allen backdated it to better

his chances in the lawsuit to obtain the official contract for publishing the federal census; see Cohen, *Calculating People*, 260.

16. A number of readers of *Hunt's Merchant's Magazine and Commercial Review* showed an interest in these figures, which confirmed popular opinion. Leon F. Litwack, "The Federal Government and the Free Negro, 1790–1860," *Journal of Negro History* 43, no. 4 (October 1958): 261–78.

17. Calhoun used the authority of the official figures in April 1844, when he defended the annexation of Texas and its entry into the Union as a slave state against European criticisms, stating that "slavery, much as it distressed whites, was actually a blessing for blacks, as the United States census demonstrated"; Cohen, *Calculating People*, 197–98.

18. "Reflections on the Census of 1840," *Southern Literary Messenger* 9 (1843): 340–52, cited by Cohen, *Calculating People*, 195.

19. Edward Jarvis, "Insanity among the Coloured Population of the Free States," *American Journal of the Medical Sciences* 7 (1845): 71–83.

20. This is the interpretation of the polemic by Patrick Gerard Feeney, who sees in it one of the practical bases of American scientific racism. Patrick Gerard Feeney, "The 200 Years' War and Counting: Power Politics and Census Controversies, 1790–1990," PhD diss., Temple University, 1994.

21. James McCune Smith, "The Influence of Climate on Longevity, with Special Reference to Insurance," *Merchant's Magazine and Commercial Review* 14 (1846): 319–29, 403–18. Robert C. Davis, who cites this article, notes that Smith had trained at the University of Glasgow. We may note that, as for Archibald Russell, European training could put one on one's guard against ideas commonly accepted as scientific in at least some parts of the United States. See also A. Deutsch, "The First US Census of the Insane (1840) and Its Use as Pro-Slavery Propaganda," *Bulletin of the History of Medicine* 15 (1944): 469–82.

22. "Memorial of a Number of Free Colored Citizens of New York, praying that the returns of the Census of 1840 may be examined and corrected, and that an Office of Registration may be established at Washington. 1844, May 25, Referred to the Com. on the Judiciary," National Archives of the United States, RG 46 (Records of the US Senate), Sen 28A-G7.2, Committee on the Judiciary, 21 May 1844 to 16 December 1844.

23. The other sources used in this petition included the doctor of the state asylum in Maine, Dr. Ray, the registers of the Lunatics Asylum at Blackwell Islands of New York County, and the registers of the Alms-Houses of New York and Philadelphia, which showed that the distortion of the figures for the insanity of blacks could also be refuted for the case of poor blacks, since these registers included only one poorhouse.

24. See note 22 above. This information would be obtained for each person twenty years old or older in 1850.

25. The American Geographical and Statistical Society was founded in New York, while the American Statistical Association was founded in Boston. The American Statistical Association, which initially attracted scientists in New England, became the national organization that brought together all the important American statisticians. The American Geographical and Statistical Society changed its name to the American Geographical Society, leaving the American Statistical Association with a monopoly on the institutional representation of statisticians.

26. "Errors in Sixth Census," House Report No. 579 (28th Congress, 1st session, 17 June 1844), cited by Edward P. Hutchinson, who notes: "It was in relation to a petition from twenty-five citizens of Pennsylvania ostensibly on the supposed errors in the 1840 census, but actually urging the petitioners' views on the slavery problem. From a quite lengthy analysis of census data the petitioners concluded that there was a natural interdependence and mutual interest between the northern and the southern states, and that with continuation of current trends of emancipation, migration, and profitability the slavery problem would eventually disappear. The brief committee reply to the petition was largely evasive, pointing out that four years after the last census it would be difficult to trace out the sources of error, and that the constructive action would be to establish a bureau of statistics to investigate the defects of past censuses and plan to improve future ones." See E. P. Hutchinson, "Population Data: Fact and Artifact,"

undated, unpublished typed manuscript, deposited at the Library of US Citizenship and Immigration Services (USCIS), Washington, DC, 31.

27. We may note that the petition by the black citizens of New York is more remarkable in showing the diffusion of a rigorous methodology of criticism of statistics than for its political impact. While Jarvis and Shattuck have received most of the credit for the success of the 1850 census over that of 1840, this petition makes no appearance in the published sources or studies of the 1840 census. The text was reproduced in part in Herbert Aptheker, *A Documentary History of the Negro People in the United States*, vol. 1 (New York: Citadel Press, 1969), 238–43.

28. Letter from Edward Jarvis to James Garfield, 19 February 1869, National Archives, RG 233 (Records of the House of Representatives), HR 41A-F 28.4, 41st Congress, Select Committee on the Ninth Census.

Part II

1. Congress, *The Congressional Globe* (Washington: Blair & Rives), 31st Cong., 1st sess., 1849–50, vol. 21, 672.

2. John R. Underwood, Whig senator from Kentucky, was one of the partisans of reform and modernization of the census, along with Sen. John Davis of Massachusetts.

3. Congress, *Congressional Globe*, 31st Cong., 1st sess., 1849–50, vol. 21, 673–74.

Chapter 04

1. In 1820 the Missouri Compromise, which Congress reached only with difficulty, made a geographic division of the United States and its western territories between a "section" north of 36 degrees of latitude, where slavery was forbidden, and another, south of this line, where slavery was tolerated. A new compromise on the geographic extension of slavery was made, with equal difficulty, in 1850. It is in this context that the question of the statistical knowledge of the slave population must be understood.

2. Opal G. Regan, "Statistical Reforms Accelerated by Sixth Census Error," *Journal of the American Statistical Association* 68, no. 343 (September 1973): 540–46.

3. *Congressional Globe, 1848–1849. Second Session of the Thirtieth Congress*, vol. 20, 1 March 1849, 627.

4. The strict interpretation of the Constitution has regularly been used in this way afterward, most recently by those opposed to correction based on sampling. The traditional defense of states' rights thus combined with short-term political calculations. For the recent period, see Margo J. Anderson and Stephen E. Fienberg, *Who Counts?: The Politics of Census-Taking in Contemporary America* (New York: Russell Sage Foundation, 1999); and Peter Skerry, *Counting on the Census? Race, Group Identity and the Evasion of Politics* (Washington, DC: Brookings Institution, 2000), 121–77.

5. *Congressional Globe*, Senate, 30th Cong., 2nd sess., 1 March 1849, vol. 20, 629. See also Anderson, *American Census*, 35.

6. The cut was not strictly geographical. Underwood represented Kentucky, and Hunter, Virginia. Margo J. Anderson relates how the Democrat majority in the Senate went after the Census Office, viewed as a Whig machine under the control of Kennedy; they eventually brought about his replacement by the southern Democrat and defender of slavery DeBow in 1853; see Anderson, *American Census*, 46–52.

7. *Congressional Globe*, Senate, 30th Cong., 2nd sess., 3 March 1849, vol. 20, 668–69.

8. Davis, "Social Research in America Before the Civil War" ; Magnuson, "Making of a Modern Census," 26, 35–37. D. L. Magnuson holds the view that the innovations of the 1850 census were not so spectacular if one considers those that had been proposed and rejected in 1839 and 1840. The model of the "modern" census, with one line per individual, was the Boston city census of 1845, conceived and carried out by Shattuck, which earned him the respect of all those who took an interest in statistics, including the future adversaries of J. C. G. Kennedy; compare J. D. B. DeBow, "Introductory Remarks," *Compendium of the Seventh Census* (Washington, DC: Nicholson, 1854), 13. See also Regan, "Statistical Reforms Accelerated by Sixth Census Error," 543, 545.

9. Census, *Seventh Census*, iv.

10. J. C. G. Kennedy's biography is not well known. Margo Anderson collected some sparse information, which she recounts in *American Census*, 36. She notes that if Kennedy was as ignorant of statistical matters as Weaver at the time of his nomination, he was able to quickly become a competent official and an ardent partisan of modernization and of the development of an American statistical apparatus, by allying himself with the experts.

11. On the essential role played by Shattuck and Russell in the conception of the schedules and the reorganization of the entire process of collection and treatment of the data, as well as on the importance of the expert community of statisticians, see Davis, "Beginnings of American Social Research," 164–65; and Anderson, *American Census*, 37, who refers to the correspondence of Chickering and Capen with Senator Davis, "Letters Addressed to the Hon. John Davis Concerning the Census . . . ," S. Misc. Doc. 64, 30th Cong., 2nd sess., 1849 (serial 553). For the biography of Lemuel Shattuck and of the best-known figures in the development of statistics in the United States in the nineteenth century (Shattuck, Jarvis, DeBow, Walker, Mayo-Smith, and Wright), see Paul J. FitzPatrick, "Leading American Statisticians in the Nineteenth Century," *Journal of the American Statistical Association* 52, no. 279 (September 1957): 301–21. Chickering seems to have been the most moderate of the experts, believing that the federal census should limit itself to the enumeration of the population, the other inquiries being left to the states. Magnuson, "Making of a Modern Census," 36–39.

12. *Congressional Globe, 31st Congress, 1st sess.*, 75, 96, 232–33, 282–92. "Report of the Census Board," 31st Cong., 1st sess., S. Ex. Doc. 38, 1850 (Serial 558). The Senate's plan for the law (S. 76) appears in *House and Senate Bills and Joint Resolutions*, 31st Cong., 1st sess., 1850. See also Anderson, *American Census*, 37–40.

13. *Congressional Globe, 31st Congress, 1st sess.*, vol. 21, 29 April 1849, 821–22.

14. Ibid., 838; italics in original.

15. The contradiction inherent in the fact that slaves were both property and persons—the Constitution called them exactly that, "all other persons"—was a source of debates and contradictory decisions by the courts, especially on the subject of the penal responsibility of slaves. For an overview of the interpretations of different southern courts and of the legal doctrine on the question during the first half of the nineteenth century, see C. N. Degler, *Neither Black nor White: Slavery and Race Relations in Brazil and the United States* (New York: Macmillan, 1971), 26–32; Mark Tushnet, *The American Laws of Slavery, 1810–1860: Considerations of Humanity and Interest* (Princeton, NJ: Princeton University Press, 1981); and Thomas D. Morris, *Southern Slavery and the Law, 1619–1860* (Chapel Hill: University of North Carolina Press, 1996). See also Robin L. Einhorn, *American Taxation, American Slavery* (Chicago: University of Chicago Press, 2006).

16. *Congressional Globe*, vol. 21, 29 April 1849, 842.

17. While it is impossible to verify this for the period, we know by comparisons from the early twentieth century that the limit for distinguishing who was black, mulatto, or white varied significantly between regions and according to the practices for recruiting agents. See chapter 14.

18. Peter Kolchin, *American Slavery, 1619–1877*, rev. ed. (New York: Hill and Wang, 2003), 44–46.

19. The names in question here are the first names of the slaves, which were generally the only way they were known. At the time of Emancipation, many slaves chose as patronyms famous names from American history, such as Jefferson or Washington. Some, however, especially those who had been freed before this date, continued to carry the family name of their master—the name that, a century later, Malcolm X and the Nation of Islam rejected as a "slave name," with "X" symbolizing the missing patronym.

20. Throughout congressional history, the committees on the census have never been sites of great power or prestige, and many of their members have distinguished themselves by their incompetence or by the extent of their ignorance of the census process. Up to the end of the century, the committees on the census were subcommittees or special committees composed in large part of recently elected members of Congress rather than more experienced members, who sat on more important committees. Moreover, the fact that these committees did not exist or were not really active except during census periods, that is every ten years, implies that one would seldom find senators, and even more rarely representatives, who had first-hand experience of the preparation of the previous census.

21. *Congressional Globe*, vol. 21, 672.

22. The practice of posting the schedules so that everyone could verify them before they were sent to Washington was usual for the first censuses. Underwood said "blacks" and not "slaves," by opposition to whites. The question concerned only slaves, since free blacks were to be enumerated on schedule no. 1, that is, with their full name. Here again, we see blacks confused with slaves.

23. *Congressional Globe*, vol. 21, 672–73. Underwood was only gradually convinced by "modernist" arguments. In 1849 Davis, who was always the Senate's enthusiastic relay for the experts, was hostile to the plan presented by Underwood, which he saw as too timid.

24. Ibid., 913, Senate, 6 May 1850. Amendments to the plan adopted by the Senate for schedule no. 2: two supplementary questions, "fugitives from the State" and "number manumitted," were adopted. This must be understood in the context of the Compromise of 1850, which reaffirmed the authority of the law on fugitive slaves, which required the states where they found refuge, even if these were non-slave states, to return them to their legal owners. The fact that this provision was being less and less respected by the free states was one of the principal grievances of the southern states.

25. "Measuring America," 11–12. In the instructions, "slaves" were opposed to the "persons" who were their owners or the free persons in the family in which they lived, which was not necessarily that of their owner. While the Constitution and the preceding census laws had spoken of slaves as "persons" ("all other persons"), this was not so much to reaffirm their humanness as to avoid mentioning slavery explicitly in the texts.

26. While schedule no. 2 had only 8 columns, schedule no. 1 had 13.

27. "Measuring America," 12.

Chapter 05

1. Indians supposedly were not counted in the census. However, a certain number of them were enumerated, and two races, Chinese and Indian, appeared on the schedules without figuring in the choices printed at the top of the columns.

2. If we except the census of 1890, which distinguished *black, mulatto, quadroon*, and *octoroon*, but without any implications, since the Census Office did not use this information and agglomerated it into a single category, *black*, for reasons which are explained in chapter 10.

3. Blacks could have Indian ancestors, but this was rarely the case for black slaves. In any case, we do find a small number of slaves enumerated in Indian tribes. We also know that some fugitive slaves found refuge among Indian tribes, but given their situation they might have tried to avoid being counted in the census. Although instructions on this point were not precise at this stage, persons issuing from a mixture of black and Indian (and white) were black or mulatto for purposes of the census. Sometimes individuals were surely classed as Indian or white if their origins were unknown or the rules were not applied strictly. For 1850 and 1860, the classification of Indians, if it existed, was still somewhat fluid in its boundaries. When the census speaks of "half-breeds," it appears to be a question of a mixture of Indian and white, while mixtures between Indians and blacks were classified as "mulattoes." See, for example, for the grouping of "half-breeds" in the zones where the black population was zero and the Indian population was significant, table 4 in Census, *Population of the United States in 1860; Compiled from the Original Returns of the Eighth Census, under the direction of the Secretary of the Interior*, by Joseph C. G. Kennedy, Superintendent of Census (Washington, DC: Government Printing Office, 1864), 29. For the population of slaves in Indian tribes in 1860, the first year when data on Indians were explicitly included, we find among the population of Indian Territory 1,998 whites, 404 "free colored," and 7,369 slaves who were the property of members of Indian tribes west of Arkansas. At this date, the enumerated population of Indian tribes was 294,431. See US Congress, *Preliminary Report on the Eighth Census, 1860* (Washington, DC: Government Printing Office, 1862), 10–11, 131, 133, 136.

4. F. James Davis, *Who Is Black? One Nation's Definition* (University Park: Pennsylvania State University Press, 1991).

5. Instructions for 1850, "Measuring America," 10, 12. The instructions for 1860 differed on one point: they proposed as another choice "Ind." for Indians, which was not printed on the schedule for 1860. See chapter 11.

6. In her dissertation on the mulatto in the 1880 census, Mary Lynn Washington points out that for Joseph C. G. Kennedy, superintendent of the Census Office in 1850 and in 1860, the author of these instructions, it seemed more important to distinguish between black and mulatto than between these two categories and white. She notes that the term "white" disappeared from the schedule and normally would not appear among the responses. Washington, "White, Black, or Mulatto," 75–76. It appears clear from the wording of the instructions that white was the rule, and that the task of census agents was to call out exceptions. The instructions, which were almost identical for schedule no. 2, clothed a different meaning: it seems that the essential distinction for the officials of the time fell across the slave population.

7. Some colonial censuses had had recourse to this distinction, and it is found in certain plans of the Continental Congress for a national census. Thus the Maryland census of 1755 gave a total of 107,208 whites, 42,764 blacks ("negroes"), and 3,592 mulattoes of whom 1,460 were free persons. The Massachusetts census of 1764–65 also distinguished between "negroes" and "mulattoes." However, this distinction was not often used in colonial censuses, especially because the categories used were generally quite rudimentary. The basic distinction between blacks and whites, sometimes along with Indians when they were counted, was more or less omnipresent in the colonial-era censuses. Census, *Century of Population Growth*, 5–6. The term *mulatto*, which comes from the Spanish, occurs in seventeenth- and eighteenth-century laws forbidding interracial unions (miscegenation). For examples of such laws, see Peggy Pascoe, *What Comes Naturally: Miscegenation Law and the Making of Race in America* (New York: Oxford University Press, 2009), 19–21. On the absence of a definition for the terms *black* and *mulatto* in 1850, see especially Census, *Negro Population in the United States, 1790–1915* (Washington, DC: Government Printing Office, 1918), 207, which notes that the instructions did not define the terms in 1850 and that in 1860 the agents did not receive any instructions. This was an error sustained for many years by the Census Bureau; there were instructions printed in 1860. A rare copy of the 1860 instructions was found in the late twentieth century. The 1860 instructions do repeat the 1850 instructions for color, but they add this important sentence: "Those who are in any degree of mixed blood are to be termed mulatto, 'M.'" Census Office, *Instructions to US Marshals, Instructions to Assistants* (Washington, DC: G. W. Bowman, 1860), 18.

8. *Congressional Globe*, vol. 21, 674.

9. Ibid. Underwood is referring to a southern racist doctor, Josiah Nott. On Nott's racial theories and his significance for the census, see Reginald Horsman, *Dr. Nott of Mobile: Southerner, Physician and Racial Theorist* (New Orleans: Louisiana State University Press, 1987). See also Anderson, *American Census*, 40–41. A representative from North Carolina, Thomas Lanier Clingman, had also demanded such changes, as we shall see below.

10. The memoirs of slaves and former slaves are full of first-hand information on children born of relations between masters and slaves, but they also bring out how impossible it was to speak of this, although the fact was certainly known and tacitly tolerated in the South. See, for example, Harriet Jacobs, *Incidents in the Life of a Slave Girl, Written by Herself* (Boston: By the Author, 1861); Frederick Douglass, *The Education of Frederick Douglass* (New York: Penguin Books, 1995 [1847]).

11. *Congressional Globe*, vol. 21, 675, italics in original. By "any proportion of blood," Underwood meant the degree of mixture between white blood and black blood. The expression was the definition of the "one drop" rule: any mixture of black blood, no matter how small, made an individual a black. The "different classes" of the population were obviously the different races.

12. Ibid.

13. Ibid., 676.

14. Polygenism, as opposed to monogenism, holds that men do not all descend from a single man (Adam, in the biblical tradition), but that there were multiple original creations corresponding to actual races. American polygenism is linked to the characters of Samuel Morton (d. 1851) and Louis Agassiz (1807–73), the latter a professor of natural history at Harvard. This was one of the first scientific domains to develop an American school, in a context very favorable to the development of racial theories justifying the American situation a posteriori. In England, polygenism was often referred to as the "American School." John S. Haller, Jr., *Outcasts from Evolution: Scientific Attitudes of Racial Inferiority, 1859–1900*

(Urbana: University of Illinois Press, 1971); William R. Stanton, *The Leopard's Spots: Scientific Attitudes Towards Race in America, 1815–1859* (Chicago: University of Chicago Press, 1960). See also Stephen Jay Gould, *The Mismeasure of Man* (New York: W. W. Norton, 1993 [1981]), 41–69. On the relationship between polygenism, the beginnings of ethnology and anthropometry, and the rationalization for the extermination of American Indians, see Robert E. Bieder, *Science Encounters the Indian, 1820–1880: The Early Years of American Ethnology* (Norman: University of Oklahoma Press, 1986).

15. In 1839 Samuel Morton published *Crania Americana*, the work in which he undertook to prove, with the assistance of reproductions of skulls and statistical tables, the inferiority of American Indians. Morton's plan was to collect enough skulls of different human races to be able to objectively establish a hierarchy of races based on the analysis of skull size. Morton did his medical studies in Paris, where he was introduced to the "numerical method," which was then in full bloom.

16. In the same period, Quételet subjected man and his behavior to quantitative analysis and the concept of the "average man." On the links between statistics and anthropometry before the Civil War, see Stanton, *Leopard's Spots*; on the Civil War period and the decades following, see Haller, *Outcasts from Evolution*, ch. 1, "Attitudes of Racial Inferiority in Nineteenth-Century Anthropometry."

17. "Finally, race as a scientific category, interpreted by medical experts or others who used the new language of physiology and ethnology, began to appear in the courtroom in the late 1840s" (Gross, "Litigating Whiteness," 133).

18. The historian George Fredrickson, in a work that has become a classic, set the fashion for polygenism into the context of the long history of American racism. He showed how this easily popularized theory facilitated the path from the older racism, which lacked a theoretical foundation, to the scientific racism of the second half of the nineteenth century. He saw the 1840s and 1850s as a turning point, something that also appears from the history of the census itself: George M. Fredrickson, *The Black Image in the White Mind: The Debate on Afro-American Character and Destiny, 1817–1914* (New York: Harper and Row, 1971).

19. J. D. B. DeBow, ed., *Encyclopaedia of the Trade and Commerce of the United States, More Particularly of the Southern and Western States*, 2nd ed. (London: Trübner & Co., 1854 [1853]). This edition combined in one bound volume the three that appeared between 1849 and 1852.

20. "Diseases and Peculiarities of the Negro Race," by Dr. Cartwright, ibid., 2:322.

21. The work reviewed was *Negro-Mania: Being an Examination of the Falsely Assumed Equality of the Various Races of Men*, by John Campbell. The review appeared in 1850; the quotations come from volume 2, 196–97. The twenty-page review gave scope for a lengthy defense of polygenist theses. On the mental illnesses of former slaves caused by freedom, see J. S. Hughes, "Labeling and Treating Black Mental Illness in Alabama, 1861–1910," *Journal of Southern History* 58, no. 3 (August 1992): 435–60. Hughes shows how, in spite of the evidence, former slaves hospitalized for mental troubles were regularly diagnosed as victims of their own freedom, a theme that lived on after abolition.

22. The term *mulatto*, borrowed from the Spanish as if American English had no word to describe the product of mixed union, had in Spanish the feminine form *mulatta*. But in English texts, the ending was anglicized. The feminine of *mulatto* is thus *mulatto*, and the plural *mulattoes*, although since the second half of the twentieth century, the term has fallen out of use and tended to become invariable in English. We have chosen to preserve the orthography that was current during the period under study.

23. DeBow, *Encyclopaedia*, 2:338.

24. The specific inferiority of "mulattoes," especially their fragility, could be found also, in a not very elaborated form, among slaveowners who became concerned about the reputed infertility of mulatto women and their lack of aptitude for hard work: they would thus be a bad investment for the fields but appeared better adapted to the house. Fragility could be a reversible stigma, at least for women. "Unproductive in the field and unprolific in the quarter, these women were the embodied opposites of the laborers/breeders slaveholders sought as field hands" (Walter Johnson, *Soul by Soul: Life Inside the Antebellum Slave Market* [Cambridge, MA: Harvard University Press, 2000], 152).

25. DeBow, *Encyclopaedia*, 2:339.
26. With independence, the states had to define who had or was denied citizenship. In 1785 Virginia defined a "Negro" as a person with a black parent or grandparent. The other states in the Upper South quickly followed. This generous legal definition of free whites as persons having less than one-quarter black blood meant that people who were visibly black, and were known as such, benefited from the rights and privileges of whites. With the sectional crisis, pressures mounted against these "abnormal" people, who were legally white and socially black, and their rights were restricted one after another in the last years of slavery: Joel Williamson, *New People: Miscegenation and Mulattoes in the United States* (New York: Free Press, 1980), 13.
27. The sexual and gender dimension of the question of mulattoes is extremely significant, but this dimension was also strongly repressed in public discourse. This is why the comparison between black slave women and white women made by Senator Seward was a provocation for the southern representatives; the uncontrolled sexuality attributed to black women was the other side of the coin of the purity attributed to southern ladies. Young women of mixed race who were very light of skin were much sought after and brought a higher price in the slave market, because they embodied the phantasm of the impossible solution of this contradiction for white men: they were at once aesthetically extremely close to the criteria of white beauty, and being black and slaves, they could be the object of socially disapproved sexual impulses toward white women. On this character of "fancy," that is to say of nearly white, mixed-race slave women sought out for their beauty, see Walter Johnson, "The Slave Trader, the White Slave, and the Politics of Racial Determination in the 1850s," *Journal of American History* 87, no. 1 (June 2000): 13–38.
28. On the subject of "white slavery" as a foil used by northern abolitionists, playing on the horror aroused by the possibility that whites could be slaves, and by the slavery proponents in the South assimilating the indentured servants of New England to white slaves, see Gross, "Litigating Whiteness," 127–29; and Roediger, *Wages of Whiteness*, 65–87. This theme disappears after abolition except in occasional references to white prostitutes.
29. Joel Williamson cites several cases of undetectable mulattoes, who appeared to be white slaves. But since such a thing as a white slave was unthinkable, these white-skinned mulattoes were legally and socially black. See *New People*, 50–54. We can see in this an early instance of the substitution of race, in its physical and social character, for color, a physical characteristic above all.

Chapter 06

1. Among the recent and most interesting contributions to this debate are those of Walter Johnson, "Slave Trader," 13–38; and Gross, "Litigating Whiteness." For the twentieth century, Peggy Pascoe, "Miscegenation Law, Court Cases, and Ideologies of Race in Twentieth-Century America," *Journal of American History* 83, no. 1 (June 1996): 44–69, belongs to the same perspective of legal history of construction of race, but she distinctly opposes the general and fluid racism of the nineteenth century to the early twentieth century when culturalists and eugenicist racists collide. Haney López, *White by Law*, analyzes a series of "racial prerequisite cases" that came before the federal courts of appeals in the course of naturalization procedures, since from 1790 to 1952 the fact of being "white" was a necessary condition of eligibility for naturalization and citizenship. John Tehranian, "Performing Whiteness: Naturalization Litigation and the Construction of Racial Identity," *Yale Law Journal* 109, no. 4 (2000): 817–48, applies the notion of race as "performance" to litigation in the 1920s relating to the "white" status of non-European immigrants (e.g., *Ozawa, Thind*). See also Cheryl Harris, "Whiteness as Property," *Harvard Law Review* 106 (1993): 1710–91; Jacobson, *Whiteness of a Different Color*.
2. Both Walter Johnson and Ariela Gross researched the manuscript censuses for information on social status and race of the persons in question, of their ancestors, and also those of the witnesses and jurors; see Johnson, "Slave Trader," 23 and note 22 for the Morrisson family in the census of 1850, and note 40, which reveals that one of the jurors in the case was a slaveowner since his name appears on the Slave Schedule; see also Gross, "Litigating Whiteness," 120n25.

3. Gross, "Litigating Whiteness," 111, 122, who notes that in all the states the customary presumption was frequently rejected by the courts.
4. Johnson, "Slave Trader," 21–22.
5. Ibid., 23. The fact that the thirty-eight-year-old black slave was enumerated after the mulatto woman and the five mulatto children may indicate that he was neither the children's father nor their mother's husband or partner.
6. Until the first half of the twentieth century, vital statistics were far from being complete in the southern states. It goes without saying that that of slaves was almost entirely unknown. Thus, the slave owner thought the young woman's first name was Jane, while Alexina Morrisson stated in court that Alexina was her only first name. Over the several years of the suit, it was impossible for the different courts that heard the case to decide it. We may note, a posteriori, that if the legislators of 1850 had not insisted on maintaining slaves in their status as chattel, the 1850 census might have enlightened us on this point.
7. In schedule no. 1 for 1850, the relation of each family member to the head of household does not yet appear, but the instructions to the census agents clearly stated the order to be used: "The names are to be written, beginning with the father and mother; or if either, or both, be dead, begin with some other ostensible head of the family; to be followed, as far as practicable, with the name of the oldest child residing at home, then the next oldest, and so on to the youngest, then the other inmates, lodgers and borders, laborers, domestics, and servants." The relation of each member to the head of the household was introduced into the schedules for 1890; "Measuring America," 10, 23.
8. From studies that have made use of this type of source, it seems that the general practice was for the owner to declare the color of his slaves, which did not correspond precisely to the usage of the census but rather reflected the existing social order. Generally, the census agent did not see slaves, but was given information about them, which would explain the significant variations in the proportion of mulattoes from one plantation to another in the same district, even when counted by the same agent. From this point of view, even if slaves were individualized on the schedules beginning in 1850, their identity was still controlled by their owner as it had been in earlier censuses. But we must not forget that the situation of slaves varied greatly, and that there were some who lived alone, at a distance from their owner. The 1850 instructions allow us to think that these slaves were enumerated in the household of the owner from which they were considered to be temporarily absent, but others were surely interviewed directly by the census agent.
9. Johnson, "Slave Trader." On the practice of physical examinations at slave sales, see Johnson, *Soul by Soul*, 135–61.
10. This is also the analysis of Ariela Gross in the cases that she studied, that is, all the cases in which racial categorization was challenged, for which records exist, around sixty-eight suits decided by the southern courts of appeals in the nineteenth century, most of them taking place between 1845 and 1861. See Gross, "Litigating Whiteness," 120, 135, 137.
11. Several studies have shown how the English colonists' views on blacks had been influenced by the discourse evolved by the English on Irish "barbarians," a discourse that had accompanied and justified the occupation of Ireland. See, among others, Ronald Takaki, *A Different Mirror: A History of Multicultural America* (Boston: Little, Brown, 1993), 24–76.
12. Gross, "Litigating Whiteness," 113–14.
13. This also applies to the choice of sources: the historians who privileged legal texts or parliamentary debates necessarily described a better organized reality than others who examined actual court cases, just as the study of the racial categories of the census as they were presented in the official reports of the census presented a more rational, "scientific" system than the study of procedures used on the ground and the rules for tabulation, which effectively put litigious cases into well-organized and mutually exclusive categories.

Chapter 07

1. The connection between military participation and freedom has been documented since the War of Independence, when the British promised freedom to the slaves who would break away from masters belonging to the insurgent side, most notably through the proclamation

of Lord Dunmore, governor of Virginia, dating from 1775. On the fate of slaves during the War of Independence and its wake, see Franklin and Moss, *From Slavery to Freedom*; Kolchin, *American Slavery*, 70–71; Philip Klinkner and Rogers Smith, *The Unsteady March: The Rise and Decline of Racial Equality* (Chicago: University of Chicago Press, 1999), 17–19. At the time of the Civil War, blacks were officially admitted to fight in the Union Army only after the Emancipation Proclamation of 1863. Nearly 180,000 black soldiers were grouped into separate units; see ibid., 62, 70, and more generally 47–71.

2. Anderson, *American Census*, 64. Margo Anderson's sources are the letter of Joseph C. G. Kennedy to James Harlan, 3 June 1865, 1860 Census File, Office of the Secretary of the Interior, RG 48, NA; the maps can be found in the Cartographic Archives Division, NA; Joseph C. G. Kennedy file, Walter Willcox Papers, box 36, Library of Congress; Lloyd Lewis, *Sherman: Fighting Prophet* (New York: Harcourt, Brace, 1932), 432. See also J. David Hacker, "Civil War and the Census," in Anderson, *Encyclopedia of the US Census*, 72–73.

3. The cartographic presentation of data had been developed in the 1850s, and the International Statistical Congresses encouraged this mode of presentation. The map of the density of slaves was published in September 1861 and "Sold for the benefit of the Sick and Wounded Soldiers of the US Army." Cartographic Archives Division, RG 29, NA. The map is reproduced in Anderson, *American Census*, 70–71.

4. *DeBow's Review* 14, n.s. 1 (New Orleans and Washington City, 1853), January 1853: 69–70: "The Colored Population of the North." *DeBow's Review* is available online: http://quod.lib. umich.edu/m/moajrnl/browse.journals/debo.html. At this date, DeBow was not yet census superintendent. He maintained cordial relations with Kennedy, who had provided him with unpublished data from the 1850 census, for purposes of the *Review*, but their relationship declined rapidly when DeBow replaced Kennedy at the head of the Census Office. Further, until the end of 1853 the Census Office was located in a building belonging to Kennedy, and he accused DeBow of having taken books and letters belonging to him, particularly those coming from European statisticians. The distinction between private correspondence and the official correspondence of the census director seems to have been somewhat fluid for Kennedy. He viewed the census as his own project and did not give up maneuvering to get back his job, which eventually happened in 1858. The relationship between DeBow and Kennedy is documented by Anderson, *American Census*, 51–52, who refers to older articles on DeBow and to Kennedy's correspondence where he complains about the actions of his successor; RG 48/ 280, Correspondence of the Secretary of the Interior/1853, 55 letters, 280, NA. Otis Clark Skipper, "J. D. B. DeBow and the Seventh Census," *Louisiana Historical Quarterly* 22 (April 1939): 479–91.

5. Anderson, *American Census*, 51, 53. DeBow edited the introduction of the 1853 volume without adding even a table to those already prepared by his predecessor. He took all the credit to himself for the impressive statistical work accomplished over more than three years, deliberately omitting Kennedy's name from the introduction. The only allusion to Kennedy is indirect, mentioning the sums remaining "when it passed under [DeBow's] control." DeBow justifies in the letter of transmittal the choice made by the secretary of the interior to entrust him with the publication of the census, given his experience as author and editor; Census, *Seventh Census*, v.

6. Hinton Rowan Helper, *The Impending Crisis of the South: How to Meet It* (New York: Burdick Brothers, 1857). Helper came from North Carolina, and if in the North he had been seen as a representative of the silent majority of the South, anti-elitist and anti-slavery, after the publication of his book his anti-slavery position led him to leave a South where criticism of slavery was no longer tolerated.

7. This was the case, for example, of Thornton Stringfellow, *Scriptural and Statistical Views in Favor of Slavery*, 4th ed. with additions (Richmond, VA: J. W. Randolph, 1856). "A comparison of the slave's condition at the South, with that of his own race in freedom at the South, shows with equal clearness, that slavery, in these States, has been, and now is, a blessing to this race of people in all the essentials of human happiness and comfort. Our slaves all have homes, are bountifully provided for in health, cared for and kindly nursed in childhood, sickness and old age; multiply faster, live longer, are free from all the corroding ills of poverty and anxious care, labor moderately, enjoy the blessings of the gospel, and let alone by wicked men,

are contented and happy" (137–38). Available online at: http://docsouth.unc.edu/church/string/menu.html.

8. On the polemic around Helper's book, which burst out in 1859, when a group of abolitionists collected sixteen thousand dollars to reprint the book for purposes of Lincoln's presidential campaign, see Anderson, *American Census*, 53–57; James M. McPherson, *Ordeal by Fire: The Civil War and Reconstruction* (New York: Alfred A. Knopf, 1982), 110–13; Kolchin, *American Slavery*, 182–83. On the racism of Helper, who in his pamphlet applies it to poor whites in the South, see Hugh C. Bailey, *Hinton Rowan Helper: Abolitionist-Racist* (Tuscaloosa: University of Alabama Press, 1965). For a discussion of Helper's heritage in the historiography of slavery, see Robert Fogel and Stanley Engerman, *Time on the Cross* (Boston: Little, Brown, 1974), 1:58–90. The authors consider Helper's conclusion to be valueless and his figures generally imprecise.

9. Thus, Edward Jarvis wrote to DeBow after the publication of the *Compendium* of the 1850 census to communicate his reservations with regard to the presentation in this volume of data on poverty in New England. The data as they appear in the *Compendium*, a work more widely distributed than the complete volumes of the 1850 census, although correct, give a mistaken impression of a considerably larger number of indigents in New England than in the southern states. The volume supervised by DeBow quite deliberately makes no reference to the different legislation of the states, especially ignoring the fact that the New England states took charge of many more paupers. The census, however, counted only those paupers whom the law required to accept public assistance. This comment received no follow-up, the census having made a practice, since Weaver's day, of not publishing corrected figures before the next census—that is, before a new superintendent could critique the work of his predecessor, which would be the case when Kennedy got his job back. Gerald Grob, *Edward Jarvis and the Medical World of Nineteenth Century America* (Knoxville: University of Tennessee Press, 1978), 146; Anderson, *American Census*, 55–56.

10. Considered iconoclastic by most traditional historians, this thesis was introduced by the economic historians Alfred H. Conrad and John R. Meyer, "The Economics of Slavery in the Antebellum South," *Journal of Political Economy* 66, no. 1 (1958): 95–130.

11. Kolchin, *American Slavery*, discusses the principal contributions and also the attempts to strike a balance on this question; see Claude Fohlen, Jean Heffer, and François Weil, *Canada et États-Unis depuis 1770* (Paris: PUF, 1997), 298–304, which gives the ten propositions of Fogel and Engerman as well as an evaluation of where things stand at the end of the intense debate they provoked. Today most historians no longer challenge the idea that slavery was profitable and that it would not have died a peaceful death without the Civil War.

12. Table 7.3 shows the concentration of mulattoes in cities in 1860.

13. Fogel and Engerman, *Time on the Cross*, table B.15, 2:108–10, and analysis, 1:131–33. Fogel and Engerman were criticized for having advanced the notion that the data showed contrasting situations. Thus the 1850 census, according to them, showed that pregnant slaves and those who were young mothers were spared severe punishments (their mortality rate was lower than that of white southern women in the same situation) but that young children fell victim to poor living conditions, which caused the infant mortality of slaves to be 25 percent higher than that of whites. "This finding appears to give credence to charges that mean treatment of infant slaves was widespread. In so doing it raises the strange paradox of planters who treated pregnant women and new mothers quite well while abusing their offspring" (1:123).

14. Herbert Gutman and Richard Sutch, "Victorians All? The Sexual Mores and Conduct of Slaves and Their Masters," in *Reckoning with Slavery: A Critical Study in the Quantitative History of American Negro Slavery*, ed. Paul A. David et al. (New York: Oxford University Press, 1976), 149.

15. The difficulty of establishing the racial identity of individuals even when we have material proof, as in the case of procedures for freeing slaves, has been shown earlier in this book.

16. Regional monographs offer a more nuanced picture, including in the Deep South. See, for example, the work of Gary Mills, who examined mixed unions in Alabama before the Civil War. Prudent with regard to the possibility of extrapolating his data to the level of the entire South, he notes that the study of families calls into question some of the commonly held views on the free blacks of the South. On the basis of the federal census of 1860, he established

that 78 percent of free blacks in Alabama were mulattoes—a very high proportion, as can be seen from Tables 7.2 and 7.3. Mills notes that the classic explanation, according to which the population of free blacks in the lower South had its origin in the emancipation of children of white fathers, is incompatible with the available data for Alabama, where only 32 percent of emancipations can be attributed to interracial relations (emancipation of the children of a white parent in 89 cases out of 361, and of concubines in 28 cases). He concludes that the majority of free mulattoes in 1860 arose from the natural growth of that population. He notes also that white mothers represented 43 percent of the identifiable mothers of mulatto children. His data contain several cases of children enumerated as white in 1850 or 1860, while one of their parents was listed as mulatto. "The number of incidences in which a parent was identified as mulatto while the child was identified as white also supports the hypothesis that an individual could be white in that society as long as he looked white. It is also worth noting that 67 percent of the 'free people of color' who moved in and out of white ranks in Anglo Alabama possessed some degree of Indian as well as Negro ancestry, and many who sought to escape racial discrimination . . . admitted only their Indian heritage." See Gary B. Mills, "Miscegenation and the Free Negro in Antebellum 'Anglo' Alabama: A Reexamination of Southern Race Relations," *Journal of American History* 68, no. 1 (June 1981): 31n37. On the persistent denial of the extent of interracial unions in American history, see also Gary B. Nash, "The Hidden History of Mestizo America," *Journal of American History* 82, no. 3 (December 1995): 941–64.

17. "Although the life expectation of slaves in 1850 was 12% below the average of white Americans, it was well within the range experienced by free men during the nineteenth century. It was, for example, nearly identical with the life expectation of countries as advanced as France or Holland. Moreover US slaves had much longer life expectations than free urban industrial workers in both the United States and Europe" (Fogel and Engerman, *Time on the Cross*, 1:126).

18. Richard H. Steckel, "Stature and Living Standards in the United States," Working Paper Series on Historical Factors in Long Run Growth, Working Paper No. 24, National Bureau of Economic Research, Cambridge, April 1991. Steckel shows that these two types of indicators are often offset in time. Thus, an economic improvement will not be perceived in the various physical measurements (notably height, weight, growth patterns, and longevity) until several years later. See also Michael R. Haines, Lee A. Craig, and Thomas Weiss, "The Short and the Dead: Nutrition, Mortality, and the 'Antebellum Puzzle' in the United States," *Journal of Economic History* 63 (2003): 382–413.

19. Steckel was able to establish that slave children were poorly nourished and showed a significant delay in growth, but that in adolescence, they were better fed because they labored. As adults, they were on average shorter than free blacks by 1.9 cm. But he also showed that these comparisons gave different results from those provided by studies of income, because of the use of two different standard-of-living indexes whose cycles did not agree. "Stature and Living Standards in the United States," 34–42.

20. Richard H. Steckel, "Miscegenation and the American Slave Schedules," *Journal of Interdisciplinary History* 11, no. 2 (1980): 260.

21. Ibid., 263.

Chapter 08

1. Éric Brian, "Statistique administrative et internationalisme statistique pendant la seconde moitié du XIXe siècle," *Histoire et mesure* 4, nos. 3–4 (1989): 201–24. Brief summaries of the different sessions up through 1872 (their author died in 1874) are presented in *Congrès international de statistique: Sessions de Bruxelles (1853), Paris (1855), Vienne (1857), Londres (1860), Berlin (1863), Florence (1867), La Haye (1869), et Saint-Pétersbourg (1872)*, by A. Quételet, president of the central statistical commission of Belgium (Brussels, 1873), 136 pp. The scattered publications, some of which can be found in Paris at the library of the institute, were listed by Éric Brian, "Bibliographie des Compte rendus officiels du congrès international de statistique (1853–1878)" (Paris: CAMS/EHESS, November 1989).

2. I am grateful to Éric Brian for sharing with me the list he drew up of the participants in the different congresses. The American representatives were Kennedy (1853 and 1855, then 1869

and 1872), Jarvis (1860 and 1869), Ruggles (1863 and 1869), Barnes and Delmar (1869 and 1872), and Young (1872 and 1876).

3. J. D. B. DeBow, "Statistical Congress of Nations," in *Seventh Census*, xxviii. For reasons set out in chapter 7, DeBow refrained from mentioning that the US representative was Kennedy.

4. "European Census System," ibid., xxvi–xxviii.

5. Ibid., xlv.

6. The sixth schedule, "Social Statistics," employed in 1850 and 1860, is reproduced in Wright and Hunt, *History and Growth*.

7. There were two in 1840, including the volume on manufactures—or even three, if we take into account that the volume on the population was published in two different editions by different publishers, as related in chapter 3.

8. "Introductory Letter," in *Seventh Census*, v.

9. Ibid., vi. Partial results had been published by Kennedy at the time of his report to Congress in December 1851.

10. "Report of the Superintendent of the Census, December 1, 1851," 142–43, in *The Seventh Census. Report of the Superintendent of the Census for December 1, 1852* [1–122], *To Which Is Appended the Report for December 1, 1851* [123–60] (Washington, DC: Robert Armstrong, 1853).

11. Ibid., 149. On the cover appears the title *Abstract of the Seventh Census*. Kennedy, who in 1849 had little experience with statistical work, traveled to Europe in the summer of 1851, then to the statistical congress in Brussels in 1853 and the one in Paris in 1855, which certainly helped establish his reputation in the United States, especially with regard to DeBow who was, by contrast, a well-known expert.

12. The earlier volumes were indeed hard to handle. For example, the population data for 1840 were presented by state, but the states were not listed in alphabetical order; instead, they appear to have been listed by their date of entry into the Union. Worse, the size of the folio volumes made it impossible to shelve them easily or to read them without difficulty. Kennedy, in his report to Congress, noted that in Brussels he had seen the oversized American volumes rotting on the floor under the bookshelves. The tables often ran for several pages without any repetition of the column titles (counties or towns). The volume on manufacturing in 1840 is a gigantic folio approximately one and a half by two feet. [Department of State], *Statistics of the United States of America, as Collected and Returned by the Marshals of the Several Judicial Districts, Under the Thirteenth Section of the Act for Taking the Sixth Census, June 1, 1840* (Washington: Blair & Rives, 1841), 410 pages.

13. Francis Amasa Walker, *A Compendium of the Ninth Census* (Washington, DC: Government Printing Office, 1872). The census volumes were distributed free of charge. See Anderson, *American Census*, 51–53.

14. *The Autobiography of Edward Jarvis (1803–1884)*, ed. Rosalba Davico, Medical History, Suppl. 12 (London: Wellcome Institute for the History of Medicine, 1992), 98–99. Jarvis's autobiography, written in the third person because he dictated it to his wife, grants him a more important role in the conception and realization of the 1850 census than he is traditionally accorded, based mainly on notes in official publications. It is clear that, at least under DeBow, the sometimes essential role of external collaborators was minimized, evidently with the aim of highlighting a flourishing institution. Jarvis also notes that he was never paid for his 1855 work, and that DeBow did not support him with Congress when he petitioned for payment for his work. This explains his wariness when he was approached again for the following census. Given that he had advised first Kennedy and then DeBow, and that he alone had done the work on the mortality statistics, he remarked that "in this way, he [gave?] to Mr. De Bow, and practically to the Government, about one third of his time for three years" (ibid., 100).

15. United States Census Office, *Statistics of the United States (Including Mortality, Property, etc.) in 1860* (Washington, DC: Government Printing Office, 1866), xxvi–xxvii.

16. Edward Jarvis to James Garfield, 17 February 1869, RG233, House of Representatives/HR 41A–F 28.4, 41st Congress, Select Committee on the Ninth Census, Committee on the Census.

17. The lectures that Jarvis mentioned having used included *Sur l'homme* by A. Quételet and the *Life Tables* of W. Farr, in charge of British statistics; *Transactions of the International Statistical*

Congress (London, 1860; Berlin, 1863). See the introduction by Jarvis in *Statistics of the United States (Including Mortality, Property, Etc.) in 1860*, 1866, 1.

18. On Kennedy as an active and enthusiastic member of the international statistical community, see Anderson, *American Census*, 59–62. Kennedy wrote in the introduction to the 1860 volume on mortality that he had personally met Adolphe Quételet at the Brussels congress in 1853. Census Office, *Statistics of the United States (Including Mortality, Property, etc.)*, iii. The lyrical style and overflowing enthusiasm of the introduction, edited by J. M. Edmunds, is characteristic of the administrative officials of the period. It forms a strong contrast with the dry reserve shown by Jarvis in his autobiography, and more still with the criticisms expressed elsewhere.

19. Ibid., xxiv–xxv.

20. Jarvis, *Autobiography of Edward Jarvis*, 99.

21. Ibid., 100–104.

22. DeBow complained of the incompetence of census agents, who were badly chosen and poorly paid. He likewise proposed the establishment of State Statistics Bureaus in the various states, and deplored the fact that the bureau in Washington was not permanent. *Seventh Census*, iv.

23. *Population of the United States in 1860*, 1:iv. The mention of generous cooperation, when we know that Jarvis complained of never having been paid, is not lacking in irony, perhaps unintended. His name is not among those mentioned here by Kennedy.

24. The report of the Special Commission on the Ninth Census of the House of Representatives described the international statistical congresses as "composed principally of men from all civilized nations, who, at their several homes, are members, leaders, and chiefs of their government bureaus of statistics, and have charge of the censuses, and of the registration of births, marriages and deaths" (*Ninth Census Report*, 18 January 1870, 41st Congress, 2d session, House Report 3, 1436, p. 101). The eight recommended questions are cited in the report on pages 101–104. See also Magnuson, "Making of a Modern Census," 48–49.

25. The question on race distinguishes the American census from other national censuses, but links it to those conducted by the European powers in their colonies.

26. "Ninth Census," *Congressional Globe*, 16 December 1869, 41st Congress, 2d session, 180.

27. *Population of the United States in 1860*, 1:xxii, xxviii, 32.

28. We recall that in 1860 the 1850 law had been renewed without changes.

29. Because of the composition of this immigration by age and sex—almost only males of working age—there were few children before the end of the century.

30. "Ninth Census," in *Congressional Globe*, 41st Congress, 2d session, 16 December 1869, 181.

31. "Ninth Census," in *Congressional Globe*, 41st Congress, 2d sessions, 7 February 1870, 1079.

32. All the laws framing the census claimed permanence, and all had as a title a formula of the type "An Act for taking the *n*th Census and following censuses."

33. We can gain some idea of the influence of representatives and senators in the recruitment of census agents by consulting the correspondence and petitions addressed to the Committee on the Census of the two chambers: most of the petitions concerned requests for recruitment as assistant marshal. See RG 233/HR 41A-F 28.4.

34. Nicolas Barreyre, *L'or et la liberté: Une histoire spatiale des États-Unis après la guerre de Sécession* (Paris: Éditions de l'EHESS, 2014), 170–76.

35. Francis A. Walker, "Statistics of the Colored Race in the United States," *Journal of the American Statistical Association* 2 (September–December 1890): 96. But another reason was that Walker, in order to defend the reform, strenuously criticized the work of Kennedy who, in return, testified before Congress against the Garfield Bill. See Anderson, *American Census*, 88.

36. Ibid., 97. Census directors would continue for a long time to deplore the recruitment of black agents where there were white residents to be enumerated. Thus, E. Dana Durand, census director in 1910, related in his memoirs, dated 1954, anecdotes that one might have found in the writings of Walker, decades earlier. "In the South it would have been impractical at that time—and perhaps also today—to have colored enumerators visit the homes of whites to take the census of population or of agriculture. In many districts only white enumerators were appointed" ("Memoirs of Edward Dana Durand," unpublished manuscript, 1954, Bureau of the Census Library, Suitland, Md., Papers of Census Officials, Folder no. 5477, 155). The period of Reconstruction has traditionally been depicted as a catastrophe, with the South delivered

over to the violence and corruption of powerful Republican officials. For almost a century, this view remained dominant in popular culture as well as in the works of historians. See Eric Foner, *Reconstruction: America's Unfinished Revolution, 1863–1877* (New York: Perennial Classics, 2002); and Nicolas Barreyre and Paul Schor, *De l'émancipation à la ségrégation: Le Sud des États-Unis après la guerre de Sécession, 1865–1896* (Paris: PUF, 2009).

37. "Interpolation back from the 1880 figures indicates a potential total undercount of 1.2 million in the South and a black undercount of over half a million—over 10 percent of the black population. In the 1870s, though, little was made of this undercount, both because the southern states were already reaping a bonus in congressional seats and electoral votes from the abolition of slavery and because few whites were seriously looking for robust growth in the black population" (Anderson, *American Census*, 89–90). In his 1890 article, Walker attempted to correct the 1870 figures on the basis of those for the southern black population in 1860 and in 1880; see Walker, "Statistics of the Colored Race in the United States," 101–102.

38. The sixth report of the special investigating committee of the National Civil Service Reform League (1891, 64–86), dealing with the recruitment of agents of the Census Bureau, was directly inspired by Walker's 1890 article, which it also cited, in its portrayal of the 1870 census as one of the worst examples of incompetence due to political clientelism. See *Civil Service Reform in the National Service, 1889–1891: Six Reports of the Special Investigating Committee of the National Civil Service Reform League* (Boston: Press of Geo. H. Ellis, 1891). File no. 7, HR52A-F49, Committee on the Census, House of Representatives, RG 233, NA.

39. Interview with Francis A. Walker in the *New York Times*, 8 March 1891, cited by James Phinney Munroe in *A Life of Francis Amasa Walker* (New York: Holt, 1923), 113.

Chapter 09

1. The Sixteenth Amendment, adopted in 1913 and creating a federal direct income tax, also had important consequences for the census, since it definitively separated it from its function of apportionment of states' fiscal contributions. Apportionment became exclusively the instrument of electoral allotment. The Sixteenth Amendment thus superseded the reference to direct taxes in Article I, Section 2, paragraph 3 of the Constitution.

2. US Congress, *Preliminary Report on the Eighth Census, 1860*, 7–8.

3. Census, *Population of the United States in 1860*, 1:xi–xii.

4. Ibid. 1:iv.

5. "Kennedy's view, further confirmed by a faulty statistical analysis in the Ninth and Tenth Censuses of 1870 and 1880, the corroborating beliefs of physicians, the investigations of American insurance companies, the statistical evidence of the United States Army, as well as countless medical reports, precipitated a belief in the negro's inevitable extinction" (Haller, *Outcasts from Evolution*, 40). For an example of medical beliefs of the period and received ideas on the insurmountable natural differences between blacks and whites, see J. Stahl Patterson, "Increase and Movement of the Colored Population I," *Popular Science Monthly* 19 (September 1881): 667.

6. Census, *Population of the United States in 1860*, 1:ix. For Kennedy, it went without saying that "more satisfactory" meant a more reassuring figure, one that heralded the progressive decline of the black population.

7. Ibid. In 1864, when this volume appeared, emancipation was under way and the Thirteenth Amendment was already under discussion in Congress.

8. When the Irish immigrants of the 1840s in the United States were considered as belonging to a different and inferior race, they were victims of a double racial prejudice: that of not being Anglo-Saxons, and that of being to some extent assimilated with blacks. The latter prejudice was reinforced by marriages between poor Irish immigrants and slaves or free blacks, and their competition in the same labor sectors, as Frederick Douglass noted in the 1840s. Takaki, *A Different Mirror*, 139; Roediger, *Wages of Whiteness*, 134.

9. Census, *Population of the United States in 1860*, 1:xi.

10. Ibid.

11. See Mills, "Miscegenation and the Free Negro," 18–19. These calculations, made from the original schedules of the 1860 census, directly contradict what Kennedy wrote in the census report, as well as a long later tradition.

12. Census, *Population of the United States in 1860*, 1:xi.
13. In contrast, there was a debate in Congress on the occasion of the adoption of the Fourteenth Amendment, concerning the possibility of going further than the "clause of equal protection under the law" to adopt a much more precise formulation, one that, instead of simply posing a principle of equality under the law without any further specification, would have given the blessing to the incorporation into the Constitution of a norm of non-usage of racial classifications by public powers—in other words, color-blindness. See Daniel Sabbagh, *L'égalité par le droit: Les paradoxes de la discrimination positive aux États-Unis* (Paris: Economica, 2003); and Andrew Kull, *The Color-Blind Constitution* (Cambridge, MA: Harvard University Press, 1992). However, even if an explicit provision in favor of color-blindness had been applied in the legal domain, it is doubtful whether the census, at this date, could have renounced classification by color, which had been the fundamental distinction it had applied to the residents of the United States since its creation.
14. Anderson, *American Census*, 72–82; Magnuson, "Making of a Modern Census," 46–54.
15. Anderson, *American Census*, 72–73.
16. Speech of 4 July 1865 at Ravenna, Ohio. Quoted by Anderson, ibid., 74. Source: Burke A. Hindsdale, ed., *The Works of James Abraham Garfield* (Freeport, NY: Books for Libraries Press, 1970 [1882]), 1:90–91.
17. This passage is indebted to Margo Anderson's discussion of the different proposals submitted to Congress, which draws on debates in both the House and the Senate. Anderson, *American Census*, 72–77.
18. Thus, we find among the documents of the House Committee on the ninth census an undated table representing an estimate of the apportionment of seats taking into account the penalties provided for in the Fourteenth Amendment, on the basis of the population figures for 1860, which would have given additional seats to all the rebel states except Florida, as well as to Missouri. Missouri, though a slave state, had remained in the Union, but this document erroneously includes it among the rebel states. "Undated Table: Apportionment of Rebel States from Last Census," HR 41A-F 28.4, 41st Cong., Select Committee on the Ninth Census, Committee on the Census, House of Representatives, RG233, NA.
19. "Ninth Census," H.R. Report 3, 41st Cong., 2d sess., 18 January 1870.
20. *Congressional Globe*, 41st Cong., 2d sess., 16 December 1869, 181. For a more complete discussion of this question, see Paul Schor, "Compter et classer: Histoire des catégories de la population dans le recensement américain, 1790–1940" (PhD diss., EHESS, 2001), 160–70.
21. To resolve the question, Representative Haldeman of Pennsylvania, member of the Committee on the Census, invoking the authority of eminent statisticians such as Quételet, Legoyt, Farr, and Engel, proposed a de facto census so that "it may be scientifically comparable with European censuses, a *de facto* enumeration, an actual enumeration in one day, is the legal, the wise, and scientific method." Haldeman, as a member of the committee, knew that this was not technically possible at the time, but he aimed to prepare for the future and to demand, for the 1880 census, a permanent bureau of statistics. His intervention is very interesting since it shows the extent to which scientific, technical, legal, and political questions overlapped, which partly explains the failure of Garfield's 1870 reform. Haldeman was clearly an enthusiastic partisan and someone well informed concerning the progress of the census, but unlike Garfield he opposed the Fourteenth Amendment and its consequences for the census. *Congressional Globe*, 41st Cong., 2d sess., "Ninth Census," 8 December 1869, 40.

　　　The US census is in fact much more a de facto census than a de jure census, since all persons physically present and alive on the reference date for the census are counted, even if the field work takes several weeks. The only exception concerns untaxed Indians, but non-naturalized immigrants, for example, are counted in the apportionment of representatives.
22. Garfield himself had insisted that the sections on apportionment, the most disputed issue, should be separated from the rest of the proposed census law. Further, he urged his colleagues to ratify the Fifteenth Amendment before the calculation of apportionment was made, showing that in 1860, in fourteen states, there were 726,635 free persons of color whose right to vote had been denied precisely because of their color or their race; Kentucky, Maryland, and Missouri represented more than half. *Congressional Globe*, 41st Cong., 2d sess., "Ninth Census," 14 December 1869, 124 and following.

23. The complete text can be found in "Measuring America," 15. "First papers" corresponds to a request for naturalization. To have obtained both meant that naturalization had been fully achieved. We shall find this distinction again in the early twentieth-century censuses.

24. Walker himself painted the picture of the exceptional difficulties census agents had to deal with. Census Office, *Ninth Census: The Statistics of the Population of the United States* (Washington, DC: GPO, 1872), 1:ix–xliv. Walker favored limiting the census to simple questions, which women could answer in the absence of their husbands, as he explained to the secretary of the interior in order to justify his opposition to the inclusion in 1880 of a question on naturalization, as well as one on the value of personal property and real estate. See Magnuson, "Making of a Modern Census," 59–60.

25. Census Office, *Ninth Census*, xxviii.

26. Cited by Anderson, *American Census*, 80.

27. *Ninth Census*, 1:xii.

28. Anderson, *American Census*, 80–81. Historians consider that the 1880 census undercounted the real number of the population, by 9 percent for blacks and 6 percent for whites, or 6.5 percent of the population, after the calculations done on the population distribution by age from 1880 to 1980. The undercounts established by this method of analysis would be 6.5 percent in 1880, 7.4 percent in 1890, 6.7 percent in 1900, 6.5 percent in 1910, 6.7 percent in 1920, 5.3 percent in 1930, 5.0 percent in 1940. Thereafter it declined, to stay between 1.5 percent and 2 percent at the end of the twentieth century. For an evaluation of the different methods, demographic analysis, comparison with other local sources, or recourse to period evidence, see Miriam L. King and Diana L. Magnuson, "Perspectives on Historical US Census Undercounts," *Social Science History* 19, no. 4 (Winter 1995): 455–66. The authors consider that the 1880 census, in which for the first time regional census officials (supervisors) were recruited on a merit basis by the Census Office and were no longer the marshals, marked a milestone of progress in the field investigation.

29. "Table of True Population," *Ninth Census*, xvii. The territory of Alaska was purchased from Russia in 1867. It would be enumerated in 1880, and its population would be counted among the American population, but like other territories that were not states and thus were not part of the Union, the population did not belong to what was called the "constitutional population," that which had to be enumerated by virtue of the Constitution in order to apportion powers among the states.

30. "H.J. Res. 108, In the H. of R., March 1, 1906, Introduced by Mr. Smith of Pennsylvania. Referred to Committee on the Census and ordered to be printed, Joint Resolution, Proposing an amendment to the Constitution providing for the repeal of the second section of the fourteenth amendment." This strange document ironically notes that, to the extent that the principles of equality of the Declaration of Independence are not to be taken literally, they would not apply to blacks, and that it would thus be appropriate to abrogate this superfluous section of the Fourteenth Amendment whose aim was to guarantee equality. RG 233/HR59A-F4.1, NA.

31. "H.R. 8132, in the House, Dec. 14, 1905, Bennet of NY, Referred and printed." Ibid.

32. Keifer, 26 February 1906, Bill H.R. 15647, presented again in the 60th Congress as H.R. 4860, 5 December 1907. Bennet introduced his proposition again, H.R. 11734, 6 January 1908, RG 233/HR60A-F6.1, NA.

33. "Petition from The Equal Suffrage League," Committee on National Affairs and Congress. A manuscript note links Bennet to this demand. "Enforcement of the 14th Amendment." RG 233/HR60A-H5.2.

34. See the detailed story of these debates that Margo Anderson gives: *American Census*, 149–56. The question of the Fourteenth Amendment was marginal, but as there was no consensus on the two proposed methods of calculation, the southern representatives profited by the opportunity to demand that non-naturalized immigrants should be excluded from the calculation, while the northern representatives proposed again that blacks deprived of the right to vote should likewise be removed from the basis of apportionment. On the polemic around apportionment in the 1920s, see also chapter 17.

35. A rather virulent letter from the National Equal Rights League of 30 December 1920 denounced the treachery of the Republican majority who voted on 17 December 1920

in favor of apportionment according to the new census without applying the Fourteenth Amendment. It threatened Republicans who acted like Democrats with electoral sanctions, and spoke of betrayal of the "Colored race." Letter of Rev. M. A. N. Shaw, President, National Equal Rights League, 30 December 1920, To the Republican Members of the House of Representatives. A petition of residents of Tolesboro, Kentucky, dated 22 January 1921, also demanded that Congress should respect the Constitution. These two documents are located in file RG 233/HR66A-D3, NA.

36. In the same file, one finds the resolution unanimously adopted on 8 January 1921 by the West Virginia State League, which tied this question to that of lynching, which a rejected legislative proposal sought to prohibit. On the question of the census and statistics on lynching, see chapter 18.

37. In this exchange, going back to the years of slavery and Emancipation, no one brought up the distinction between blacks and slaves. The term used was the neutral term "Negroes," in reference to the situation of slaves. Representative Larsen of Georgia several times used the derogatory term "niggers" when addressing George Murray, of the National Association for the Advancement of Colored People. *Statement of Mr Joseph A. Hill, Chief Statistician, Revision and Results, Bureau of the Census, December 28. Hearings before the Committee on the Census on H.R. 14498, 15021, 15158, 15217, December 28, 29 1920, January 4, 5, 6 1921. Apportionment of Representatives. Chairman: Isaac Siegel* (Washington, DC: GPO, 1921), 26. On the pressure exerted by the NAACP on one side, and the southern representatives on the other, to modify the calculation of apportionment, see chapter 17.

38. Slaves disappeared from the census, but not from the retrospective statistics that would figure in later reports, in which this category would frequently be distinguished from that of free blacks.

Chapter 10

1. Column 6 of Schedule no. 1, Population, 1870, reproduced in "Measuring America," 13.

2. Instructions to Assistant Marshals, 1870, ibid., 14 (italics in original). The fact that a person was no longer white by default grew out of the experience of the previous census, where for whites the column was to be left blank, which carried the consequence of counting as white all those for whom information was lacking. Schedule no. 2 covered mortality statistics, which likewise distinguished the dead by color.

3. In 1870, penalties were prescribed for censustakers who failed to fill out forms correctly, but in 1880 these penalties were abandoned, to be replaced by a system more conducive to a posteriori control of data by the population itself, as set forth in the law of 20 April 1880, Section 6. See Hutchinson, "Population Data: Fact and Artifact," 135–36.

4. The census seems to have been especially preoccupied with erroneous responses about age, whether deliberate or accidental. Still, the fact that color also figured on these public lists had to make it more difficult, for example, to classify as mulatto a family that locally was considered black, or to list different colors within a single family, not to mention the possibility of blacks passing as white and who were obviously white for the census.

5. Edward Jarvis, in a letter to Garfield in 1869, emphasized the scientific importance of the mulatto category, in particular with regard to mortality statistics, the subject of Jarvis's attention in the previous census. See Grob, *Edward Jarvis and the Medical World*, 195.

6. Fredrickson, *Black Image in the White Mind*, 232.

7. The opposite hypothesis, according to which American blacks, through mixing with mulattoes, were going to become a new people characterized by their mixed origins, was already being proposed by some writers, mostly blacks. However, it was diametrically opposed to the theories of the conservatives, which included all the nineteenth-century census officials. On the birth of the idea of a new, mixed black people, see Williamson, *New People*.

8. Department of the Interior, Census Office, "Instructions to Enumerators, 1880," 1 May 1880, reproduced in Wright and Hunt, *History and Growth*, 170–71, and in "Measuring America," 19.

9. A census publication in 1904, with regard to the identification of blacks (in 1900, there had been no distinction within the black population, only the category "black" or "negro"), used a

formula that went in exactly the same direction as the 1880 instructions as far as the method of inquiry was concerned: "For census purposes a negro is a person who is classed so in the community in which he resides. The enumerator is supposed to know this fact or to ascertain it by observation or inquiry" (US Bureau of the Census, *Negroes in the United States, Census Bulletin* [Washington, DC: GPO, 1904], 14). This bulletin was the first official statistical publication of any importance devoted to the black population. It was compiled for the census by the economist Walter Willcox (a white statistician linked to the Progressive movement) and W. E. B. DuBois (the first African American to collaborate on the census).

10. Washington, "White, Black, or Mulatto." Her statistical analysis included the 502,913 individuals in the 1880 IPUMS sample (one household out of one hundred). She concludes that "there is a significant and consistent positive effect between being female, young, not fully literate, and working in low paying occupation (for men), and being classified as 'mulatto' rather than 'white,' " 208. On the effect of the occupation held on the perception of color, see p. 170 and following; on age, p. 185; on gender, p. 212.

11. Ibid., 109.

12. We can gain some idea of the prohibitions and invalidations applied to interracial marriages in almost all the southern states and some northern and western states in Department of Commerce and Labor, Bureau of the Census, S. N. D. North, director, *Special Reports: Marriage and Divorce, 1867–1906* (Washington, DC: GPO, 1909), Digest of Marriage Statutes, 200–63, which summarizes the laws regarding marriage state by state at the beginning of the twentieth century. Out of the forty-five states, three territories, and the District of Columbia, twenty-three had no restriction by race. Among the twenty-six states that either prohibited or invalidated interracial marriages or punished them by fines, only four addressed marriages between whites and blacks ("Negroes" or "colored") without any further specification, while the others specified invalidation to explicitly include mulattoes, "or persons of negro descent to the third generation, inclusive" (Maryland) or specified "a mulatto having one-eighth negro blood being a colored person" (Florida). All the prohibitions applied only to marriages between whites and blacks, Indians, or Asians, never to marriages between members of these non-white groups. The exception was North Carolina, which in 1887 invalidated marriages between Croatan Indians (descendants of Indians, whites, and blacks) and persons of black descent up to and including the third generation. See also Albert Ernest Jenks, "The Legal Status of Negro-White Amalgamation in the United States," *American Journal of Sociology* 21, no. 5 (March 1916): 666–78; Pascoe, *What Comes Naturally*; Daniel Sabbagh, "La normalization juridique des rapports sexuels interraciaux aux États-Unis," *Tocqueville Review/Revue Tocqueville* 21, no. 2 (2000): 9–30.

13. Quoted by Nobles, *Shades of Citizenship*, 55–56. As she notes, the text has an ambiguity that is impossible to pin down. It refers to "the amalgamation of human species," while *species* is an invariable word in English. Therefore, it could be plural, referring to the various human species, in which case the text fits into the polygenic tradition. It could also be singular, in which case it would be a more modern version of racial theories influenced by Darwinism. The period (1888) would seem to indicate the singular, while the syntax would appear to call for the plural: it is a question of the mixture of the species, since otherwise the author would have written "amalgamation among the human species." Members of Congress often used the terms *race, color, people,* or *species* indifferently. Thus, in the last line, Wheeler spoke of "the human race," which evidently does not exclude the existence of several human races.

14. Wright was statistician for the Commonwealth of Massachusetts before moving on to federal labor statistics.

15. *Congressional Record,* 1889, 2244–46. Quoted in Nobles, *Shades of Citizenship*, 58.

16. From 1850 to 1880, only the term *color* appeared on the schedules and in the accompanying instructions. The instructions for the 1890 census used the expression "color or race," which also appeared on schedules from 1900 to 1940. In 1950, only the term *race* appeared on the schedule. In 1960 and 1980 the question was "Is this person—White, Negro, American Indian etc." In 1970, the heading "Color or race" again appeared on the schedule. In 1990 and in 2000, the question was "What is this person's race?" Congress decided to use the expression "color or race" from 1890 onward, precisely in order to account for the presence of non-whites who were not covered by the term *colored*, which was reserved for blacks. In other

words, *color* applied to blacks, *race* to others. US Senate, 50th Cong., 2d sess., Congressional Record, 1889, 2019.

17. "Instructions to enumerators, Census of 1890," reprinted in "Measuring America," 19 (schedule) and 27 (instructions). Italics and quotes in original.

18. US Bureau of the Census, *Negro Population, 1790–1915*, 207–208. This point is discussed in more detail in chapter 14.

19. Francis A. Walker, "The Colored Race in the United States," *Forum* 11 (1891): 502.

20. US Census Office, *Report on Population of the United States at the Eleventh Census: 1890*, Part 1 (Washington, DC: GPO, 1895), xciii.

21. Ibid., 387.

22. It was simpler and less costly to proceed to a tabulation of cards already perforated than to a new count. If, as was likely, the cards had never been coded for "mulatto," "quadroon," and "octoroon," once the temporary censustakers in Washington had been laid off, it would have been impossible to redo the work on the scale of the national population.

23. We know that this was the case in the Southwest in the 1920 census, where numerous persons categorized as "Mu" (mulatto) in districts with no black inhabitants were in fact persons whose family name and possibly place of birth indicated Mexican origin.

24. This is what appears from the comparison of data for the category "mulatto" in the 1880 census, where in Colorado Hispanics were categorized as whites, while in New Mexico they were counted as "mulatto." Brian Gratton and Myron P. Gutman, "Hispanics in the United States, 1850–1990: Estimates of Population Size and National Origin," *Historical Methods* 33, no. 3 (Spring 2000): 137–53.

25. US Census Office, *Report on Population of the United States at the Eleventh Census: 1890*, Part 2: "Insane, Feeble-minded, Deaf and Dumb, and Blind" (Washington, DC: GPO, 1895). At issue is a table on the "Insane" population divided into "White (Native Born [Parents native/One or both parents foreign born]/Foreign born)" and "Colored (Black/Mixed blood)," 157. The sole passage mentioning the category "mixed blood" does so in one line: "Of the 6,535 colored insane, 5,440 were reported as black and 1,095 as of mixed blood" (10).

26. For Porter's criticisms, see, for example, Census Office, *Preliminary Results as Contained in the Eleventh Census*, Bulletin no. 199, "Colored Population in 1890. Classified as Persons of African Descent, Chinese, Japanese, and Civilized Indians. By States and Territories," 14 July 1892 (Washington, DC: Government Printing Office, 1892), 1. In these bulletins, the expression "colored population" included all these categories. Later, in conformity with common usage, the census would tend to reserve the expression "colored" for the black population, and to designate what it here called "colored population" as "non-white races." Reading the bulletins on the colored population state by state shows that the meaning of the expression varied according to region, either including or excluding Indians and Chinese. See Census Office, *Population by Color, Sex, and General Nativity as Returned at the Eleventh Census, June 1, 1890* (Washington, DC: Government Printing Office, 1893), which gathers in one bound volume the bulletins that had appeared up to that point that presented data by color or by race. We shall see how in the 1930s Mexicans and Hawaiians mobilized so as not to be designated as "colored" in the census. Hawaiians were included in the total for whites in 1900, while Asians in Hawaii were described as comparable in the balance of the population to blacks in South Carolina. Census Office, *Twelfth Census of the United States Taken in the Year 1900, Population Part 1* (Washington, DC: GPO, 1901), cxvii.

27. US Bureau of the Census, *Report of the Director to the Secretary of Commerce and Labor, Concerning the Operation of the Bureau for the Year 1903–1904* (Washington, DC: Government Printing Office, 1904), 9.

28. Jennifer L. Hochschild and Brenna M. Powell, "Racial Reorganization and the United States Census, 1850–1930: Mulattoes, Half-Breeds, Mixed Parentage, Hindoos, and the Mexican Race," *Studies in American Political Development* 22 (2008): 70.

Chapter 11

1. See William Seltzer, "Excluding Indians Not Taxed: Federal Censuses and Native Americans in the Nineteenth Century," communication to the 1999 Joint Statistical Meetings, Baltimore,

9 August 1999. Seltzer also refers to a certain number of censuses specifically of Indian populations conducted by the federal government.

2. "Measuring America," 10.

3. Francis A. Walker discussed in his reports the concept of the constitutional population, that which served for the apportionment calculation, as distinct from the real population, which he also aimed to enumerate.

4. *Seventh Census*, iv.

5. Nobles, *Shades of Citizenship*, 36.

6. "Instructions to Assistant Marshals," 1860, 14–15 (italics in original).

7. Census, *Population of the United States in 1860*, 1:220, 1:22–36.

8. Ibid., 1:32n and Table 3, 1:29–32.

9. Ibid., 1:33.

10. Ibid., 1:29.

11. "Instructions to Assistant Marshals," 1870. See "Measuring America," 13, 15.

12. "Table of True Population," in *Ninth Census*, xvii. Walker justified the extension of the census to populations whose inclusion the law did not require but also, in his view, did not prohibit. In the case of Alaska, acquired in 1867, he included on his own initiative statistics that were not part of the legal scope of the census and compiled existing data, generally lists of names rather than enumerations. Census Office, *Compendium of the Ninth Census*, 22.

13. *Ninth Census*, xvi. Later, however, Walker, on the basis of his experience as superintendent of Indian affairs, would say that Indians were savages, who were to be treated by whites as wild animals—that is, by avoiding confrontation wherever possible—because the dignity of "Anglo-Saxons" was not at risk in contact with Indians. Francis A. Walker, *The Indian Question* (Boston, 1874), 34–35; quoted by Takaki, *A Different Mirror*, 231. For Walker, the only solution was to stabilize the Indians geographically so that they could become farmers or workers. From this point of view, the opposition between Indians haunting the margins of cities and Indians living in tribes did not amount to having two agencies competent to enumerate them.

14. *Congressional Globe*, 41st Cong., 2d sess., "Ninth Census," 14 December 1869, 125 and following. Niblack concluded his proposal in these words: "We must treat them as citizens of the United States, entitled to all the privileges of such citizens, ridiculous as it may seem to have to do so."

15. According to the commissioner for Indian affairs in a later evaluation, in 1870 there were 278,000 Indians in the territories, to which were to be added about 10,000 "freedmen" and "intermarried whites," that is, freed blacks and whites who had married into Indian tribes. US Bureau of the Census, *Indian Population in the United States and Alaska, 1910* (Washington, DC: General Printing Office, 1915), 10.

16. Munroe, *Life of Francis Amasa Walker*, 195. Munroe notes that Walker continued his work at the head of the census without pay even after the authorized funds had run out. Walker was a professor of political economy at Yale until his return to Washington in 1879 to manage the 1880 census. He resigned in 1881 in response to congressional hostility over his intransigence on the question of recruitment of censustakers. He served as president of MIT and president of the American Statistical Association from 1882 until his death in 1897, and served as president of the American Economic Association from its creation in 1885 until 1892.

17. *Ninth Census*, xiii.

18. "Instruction to Enumerators," 1880; see "Measuring America," 18.

19. The 1879 law authorized the superintendent of the census henceforth to engage special agents in charge of a particular area. It appears that Walker did not fail to take advantage of this, given the twenty-two published volumes of the 1880 census, of which only two deal mainly with population.

20. "Indian Division. Schedule no. 1. Population," Tenth Census. Reprinted in *200 Years of US Census Taking*, 31–33. The tribal name appeared on the first page of the schedule along with that of the reservation, in the spot where the ordinary census form would have the name of the city or town.

21. "Annual Report of the Superintendent of the Census for the Fiscal Year 1888–1889," 26, quoted in "Measuring America," 21.

22. Census Office, Bulletin no. 25, "Enumeration of Indians living within the Jurisdiction of the United States (except Alaska) Taxed or Taxable and Untaxed," 29 January 1891, by Thomas Donaldson. Donaldson, according to Superintendent Porter, had devoted his life to the study of Indians on each reservation. On this topic see Robert P. Porter, "The Eleventh Census," *Publications of the American Statistical Association* 2, no. 15 (September 1891): 369.

23. Census Office, Bulletin no. 25, 3.

24. The case is reported by Seltzer, "Excluding Indians Not Taxed," 9–10. Seltzer's source was John R. Finger, *The Eastern Band of Cherokees: 1819–1900* (Knoxville: University of Tennessee Press, 1984).

25. "Instructions to Enumerators—Census of 1890," Special Enumeration of Indians, reprinted in *200 Years*, 34.

26. Frederick Jackson Turner, "The Significance of the Frontier in American History," *Annual Report of the American Historical Association* (1893): 199–227. See also Gerald Nash, "The Census of 1890 and the Closing of the Frontier," *Pacific Northwest Quarterly* 71 (July 1980): 98–100.

27. The archives of Ivan Petroff contain a biographical notice that summarizes his busy life. Petroff Papers, Bancroft Library, Special Collections, University of California, Berkeley, MSS C-B 989, 2. See also Schor, "Compter et classer" (2001), 395–414.

28. One of these agents, Frank Lowell, sent his logbook to Washington. The logbook, which has been preserved, shows the enormous material difficulties encountered by federal agents in a vast but sparsely populated territory. See "Alaska, Logbook, 1890. Frank Lowell. Special Agent. Dist. #2 Alaska," Records of the Twenty-first Division, Entry 118 (Records of the Eleventh Census), RG29. Such tales of adventure became a distinct genre in the internal literature of the Census Bureau. A similar story for 1940 was written by W. A. Goddard, as if in fifty years things had scarcely changed; see letter of 4 January 1940 from W. A. Goddard, enumerator in the district of Rethel at Arend and assistant to Supervisor Hammack, who passed it, with others, along to his staff as an illustration of the extreme conditions of the Alaska census. File 107 (Dwight R. Hammack), Entry 250 (Assistant Director for Demographic Files; Records of the Division of Territorial, Insular, and Foreign Statistics; General Subject File, 1935–1942), RG 29.

29. Census Office, *Statistics of the Population of the United States at the Tenth Census (June 1, 1880)*, vol. 8 (Washington, DC: General Printing Office, 1884), "Alaska: Its Population, Industries and Resources" by Ivan Petroff, Special Agent, v.

30. Ibid., 32–38.

31. United States Census Office, *Report on Population and Resources of Alaska at the Eleventh Census: 1890* (Washington, DC: GPO, 1893), xi. The five classes were white, mixed Indian, Indian, Mongolian, and all others.

32. Ibid. The report sometimes also used the term *creole* to designate persons having one white parent and the other indigenous. Very few Russians born in Russia had remained in Alaska after 1867.

33. See the sample form for 1909, RG 29/251, Records Relating to Territorial and Insular Census. 15th Decennial Census 1920–1934. Classified File/Alaska File. On the increase in the number of persons categorized as Indian due to this definition, see Bureau of the Census, *Indian Population in the United States and Alaska, 1910* (Washington, DC: GPO, 1915), 10.

34. "Mixed" and "mulatto" were mutually exclusive categories, as was explicitly stated in the coding instructions at the beginning of the twentieth century: "A mixture of Indian with any race other than Negro should be reported as "Mxd" in column 6" ("Supplemental Coding Instructions for Population Schedule. Outlying Possessions (Alaska)," 1; RG 29/251/802).

35. "Instructions for Filling the Population Schedule," 1909, RG 29/254, Assistant Director for Demographic Fields. Records of the Division of Territorial, Insular, and Foreign Statistics. Miscellaneous Records Relating to Territorial Censuses, 1900–1938/Alaska 1910.

36. "Illustrative Example of the Method of Making Returns on Schedule for Population," Form 8-1507, ibid. An example of a "mixed family" is a fictitious family where the father is "Mxd," the mother is "Indian" (In), and the children are classified as "Mxd." On the other hand,

the "mulatto" family in the example is made up of a "Mu" father, a "Mu" mother, and "Mu" children.

37. "Memorandum—Editing," ibid.

Chapter 12

1. See chapter 16.
2. Roger Daniels, *Asian America: Chinese and Japanese in the United States since 1850* (Seattle: University of Washington Press, 1988), 9. If we compare these entry figures with the 100,686 Chinese enumerated in 1880, it appears that the number of returnees was quite high. The Chinese term for "immigrant" literally means "visitor."
3. *Seventh Census*, xxxvii.
4. Ibid., lxi. California achieved statehood in 1850.
5. Naomi Mezey lays out the stages and pauses in the process of the Chinese becoming a separate race. See N. Mezey, "Erasure and Recognition: The Census, Race, and the National Imagination," *Northwestern University Law Review* 97 (2003): 1701–68.
6. There were 9,809 Chinese enumerated in the California state census, added to the official census of 1850. *Ninth Census*, 5.
7. Daniels, *Asian America*, 35.
8. Census Office, *Population of the United States in 1860*, 1:xxviii.
9. Ibid.; italics added.
10. The term used was "free colored," even though California entered the Union as a non-slave state in 1850, so that these were the only possible "colored," but the term implied a comparison with other states where slavery existed.
11. Census Office, *Population of the United States in 1860*, 1:32.
12. One possible instruction would have been to note, as in the reports, that the term "Chinese" was intended to include Japanese. It is hard to know if the term "Japanese" appeared spontaneously on the schedules filled out by census agents or if it was the Census Office that produced these figures based on places of birth. At this time, all the "Japanese" were born in Japan.
13. *Ninth Census*, xii.
14. Ibid., 8.
15. Ibid., 318.
16. Edward P. Hutchinson, *Immigrants and Their Children, 1850–1950*, Census Monograph Series (New York: John Wiley & Sons, 1956), 334. Hutchinson's figures, pulled from a retrospective table of volume 2 of the 1930 census (p. 233), are a little problematic, because these were corrected figures, which varied slightly from those of the original volumes. Thus, for 1870, he gives 63,042 persons born in China and 73 born in Japan. But in both cases, we see that persons born in India are much more numerous than those born in Japan.
17. *People v. Hall*, 4 Cal. 309 (1854), quoted by Daniels, *Asian America*, 34.
18. Census Office, *Statistics of the Population of the United States at the Tenth Census*, Table XII: "Native Colored Population of the United States According to State or Territory of Birth," 488.
19. In all, 89,863 persons were counted in 1900, 71,531 in 1910, 61,639 in 1920, 74,954 in 1930, and 77,504 in 1940. According to Daniels, *Asian America*, 67, the population might have reached a peak of 125,000 in 1882.
20. The remaining category was "Indian," that is, Native American. The eight racial categories in 1890 were: white, black, mulatto, quadroon, octoroon, Chinese, Japanese, and Indian.
21. The population was 24,326 in 1900, 72,157 in 1910, 111,010 in 1920, 138,834 in 1930, and 126,948 in 1940. In percentage terms, the peak nationally was reached in 1930, when they reached 0.11 percent of the total population. For the West Coast (1.7 percent) and California (2.1 percent) the peak was reached in 1920. "More Italians entered the United States (283,000) in the one year from July 1, 1913 to June 30, 1914 than Japanese entered (ca. 275,000) in the whole period of emigration through 1924. In 1907, the heaviest year of immigration from Japan, 30,842 Japanese were recorded as entering the United States, just 2.4% of the 1,285,349 who came from all countries that year" (Daniels, *Asian America*, 115).
22. Ibid., 100–54.

23. Ibid., 56–57.
24. H.R. 6420, 17 March 1890, 51st Cong., 1st sess.
25. "Enumeration of the Chinese Population of the United States," Report no. 486, 51st Cong., 1st sess., House of Representatives, 27 February 1890. Copy in file RG 46/Sen 51A-F3, Committee on Census, cf. HR Bill 6420, and Remonstrances against its passage (Chinese exclusion).
26. On the basis of the Scott Act, Chinese immigrants were to come forward on their own in order to be recorded.
27. H.R. 6420, sec. 1, Amendment to the Eleventh Census Act, sent by the House, read in the Senate March 17, 1890; RG 46/Sen 51A-F3, Committee on Census.
28. Report of the secretary of the treasury, quoted in "Report no. 486," 51st Cont., 1st sess.
29. Resolution of the Minneapolis Board of Trade, 5 May 1890, approving the action of the New York State Chamber of Commerce of 3 April 1890, and addressed to Rep. C. R. Davis of the Philadelphia Board of Trade, 29 April 1890. From the Chamber of Commerce of Duluth, Minnesota, 10 April 1890. From the Chamber of Commerce of Pittsburgh, File RG 233/HR51A-H26.4, Committee on the Census/"Various subjects." These petitions are those found in the archives of the committee, so the list may be incomplete.
30. Letter from the Chamber of Commerce of Pittsburgh.
31. Chamber of Commerce of the State of New York, 4 April 1890. Resolution proposed by the House Committee on Foreign Trade and addressed to all the Chambers of Commerce and all the important Boards of Trade of the nation, asking them to adopt similar resolutions and to communicate them to their members of Congress. File RG 233/HR51A-H26.4.
32. Docket volume, Committee on the Eleventh Census. The committee reported back Bill 6420 favorably with an amendment on 26 February 1890 and received the petitions between 16 April and 2 May 1890; RG 233/HR51A-F.45.3.
33. The starting date of the census was 1 June 1890.

Chapter 13

1. This was also the date from which statistics, though of poor quality, became available on entrances into the country, but not on departures.
2. Jarvis, among others, had asked in his hearing before the census committee in 1869 that the next census should be a genuinely de facto enumeration (*Congressional Globe*, 41st Cong., 2d sess., 181). The census reported first of all the figures for the legal, or "constitutional," population for purposes of apportionment, and then, in its published reports, took account of the population of the territories and that of untaxed Indians.
3. We recall that the right of naturalization had been established by the First Congress in 1790. If courts debated the right to naturalization of one individual or another, especially in the case of racial minorities, birthright citizenship had always been the rule for residents of European origin. This explains how the statistics on nationality could concern only first-generation immigrants. Challenges to or denials of naturalization only rarely came before the courts before the late nineteenth century. On the discussions concerning citizenship, naturalization, and immigration at the beginning of this period, see James H. Kettner, *The Development of American Citizenship, 1608–1870* (Chapel Hill: University of North Carolina Press, 1978).
4. US Bureau of the Census, *200 Years of US Census Taking*, 24, reprinting the 1860 schedule, similar to that for 1850.
5. By "social," we mean that the distinction by national origin also responded to a demand for information on the composition of the American population as it was layered on American soil. This is based on the idea that national origin is an important element of American social organization, so that what we have here is a matter of ethnic statistics.
6. *Seventh Census. Report of the Superintendent of the Census*, 10, 14, 8.
7. Between 1820 and 1850, we have only the raw number of immigrant entries by year, with no information on returns or reentries. These raw entries increased from 8,385 in 1820 to 10,199 in 1825, 23,322 in 1830, 45,374 in 1835, and 84,066 in 1840. US Bureau of the Census, *Historical Statistics of the United States, Colonial Times to 1970* (Washington, DC: GPO, 1975).

8. US Bureau of the Census, *Historical Statistics of the United States, Colonial Times to 1970.* Until 1870, the figure was surpassed only once, in 1854 with 427,833 entries.

9. *Seventh Census*, Table xxx: "Nativities of Deaf, Dumb, Blind, Insane and Idiotic Persons in the United States," l. The data are also more precise than in Kennedy's preliminary report of 1852; the 1853 volume distinguished Prussia from the rest of Germany, and Sardinia from Italy, as places of birth. Ibid., Table xv, p. xxvii.

10. Alan M. Kraut, *Silent Travelers: Germs, Genes, and the "Immigrant Menace"* (Baltimore: Johns Hopkins University Press, 1994), 39–40. See also Gerald Grob, *Mental Illness and American Society, 1875–1940* (Princeton, NJ: Princeton University Press, 1983), 169–70.

11. *Population of the United States in 1860*, 1: xxxii.

12. "Instructions to Assistant Marshals," 1860, 16.

13. After the third division of Poland, in 1795, there remained of the country only the tiny republic of Krakow, which was annexed by the Austrian empire in 1846.

14. "Although Poland was not restored to its original status as an independent country until the close of the World War, many persons reported their birthplace as Poland and were so tabulated for several censuses" (*The Fourteenth Census of the United States*, vol. 2, "Population," 688). On the other hand, in 1870, the scattered instances where the place of birth was recorded as "Finland" were reclassified as "Russia" (*Ninth Census: The Statistics of the Population of the United States*, vol. 1, 317). The number of responses was clearly the determining factor for the existence or nonexistence of these countries in the census.

15. The following cases all point in this direction, and this is the interpretation found in later studies, especially that of E. A. Goldenweiser, "The Mother Tongue Inquiry in the Census of Population," *Journal of the American Statistical Association* (1913): 648–55. The absence of precise instructions on this point is an indication that the census once again adapted a posteriori to the responses that were given.

16. The political influence of Polish Americans was negligible at that time. By the eve of World War I, their influence was still limited compared to that of other groups such as Czechs, who had for a long time advocated with President Woodrow Wilson the cause of an independent Czech state. On this point, see Alexander Deconde, *Ethnicity, Race, and American Foreign Policy: A History* (Boston: Northeastern University Press, 1992), 89–90. The classifications of the census, although it was a federal agency, should not be read as an official government position. However, the retention of this category indicates that, from the point of view of the census, the groups present in the United States did not necessarily have to correspond to nation-states. Ethnicity does not strictly correspond to nationality of origin.

17. Paul Schor and Alexis Spire, "Les statistiques de la population comme construction de la nation: La mesure des origines nationales dans les recensements français et américains (1850–1920)," in *Les codes de la différence: Race–Origine–Religion; France–Allemagne–États-Unis*, ed. Riva Kastoryano (Paris: Presses de la FNSP, 2005): 91–121.

18. US Bureau of the Census, *Thirteenth Census of the United States Taken in the Year 1910* (Washington, DC: GPO, 1913), 1:959. See also Susan Cotts Watkins, ed., *After Ellis Island: Newcomers and Natives in the 1910 Census* (New York: Russell Sage Foundation, 1994), 13.

19. This rule was modified in 1900, when the instructions on place of birth stated: "In case the person speaks Polish, as Poland is not now a country, inquire whether the birthplace was what is now known as German Poland or Austrian Poland or Russian Poland, and enter the answer accordingly as Poland (Ger.), Poland (Aust.), or Poland (Russ.)" (*Measuring America*, 37). Beginning in 1910, the question of mother tongue would be asked of all persons born abroad, as we shall see.

20. *Congressional Globe*, House, 41st Cong., 2d sess., 16 December 1869, 181.

21. Massachusetts statisticians especially had directed attention to the differential demography of these two populations in their commonwealth. Anderson, *American Census*, 90.

22. *Ninth Census*, 1:xxix.

23. Ibid., 299. See also the analysis by E. P. Hutchinson, *Immigrants and Their Children*, 288–89.

24. [Francis A. Walker], *Statistical Atlas of the United States, Based on the results of the Ninth Census 1870.* With contributions from many eminent men of science and several departments of government. Compiled under the authority of Congress by Francis A. Walker, M.A.

Superintendent of the 9th Census, Professor of Political Economy and History, Sheffield Scientific School of Yale College, Julius Bien, Lith., 1874.

25. Ibid., 3. We must note that the census used the term "foreign" or "foreigner" to indicate foreign birth, with no concern for the nationality of these immigrants who could well be US citizens.

26. The census law of 1880 took up Garfield's proposal that had been rejected ten years earlier. The authority of the census superintendent was significantly strengthened, as Walker had hoped. Henceforth it was the Census Office that would name supervisors and would have oversight of the recruitment of enumerators. The work was centralized in Washington, where the number of agents was enormously increased. It had tripled between 1860 and 1870, and Walker tripled it again in 1880, bringing it up to 1,495. The number of published volumes grew from five in 1860 and 1870 to twenty-three in 1880 and thirty-two in 1890. See Anderson, *American Census*, 84. The most detailed account of the administrative development of the census under Walker is that of Magnuson, "Making of a Modern Census," ch. 4, "Walker Gets His Way: The Censuses of 1880 and 1890."

27. Census Office, *Statistics of the Population of the United States at the Tenth Census*, 1:674–75.

28. Magnuson, "Making of a Modern Census," 59–60.

29. "The Census," *Congressional Record. House*, 1 April 1880, 46th Cong., 2d sess., 2033.

30. Census Office, *Statistics of the Population of the United States at the Tenth Census*, 1:677, 460.

31. Herman Hollerith, "The Electrical Tabulating Machine," *Journal of the Royal Statistical Society* 57, no. 4 (December 1894): 678–89; Leon E. Truesdell, *The Development of Punch Card Tabulation in the Bureau of the Census, 1890–1940. With Outlines of Actual Tabulation Programs*, US Department of Commerce, Bureau of the Census (Washington, DC: GPO, 1965).

32. Porter, "Eleventh Census," 331. The term "foreign" as used here evidently refers to place of birth and not to nationality.

33. Ibid. We have explained why the classification of blacks into blacks, mulattoes, quadroons, and octoroons was not published. It seems dubious that this tabulation would have been done if it were not to be published. In Census *Bulletin* no. 48, "The White and Colored Population of the South: 1890" (7 April 1891), which appeared before this article by the census superintendent, blacks were classified in only one category, "colored." In the *Bulletin* on the population of the nation by color, published in July 1892 and reprinted in the population volume of 1893, it was the same thing. On the other hand, in the *Bulletin* on California, it was stated that by request of the local authorities, a special tabulation had been done to establish the representative population without Indians and persons of color. The Census Office had the capability to conduct this classification of blacks into four categories, but either it did the tabulation and then decided not to publish it nor to aggregate the data, or else, which is more likely, and contrary to what Porter says here, the tabulation was not done because the idea was dismissed as worthless, something that Porter himself admits: "The present census law also calls for a subdivision of the colored population into blacks, mulattoes, quadroons, and octoroons. The result of this special requirement can furnish, however, only an approximation at most as to the real facts" (ibid., 333). See also Department of the Interior, Census Office, *Bulletin* no. 119, 14 July 1892, "Colored Population in 1890. Classified as Persons of African Descent, Chinese, Japanese, and Civilized Indians. By States and Territories."

34. Porter, "Eleventh Census," 335.

35. W. F. W., "Migration of Negroes," *Publications of the American Statistical Association* 5, no. 40 (December 1897): 371–72. Review of a work by F. J. Brown, *The Northward Movement of the Colored Population* (Baltimore: Cushing & Co., 1897). This was a statistical study based on data published by the censuses of 1880 and 1890. The author of the review may have been the statistician W. F. Willcox.

36. The brevity of the comments appearing in the *Compendium* of the 1890 census, which concluded that the distribution of immigrants of the first and second generations was very close, was the subject of a critical note in the *Publications of the American Statistical Association*, stating that this generalization was incorrect and false in its detail: in certain states, the first generation was more numerous, while in others the second was larger. L. W. Hatch, "Foreign Parentage and Foreign Born," *Publications of the American Statistical Association* 4, nos. 28–29 (December 1894–March 1895): 116–18.

37. In the case of Bohemia, census agents recorded this country and not Austria as the place of birth only when the persons in question spoke Czech (Bohemian). See Goldenweiser, "The Mother Tongue Inquiry in the Census of Population," 649.
38. See the instructions for 1870 and 1900 in "Measuring America," 15, 37.
39. Ibid., 28, Instructions for 1890.
40. The expression "race suicide" does not appear as such before 1901, in an article by Edward A. Ross, "The Causes of Race Superiority," *Annals of the American Academy of Political and Social Sciences* 18 (1901): 67–89. It was later taken up by President Theodore Roosevelt. On the spread of this concept and this term, see John R. Keeling, "The Role of Academic Social Science and the Dillingham Commission in American Immigration Restriction, 1890–1917" (MA thesis, University of Southwestern Louisiana, 1992).
41. Walker's principal articles were reprinted in Francis Amasa Walker, *Discussions in Economics and Statistics*, ed. Davis R. Dewey, 2 vols. (New York: Henry Holt, 1899). An exhaustive bibliography was published by James P. Munroe, *A Life of Francis Amasa Walker* (New York: Henry Holt, 1923).
42. Miriam L. King went back to the data and redid the calculations based on the sample of historical census data made available by the IPUMS-USA database (http://www.ipums.org) for 1900 and showed that "race suicide" never happened: the fertility differences between "natives" and "foreigners" were small and were compensated by differences in fertility between first- and second-generation immigrants. She concluded that the belief that immigrants and their children had higher fertility rates than the "native-born of native parentage" reflected nativist fears more than demographic reality. See Miriam L. King, "The Quantum of Happiness: The Politics of American Population Debates, 1850–1930" (PhD diss., University of Pennsylvania, 1990).
43. Francis A. Walker, "Immigration and Degradation," *Forum* 11 (1891): 634–43, reprinted in Walker, *Discussions in Economics and Statistics*, vol. 2. Quote p. 420, italics in original.
44. Ibid., 423, 426.
45. We find the same pessimistic argument in the famous work of Madison Grant, *The Passing of the Great Race* (New York: Charles Scribner's Sons, 1916).
46. "Instructions to Enumerators—Census of 1890," Schedule no. 1, Population, Paragraphs "Naturalization" and "School Attendance, Illiteracy, and Language Spoken"; reprinted in "Measuring America," 28 and 32; italics in original.
47. Kathleen N. Conzen, *Immigrant Milwaukee, 1836–1860: Accommodation and Community in a Frontier City* (Cambridge, MA: Harvard University Press, 1976).
48. Porter, "Eleventh Census," 333. Contrary to what the census superintendent implies here, the question of language spoken was posed to all residents ten years old or older, and not only to those of foreign birth or foreign extraction, unless we consider that all Americans were of foreign extraction, which was surely not Porter's intention, he himself being of English birth.
49. Richmond Mayo-Smith, "Statistical Data for the Study of the Assimilation of Races and Nationalities in the United States," *Publications of the American Statistical Association* 3, no. 24 (December 1893): 430. Mayo-Smith's biography and list of principal publications were compiled by FitzPatrick, "Leading American Statisticians in the Nineteenth Century," 312–13.

Part IV

1. On the ties between the Bureau of the Census and the Department of Commerce, its oversight body, and more generally on the attempts in the 1930s to integrate the work of the Bureau of the Census with the ensemble formed by all the federal agencies that produced statistics under the direction of the Central Statistical Board, see Joseph W. Duncan and William C. Shelton, *Revolution in United States Government Statistics, 1926–1976* (Washington, DC: GPO, 1978).
2. In examining the profiles of the seven principal American statisticians of the nineteenth century, of whom five had, to one degree or another, worked for the census, Paul J. FitzPatrick noted that four of them (Jarvis, DeBow, Mayo-Smith, and Walker) were college graduates, while three (Shattuck, Pidgin, and Wright) were not. Only one (Mayo-Smith) had been trained as a statistician. Mayo-Smith and Walker were the only ones with postgraduate training. See FitzPatrick, "Leading American Statisticians in the Nineteenth Century," 317.

Chapter 14

1. We mentioned Mary Lynn Washington's study on mulattoes in the IPUMS census sample (http://www.ipums.org) of 1880. With rare exceptions, the raw data of 1880 were not consulted, as other authors used census publications, some going so far as to write that the distinction was not made in 1880.
2. "Measuring America," 36.
3. US Census Office, *Twelfth Census of the United States Taken in the Year 1900: Supplementary Analysis* (Washington, DC: GPO, 1906), 177.
4. William Z. Ripley, "Colored Population of African Descent," in *The Federal Census: Critical Essays*, ed. American Economic Association (New York: Macmillan, 1899), 38–48; quote on 44–45. S. N. D. North, who headed the Census Bureau in 1909, referred to southern men as authorities on the question of racial mixtures. US Immigration Commission, *Dictionary of Races or Peoples: Reports of the Immigration Commission*, vol. 5 (Washington, DC: GPO, 1911) (Senate Doc. 662, 61st Cong., 3d sess.). See chapter 17.
5. In 1890, the term "black" was confined to blacks having three-fourths of black blood or more.
6. The old theme of the "tragic mulatto" was revived in 1908 by the journalist Ray Stannard Baker, *Following the Color Line: American Negro Citizenship in the Progressive Era* (New York: Doubleday, 1908; rpt., New York: Harper & Row, 1964). Chapter 2 of this collection of articles addresses a "curious and apparently absurd" question, "What is a Negro?" under the title "The Tragedy of the Mulatto." The theme of the "tragic mulatto" in literary, sociological, and journalistic writings of the period has been studied in detail by Ardizzone, "Red Blooded Americans," 90–159. See also Werner Sollors, ed., *Interracialism: Black-White Intermarriage in American History, Literature, and Law* (New York: Oxford University Press, 2000); Kathy Russel, Midge Wilson, and Ronald Hall, *The Color Complex: The Politics of Skin Color among African-Americans* (New York: Harcourt Brace Jovanovich, 1992).
7. Shirley Taylor Haizlipp, *The Sweeter the Juice: A Family Memoir in Black and White* (New York: Simon & Schuster, 1994), 54–60. See also the review in the *Chicago Tribune*, 26 February 1995, sec. 4, pp. 1 and 4, for a photographic reproduction of the census entries for Sumner Morris, who was black in 1910 and white in 1920. See also Paul Schor, "Un prisme en noir et blanc: l'invisibilité des familles multiraciales dans le recensement américain au début du vingtième siècle," in *Faire figure d'étranger: Regards croisés sur la production de l'altérité*, ed. C. Cossée, E. Lada, S. Lamri, and I. Rigoni (Paris: Armand Colin, 2004), 39–56.
8. Caleb Johnson, "Crossing the Color Line," *Outlook*, 26 August 1931, 526; cited by Ardizzone, "Red Blooded Americans," 136–37, who gives other examples of sociologists in the 1920s and 1930s moving in the same direction. The analogy, based on etymology, was present in congressional debates as early as 1849.
9. This new perspective, which saw mulattoes as the elite among blacks, can be found in the work of, among others, the influential Alfred Stone, *Studies in the American Race Problem* (New York: Doubleday, 1908), which bemoaned their rise because, according to him, "true blacks" accepted segregation, and also Edward Byron Reuter, whose position was more complex ("The Superiority of the Mulatto," *American Journal of Sociology* 23, no. 1 [July 1917]: 83–106). This idea also appears, more surprisingly, in the work of the historian Joel Williamson, *New People*.
10. US Congress, *Congressional Record*, 60th Cong., 2d sess., vol. 43, I, 9 December 1908, 85–86. Cited by Ardizzone, "Red Blooded Americans," 196–97.
11. *Congressional Record*, 60th Cong., 2d sess., 9 December 1908, 85–86.
12. S. N. D. North, Director, Bureau of the Census, to Sen. Chester Long, Chair, Senate Committee on the Census, 11 January 1909, *Congressional Record*, 60th Cong., 2d sess., 20 January 1909, 1154. Cited by Ardizzone, "Red Blooded Americans," 198–99.
13. "The Statistics of Population," 13–14, 18. RG 29/File 140: Lectures and Papers of S. N. D. North/Folder 5: "The Census of Population: 1900." The text is undated but later than 1910 although bearing on the results of the 1890 census and earlier.
14. Since 1830, there had been no more than two consecutive censuses that had had identical combinations of racial classifications.
15. US Bureau of the Census, *Instructions to Enumerators* (Washington, DC: GPO, 1910). Copy in "Measuring America," 48.

16. See table 7.4, p. 72, for the numbers of mulattoes from 1850 to 1920.
17. Joseph A. Hill, "Population Classified by Race and Nativity: Black and Mulatto," a study addressed by Hill to the members of the Census Advisory Committee, 9 April 1932, RG29/ File 148: Census Advisory Committee, 1919–1949.
18. US Bureau of the Census, *Negro Population, 1790–1915* (Washington, DC: GPO, 1918), ch. 11: "Color—Black and Mulatto Elements," 207–17.
19. US Bureau of the Census, *Negro Population, 1790–1915*, 207.
20. Bureau of the Census, *Negroes in the United States*, Bulletin no. 8 (Washington, DC: GPO, 1904), "prepared under the supervision of W. F. Willcox, Section on the negro farmer prepared by W. E. B Du Bois," 11, 14. W. E. B. Du Bois conducted his own statistical inquiries on southern blacks, and he believed the census had fallen short in several respects: "The Twelfth Census and the Negro Problems," *Southern Workman* 29, no. 5 (1900): 305–309 (1900); and W. E. B. Du Bois, ed., *The Health and Physique of the Negro American* (Atlanta: Atlanta University Press, 1906).
21. Maria Farland, "W. E. B. Du Bois, Anthropometric Science, and the Limits of Racial Uplift," *American Quarterly* 58, no. 4 (2006): 1017–45; Shawn Michelle Smith, "'Looking at One's Self Through the Eyes of Others': W. E. B. Du Bois's Photographs for the 1900 Paris Exposition," *African American Review* 34, no. 4 (Winter 2000): 581–99.
22. See "Executive Board of Women's League, Newport, RI," African American Photographs Assembled for the Paris Exposition of 1900: https://www.loc.gov/item/98502151/.
23. African American Photographs Assembled for the Paris Exposition of 1900, lot 11931, Plate 69: https://www.loc.gov/item/97506054/.
24. US Bureau of the Census, *Negro Population, 1790–1915*, 209. The term *discrimination* must be understood here in its literal sense of "distinction."
25. It is generally acknowledged that the 1870 census undercounted the southern population, and especially the black population, but this does not mean that mulattoes were necessarily more undercounted than blacks, especially because their proportion was higher among the black population of the North, but better accounted for. In order to say that mulattoes were undercounted in 1870, it would be necessary to break the analysis down to the local level, which the 1918 report did not do. Ibid., 208. On the other hand, in view of the decrease in the proportion of mulattoes in 1920, the Census Bureau would test this hypothesis for the results of 1910 and 1920 by conducting special tabulations. One of the benefits of the transformation of the Census Bureau into a permanent agency was its ability to work outside of census periods and perform extra tabulation and analysis.
26. Resolution 85 (November 1921), RG29/File 148: Census Advisory Committee, 1919–1949. See also the resolution "Black and Mulatto," 14–15 December 1928. It requested once again the abandonment of the distinction between blacks and mulattoes for 1930, because of the poor past results.
27. Among its first members in 1919 was Walter F. Willcox. On the committee's role with regard to the director, see Magnuson, "Making of a Modern Census," 73–78.
28. US Bureau of the Census, *The Fourteenth Census of the United States* (Washington, DC: GPO, 1922), 2:16–17. In fact, the instructions for 1920 differed in one point from those of 1910. In 1910, all persons "having some proportion or perceptible trace of black blood" were to be classified as mulatto. In 1920, the "perceptible trace" disappeared from the instructions. US Bureau of the Census, *Fourteenth Census*, vol. 2, Appendix B: Instructions to Enumerators, 1382. The expression "considerable uncertainty" was already present in the report of the 1910 census, although North, who had wanted that distinction to be made, was no longer director; US Bureau of the Census, *Thirteenth Census*, 79. North was abruptly replaced in 1909 by E. Dana Durand, a director who would later be criticized for having been too much the scientist and not enough of an administrator. North had a much more political sense of the census, and felt that its data could not be trusted 100 percent. In his opinion, the census should confine itself to the administrative use of the statistics; "Lectures and Papers of S. N. D. North," RG29/140; Durand, "Memoirs of Edward Dana Durand," ch. 7: "Work as Director of the Census, 1909–1913," 153–66.
29. US Bureau of the Census, *Fourteenth Census*, 2:17.

30. Thus, in 1913 and in 1914, census director William Harris received letters asking for the creation of a special division of the Census Bureau devoted to statistics on the black population. It was the work of a campaign organized by a Census Bureau agent, William Jennifer, clergymen from black churches, and the leaders of the NAACP, W. E. B. Du Bois and Oswald Garrison Villard. Harris responded that he lacked the means, but that he was planning to publish a special bulletin on the black population, which was entrusted to Joseph A. Hill. See correspondence in RG29/File 149, Office of the Chief Clerk, 1899–1941/Folder 309: "Negro Statistics." On the Bureau's relations with representatives of black organizations, see chapter 18.

31. Ardizzone, "Red Blooded Americans," 191.

32. The census effectively created a special section, "Negro Statistics," under the leadership of a black statistician, Charles E. Hall, presenting him in a press release as the "highest colored agent in civil service" in 1935. See chapter 18.

33. The argument set out in the 1920 report was reprised by Hill: "It may well be that the Negro enumerators take more pains than the white enumerators to distinguish and report the mulattoes." Joseph A. Hill, "Population Classified by Race and Nativity: Black and Mulatto," study addressed by Hill to the members of the Census Advisory Committee, 9 April 1932, RG29/148.

34. Ibid. The copy is dated April 1932, but the study is older, bearing on the 1920 census and obviously prior to that of 1930.

35. Calvert L. Dedrick, acting chief statistician, "Social Psychological Factors in the Enumerative Process," for presentation at a joint meeting of the American Statistical Association and the American Sociological Society, 28 December 1938, at Detroit, Michigan, p. 5; copy in RG 29/142/NN 367-1/W. L. Austin Files, 1933–1941/Box 3.

36. This law stipulated that "every person in whom there is ascertainable any Negro blood shall be deemed and taken to be a colored person" and prohibited interracial marriages of whites with non-whites. "The term 'white person' shall apply only to the person who has no trace whatsoever of any blood other than Caucasian." Sections 1-14 and 20-54 of Virginia Code.

37. For a systematic refutation of the thesis of the inferiority of mulattoes and blacks, based both on the works of Boas, who directly challenged the assumption of the inequality of the races, and on the studies done of mulattoes in the 1920s, especially by disciples of Boas and Park, see the January 1935 article by W. E. B Du Bois, "Miscegenation," in *Against Racism: Unpublished Essays: Papers, Addresses, 1887–1961, by W. E. B. Du Bois*, ed. Herbert Aptheker (Amherst: University of Massachusetts Press, 1985), 90–102; reprinted in Sollors, *Interracialism*, 461–73.

Chapter 15

1. For a more detailed account, see Paul Schor, "Compter et classer par race: Hawaii, les Îles Vierges et le recensement américain, 1900–1940," *Histoire et Mesure* 13, nos. 1–2 (1998): 113–34, available online at http://histoiremesure.revues.org/persee-128484. See also "Compter et classer" (2001), 382–450.

2. Bureau of the Census, *Census of the Virgin Islands of the United States, November 1, 1917* (Washington, DC: GPO, 1918), 44–45.

3. Undated memo, apparently from census director Rogers, in order to prepare for the census that would take place at the end of 1917. Memorandum "Virgin Islands," p. 2, RG29/File 149, Miscellaneous Records 1900–1953, Assistant Director for Operations, Office of the Chief Clerk (c. 1899–1941), Administrative Service Division/Folder 17:5 (317), Virgin Islands, Census of.

4. Bureau of the Census, *Census of the Virgin Islands*, 44.

5. Ibid.

6. "Urgently recommend your approval for Virgin Islands of third classification quote mixed unquote as was done in 1917. This will allay race feeling and obviate further protest and dissension." Telegram of W. Evans, governor of the Virgin Islands, to the director of the Census Bureau, 24 March 1930, and response from J. A. Hill, acting director of the Census, same date, RG 29/251/502, "Virgin Islands, Correspondence with Governor."

7. "Virgin Islands of the United States. Population," prepared under the supervision of LeVerne Beales, September 1940. RG 29/250/137. The expression "full-blooded white" appears nowhere else in census documents.

8. All the tables relating to the population of the Virgin Islands make this distinction in the report of the 1930 census. See Bureau of the Census, *Fifteenth Census of the United States: 1930, Outlying Territories and Possessions*, 259–76.

9. On censuses in the Canal Zone of Panama and other, smaller American possessions such as Guam and Samoa, see Schor, "Compter et classer" (2001).

10. RG 29 UD 75 (NC 3-29-81-4), "Field Division of the Census Bureau. Methods and Procedures of the 1930 Decennial Census. Fifteenth Census of the United States," Scrapbook, 1930, vol. 1: *Field and Office Work*, Section on Census of Outlying Possessions, 65–66.

11. The main divergences of the 1910 Puerto Rico census with respect to the mainland United States were the replacement of the question "Able to speak English" with "Able to speak Spanish" and the failure to pose the question on mother tongue, which had been introduced by a last-minute amendment and arrived in Puerto Rico after the census was already under way. Questions on citizenship and nationality were similarly adapted to the particular situation of the island. They were modified in 1920, since the 1917 law collectively assigned American citizenship to all the inhabitants except those who explicitly rejected it. Up through 1930, the census asked immigrants and persons born in Puerto Rico if they owed allegiance to another nation. On the other hand, in principle, categories of color and race had to conform to the American model. See "Instructions for Filling the Population Schedule," Porto Rico, 1920, para. 41: "Country of allegiance," RG 29/254/PR 1920.

12. Anderson, *Imagined Communities*.

13. *Census of Porto Rico*, 1900, Bulletin 1, p. 8.

14. *Instrucciones á los enumeradores*, 1920, p. 20, RG 29/254/PR 1920.

15. The other major adaptation of the schedule to Puerto Rico was to take account of concubinage. See especially "Single, married, consensually married, widowed, and divorced persons in the population of Porto Rico" (1930), Census Bureau communication, 7 July 1931, RG 29/251/Press Releases Puerto Rico.

16. Mara Loveman, "The US Census and the Contested Rules of Racial Classification in Early Twentieth-Century Puerto Rico (1910–1920)," *Caribbean Studies* 35, no. 2 (July–December 2007): 79–114.

17. Bureau of the Census, *Negro Population, 1790–1915*, 22–23, 207.

18. Jorge Duany, *The Puerto Rican Nation on the Move: Identities on the Island and in the United States* (Chapel Hill: University of North Carolina Press, 2002), 250; cited by Mara Loveman and Jeronimo O. Muniz, "How Puerto Rico Became White: Boundary Dynamics and Intercensus Racial Reclassification," *American Sociological Review* 72, no. 6 (2007): 915–39.

19. US Bureau of the Census, *Fifteenth Census*, vol. 3, *Outlying Territories and Possessions*, 133. In 1939, the Central Statistical Board requested that the term "colored" should no longer be used in publications on Puerto Rico, but that "Negro" should be used instead, as in the continental United States. Memorandum of 13 June 1939, "Sixteenth Census Schedules for Outlying Areas of the United States. Minor Suggestions," RG 29/250/38 (Fifteenth Census Act).

20. Memorandum of LeVerne Beales, "Population Schedule for Puerto Rico," 28 March 1939, RG 29/250/125. Beales added later in the document: "It is my understanding that the great majority of the so-called 'white' population in Puerto Rico are of mixed white and Negro blood, or of mixed white, Negro and Indian blood."

21. Loveman and Muniz, "How Puerto Rico Became White." The racial reclassification is very important in every way: nearly 30 percent of a reconstructed subsample in 1920 had a different race than in 1910, but most numerous were those who went from being something else to being white.

22. Memorandum of Starke Grogan to the director, 1 November 1928, p. 8, RG 29/251/Puerto Rico/Box 13/Correspondence with Director. On the gap between official instructions and the practice of census agents, see Loveman, "US Census and the Contested Rules of Racial Classification."

23. See figure 11, and other photos from the series 350-PR-44C on Puerto Rico in the National Archives.

24. Robert C. Schmitt, *Demographic Statistics of Hawaii: 1778–1965* (Honolulu: University of Hawaii Press, 1968).
25. Domínguez, "Exporting US Concepts of Race," 369–99.
26. Christian Topalov, "L'individu comme convention: Le cas des statistiques professionelles du XIXe siècle en France, en Grande-Bretagne et aux États-Unis," *Genèses* 31 (June 1998): 73.
27. US Census Office, *Twelfth Census*, Population, Part 1, cxvii.
28. See table "Statistically Unrecognized Mixed-bloods," in Romanzo Adams, *Interracial Marriage in Hawaii: A Study of the Mutually Conditioned Processes of Acculturation and Amalgamation* (New York: Macmillan, 1937), 346–47.
29. Letter of R. Adams to W. M. Steuart, director of the census, 27 March 1931, and response of 12 May 1931, RG 29/251/627 (Hawaii, Suggestions in Tabulation). Adams redid the calculations, compared the data to those of the Hawaiian registry office, and scrutinized the Census Bureau's arbitration in the cases of multiracial children as a source of the disagreement.
30. Adams's influence is attested by internal reports discussing modifications of instructions or statistical treatments made at his request, as well as by the summaries of discussions with him, or the place of his writings in the bibliography on Hawaii used by the statistical division for the territories. See "Memorandum for Dr. Hill; Citizenship in Hawaii," S. M. Grogan, 8 May 1931, RG 29/251/622; Discussion of Romanzo Adams with M. Birge, assistant to LeVerne Beales, division chief, RG 29/250/122; "Books Read by the Division," list of February 1937, RG 29/250/box 17/folder 13. Many of these references deal with racial questions.
31. Adams stated in discussions that counting 27,558 inhabitants as being of the "Portuguese" race in 1930 made no sense, because if the term had initially been used to designate the descendants of the 150 blacks who had arrived from a Portuguese possession in 1870, most of the persons so categorized were the descendants of European immigrants. This oddity parallels the 1930 creation in the continental United States of a "Mexican" race, discussed in chapter 16. In the same discussion, he added that Puerto Ricans should not be classified as whites since they mostly resulted from a mixture of black and Indian blood. See discussion of Romanzo Adams with M. Birge, assistant of LeVerne Beales, division chief, RG 29/250/122.
32. Andrew W. Lind, *Hawaii's People*, 4th ed. (Honolulu: University Press of Hawaii, 1980 [1955]), and "Economic Succession and Racial Invasion in Hawaii" (PhD diss., University of Chicago, 1931), published as *An Island Community: Ecological Succession in Hawaii* (Chicago: University of Chicago Press, 1938).
33. Bernhard L. Hormann, "'Racial' Statistics in Hawaii," *Social Process in Hawaii* 12 (1948): 34.
34. We saw in chapter 10 how Congress in 1889 added the words "or race" to the heading "color" for this reason.
35. Letter from Delegate V. S. K. Houston to Wm. Steuart, 2 May 1928, and Steuart's response, 23 May 1928. This request was supported by the governor of Hawaii, who emphasized the need to use a term that did not apply to blacks in the continental United States. Letter of W. R. Farrington to Steuart, 6 June 1928, RG 29/198, General Subject File of the Statistical Research Division/163: Hawaii 1930. See also the memorandum of Starke Grogan for the director, who complained of these repeated applications, 26 March 1932, RG 29/251/613-1.
36. "Monthly Reports," 7 February 1939 and 7 April 1939, RG 29/250/Box 17.
37. See, for example, the letter of LeVerne Beales of 23 September 1940 to a correspondent in California, Gerald A. Estep. Beales says that this was done following the recommendations of the Hawaii Bureau of Governmental Research, a point of view upheld by Andrew Lind when he visited the Census Bureau, 1 September 1938, RG 29/250/General Correspondence, "E" and file on "Hawaii Supervisors."

Chapter 16

1. US Census Office, *Twelfth Census: Supplementary Analysis*, 176.
2. Ibid., 176–77. A footnote refers to the example of the Croatans, reported as whites in 1890 and as Indians in 1900, who "are said, however, to be 'generally white showing the Indian mostly in action and habits.'"
3. Mongolian was the term used by the census to talk about the various Asian races it used in the schedules; the term Mongolian was not a census category.

4. These Hollerith machines developed for the census, which were state of the art in 1920, were used in some Florida counties for counting ballots in the 2000 presidential election.

5. "Instructions to Enumerators, 1930, Revised," p. 26, 1930, Form 15-100, RG 29/212, Forms and Schedules, Collections of the Statistical Research Division, Instructions to Assistant Marshals and Enumerators etc., 1850 to 1939/738.

6. "Instructions to Supervisors, 1930, Revised," 1930, paras. 121 and 122, pp. 25–26 (15-13a). Paragraphs 121, 122, and 126 (mother tongue) did not appear in the unrevised version (15-13) of 1929. Schedule 15-13a, ibid. On Du Bois and the 1900 census, see chapter 14.

7. In the case of Alaskan Indians, between 1910 and 1940, the linguistic grouping played the role of race. The census identified some mixed-race Indians, the offspring of different tribes or linguistic groups, which allowed for measurement of "purity of blood." Here again, the father's race was the determining factor. See *Indian Population in the United States and Alaska, 1910*, 32–33, 123, 154; *Fourteenth Census*, 3:1158; Bureau of the Census, *Sixteenth Census of the United States—1940, Population*, [Bulletin] Second Series, "Characteristics of the Population. Alaska" (Washington, DC: GPO, 1943), 1. See also, for the determination in 1940 whether Alaskan natives were racially Indian or Eskimo, "Subjects to be discussed with the Governor of Alaska," RG 29/251/Material to be taken to Alaska by Mr Beales. More generally, see Schor, "Compter et classer" (2001), 403–14.

8. US Bureau of the Census, *Coding Instructions for the Population Schedule. Individual Card. Fifteenth Census* (Washington, DC: GPO, 1930), 4.

9. Editing Instructions, Individual Card, 9-512, RG 29/212/Folder 26, Population 1920. See also figure 14.

10. "F" for Foreign-Birth indicated that a person was not American by birth; "Instructions for card verification. Individual card. 9-584," ibid. See also figures 22 and 23. For an example of a 1940 coding card, see figure 1.

11. Instructions Manual of 29 April 1939, Part I, Personal Particulars and Geographic Coding: Punching Instructions, 5th ed., p. 12, RG 29/231 Records Relating to Vital Statistics, General Records, 1936–1946/704.34, Instructions Manuals.

12. "**83. Color or race.**—Punch 'White,' 'Black,' 'Mulatto,' 'Indian,' 'Chinese,' 'Japanese,' 'Filipino,' 'Hindu,' or 'Korean,' as the case may be. For any other color or race, punch 'Other' and write information on card." 1918 Special Census of Okmulgee County, Oklahoma, 15 August 1918, Instruction to Enumerators, RG 29/212.

13. *United States v. Thind* (261 US 204, 1923). See Haney López, *White by Law*, 67–109; Joan Jensen, *Passage from India: Asian Indian Immigrants in North America* (New Haven, CT: Yale University Press, 1988), 247–69; Tehranian, "Performing Whiteness," 817–48.

14. US Bureau of the Census, *Fourteenth Census*, 2:29.

15. Since 1990, the Asian races have been consolidated under the designation "Asian or Pacific Islander" (API), but they remain separately enumerated on the schedules. On the short form (D-10) for 2000, the choices were: "White; Black, African Am., or Negro; American Indian or Alaska Native—Print name of enrolled or principal tribe; Asian Indian; Chinese; Japanese; Korean; Filipino; Vietnamese; Other Asian—Print race; Native Hawaiian; Guamanian or Chamorro; Samoan; Other Pacific Islander—Print race; Some other race—Print race." US Department of Commerce, Bureau of the Census, Form D-10, United States Census 2000. Of the fifteen choices proposed (for the first time in 2000, it was possible to check more than one box and thus to combine races), a unique box corresponds to Americans of European origin, of North Africa, or of the Middle East, one to black Africa, one to Amerindians, one to a choice different from those offered, and eleven to the races corresponding to peoples of Asia and the Pacific. If we set aside the US territories of the Pacific, the choices offered for Asia are all nationalities or countries of origin, exactly as they were a century earlier.

16. On the anti-Asian racism that was central to the 1924 immigration law, see Mae M. Ngai, "The Architecture of Race in American Immigration Law: A Reexamination of the Immigration Act of 1924," *Journal of American History* 86, no. 1 (June 1999): 67–92.

17. Thirteenth Census, Special Instruction to enumerators relating to the enumeration of Indians, 33258-10, 1910, RG 29/212. Note that these instructions speak of "white" families and communities as a way to designate all non-Indian families. See instructions for the special schedule in "Measuring America," 55–57. The instructions deal mainly with fractions of blood

(Indian and other), polygamy, and tribal lands. See also the facsimile in Bureau of the Census, *200 Years of US Census Taking*, 56–57. For the "percentage of blood," agents were told to speak to tribal elders, since "an Indian is sometimes of mixed blood without knowing it."

18. Bureau of the Census, *Fourteenth Census*, vol. 2, Appendix B: "Instructions to Enumerators."

19. "Illustrative Example of Manner of Filling Population Schedule," 1910, US Bureau of the Census, *Thirteenth Census*, 1:1368–69; and "Illustrative Example of Manner of Filling Population Schedule, 1920," US Bureau of the Census, *Fourteenth Census*, 2:1376–77. See also figure 14.

20. Form 16-2700, P-104, Department of Commerce, Bureau of the Census, Sixteenth Census of the United States: 1940, Test 1, Based on abridged instructions to enumerators for population schedule, RG 29/142 (NN 367-1), Records of William Lane Austin, Director 1933–1941/ File 29a, Executive Assistant to the Director.

21. Sixteenth Census, Instructions to enumerators, Form PA-1, 16-380, Scrapbook 4 of 5, p. 43, RG 29/238, Assistant Dir. for Demographic Fields, Records of the Population and Housing Division, Scrapbooks relating to the censuses of population, 1920–1940.

22. "The strictly personal characteristics which appear in the census classifications are three, namely, color, sex, and age. Color is significant primarily because of the social and economic differentiation between the white and the Negro population, especially in the southern states, though statistics by color or race are of importance in many other connections. This classification is made less accurately than some of the others because of difficulty in getting reliable information with respect to persons of mixed blood. A person with any fraction of Negro blood is theoretically classified as a Negro. Actually, however, many individuals of mixed blood whose Negro characteristics are not physically prominent are without doubt classified as white." (Leon E. Truesdell, "Value of the Population Census for Research," reprinted from *Annals of the American Academy of Political and Social Science*, Philadelphia, November 1936, 331; Leon E. Truesdell files, Bureau of the Census Library, Suitland, MD). "The fundamental classification in the statistics of population is that based on color or race. This distinction is probably, next to sex, the most definite and specific of all the classifications. Yet its application requires at the outset certain arbitrary definitions: one, to the effect that all persons having any Negro blood whatsoever shall be returned as Negroes; and another, somewhat inconsistent, that persons of mixed white and Indian blood shall be returned as Indians only when they are so regarded in the locality where they are found" (Leon E. Truesdell, "Methods Involved in the Federal Census of Population," excerpted from *Methods in Social Science*, ed. Stuart A. Rice [Chicago: University of Chicago Press, 1931], 203–204); Leon E. Truesdell files, Bureau of the Census Library. Truesdell's text was written in 1928.

23. The outline of the political history of the episode has been sketched by Linda Chavez, "Promoting Racial Harmony," in *The Affirmative Action Debate*, ed. George E. Curry and Cornel West (Reading, MA: Addison Wesley, 1996), 317. According to this version, while Mexicans had been classified as white since 1848 (the date of signing of the Treaty of Guadalupe-Hidalgo, which put an end to the US–Mexican War), the 1930 census assigned them the status of a racial group, which aroused protests from the Mexican government and led to the classification being dropped. We shall see that the history is more complex, since the target of the classification was not the descendants of Mexicans of 1848 but rather more recent immigrants.

24. In 1900, the Bureau's official name was still Census Office; in 1902, the permanent agency adopted the name Census Bureau and then, definitively, Bureau of the Census.

25. US Census Office, *Twelfth Census: Supplementary Analysis*, 177.

26. In this table, "Part Mexican" and "Other unknown" are not included in the total number or total percentage, as the focus is on part white-part Indian mixture; being anything other than white or Indian obviously put persons outside of the Indian population. For that reason, the total seems to be over 100%. US Bureau of the Census, *Indian Population in the United States and Alaska, 1910*, Table 15, p. 35.

27. Although we know the circumstances of the abandonment of this racial classification, those of its introduction have left no trace in the archives and seem to have given rise to very little discussion, unlike other difficult questions that were discussed in preparation for the census. The classification of Mexicans as a race did appear on the agenda for the meeting of the Census

Advisory Committee on 14 and 15 December 1928, but the minutes contain no record of such a discussion. "The Fifteenth Census Schedule," Memorandum for the meeting of 14–15 December 1928, RG 29/148. The Census Bureau had decided to seek broad input from the public a year before the census and then to evaluate the suggestions by means of specially constituted committees. The questions on unemployment (the final version of the question was "Whether actually at work yesterday?") were the ones that had raised the most concern and had the longest discussion. See Magnuson, "Making of a Modern Census," 86–92.

28. Census, *Fifteenth Census*, Population, 2:27. Italics in original. The report also mentions "a very considerable influx of Mexicans between 1920 and 1930" and makes an attempt at retroactively reclassifying whites as Mexicans from the 1920 census (700,541 persons) and the 1910 census (367,510), pp. 25 and 27.

29. See Gratton and Gutman, "Hispanics in the United States, 1850–1990," 137–53. Gratton and Gutman note that in 1880 Hispanics were classified as mulatto in Colorado but not in New Mexico, which seems to validate the hypothesis that Hispanic census workers were recruited in one state but not in the other. According to Gratton and Gutman, the mulattoes with Hispanic names enumerated in the Southwest in 1920 were mainly Hispanic blacks, especially Cubans of African origin. They therefore believe this classification to be correct.

30. Myron P. Gutman, W. Parker Frisbie, and K. Stephen Blanchard, "A New Look at the Hispanic Population of the United States in 1910," *Historical Methods* 32, no. 1 (Winter 1999): 10n5. The authors estimate the Hispanic population, all generations combined, as 845,000 in 1910, rather than the traditional figure of 500,000 (p. 6).

31. It is doubtful that the Census Bureau in Washington would have wanted to encourage discordant local interpretations of racial categories, or that it would have viewed favorably the confusion between Mexicans and Americans of color, that is, blacks. In fact, the Bureau in the 1920s appears not to have been concerned with, or even aware of, this particular application of the mulatto category.

32. *Fifteenth Census*, vol. 2, *Population*, 233. Mexican immigrants constituted the base of Spanish-speaking immigration in 1930, at a time when there were only 10,514 inhabitants born in Central America and 33,623 from South America.

33. Tomás Almaguer, *Racial Fault Lines: The Historical Origins of White Supremacy in California* (Berkeley: University of California Press, 1995).

34. Form 15-100, "Instructions to enumerators, Population and agriculture, Revised," RG 29/212/738.

35. Ngai, "Architecture of Race," 91, and *Impossible Subjects*).

36. Material for press release on 1930 schedule, RG 29/215. "Population of the United States by Color or Race," Released for use of afternoon papers on Aug. 4, 1931, ibid. In this document, the census retroactively extracted from the white population of 1920 some 700,541 persons of Mexican race, although without stating how this "estimate" was formed. See also Nobles, *Shades of Citizenship*, 73–74.

37. Mario T. Garcia, *Mexican Americans: Leadership, Ideology and Identity, 1930–1960* (New Haven, CT: Yale University Press, 1989), 29–31.

38. F. Arturo Rosales, "Shifting Self Perceptions and Ethnic Consciousness among Mexicans in Houston, 1930–1946," *Aztlan* 16, nos. 1–2 (1985): 82–84. In his research Rosales made use of both Mexican and American government archives.

39. Letter of Joseph A. Hill, Acting Director, to Alonso S. Perales, 4 February 1930, RG 29/215/File S3. Hill also sent Perales several copies, in Spanish and English, of the presidential proclamation for the 1930 census. Perales had been recommended to Hill by the Berkeley economist Paul S. Taylor, an expert on southwestern migrant labor. Taylor had told Hill that there ought to be articles in the newspapers that Mexicans read, which might lead them to see participation in the census as "a patriotic duty toward their country, whether the United States or Mexico."

40. "The Director [Steuart] brought up the subject of Mexicans and asked the Committee how they thought Mexicans should be classified. The Committee agreed that they should not be classified as white and that it would be best to include them with 'Other races'" (Minutes of the meeting of 13 March 1931, RG 29/148).

41. Minutes of the meeting of 21 April 1934, RG 29/148.

42. This was the point of view defended by the consumer economist Cherlingon at the same meeting, for Mexicans as well as for Asians, especially in order to study the prevalence of certain diseases. For the debate on the relevance and legality of tables of life expectancy and differential rates of coverage or eligibility for life insurance for blacks, see "Mortality and Insurance of Colored Persons," *Publications of the American Statistical Association* 3, nos. 21–22 (March–June 1893): 350–52. On the question of life insurance policies and insurance companies specializing in this segment of the market, see John S. Haller Jr., "Race, Mortality, and Life Insurance: Negro Vital Statistics in the Late Nineteenth Century," *Journal of the History of Medicine and Allied Sciences* 25 (July 1970): 247–61.

43. Willard C. Smith, Assistant Chief Statistician for Vital Statistics, to Dr. Hill, 13 August 1934, RG 29/230, Records of the Office of Ass. Dir. for Stat. Standards, Records Relating to Vital Statistics/351, Classification of Mexican Births and Deaths, 1934.

44. Director of the Census to Dr. Halbert L. Dunn, Chief Statistician for Division of Vital Statistics, "Instructions for classification of Births and Deaths, by race or color, for all publications of the Division of Vital Statistics," 15 October 1936, RG29/149/321 (17/12).

45. Memorandum from the Director, "Population," without recipient name, 3 December 1936. RG29/149/321 (17/12).

46. Letter from the chargé d'affaires of the Mexican embassy in Washington, DC, to the US secretary of state, 29 July 1937, RG 85, Records of the Immigration and Naturalization Service/ 26, Administrative files relating to Naturalization, 1906–1940/File 19783:155, Mexican as white.

47. Memorandum of Edw. J. Shaughnessy, Acting Commissioner, no. 111, 18 May 1937, ibid.

48. For mention of several courts denying naturalization to Mexicans as "racially ineligible" despite the fact that the Naturalization Service had adopted a policy classifying Mexicans as of the white race, see letter from Lemuel B. Schoffield, Special Assistant to the Attorney General, 21 October 1941, to Mrs. Franklin Roosevelt, The White House (after a complaint made to her by a Mexican woman), ibid.

49. A circular from the deputy director of the Immigration and Naturalization Service, 15 August 1937, directed that on all the necessary documents concerning immigration or naturalization, the race of persons of Mexican origin should be given as "white" rather than "Mexican." The letter explained that use of the term "white" instead of "Mexican" was intended to apply to all situations and not just the compilation of statistics. Letter of Edw. J. Shaughnessy, Deputy Commissioner, to District Director, Galveston, Texas, 27 August 1937, citing the circular on this subject, Central Office Circular No. 154 of 17 August 1937, ibid.

50. Formed in 1933 by the Franklin D. Roosevelt administration, the Central Statistical Board was headed by Stuart Rice, president of the American Statistical Board and assistant director of the census, with the particular charge of achieving convergence—by authority, if necessary—between the various government statistical agencies. See Duncan and Shelton, *Revolution in United States Government Statistics*; and Robert M. Jenkins, *Procedural History of the 1940 Census of Population and Housing* (Madison: University of Wisconsin Press, 1985), 5–6.

51. Figure 12 shows the members of the committee in 1941, with Director Austin and Assistant Director Dedrick presiding.

52. Minutes of the Census Advisory Committee, 5 January 1940, RG 29/File UD 10 (NN 3-29-80), Census Advisory Committee.

53. "Although the statistics of persons of Spanish mother tongue could hardly be said to cover exactly the same segment of the population as covered by the 1930 statistics on 'Mexicans,' the two sets of statistics would seem, on an a priori basis, to do so to a considerable extent"; US Bureau of the Census, *US Census of Population: 1950. Special Reports. Persons of Spanish Surname*, 1950, Population Census Report P-E No. 3C, preprint of Vol. 4, part 3, chap. C (Washington, DC: GPO, 1953), 3C-4.

54. Recommendations of the CSB, 12 June 1939, discussed at the meeting of 16–19 June 1939, RG 29/148.

55. On the persistent resistance of Hispanics to be placed in the context of American racial categories, see Clara E. Rodríguez, *Changing Race: Latinos, the Census, and the History of Ethnicity in the United States* (New York: New York University Press, 2000) and Kenneth Prewitt, *What Is*

Your Race? The Census and Our Flawed Efforts to Classify Americans (Princeton, NJ: Princeton University Press, 2013).

56. Rosales, "Shifting Self Perceptions," 89–90. His conclusion is that Mexican-Americans experimented with a strategy to fight discrimination in the 1930s, in the belief that not being seen as white was the main economic and social obstacle they faced, and for lack of definitive results, in the postwar years they turned toward another strategy: "The fact that Chicano leaders are willing today [1985] to be identified with racial minorities suggests the abandonment of that strategy, perhaps because it was not effective. The perceived success of the civil rights movement in the nurturing atmosphere of the 1960s and 1970s, created a tacitly accepted, albeit vague notion that admitting to 'non-whiteness' could pay off. The acceptance of racial minority status acquires an even greater significance when one considers the investment which Mexican Americans put into the struggle to be classified as white. In fact, this historical shift parallels the struggle beginning in the 1930s to be considered white because projecting a Mexican image, no matter how positive it might seem to Mexicans, would not be accepted by Anglo society."

57. This is what Kenneth Prewitt calls the democratization of the census, although he applies the notion to a later period. Prewitt, *What Is Your Race?*

Chapter 17

1. The question of legal status at this point seemed to take such a back seat that the director of citizenship in the Naturalization Bureau, Raymond F. Christ, could put into writing an astonishing error in the definition of the term *alien*, stating that "the word 'aliens' means foreign-born persons and includes those who are naturalized." LeVerne Beales, assigned in 1919 to handle statistics on foreigners, justly reminded him that not only census usage but immigration laws unambiguously defined *alien* as a person of foreign nationality. One can see how Christ could disagree with census figures on the number of foreigners, or "aliens," given that census statistics (which according to him underestimated the reality) and those of the Immigration and Naturalization Service were in conflict. But such a misunderstanding regarding a term so central to immigration and nationality law, on the part of so senior an officer, was unheard-of and disturbing—especially between the concern over "enemy aliens" of the war and the reform of immigration laws that came two years after this letter. See the letter of Raymond F. Christ, Director of Citizenship, Bureau of Naturalization, 14 May 1919, RG 29/205, Records of the Office of the Assistant Director for Statistical Standards Records of the Chief Statistician, Correspondence of LeVerne Beales 1915–1919/Beales, Personal.

2. US Census Office, "Eleventh Census, 1890," Bulletin no. 19, "Vital Statistics of the Jews in the United States," 30 December 1890. The data were obtained for ten thousand families that were "members of the Jewish race," contacted through religious organizations. A comment on this bulletin appears in Dr. Vacher, *Considérations sur le Census Américain de 1890*, extract from the *Journal de la Société de statistique de Paris*, October 1891 (Nancy: Berger-Levrault, 1891), 14 pages: "The figure on mortality [7.1 per thousand] seems rather dubious: statistics in our country have long since highlighted the remarkable vitality of the Jewish race."

3. Letter of Superintendent Porter to Benjamin Peixota (*The Menorah Monthly*), 29 August 1889. He cited a letter from Billings, who was not in favor of enumerating Hebrews unless other religions were also enumerated. He preferred the solution, finally adopted, of an investigation undertaken through the leaders of the community. "It should be understood in making this arrangement that we propose to treat the Hebrews as a race, and not as a religious sect." Billings and Porter proposed a meeting with this editor of a Jewish newspaper in New York. RG29/83, Records of the Eleventh Census, Records of the Superintendent, Record of Letters Sent Feb.–Nov. 1889.

4. "The question of statement of Jewish or non-Jewish should be obtained if it can be done without conflicting with religious ideas. Therefore an expression of opinion from prominent Jewish authorities should be obtained and perhaps the express sanction of Congress for this part of the work." Letter of Cressy L. Wilbur, Chief Statistician, to William C. Hunt, Acting Director, 17 June 1909. RG 29/145, Correspondence of William Fl. Willoughby, Assistant Director 1910. See also Schor, "Compter et Classer" (2001), 306–309.

5. On the use of the term "race" for European immigrants, Husband noted, in a letter to the Assistant Secretary of Labor, that he considered "race" or "people" interchangeable, but that the example of Austria-Hungary and its many races showed that the term "nation" was utterly unsuited for the study of immigration; see letter from W. W. Husband to Hon. William R. Wheeler, Assistant Secretary of Commerce and Labor, Washington, DC, 15 December 1909, W. W. Husband Papers/Correspondence/File 1, William Walter Husband Papers, Chicago History Museum, Chicago.

6. "Physically the Hebrew is a mixed race, like all our immigrant races or peoples, although to a less degree than most. . . . The 'Jewish nose,' and to a less degree other facial characteristics, are found well-nigh everywhere throughout the race, although the form of the head seems to have become quite the reverse of the Semitic type. The social solidarity of the Jews is chiefly a product of religion and tradition. Yet, taking all factors into account, and especially their type of civilization, the Jews of to-day are more truly European than Asiatic or Semitic. The classification of the Bureau of Immigration separates the Hebrews from the Semites and places them in the Slavic grand division of the Aryan family, although, as is explained above, they are not Aryan. Nine-tenths of our Jewish immigrants come, however, from Slavic territory." US Immigration Commission, *Dictionary of Races or Peoples*, 73–74. For the editor, W. Z. Ripley, see chapter 14.

7. For an in-depth discussion of this question, see Joel Perlmann, *"Race or People?" Federal Race Classifications for Europeans in America, 1898–1913*, Working Paper No. 320 (Annandale-on-Hudson, NY: Bard College, Levy Economics Institute, 2001). See also Hochschild and Powell, "Racial Reorganization and the United States Census 1850–1930," 76–77, showing the senators' uncertainty over the meaning of terms for race and nationality.

8. "Jews a Race No More?" *Chicago Record Herald*, 26 April 1909.

9. See Louis Wirth, *The Ghetto* (1928; rpt., New Brunswick, NJ: Transaction Books, 1998).

10. For a more detailed study of reactions in the city of Chicago, see Paul Schor, "Origines nationales, race et ethnicité dans le recensement américain, de l'indépendance à 1920" (MA thesis, EHESS, 1994), 59–62.

11. Hebrew as a race in naturalization forms, 1930. Contested by the American Jewish Committee. Opinion of Solicitor, 16 July 1930, RG 85/26, Administrative files relating to Naturalization, 1906–1940/79-53.

12. Dr. Dewhurst stated that in view of Nazi programs, such a question risked widespread rejection by Jewish immigrants, which would cause public relations problems, something the Census Bureau feared, especially just before a census. "He would not counsel the inclusion of the question, he said, if the Bureau wanted to keep its public relation straight with immigrant people." Minutes of the session of 17–18 June 1938, 1940, "Population schedule," RG 29/148. As a comparison, in the Canadian census of 1991, 405,995 persons declared themselves Jewish, either by religion or by ethnicity, or both. The United Kingdom at the end of twentieth century debated the inclusion of an ethnic category, "Jewish," in its censuses. The arguments in favor are presented in Barry Kosmin, "Ethnic and Religious Questions in the 2001 UK Census of Population Policy Recommendations," *Jewish Policy Research Policy Papers* 2 (1999), available online: http://www.bjpa.org/Publications/details.cfm?PublicationID=4103.

13. See especially *Congressional Record*, 1910, 3129–30. Representative Sabath, who was of Czech origin and came from Chicago, played a very active role in favor of the adoption of this amendment. His role was clearly that of an ethnic leader defending the interests of his constituents.

14. RG 233/HR 61A-H4.1.

15. Ibid.

16. The list of ethnic leaders drawn up for the 1920 census can be found in File 66, Foreign Language Appeals Letters Census of 1920, RG 29/198, General Subject File of the Statistical Division.

17. Letter of Thor J. Benson to Sam L. Rogers, Director of the 1920 Census, ibid.

18. See figures 3 and 4 for the proclamation of the 1940 census, translated into twenty-two languages.

19. *Denni Hlasatel*, 4 May 1912, Chicago Foreign Language Press Survey (CFLPS) Records, Special Collections, Joseph Regenstein Library, University of Chicago. For a more detailed analysis, see Schor, "Origines nationales, race et ethnicité dans le recensement américain."

20. Rather than believe that there are accurate figures and false figures, we can see that these figures were produced in a specific historical context, which must be recognized. In other words, for us, their interest lies not so much in methodological rigor as in the social value that was accorded them.

21. Identifying one's mother tongue as Yiddish, the method used by the census to estimate the Jewish population, amounted to identifying oneself as a Jew. Because of the separation of church and state, the federal agency could not ask questions about religion, so it used this method to cross-check the figures for the Jewish population, estimating that 90 percent of American Jews had Yiddish as their mother tongue. Census figures were not generally challenged by Jewish organizations, even if the registers of the community continued to serve equally as a source. The quotation is found in the CFLPS Collection of the Regenstein Library.

22. The Census Bureau explored various methods for establishing the quotas, especially for the second law (1924). One of the discarded plans was to reconstitute the national origin, with no limit on generations, of the cumulative general population having lived in the United States. To this end, linguists and anthropologists were tasked with re-attributing into their "true" groups of origin persons who had Anglicized their names. Given the huge margins of error of such methods, this plan was discarded in favor of the much simpler one of taking as a point of reference the cumulative immigration, projected onto the actual population. The archives of the Census Bureau hold part of the correspondence relating to these abortive plans; see RG 29/NN 374-63, Reports, Correspondence, and Other Records Relating to Immigration Quota Laws and National Origin Statistics, c. 1920–1936. See also Ngai, "Architecture of Race," 67–92.

23. Memorandum of Joseph A. Hill to Director, 5 February 1919, concerning border changes in Europe and the questions of birth and mother tongue. Hill relied on the analysis of E. A. Goldenweiser, who worked for the Census Bureau on mother tongue data in 1910. The document was discussed again in 1929 by the Census Advisory Committee. In October 1929, the committee ruled against the inclusion of this question on the schedules for 1930, whether for the native or foreign-born population; see Resolution 193 (18 and 19 October 1929). Both documents are in RG 29/148/Box 1 (1919–1923). See also Goldenweiser, "The Mother Tongue Inquiry in the Census of Population," 648–55.

24. "100 percent of those of Polish speech and a small proportion of the Jews." Memorandum of S. W. Boggs, Geographer, State Department, January 1928, and "Foreign-born Factor" (February 1928), for Joseph Hill, RG 29/NN 374-63, Population Division Re Immigration Quotas, 1920–1935. Boggs was the secretary of the Quota Board, to which we shall return.

25. Hearing of Mr. Boggs, State Department, by the Census Advisory Committee, meeting of 18–19 October 1929, RG 29/148.

26. On the difficulties of trying to unify methods between these two agencies, in particular the treatment and mechanical tabulation of INS data by Census Bureau statisticians during a two-year period (1903–1905), see S. N. D. North's reply, *The Census Office and Coordination of Statistics*, Reply of the Director of the Census to the Inquiries of the Interdepartmental Statistical Committee, 8 January 1909 (Washington, DC: GPO, 1909), 19.

27. For a thorough study of the history of the list of races used by the immigration services from 1898 to 1952, and the importance of the often overlooked conceptual differences between the 1921 and 1924 laws, see Patrick Weil, "Races at the Gate: A Century of Racial Distinctions in American Immigration Policy (1865–1965)," *Georgetown Immigration Law Journal* 15, no. 4 (Summer 2001): 625–48. Weil shows that the 1911 *Dictionary of Races and Peoples* was an explanatory document, while in practice the working tool was the list drawn up in 1898 and used, with some changes, until 1952. Weil shows that this list was not drawn up by the Smithsonian Institution, as stated repeatedly by the State Department and Labor Department in the 1920s, 1930s, and 1940s, but by three civil servants with connections to labor unions and the Immigration Restriction League.

28. This directive orders all federal agencies to use what the historian David Hollinger has called the "racial pentagon." The official races are white, black, American Indian, Asian, or Pacific Islander, while within the white category, a distinction is made between Hispanic white and non-Hispanic white. This directive is still in force today, and served as a point of reference for

the 2000 census, although in several instances its meaning has been changed. See David A. Hollinger, *Postethnic America: Beyond Multiculturalism* (New York: Basic Books, 1995).

29. This was a committee of the Commerce Department, different from the Census Advisory Committee of the Census Bureau; see RG 29/149, Miscellaneous Records 1900–1953, Assistant Director for Operations, Office of the Chief Clerk (c. 1899–1941), Administrative Service Division/File 321 #3, 17-14, Files of the Advisory Committee on Census of Population.

30. RG 29/148/Box 2, 1926–1932.

31. H. H. Laughlin, Secretary of the Eugenics Research Association, copy of a letter of 23 August 1929 addressed to several senators, the president, and the secretary of commerce, who forwarded it to the census director. Steuart replied that it was interesting, but that he had already said no, that the data were impossible for the census to obtain. Response of W. M. Steuart, 13 September 1929, RG 29/198/170, Correspondence relative to the racial origin of the inhabitants of the United States, Laughlin, Harry H.

32. "Measuring America," 59.

33. Ibid., 63.

34. Ibid., 85.

35. Since the classic work of John Higham (*Strangers in the Land: Patterns of American Nativism, 1865–1925* [1955; rpt., New Brunswick, NJ: Rutgers University Press, 1988]), this question has given rise to a large output that we cannot take account of here. Instead, we simply refer readers to Edward Hutchinson, *Legislative History of American Immigration Policy, 1798–1965* (Philadelphia: University of Pennsylvania Press, 1981). The historiography of immigration has long been characterized by a focus on immigration from European countries. For a perspective that restores non-European groups to immigration history, see Silvia Pedraza, "Beyond Black and White: Latinos and Social Science Research on Immigration, Race, and Ethnicity in America," *Social Science History* 24, no. 4 (Winter 2000): 697–726; and especially Mae M. Ngai, "Architecture of Race" and *Impossible Subjects*, which offer a fruitful rereading of the 1924 legislation. See also Weil, "Races at the Gate."

36. The literacy test was clearly conceived by its advocates as a method of triage, a way of refusing entry to the largely rural and Catholic immigrants from southern and eastern European countries, who had the reputation of being uncivilized and undeserving of American citizenship. Advocates of the literacy test were found among the ruling classes of New England, such as Henry Cabot Lodge and Prescott Hall with his Immigration Restriction League, as well as among unionized workers, themselves very often immigrants or the children of immigrants. See Catherine Collomp, "Unions, Civics, and National Identity: Organized Labor's Reaction to Immigration, 1881–1897," in *In the Shadow of the Statue of Liberty: Immigrants, Workers, and Citizens in the American Republic, 1880–1920*, ed. Marianne Debouzy (Urbana: University of Illinois Press, 1992), 229–56; and *Entre classe et nation: Mouvement ouvrier et immigration aux États-Unis* (Paris: Belin, 1998), chs. 6 and 7.

37. See Historical Statistics, Immigration, US Census: http://www2.census.gov/library/publications/1975/compendia/hist_stats_colonial-1970/hist_stats_colonial-1970p1-chC.pdf.

38. Hutchinson, *Legislative History of American Immigration Policy*, 210–11.

39. Congress had first considered a quota of 5 percent.

40. Ngai, "Architecture of Race," 71; Weil, "Races at the Gate."

41. Lawrence H. Fuchs, *The American Kaleidoscope: Race, Ethnicity, and the Civic Culture* (Middletown, CT: Wesleyan University Press, 1990), 60.

42. Quoted in ibid.

43. Ngai, *Impossible Subjects*; and Aristide Zolberg, *A Nation by Design: Immigration Policy in the Fashioning of America* (Cambridge, MA: Harvard University Press, 2006).

44. Immigration Act of 1924, 43 Stat. 153, 1924, Section 11 (Numerical Limitations), para. c.

45. Immigration Act of 1924, section 12 (Nationality), para. a. The law allowed for reassigning territories or regions of birth of 1890, when known, according to new national boundaries, provided they were recognized by the United States (para. c).

46. "Aliens ineligible to citizenship or their descendants," section 11, para. d. The Japanese government unsuccessfully protested this measure, on the grounds that it violated the "Gentlemen's Agreement."

47. See, for example, "Racial Origins of White Persons in the United States on January 1, 1920 (for Dr. Hill's Article, September 1936) Determined by Taking into Account Persons from All Countries—'Quota' and 'Non-quota,'" RG 29/NN 374-63. The article referred to is Joseph A. Hill, "Composition of the American Population by Race and Country of Origin," *Annals of the American Academy of Political and Social Science* 188 (November 1936): 177–84. The article concludes: "Few persons could then boast of unmixed descent from any single country or people. That is to say, there would be few whose immigrant ancestors all came from the same country. The average or typical white American would be about 37 percent English, including a small admixture of Welsh, 8 percent Scotch, 11 percent Irish, and 17 percent German. The rest of the blood in his veins would be of very mixed origin, derived from many countries with no one country predominant. Italy, Poland, and France each contributing about 4 percent of the total, Russia, Czechoslovakia, the Netherlands, and Sweden about 2 percent each, Norway 1.5 per cent, and no other country as much as 1 per cent."

48. Immigration Act of 1924, section 11 (Numerical Limitations), para d. See also Ngai, "Architecture of Race," 72–73.

49. "Contributions of Irish to American Blood in 1790," by Howard F. Barker, American Council of Learned Societies, 27 November 1927. Barker sent to Willcox, who was the chairman of the ACLS, his reports, such as "The Proportion of English among Early Settlers in Maryland," based on the study of family surnames. See RG 29/NN 374-63. A very negative evaluation of Barker's methodology was made for the Census Bureau by Marcus Hansen, who worked alongside Hill for the Quota Board. See "A Consideration of the System of 'Distinctive Names' as a Method for Determining the National Origins of the American Population," RG 29/298/158.

50. "Note Bearing on the Question of the Reliability of the National Origin Quotas," 14 March 1928, RG 29/NN 374-63.

51. "Strike Out the 'National Origins' Clauses from the Immigration Act!" American Irish Historical Society, 12 March 1928. This document also complained about how countries that were not assigned quotas, such as Canada and Mexico, would see their immigration increase. It concluded: "No shuffling of unreliable figures or hypothetical averages, and no amount of camouflage can bring truth or justice out of the 'National Origins' mess." See text in RG 29/198/147, Social Sciences Research Council, 1927–1928.

52. Proclamation of President Hoover, 22 March 1929. Great Britain had an annual quota of 65,721 (34,007 in 1924); Germany, 25,957 (51,227); Ireland, 17,853 (28,567); some countries saw their quota increase in 1929, but it remained very low: Italy, 5,802 (3,845); Poland, 6,524 (5,982); Russia, 2,784 (2,248). See the proclamation of President Coolidge, 30 June 1924, copies of proclamation no. 1872 (1929) and no. 1703 (1924), RG 29/NN 374-63.

53. On the training of teams and the work done by the Census Bureau during its first professional period, see Diana L. Magnuson, "US Census of Population Office Culture, 1902–1928," unpublished article presented at Social Science History Association Conference, Fort Worth, TX, November 1999, in possession of author.

54. Margo Anderson finds a very convincing parallel between immigration legislation and the impossibility for Congress, throughout the 1920s, to settle on a modified formula for apportionment, so as not to give too much weight to cities and regions where immigrants had settled. In both cases, Congress, in the face of significant demographic changes with significant political consequences, sought a mechanism to go backward, and in both cases it turned toward the census. The results of the 1920 census, showing a predominantly urban population (cities of more than 2,500 inhabitants), shocked representatives. The first projections of apportionment showed that nineteen states would lose or gain seats. The urban population had grown by 19 million, and the rural population had declined by 5 million. This was the only decade in which no agreement was found for the publication of apportionment required by the Constitution. See Anderson, *American Census*, 131–58. Joseph Hill was responsible for the two methodologies and was in contact with congressional committees for apportionment as well as for quotas.

55. "Punching of place and birth and mother tongue of foreign-born parents takes much longer than punching place of birth of American parents, and that many operatives could not keep up to an average of 840 cards per day on any of these schedules unless they worked overtime";

report of the US Department of Labor, Women's Bureau, 19 October 1920, addressed to the Census Bureau on the subject of favoritism and women's working conditions in the Division of Population, RG 29/149/File 3/12 (110), Personnel complaint. The same criticism of the work problems raised by these questions is found in the director's annual report for 1929: "But it is proposed to omit the inquiry as to the mother tongue or native language of foreign-born persons and foreign-born parents, which was first introduced in the census of 1910 and repeated in 1920. This question imposed a heavy additional burden on the enumerators and on the office force engaged in tabulation. It is believed that the questions as to the nativity and parent nativity permit an adequate classification by origin of the population of foreign birth or parentage, and that the added information that might be obtained by the mother-tongue question is not of sufficient value and reliability to justify the retention of that question, especially as the political boundaries of Europe now conform more closely to racial divisions than was the case in 1910." Report of the Director of the Census to the Secretary of Commerce, 1929, p. 6, RG 29/192, Annual Reports 1899–1949.

56. Minutes of the meeting of the Census Advisory Committee of 12 November 1927, RG 29/148. For the long list of languages appearing in the instructions given to census workers for 1910 and 1920, see US Bureau of the Census, *200 Years of US Census Taking*, 51. On the question of changes in borders within Europe after World War I—a question that gave the Census Bureau a great deal of work—see the undated Census Bureau press release for the 1930 census, "Census-Takers Will Need World Atlas and History," RG 29/215/V-1.

57. On the same day, the decision was made to abandon the distinction between black and mulatto. Resolutions adopted 14–15 December 1928, RG 29/148. An identical argument, almost word for word, is in the report of the director for 1929, cited above, p. 6. We have already noted that, when speaking of European peoples, the terms "nationalities" and "races" were interchangeable. The memorandum "The Fifteenth Census Schedule," which served as the basis for the discussion, points out that this would make a significant savings in the printing of the schedules, the perforation of cards, and the tabulation of data. In fact, after the censuses of 1910 and 1920, cross-tabulations of country of birth and mother tongue had been done. This text also stated: "It is a fair question whether the population schedule has not heretofore devoted a disproportionate amount of detail to the foreign born population." This was indeed a complete turnaround of developments since 1850.

58. Minutes of the meeting of 18–19 October 1929, RG 29/148.

59. Letter of Read Lewis to Steuart, 17 September 1929, RG 29/148/File of correspondence between Lewis and Steuart.

60. "The 1930 Census and Our Foreign Born People," ibid.

61. Letter from Steuart to Lewis, 25 September 1929, ibid.

62. The Census Bureau and the Census Advisory Committee were at first against this question on unemployment. See Magnuson, "Making of a Modern Census," 86–87.

63. Fifteenth Census of the United States, 1930, vol. 1, *Field and Office Work*, p. 86, RG 29/UD75 (NC 3-29-81-4), Field Division of the Census Bureau, Methods and Procedures of the 1930 Decennial Census.

64. Minutes of the meeting of the Census Advisory Committee, 7 January 1938, RG 29/148.

65. Minutes of the meeting of 17–18 June 1938, 1940 Population Schedule, ibid.

66. "Measuring America," Supplementary Questions, 63. The sample thus obtained was unsatisfactory from a statistical point of view, but much simpler and more economical. On the question of sampling, and the theoretical and political difficulties it posed for the Census Bureau in the late 1930s, see Anderson, *American Census*, 182–90. The older generation (Truesdell, Austin, and others) were skeptical, even hostile, while the younger generation (Dedrick, Hauser, and others) were to some extent identified with this development in statistical research. For a very detailed study of the complex stakes of the question of sampling and their legitimacy, see Emmanuel Didier, "De l'échantillon à la population, sociologie de la généralisation par sondage aux États-Unis avant 1945" (PhD diss., ENSMP, 2000); and Didier, *En quoi consiste l'Amérique? Les statistiques, le New Deal et la démocratie* (Paris: La Découverte, 2009).

Part V

1. A complete list of suggestions received by 1 December 1928, with the names and addresses of the parties, is in RG 29/148/Suggestions 1930.
2. Magnuson, "Making of a Modern Census," 85–86, evokes the feelings of despair and frustration that overcame Hill in reading the innumerable requests, some of which had the support of influential organizations.
3. The archives concerning the census for the nineteenth century are divided up among different administrations and thus dispersed into different holdings. But the archives of the Department of the Interior for the period during which it had authority over the Census Office show that the shape of the schedule or publications of the census occupied only a minuscule place in the archived correspondence, compared to letters concerning financial claims by agents and requests for proof of age. Comments on the quality of the census are quite rare, except in the form of criticisms of apportionment. Correspondence with experts took the form of private letters, mainly retained in their personal archives, with only a small number appearing in the public archives. The case of Ivan Petroff (see chapter 11) is one example: his personal archives contain Census Office letters, but the official archives show no trace of them. Overall, it appears that there is nothing in these holdings (RG 48) that might have led the Census Office to modify its methodology, but that is due both to the nature of the sources and to the selection of records conserved (see the list of primary sources, at the end of this volume).
4. On the role of Congress as a central actor of the administration during this period, see Nicolas Barreyre, "Administration et franchise: La Poste, le Congrès, et les formes de l'Etat américain au XIXe siècle," *Revue française d'études américaines* 112 (June 2007): 52–64.
5. See, for example, "The Fraudulent Census: Porter and His Democratic Allies," *The News*, Washington, DC, 2 August 1891, which accused Porter of being a Democrat and of English origin. A file of clippings on criticism of Porter and his Census Office can be found in RG 233/HR52A-F49.1, Committee on the Census.

Chapter 18

1. Bureau of the Census, *Negroes in the United States*, Bulletin No. 8 (Washington, DC: GPO, 1904), prepared under the supervision of W. F. Willcox, section on the negro farmer prepared by W. E. B. Du Bois. See also chapter 14.
2. Walter Willcox later published a study that forms part of the tradition of anxiety about the future of blacks in the United States, even if its conclusions were nuanced: "The Probable Increase of the Negro Race in the United States," *Quarterly Journal of Economics* 19, no. 4 (August 1905): 545–72. In his conclusion, Willcox stated clearly that one of the main causes of income differentials between blacks and whites was "economic discrimination," while another was the possible lack of aptitude of blacks for certain tasks, which was often accepted as the sole explanation in that period. The historian Mark Aldrich has written a study very critical of Willcox: Mark Aldrich, "Progressive Economists and Scientific Racism: Walter Willcox and Black Americans, 1895–1910," *Phylon* 40, no. 1 (1979): 1–14. Aldrich states that Willcox was responsible for the Census Bureau's abandonment in 1906 of the plan to collect statistics on lynchings in the South. Willcox's relations with the Census Bureau were significant and long-lasting. In the 1920s, he defended, against Hill, an alternative method of apportionment, but found himself isolated within the scientific community, which did not prevent him from continuing his involvement in Census Bureau activity, through the Census Advisory Committee of which he was a long-time member.
3. Bureau of the Census, *Negro Population 1790–1915* (Washington, DC: GPO, 1918), 850 pages. The report was prepared by Dr. John Cummings and the Division of Revision and Results, under the general supervision of Dr. Joseph A. Hill. Hill virtually embodies the census, immovable for forty years while census directors were replaced following the election of new presidents. He came to the Census Office in 1898 and remained there until his death at age seventy-eight in 1937.
4. Thus on the drop in birth rate for free blacks, less than that of slaves, which fed speculation on the extinction of blacks unsuited for freedom, the report notes prudently that "Census

data do not very clearly account for this decline in the rate of increase of the free element in the Negro, population, so far below the rate of the slave population, but it may be noted that, as compared with the slave population, the free colored were somewhat older, and on that account naturally subject to a higher mortality rate, and somewhat less normally distributed by sex, and, therefore, probably characterized by a marital condition less favorable to rapid natural increase" (ibid., 54). These common-sense hypotheses, as we have noted, had totally escaped the nineteenth-century experts.

5. Ibid., 13.

6. Bureau of the Census, *Negroes in the United States 1920–1932* (Washington, DC: GPO, 1935), 850 pages. The publicity material for this volume and for statistical bulletins on blacks is located in RG 29/185/Publicity, 1940 Census. See figure 31, which reproduces a publicity item for this work.

7. See RG 29/149/14:9 (305), which contains 135 letters of congratulation on the 1915 bulletin no. 129, "Negroes in the United States" (mostly focused on the 1910 census and which prepared the publication of the 1918 volume) from blacks who said they felt proud and inspired by reading these statistics, and also from persons, whose skin color is not always specified in their letters, who said that it would be useful to them in their work in life insurance or as a probation officer and judge in family court.

8. See, for example, the letter of Wm. Preston Moore, Brooklyn. A letter of 10 March 1915, from Director Rogers to the secretary of commerce, strikes a similar note in saying that it was already the bureau's policy, in response to complaints. Ibid. See also Ardizzone, "Red Blooded Americans."

9. "Hall Appointed Specialist in Census Bureau," Press Release, 23 May 1935, "Personnel File" of Hall. Most of the information on Hall comes from an archive compiled by Rodney Ross, archivist at the National Archives, who kindly allowed me to consult these files, which fill out what can be learned about him from the public archives of the census. The basics come from the personnel file on Hall, the originals of which are in the central civil service personnel files of the federal government in St. Louis. These documents contain evaluations of Hall by his superiors and confidential notes on his career. Hereafter cited as "Personnel File." See also Rodney A. Ross, "A Centennial Celebration of Federal Employment: Charles E. Hall (1868–1952), 'Specialist in Negro Statistics' with the Census Bureau," paper presented at OAH annual meeting, St. Louis, 1 April 2000. Rodney Ross found Hall at age two in the 1870 census, where he was classified as "mulatto."

10. RG 29/149/File 3:12 (110), Personnel complaint, and letter from Hall to Secretary of Commerce Herbert Hoover, 19 March 1921, in which Hall notes that on 26 April 1920, he refused "the humiliating verbal order" to impose segregation of restrooms used by the employees he supervised ("Personnel File" of Hall).

11. Memorandum of the Bureau of the Census, with no author name, 18 July 1930, "Personnel File" of Hall.

12. "Charles E. Hall, Specialist in Negro Statistics," *New York Age*, 8 June 1935. Another article described him as the "Most Important Negro in Black Cabinet," *Black Dispatch*, 8 January 1938, which was an exaggeration ("Personnel File" of Hall).

13. Letter of S. N. D. North to Senator A. J. Hopkins, 16 March 1907, "Personnel File" of Hall. The approximation seems to indicate that the Census Bureau was well aware of the rising migration of African Americans from the South, but between two censuses they did not have exact numbers.

14. Except for two years with the Department of Labor, Hall spent his entire career with the census.

15. Memorandum of 24 October 1904, "Personnel File."

16. Memorandum of 2 October 1907 of Mark Hansen, Chief of Division, "Personnel File." Field inquiries, outside of the census period, consisted of visiting local institutions to collect statistics.

17. Memorandum of Steuart, Chief Statistician for Manufactures, 9 December 1909, "Personnel File." Hall, who had connections, had been recommended by Senator Lorimer for assignment to the industrial census in Chicago, where he was from.

18. Ralph Tyler was also national organizer at the National Negro Business League. In this capacity, he regularly asked the Census Bureau for information about statistics on black-owned business and farms; see RG 29/149/16:12 (309).
19. Letter signed by Charles E. Hall, Wm. Jennifer, and Robert A. Pelham, to the Editor of the *Chicago Defender*, 21 May 1915; transcribed copy in archives of the Chief Clerk, who was in charge of personnel at the Census Bureau; see RG 29/149/16:12 (309).
20. Letter of the director to Mr. Simpie Patterson, 6 January 1930, RG 29/215/E 2, Experiences of 1930 Census, Supervisors and enumerators.
21. Ardizzone, "Red Blooded Americans," 191–92.
22. Nobles, *Shades of Citizenship*, 137.
23. See *Civil Service Reform in the National Service, 1889–1891*, 74–75, on the case of a black lawyer hired in Indianapolis; RG 233/HR52A-F49.1.
24. "I recall two amusing experiences in connection with the appointment of census enumerators. In the South it would have been impractical at that time—and perhaps also today—to have colored enumerators visit the homes of whites to take the census of population or of agriculture. In many districts only white enumerators were appointed.
"In a considerable number of districts, however, where there was a large negro population, both a white and a colored person were appointed, but the colored appointee was instructed to enumerate only colored families. Down in Mississippi there was a district in which a few whites lived in a distant corner surrounded by negroes. The white enumerator asked the colored enumerator to canvass these few white families. The colored man wrote me afterwards: 'I got along all right with the colored families but when I tried to visit a white family the man told me to get the hell out of there and never show my face there again, and I politely took him at his word.' " Durand, *Memoirs of Edward Dana Durand*, 156.
25. "List of Supervisors for Whom Negro Advisors Have Been Suggested," RG 29/215/N1.
26. "Form Letter to Supervisors, Negro Advisers," Joseph A. Hill, Acting Director, undated, probably February or March 1930 (emphasis in original), RG 29/215/57.
27. Report of Frederick Kuhlman, Chicago, 29th District, Illinois, Supervisors' Reports and Chamber of Commerce Letters, vol. 7, pp. 174–75, RG 29/UD75 (NC 3-29-81-4), Field Division of the Census Bureau, Methods and Procedures of the 1930 Decennial Census.
28. "It is found that in the more prosperous districts of the city, people did not regard the taking of the census seriously and caused many back calls for enumerators. This could easily have been avoided had they cooperated" (Alfred M. Mendel, Tenth District, Milwaukee, Wisconsin). "In the wealthy and stylish districts of the city, the homes were in some instances difficult of access for the enumerators, and the people themselves indifferent or haughty and uncivil" (John W. Stitt, Ninth District, Fort Worth, Texas). Both in id. On the discrepancy between the Census Bureau's communication on anticipated difficulties in poor black and immigrant neighborhoods, and the reports from field workers that often told the opposite story, see Paul Schor, "The View from Below and the View from Above: What US Census-Taking Reveals about Social Representations in the Era of Jim Crow and Immigration Restriction," in *A World of Populations: Transnational Perspectives on Demography in the Twentieth Century*, ed. Heinrich Hartmann and Corinna R. Unger (New York: Berghahn Books, 2014), 19–35.
29. In this memo, the census director noted, with respect to the toilet incident mentioned above, that black employees were grouped together because they worked on the same tasks, and that instructions had been given to section chiefs to inform their subordinates to use the toilets closest to their work station in order to avoid loss of work time. The vast majority of colored employees were in Building D. Thus, segregation and rational workplace organization overlapped. Rogers also noted that Hall was paid the same salary as white section chiefs, and that the average number of punched cards processed daily by colored employees was no less than the average for white workers. From his point of view, there was no discrimination, and recruitment in particular was made in order "to avoid the possibility of any discrimination being made in favor or against any class." Memorandum of Sam L. Rogers, Director, to Mr. Libbey, 22 March 1921, "Personnel File" of Hall. The organization of Census Bureau buildings during this period has been studied by Diana L. Magnuson, "US Census of Population Office Culture, 1902–1928."

30. "Importance of Factual Information," speech of Hall, official representative of the Census Bureau, at Cleveland, before the Cleveland Board of Trade, 21 March 1937. Italics and capital letters in original. From the speech, it appears that this may have been a meeting of black businessmen in Cleveland and not of local businessmen generally. RG 29/194, Records of the Assistant Director for Statistical Standards, General Bureau of Records, Records Concerning Trips, Papers Read, and Meetings Attended ("TPM" files), 1934–1949/Box 81/Population 1937 and earlier. File 194 documents Hall's extensive travel on behalf of the Census Bureau. He mainly traveled to conferences, where he tirelessly explained to black audiences how statistics were the tool that could show everyone the progress made by African Americans in the United States—especially statistics on black-owned small businesses, which were a focus of the Bureau's attention, along with black-owned farms, which had been a traditional element since 1900. Hall's successor from 1938 on, Houchins, who was likewise African American, would take to black economic actors his message on the purchasing power of African Americans, which required them to buy from black businesses. The statistics used in his travels were mostly drawn from the industrial and agricultural censuses, which—like the population census—noted the color of business owners or managers and of farm operators. This made it possible to show not only an increase in numbers but also in sales of the black-owned businesses in a given area.

31. See, for example, Census Photographs, National Archives no. 29-C-1A-17, "Review Section in Machine Tabulation Division," or no. 29-C-1A-20, "Result Work. Critical Analysis. Agriculture Division."

Chapter 19

1. Bureau of the Census, *Thirteenth Census*, 1:133. See also Hochschild and Powell, "Racial Reorganization and the United States Census 1850–1930," 76.

2. On women census workers in 1880, see Magnuson, "Making of a Modern Census," 146. The tabulating machines used for verification were set to reject punchcards showing women in a traditionally male occupation and vice versa in 1900; see the report of 18 August 1902, Wm. C. Hunt, Chief Statistician for Population, to William R. Merriam, director, RG 29/145, Correspondence of William Fl. Willoughby, Assistant Director, 1910/Work of the Population Division.

3. "The attention of enumerators should be particularly called to the change in the naturalization laws as relating to women. Prior to 1922 a foreign-born woman became a citizen when her husband was naturalized. The foreign born wife of a man naturalized in 1922 or later remains an alien, unless she has taken out naturalization papers in her own name," *Instructions to supervisors, 1930, Revised*, 1930 (15-13 a), p. 27, RG 29/212. See Patrick Weil, "Le statut de la femme en droit de la nationalité: Une égalité tardive," in *Les Codes de la différence: Race–origine–religion; France, Allemagne, États-Unis*, ed. Riva Kastoryano (Paris: Presses de Sciences-Po, 2005), 123–43.

4. RG 29/215/File W-2.

5. Compare the all-male workforce in 1910 (figure 15) and the women employees in 1941 (figures 16 and 22), male supervisors being present in some pictures.

6. In 1930, there were a total of 575 supervisors of the census of the population. We have mentioned the opening of the post of supervisor to African Americans, also in 1930, in very small numbers. There do not appear to have been any women among the few black supervisors we have been able to identify for 1930.

7. Press release, For Immediate Use, 29 December 1929, "Women employed in taking the Census," RG 29/215/Folder W-4.

8. "Many Women Will Take the Census in New York," *Atlanta Journal*, 11 April 1910. The article stated that these women were generally high-school graduates, and that they would be assigned to the better neighborhoods of the city.

9. RG 29/215/Folder E-2.

10. Thus, supervisor P. P. Boli, Hamilton, 22nd District, Ohio, stated: "We found that married women from about 28 to 45 years of age made the best enumerators. Their work was thorough,

conscientious, and efficient. A very large majority of our enumerators were women" (RG 29/UD75).

11. "Women Employed in Taking the Census," RG 29/215/Folder W-4.
12. For 1930, see the accounts in RG 29/UD75.
13. "Number of Enumerators appointed in connection with all phases of the 1940 Census, by State, sex and color," RG 29/UD78, NN 364-101, Field Division, Records documenting plans, decision and procedures of the 1940 Census of population and housing, c. 1940–1945/Box 13, Field memoranda/Enumerators appointed.
14. Memo for Dr. Kerlin, by W. L. Austin, Director, 12 December 1938, Bureau of the Census Archives (Suitland, MD)/Census History Files/1940 Census, Special Advisory Committee.
15. See the accounts of census workers in RG 29/UD 75 (NC 3-29-81-4), Field Division of the Census Bureau, Methods and Procedures of the 1930 Decennial Census/Chambers of Commerce, Criticisms, Enumerators.
16. "The Woman in the Home," by William M. Steuart, director of the census, RG 29/215/W-4, 1930. Four photos accompanied the two pages of text: on the cover, an image of a man interviewing an older woman at the door of a middle-class home; a photo of Steuart, stern, aged, and upper-middle-class, signing a document; one of a tabulating machine; and the photo of the tabulation room, which had already appeared in "What Census Bureau Does." One section's title was "Tell the Wife." Although signed by Steuart, the article appears to have been prepared by Hill. It was published in the newsletters of at least four state Chambers of Commerce (Arkansas-Texas, Iowa, North Carolina, and Ohio).
17. Letter from Steuart to J. M. Guild, President, Community Service Company, Kansas City, Missouri, 9 December 1929, RG 29/215/Folder C-5.
18. RG 29/215/S-7.

Chapter 20

1. The proclamation for 1930, signed by President Hoover, is identical to that of 1920, initialed by President Wilson. The presidential proclamations are the oldest and most consistent evidence of census external communications. Those of 1930, in different languages, are archived in RG 29/141. That of 1940, surrounded by its various translations, is shown in figure 3.
2. Photos of census leaders (Hill, Austin, Steuart, and Truesdell) appeared next to those of IBM machines in the IBM magazine *Business Machines*, 19 April 1930, a special number on IBM's contribution to the 1930 census, RG 29/215/Material from the files of Alice Short/B-1, The Hollerith Machines.
3. RG 29/215/E-2.
4. The films can be viewed at the National Archives, College Park, Film Reels, Census, 29.1 to 29.6 for 1940. Still photos of the films, by the Motion Picture men of the Division of Statistical Research, as well as photos made for the instruction of the 1940 census workers and photos of the test-census in Indiana in January 1939, are in RG 29/215/ "Alice Short, Publicity, Census of 1940." See also the Photos of the Census Training School of the 16th Census, in the same file. On the important development of agent training during preparation of the 1940 census, see Magnuson, "Making of a Modern Census," 186–87, 196.
5. Census Photographs, Series RG 29-C.
6. As noted by Calvert Dedrick, Acting Chief Statistician, on the basis of supervisors' reports, in his lengthy study, "Social Psychological Factors in the Enumerative Process," copy in RG 29/142-NN 367-1/Box 3. This question was introduced at the request of the Department of Commerce, with the purpose of collecting information that would help in regulating radio frequencies at a time when the new medium was expanding, but it might relate more broadly to the numerous questions that economic actors tried to impose on the schedule for 1930 in order to obtain, for free, information that would be valuable for their businesses. The question on ownership of radio sets, which would not be retained in 1940, did not yield results that could be exploited in detail, because of the very high rate of ownership that made it irrelevant. It was one of only a few external suggestions included in the 1930 schedule; although it was not one of those that came up most often in public meetings, it had the support of the Federal Radio Commission, which carried more weight than private interests, even if the agency

seemed in this case to be using the census for a very specific purpose. Magnuson, "Making of a Modern Census," 94–95.

7. This program was broadcast on radio station WOWO, Fort Wayne, Indiana, on 24 March 1930, about one week before the beginning of the census. It was made on the initiative of the local supervisor; RG 29/215/E-2.

8. Ibid.

9. Magnuson, "Making of a Modern Census," 196.

10. Dedrick, "Social Psychological Factors in the Enumerative Process," 12. Dedrick cited a supervisor as stating: "Perhaps the best publicity was the Amos and Andy census hour on the radio. Prior to that we had a great deal of difficulty in some of our colored areas. The morning after the Amos and Andy radio discussion of the census, the change in attitude of the colored people especially was very appreciable. They usually referred to the fact that they had heard Amos and Andy tell them about the census, and they understood all about it."

11. A to-do list for the preparation of the 1930 census, compiled by public relations officers, gives the heading: "Publicity. Ways and Means." RG 29/215/F-3.

12. The head of the Postal Service responded to the census director, on 26 February 1930, that the proclamation would be displayed prominently by its 49,244 postmasters in their post offices. They would also display translations into twenty-two languages. RG 29/215/P-4.

13. RG 29/215/F-3. The folder also contains leaflets from the Naturalization Bureau intended to reassure the foreign born.

14. The order for printing the proclamations on 11-by-14-inch card stock was given to the census printer on 15 February 1930, with a total print run of 201,500. At that time, there were still no translations into Lithuanian, Hungarian, or Japanese, but their numbers were included in the total. Ibid.

15. The Census Bureau anticipated at this time 200,000 proclamations in English, as opposed to 100,000 in 1920. Ibid.

16. The language of reference is Yiddish, the language used for the proclamation; added to the Jewish population were speakers of Hebrew, a very small group. Bureau of the Census, *Thirteenth Census*, 960. On the link between the Yiddish language and the Jewish community for the Census Bureau, see the study by Susan Cotts Watkins in Watkins, *After Ellis Island*, 11–33.

17. These figures correspond to the number of persons who had this language as their own native language, or that of their parents, in 1920. These questions were asked only of foreign-born persons, as we have seen, which explains the small number of persons whose language was Spanish, and makes room for other underestimates as well: US Bureau of the Census, *Fourteenth Census*.

18. It is difficult to establish the precise size of the English-speaking population on the basis of census data, because on the one hand certain immigrants (mainly English and Irish) were English speakers, and on the other hand we cannot take into account here the estimates that were made to measure the ethnicity of the nonimmigrant population. Here, we merely use an approximation that substitutes for size ranking.

19. See, for example, the *Chicago Record Herald*, 31 January 1910, where the information provided by a local census supervisor expressed the position of many in the Census Bureau: "The difficulties of census taking are enormously increased by the 'melting-pot' character of the country. Something can be done by the foreign newspapers and by special circulars printed and widely distributed in as many tongues as Chicago boasts of, but this will not suffice. . . . To reassure the suspicions, brought up under very different conceptions of 'officialism,' to make them feel that the objects of the census are merely scientific and that no danger to life, liberty or the pursuit of happiness lurks in frank and full answers will be no easy task." Along the same lines, census officials made a distinction between immigrants coming from democracies and those coming from countries whose governments were identified with repression, as well as between countries with a history of census-taking and the rest.

20. In the context of the 1930 census, the Commissioner of Naturalization Raymond F. Crist sent out a circular that spoke of the confidentiality of census data in these terms: "Do not be afraid to answer all the questions, for the President has promised that the census-taker will be the

only person who will know what your answers are." He emphasized the fact that enumerators were furnished with government credentials. RG 29/215. F-3.

21. Kellee Green notes that if the raids had been planned for some time, their timing with the regard to the census and the consequences for its success would warrant further study. Kellee Green, "The Fourteenth Numbering of the People: The 1920 Federal Census," *Prologue* 23, no. 2 (Summer 1991): 135.

22. The lists of prominent members of ethnic communities drawn up by the Census Bureau seem quite solid, since the contact in the large Czech community of Chicago was Anton Cermak, who later became mayor of the city. See the letter of Director Rogers to Cermak, 13 December 1919, RG 29/198/66.

23. See also the special poster in Chinese, prepared by the Census Bureau in 1919 for the population of Chinese origin, which was reviewed by the Chinese consulate. Memorandum of Joseph A. Hill to director, 3 December 1919, RG 29/149/File 2123, Fourteenth Census, Publicity/72:11. Traditionally, for the Census Bureau, the representatives of the Chinese and Japanese populations were their consulates, rather than prominent individuals in the United States, as if it were impossible to imagine these immigrants putting down American roots. This poster had a print run of ten thousand copies, and bore the seal of the consuls-general of China in New York and San Francisco.

24. See the appeal by Thor J. Benson (chapter 17).

25. RG 29/238/Scrapbooks, vol. 4, p. 2.

26. Diana Magnuson analyzed a large body of newspapers that covered the censuses from 1880 to 1940; see Magnuson, "Making of a Modern Census," ch. 12 ("Trials and Tribulations of Census Takers"), 214–31.

27. *Chicago Daily Tribune*, 17 April 1910. See also Schor, "The View from Below and the View from Above," 19–35.

28. *Instructions to the Enumerators*, 1919.

29. *Chicago Daily News*, 2 June 1920.

30. *Chicago Daily Tribune*, 17 April 1910.

31. Letter from Geo. W. Wickersham, Attorney General, to Sec. of Commerce and Labor, 19 March 1910, RG 29/149/1002 (49-21), Opinions of the Attorney General, 1910.

32. Before the law explicitly prohibited their hiring, there do not seem ever to have been any foreign supervisors.

33. See chapter 17; see also Gratton and Gutman, "Hispanics in the United States, 1850–1990," 137–53.

34. One of the Pennsylvania supervisors sent the Census Bureau a copy of the accounts he had requested from his censustakers. From the responses, it appears that this supervisor gave his subordinates a questionnaire that contained a question on what kind of reception they had gotten from immigrant families. These accounts came from their responses. Folder 74-14 contains a bundle of extracts of Reports of Enumerators to H. R. Campbell, Supervisor, Twenty-third District, Pennsylvania, Originals on File in the Office of Chamber of Commerce, Washington, PA. RG 29/149/3309, Fifteenth Census, Amusing Incidents/74-14. This may be a selection, the majority of the census workers reporting their satisfaction and the pleasant surprises encountered in the course of their work, while other sources, such as newspapers and petitions addressed to the Census Bureau, emphasized negative aspects.

35. Anonymous ten-page account entitled "Counting Uncle Sam's Children (By One of Them)," submitted by Mrs. R. J. Berry, King City, CA, RG 29/149/74-16.

36. RG 29/149/3309/74-14. As often noted, use of the term "foreign" in this period signified "born in a foreign country" or "of foreign origin," without reference to a person's citizenship.

37. See testimony to this effect, for 1930, by Alfred M. Mendel, Milwaukee, 10th District, Wisconsin, or John W. Stitt, Fort Worth, 9th District, Texas, RG 29/UD 75/Scrapbook 7.

38. "Field Division Report 1930," vol. 1, p. 44, RG 29/UD 75.

39. See, for example, the letter of LeVerne Beales, 26 March 1917, giving the number of Germans and Austrians, naturalized and non-naturalized, more than twenty-one years old—that is, old enough to be citizens—in response to a request from an individual. Beales also informed the person that these figures were much lower than those given by the newspapers for non-naturalized Germans. RG 29/205/G.

40. RG 29/205/War Work.
41. Letter of 26 November 1917 from a retired chief of police asking the age of an individual who was suspected, among other things, of having exaggerated his age in order to avoid conscription. The Census Bureau affirmed that according to the 1910 census, he was twenty-four years old, which meant he was over thirty in 1917. Providing this information violated the rules of confidentiality, and worse, did so for someone who no longer occupied an official role as a police officer. RG 29/149/1-1, "Confidential."
42. The census director responded to a correspondent who informed him of their suspicions about a fellow inhabitant of their city: "I note your statement that Mr. Wohler has been active in furnishing a hiding place for Germans coming over from Canada, and I shall be glad to see that this matter is given careful consideration. Permit me to thank you for bringing this matter to the attention of the government." Letter from Census Director Rogers, 3 December 1917, transmitting the file to the Secretary of Commerce who had authority over the Census. The Department of Justice opened an investigation on Mr. Wohler following this correspondence. RG 29/149/1-1, "Confidential."
43. RG 29/149/1-1, "Confidential."
44. RG 29/149/2205, Work for War Agencies—Department of Justice, 72/19, Memorandum of the Acting Solicitor to Secretary of Commerce, 25 June 1917.
45. Letter of the Assistant Attorney General to the Secretary of Commerce, 7 February 1920, RG 29/149/1002 (49/23) 1919 and 1920.
46. RG 29/148/June 1939.
47. See chapter 9.
48. Resolution "Alien Registration," 31 March–1 April 1939, Items 12–54, RG 29/142 (NN367-1).
49. "List of cases involved alleged affiliation with subversive organizations," 5 December 1940, "Confidential Files," Unnumbered files, RG 29/142/Box 12.
50. Information on the deportation of the Japanese comes from Margo Anderson and William Seltzer, "After Pearl Harbor: The Proper Role of Population Data Systems in Time of War," Population Association of America, 23–25 March 2000, available online along with other articles on the subject of confidentiality: https://pantherfile.uwm.edu/margo/www/gov-stat/integrity.htm
51. According to Margo Anderson, there are known individual cases in which the Census Bureau gave people's names to the authorities, especially in Washington, DC.
52. RG 29/148/10 January 1942; cited by Anderson and Seltzer, "After Pearl Harbor," 10.
53. See, for example, Charles A. H. Thomson, "Public Relations of the 1940 Census," *Public Opinion Quarterly* 4, no. 2 (June 1940): 311–18.

Epilogue

1. See chapter 17 on this point. The expression was coined by David A. Hollinger in *Postethnic America*. The four races are white, black, American Indian, Asian or Pacific Islander. Within the white category, a distinction is made between Hispanic white and non-Hispanic white.
2. 1950 instructions to enumerators. See Nobles, *Shades of Citizenship*, 190.
3. See the reproduction of the schedules in *Measuring America*, 72–75; and *200 Years of US Census Taking*, 79.
4. *Measuring America*, 77.
5. Ibid., 78. This wording led many inhabitants of states in the central or southern United States (Alabama, Georgia, etc.) to answer yes to the question. The terms "Central or South America" were later eliminated. See Jorge Chapa, "Hispanic/Latino Ethnicity and Identifiers," in Anderson, *Encyclopedia of the US Census*, 245.
6. See, among others, Chapa, "Hispanic/Latino Ethnicity and Identifiers"; Rodriguez, *Changing Race*; Rodriguez, "Latinos and the Census," in *The Oxford Encyclopedia of Latinos and Latinas in the United States*, ed. Suzanne Oboler and Deena J. González (New York: Oxford University Press, 2005), 288–93.
7. On the fact that official designations of minorities as they exist today were produced by the administration between the 1940s and mid-1960s, before the advent of preferential

policies, see Hugh Graham, "The Origins of Official Minority Designation," in *The New Race Question: How the Census Counts Multiracial Individuals*, ed. Joel Perlmann and Mary Waters (New York: Russell Sage Foundation, 2002), 288–99. See also Daniel Sabbagh, *L'égalité par le droit*, and Kenneth Prewitt, who argues that path dependency and bureaucratic reasons played an important role in keeping the same categories before and after the Civil Rights Act of 1964: *What Is Your Race?*.

8. *200 Years of US Census Taking*, 89.

9. Reynolds Farley, "Racial Identities in 2000: The Response to the Multiple-Race Response Option," in Perlman and Waters, *The New Race Question*, 33–61.

10. Ibid. More generally, see Perlmann and Waters, *The New Race Question*, which deals with all aspects of the question and the major debates.

Conclusion

1. Melissa Nobles, "Racial Categorization and Censuses," in *Census and Identity: The Politics of Race, Ethnicity, and Language in National Censuses*, ed. David I. Kertzer and Dominique Arel (Cambridge: Cambridge University Press, 2002), 43–70; Skerry, *Counting on the Census?*; Anderson and Fienberg, *Who Counts?*

2. For an example of historical comparison between France and the United States, see Schor and Spire, "Les statistiques de la population comme construction de la nation."

3. One notable exception being the former director of the census, Kenneth Prewitt, in *What Is Your Race?*

4. This book is not a comparative study, but as it is written from a distance, by an outsider, it could be described as implicitly comparative, being informed by scholarship and debates on other parts of the world. On the advantages and challenges of writing US history from outside, see Nicolas Barreyre, Michael Heale, Stephen Tuck, and Cécile Vidal, eds., *Historians Across Borders: Writing American History in a Global Age* (Berkeley: University of California Press, 2014); and Manfred Berg, Isabel Soto, and Paul Schor, "The Weight of Words: Writing about Race in the United States and Europe," *American Historical Review* 119, no. 3 (June 2014): 800–808, part of the AHR roundtable on European historians writing US history ("You, the People," ibid., 741–823).

5. Matthew Frye Jacobson, "History, Historicity, and the Census Count by Race," in Perlmann and Waters, *The New Race Question*, 259. Jacobson specifies that this is only very partially the case.

6. Rogers Brubaker, Mara Loveman, and Peter Stamatov, "Ethnicity as Cognition," *Theory and Society* 33 (2004): 31–64.

7. In another domain, that of national statistical institutes in Europe at the close of the twentieth century, this is also the approach of Alain Desrosières: "Les qualités des quantités: Comment gérer la tension entre réalisme et conventionnalisme," *Enquête* 6 (2007): 271–92.

SOURCES AND BIBLIOGRAPHY

Sources

NATIONAL ARCHIVES

Record Group 29 Administrative Records of the Bureau of the Census

Entry 83: Records of the Eleventh Census. Records of the Superintendent. Record of Letters Sent Feb.–Nov. 1889.

Entry 118: Records of the Eleventh Census. Records of the Twenty-first Division—Alaska.

Entry 140: Lectures and papers of S. N. D. North.

Entry 141: Office Records of William M. Steuart, 1922–1932.

Entry 142: (NN 367-1), Records of William Lane Austin, Director 1933–1941.

Entry 145: Correspondence of William Fl. Willoughby, Assistant Director 1910.

Entry 148: Census Advisory Committee, 1919–1949.

Entry 149: Miscellaneous Records 1900–1953. Assistant Director for Operations. Office of the Chief Clerk (c. 1899–1941). Administrative Service Division.

Entry 192: Annual Reports 1899–1949.

Entry 194: Records of the Assistant Director for Statistical Standards. General Bureau of Records. Records Concerning Trips, Papers Read, and Meetings Attended ("TPM" files) 1934–1949.

Entry 198: General Subject File of the Statistical Division.

Entry 202: Records of the Office of the Assistant Director for Statistical Standards. Records of the Chief Statistician. Correspondence of Joseph A. Hill 1911–1940.

Entry 203: Office File of Joseph A. Hill 1912–1940.

Entry 205: Records of the Office of the Assistant Director for Statistical Standards. Records of the Chief Statistician. Correspondence of Le Verne Beales 1915–1919.

Entry 207: Records of the Chief Statistician. Correspondence of the Statistical Research Division, 1935–1938.

Entry 208: Records of the Office of the Assistant Director for Statistical Standards. Records of Chief Statistician. Miscellaneous Correspondence ("Inactive Correspondence"), 1937–1943.

Entry 210: Records of the Office of the Assistant Director for Statistical Standards. Records of the Chief Statistician. General Records Maintained by Calvert Dedrick, 1935–1942.

Entry 212: Forms and Schedules. Collections of the Statistical Research Division. Instructions to Assistant Marshals and Enumerators, etc., 1850–1939.

Entry 215: Publicity Materials Files of the Statistical Research Division.

Entry 227: Records of the Office of Assistant Director for Statistical Standards. Records Relating to Apportionment.

Entry 229: Records of the Office of Assistant Director for Statistical Standards. Records Relating to Apportionment. Office File of Morris B. Ullman, 1939–1950.

Entry 230: Records of the Office of Asst. Director for Statistical Standards. Records Relating to Vital Statistics. Office Records of Joseph A. Hill, 1932–1938.

Entry 231: Records Relating to Vital Statistics. General Records, 1936–1946.

Entry 238: Assistant Director for Demographic Fields. Records of the Population and Housing Division. Scrapbooks Relating to the Censuses of Population, 1920–1940.

Entry 250: Assistant Director for Demographic Fields. Records of the Division of Territorial, Insular, and Foreign Statistics. General Subject File, 1935–1942.

Entry 251: Records Relating to Territorial and Insular Census. 15th Decennial Census 1920–1934. Classified File.

Entry 252: Assistant Director for Demographic Fields. Records of the Division of Territorial, Insular, and Foreign Statistics. Classified File for the 16th Decennial Census, 1938–1943, 1946–1948.

Entry 253: Records Relating to Territorial and Insular Census. Scrapbooks Relating to Territorial Decennial Censuses, 1920–1941.

Entry 254: Assistant Director for Demographic Fields. Records of the Division of Territorial, Insular, and Foreign Statistics. Miscellaneous Records Relating to Territorial Censuses, 1900–1938.

Entry 255: Assistant Director for Demographic Fields. Records of the Division of Territorial, Insular, and Foreign Statistics. Office Files of Margaret O. Strahorn, 1940–1941.

Entry NN 374-63: Population Division Re Immigration Quotas, 1920–1935. Reports, Correspondence, and Other Records Relating to Immigration Quota Laws and National Origin Statistics, c. 1920–1936.

Entry NN 396-58: Records of the Bureau of the Census. Population and Housing Division. History of the 1940 Census of Housing and Other Records.

Entry UD 10 (NN 3-29-80): Census Advisory Committee.

Entry UD 75 (NC 3-29-81-4): Field Division of the Census Bureau. Methods and Procedures of the 1930 Decennial Census.

Entry UD 76 (NC 3-29-81-4): Field Division of the Census Bureau. National Weekly Reports for the 1940 Decennial Census.

Entry UD 78 (NN 364-101): Field Division. Records Documenting Plans, Decisions, and Procedures of the 1940 Census of Population and Housing, c. 1940–1945.

Entry UD 87 (NN 364-101): Field Division. 1930 Territorial Census Alaska–Virgin Islands, 1929–1930.

Entry UD 88 (NN 364-101). Field Division. Records Relating to the 1940 Census of Territories, 1937–1940.

Entry UD 184 (NN 364-101). Scrapbook Concerning Legislation for the 14th Census (1920), 1917–1919.

Entry UD 185 (NN 364-101): Scrapbook of Publicity Material Relating to the 1940 Census, 1935–1942.

Record Group 46 Records of the US Senate, Congress

Sen 28a-G7.2: Committee on the Judiciary. May 21, 1844, to December 16, 1844.

Sen 51A-F3: Committee on Census cf. HR Bill 6420, and Remonstrances Against Its Passage (Chinese Exclusion).

Record Group 48 Records of the Office of the Secretary of Interior, Records of the Patents and Miscellaneous Divisions

Entry 280: Records Relating to Decennial Censuses, Letters Received Relating to the Seventh Decennial Census (1850), 1850–1857.

Entry 282: Records Relating to Decennial Censuses. Records Relating to the 8th Decennial Census (1860).
Entry 284: Records Relating to the 9th and 10th Decennial Censuses (1870 and 1880), 1870–1881.
Entry 285: Records Relating to the Census of South Carolina, 1880.
Entry 286: Records Relating to the 11th (1890) Census, 1889–1895.
Entry 288: Records Relating to the Decennial Censuses. Miscellaneous Letters Received, 1894–1904.

Record Group 85 Records of the Immigration and Naturalization Service

Entry 26: Administrative Files Relating to Naturalization, 1906–1940

Record Group 233 Records of the United States House of Representatives, Congress

HR 41A-F 28.4: 41st Congress, Select Committee on the 9th Census.
HR 51A-H 26.4: Various Subjects. Records of the United States House of Representatives, Congress. Committee on the Census, House of Representatives.
HR 52A-F 49.1: Committee on the Census, House of Representatives.

Other Archives

Bureau of the Census Library, Suitland, MD. Papers of Census Officials. Census History Files, Bureau of the Census, Room 3031.
William Walter Husband Papers, Chicago History Museum.
Ivan Petroff Papers, MSS C-B 989, Bancroft Library, University of California Berkeley.
Chicago Foreign Language Press Survey (CFLPS), Special Collections, Joseph Regenstein Library, University of Chicago.

Official Census Publications in Chronological Order

The name of the Census Bureau as author is United States Census Office until 1901, thereafter United States Bureau of the Census. Unless listed otherwise, the place of publication is Washington, DC, and the publisher is the Government Printing Office (GPO). Titles are given in short form.

The decennial reports are available in full online: https://www.census.gov/prod/www/decennial.html
An exception is the Blair & Rives publication of the 1840 census which is unavailable online and was published as: [Department of State]. *Volume 1. Sixth Census or Enumeration of the Inhabitants of the United States, as Corrected at the Department of State, in 1840.* Washington, DC: Blair & Rives, 1841. *Volume 2. Statistics of the United States of America, as Collected and Returned by the Marshals of the Several Judicial Districts, Under the Thirteenth Section of the Act for Taking the Sixth Census, June 1, 1840.* Washington, DC: Blair & Rives, 1841.
Compendium of the Enumeration of the Inhabitants and Statistics of the United States. Washington, DC: T. Allen, 1841.
The Seventh Census of the United States: 1850. Washington, DC: Robert Armstrong, 1853.
US Congress [Superintendent of the Census]. *The Seventh Census. Report of the Superintendent of the Census for December 1, 1852, To Which Is Appended the Report for December 1, 1851.* Washington, DC: Robert Armstrong, 1853.
Compendium of the Seventh Census. Washington, DC: Nicholson, 1854.
US Congress. *Preliminary Report on the Eighth Census, 1860.* By Jos. C. G. Kennedy, Superintendent, 37th Congress, 2d Session, House of Representatives, Ex. Doc. No. 116. 1862.
Census Office. *Instructions to US Marshals, Instructions to Assistants.* Washington, DC: G. W. Bowman, 1860. http://www2.census.gov/prod2/decennial/documents/1860f-01.pdf

Population of the United States in 1860: Compiled from the Original Returns of the Eighth Census, under the direction of the Secretary of the Interior, by Joseph C. G. Kennedy, Superintendent of Census. 1864.

Statistics of the United States (Including Mortality, Property, Etc.) in 1860. 1866.

Ninth Census: The Statistics of the Population of the United States, Embracing the Tables of Race, Nationality, Sex, Selected Ages, and Occupations. 1872.

[Walker, Francis A.] *A Compendium of the Ninth Census, June 1, 1870.* 1872.

[Walker, Francis A.] *Statistical Atlas of the United States, Based on the Results of the Ninth Census 1870.* Julius Bien, Lith. 1874. See: http://hdl.loc.gov/loc.gmd/g3701gm.gct00008

Statistics of the Population of the United States at the Tenth Census (June 1, 1880). 1883–84.

Preliminary Results as Contained in the Eleventh Census. Bulletin no. 15: "The Census of Alaska," Report of Ivan Petroff. 1890.

"Eleventh Census, 1890." Bulletin no. 19: "Vital Statistics of the Jews in the United States." 30 December 1890.

"Eleventh Census, 1890." Bulletin no. 25: "Enumeration of Indians Living within the Jurisdiction of the United States (except Alaska) Taxed or Taxable and Untaxed." 29 January 1891.

Preliminary Results as Contained in the Eleventh Census. Bulletin no. 48: "The White and Colored Population of the South: 1890." 7 April 1891.

Preliminary Results as Contained in the Eleventh Census. Bulletin no. 199: "Colored Population in 1890. Classified as Persons of African Descent, Chinese, Japanese, and Civilized Indians. By States and Territories." 14 July 1892.

Population by Color, Sex, and General Nativity as Returned at the Eleventh Census, June 1, 1890. 1893.

Report on Population and Resources of Alaska at the Eleventh Census: 1890. 1893.

Report on Population of the United States at the Eleventh Census: 1890. 1895.

Twelfth Census of the United States Taken in the Year 1900. 1901.

"Negroes in the United States, Census Bulletin." Bulletin no. 8. 1904.

Report of the Director to the Secretary of Commerce and Labor, Concerning the Operation of the Bureau for the Year 1903–1904. 1904.

Special Reports. Occupations at the Twelfth Census. 1904.

Twelfth Census of the United States Taken in the Year 1900: Supplementary Analysis. 1906.

Special Reports. Marriage and Divorce, 1867–1906. 1909.

A Century of Population Growth. From the First Census of the United States to the Twelfth, 1790–1900. 1909.

The Census Office and Coordination of Statistics. Reply of the Director of the Census to the Inquiries of the Interdepartmental Statistical Committee, 8 January 1909. 1909.

Instructions to Enumerators. 1910. [62 pages, plus 2 pages glued into the cover, at the end of fascicles concerning the question on "nationality or mother tongue."]

Thirteenth Census of the United States Taken in the Year 1910. 1913.

Indian Population in the United States and Alaska, 1910. 1915.

"Negroes in the United States." Bulletin no. 129. 1915.

Negro Population in the United States, 1790–1915. 1918.

Census of the Virgin Islands of the United States, November 1, 1917. 1918.

The Fourteenth Census of the United States. 1922.

Coding Instruction for the Population Schedule. Individual Card. Fifteenth Census. 1930.

Fifteenth Census of the United States: 1930. Vol. 1, Number and Distribution of Inhabitants, 1931; vol. 2, General report. Statistics by subjects, 1933; Special Volume, Outlying Territories and Possessions. 1932.

Negroes in the United States, 1920–1932. 1935.

Sixteenth Census of the United States—1940. Population and Housing. 1943.

"16th Census of the United States. Population." [Bulletin] Second Series, "Characteristics of the Population, Alaska," 1943.

US Census of Population: 1950. Special Reports. Persons of Spanish Surname. 1950 Population Census Report P-E no. 3C. Preprint of Volume IV, Part 3, Chapter C. 1953.

Historical Statistics of the United States: Colonial Times to 1970. 2 vols. 1975.
200 Years of US Census Taking: Population and Housing Questions, 1790–1990. 1989.
"Measuring America: The Decennial Censuses from 1790 to 2000." 2002. Available online: http://www.census.gov/prod/2002pubs/pol02marv.pdf

Bibliography

Adams, Romanzo. *Interracial Marriage in Hawaii: A Study of the Mutually Conditioned Processes of Acculturation and Amalgamation.* New York: Macmillan, 1937.

Aldrich, Mark. "Progressive Economists and Scientific Racism: Walter Willcox and Black Americans, 1895–1910." *Phylon* 40, no. 1 (1979): 1–14.

Allen, Theodore. *The Invention of the White Race.* Vol. 1, *Racial Oppression and Social Control.* London: Verso, 1994.

Almaguer, Tomás. *Racial Fault Lines: The Historical Origins of White Supremacy in California.* Berkeley: University of California Press, 1995.

Anderson, Benedict. *Imagined Communities: Reflections on the Origin and Spread of Nationalism.* London: Verso, 1983; rev. ed., 1991.

Anderson, Margo J. *The American Census: A Social History.* New Haven, CT: Yale University Press, 1988.

Anderson, Margo J., ed. *Encyclopedia of the US Census.* Washington, DC: CQ Press, 2000.

Anderson, Margo J., and Stephen E. Fienberg. "The History of the First American Census and the Constitutional Language on Census-taking: Report of a Workshop." February 1999. Available online: http://lib.stat.cmu.edu/~fienberg/DonnerReports

Anderson, Margo J., and Stephen E. Fienberg. *Who Counts?: The Politics of Census-Taking in Contemporary America.* New York: Russell Sage Foundation, 1999.

Anderson, Margo J., and William Seltzer. "After Pearl Harbor: The Proper Role of Population Data Systems in Time of War." Population Association of America, 23–25 March 2000. Available online: https://pantherfile.uwm.edu/margo/www/govstat/integrity.htm

Aptheker, Herbert. *A Documentary History of the Negro People in the United States.* Vol. 1. New York: Citadel Press, 1969.

Ardizzone, Heidi. "Red Blooded Americans: Mulattoes and the Melting Pot in US Racialist and Nationalist Discourse, 1890–1930." PhD diss., University of Michigan, 1997.

Arendt, Hannah. "Reflections on Little Rock." *Dissent* 6, no. 1 (Winter 1959): 45–56.

Bailey, Hugh C. *Hinton Rowan Helper: Abolitionist-Racist.* Tuscaloosa: University of Alabama Press, 1965.

Baker, Ray Stannard. *Following the Color Line: American Negro Citizenship in the Progressive Era.* New York: Doubleday, 1908; rpt., Harper & Row, 1964.

Balinski, Michel. *Le suffrage universel inachevé.* Paris: Belin, 2004.

Balinski, Michel, and H. Peyton Young. *Fair Representation: Meeting the Ideal of One Man, One Vote.* New Haven, CT: Yale University Press, 1982.

Barreyre, Nicolas. "Administration et franchise: La Poste, le Congrès, et les formes de l'État américain au XIXᵉ siècle." *Revue française d'études américaines* 112 (June 2007): 52–64.

Barreyre, Nicolas. *L'or et la liberté: Une histoire spatiale des États-Unis après la guerre de Sécession.* Paris: Éditions de l'EHESS, 2014.

Barreyre, Nicolas. "Sectionalisme et politique aux États-Unis: Le Midwest et la Reconstruction, 1865–1877." PhD diss., EHESS, 2008.

Barreyre, Nicolas, Michael Heale, Stephen Tuck, and Cécile Vidal, eds. *Historians Across Borders: Writing American History in a Global Age.* Berkeley: University of California Press, 2014.

Barreyre, Nicolas, and Paul Schor. *De l'émancipation à la ségrégation: Le Sud des États-Unis après la guerre de Sécession, 1865–1896.* Paris: PUF, 2009.

Benoit, Simonne M. *Histoire et méthodologie du recensement de la population aux États-Unis (1787–1930), suivies de l'étude des bulletins démographiques dans la même nation.* Paris: Sirey, 1931.

Berg, Manfred, Isabel Soto, and Paul Schor. "The Weight of Words: Writing about Race in the United States and Europe." *American Historical Review* 119, no. 3 (June 2014): 800–808.

Bieder, Robert E. *Science Encounters the Indian, 1820–1880: The Early Years of American Ethnology.* Norman: University of Oklahoma Press, 1986.

Brian, Eric. "Bibliographie des comptes rendus officiels du Congrès international de statistique (1853–1878)." Paris: CAMS/EHESS, November 1989.

Brian, Eric. "Statistique administrative et internationalisme statistique pendant la seconde moitié du XIXᵉ siècle." *Histoire et mesure* 4, nos. 3–4 (1989): 201–24.

Brubaker, Rogers, Mara Loveman, and Peter Stamatov. "Ethnicity as Cognition." *Theory and Society* 33 (2004): 31–64.

Chapa, Jorge. "Hispanic/Latino Ethnicity and Identifiers." In Anderson, *Encyclopedia of the US Census*, 243–46.

Chavez, Linda. "Promoting Racial Harmony." In *The Affirmative Action Debate*, edited by George E. Curry and Cornel West, 314–25. Reading, MA: Addison Wesley, 1996.

Civil Service Reform in the National Service, 1889–1891: Six Reports of the Special Investigating Committee of the National Civil Service Reform League. Boston: Press of Geo. H. Ellis, 1891.

Cohen, Patricia Cline. *A Calculating People: The Spread of Numeracy in Early America.* Chicago: University of Chicago Press, 1982.

Collomp, Catherine. *Entre classe et nation: Mouvement ouvrier et immigration aux États-Unis.* Paris: Belin, 1998.

Collomp, Catherine. "Unions, Civics, and National Identity: Organized Labor's Reaction to Immigration, 1881–1897." In *In the Shadow of the Statue of Liberty: Immigrants, Workers, and Citizens in the American Republic, 1880–1920*, edited by Marianne Debouzy, 229–56. Urbana: University of Illinois Press, 1992.

Conk, Margo A. *The United States Census and Labor Force Change.* Ann Arbor, MI: UMI Research Press, 1980.

Conrad, Alfred H., and John R. Meyer. "The Economics of Slavery in the Antebellum South." *Journal of Political Economy* 66, no. 1 (1958): 95–130.

Conzen, Kathleen N. *Immigrant Milwaukee, 1836–1860: Accommodation and Community in a Frontier City.* Cambridge, MA: Harvard University Press, 1976.

Daniels, Roger. *Asian America: Chinese and Japanese in the United States since 1850.* Seattle: University of Washington Press, 1988.

Davis, F. James. *Who Is Black? One Nation's Definition.* University Park: Pennsylvania State University Press, 1991.

Davis, Robert C. "The Beginnings of American Social Research." In *Nineteenth-Century American Science: A Reappraisal*, edited by G. H. Daniels, 152–78. Evanston, IL: Northwestern University Press, 1972.

Davis, Robert C. "Social Research in America Before the Civil War." *Journal of the History of Behavioral Sciences* 3 (January 1972): 69–85.

DeBow, J. D. B., ed. *Encyclopaedia of the Trade and Commerce of the United States, More Particularly of the Southern and Western States.* 2d ed. London: Trübner & Co., 1854 [1853].

Deconde, Alexander. *Ethnicity, Race, and American Foreign Policy: A History.* Boston: Northeastern University Press, 1992.

Degler, C. N. *Neither Black nor White: Slavery and Race Relations in Brazil and the United States.* New York: Macmillan, 1971.

Desrosières, Alain. *La politique des grands nombres: Histoire de la raison statistique.* Paris: La Découverte, 1993.

Desrosières, Alain. "Les qualités des quantités: Comment gérer la tension entre réalisme et conventionnalisme." *Enquête* 6 (2007): 271–92.

Desrosières, Alain, and Laurent Thévenot. *Les catégories socio-professionelles.* Paris: La Découverte, 1988.

Deutsch, A. "The First US Census of the Insane (1840) and Its Use as Pro-Slavery Propaganda." *Bulletin of the History of Medicine* 15 (1944): 469–82.

Didier, Emmanuel. "De l'échantillon à la population, sociologie de la généralisation par sondage aux États-Unis avant 1945." PhD diss., ENSMP, 2000.

Didier, Emmanuel. *En quoi consiste l'Amérique? Les statistiques, le New Deal et la démocratie.* Paris: La Découverte, 2009.

Domínguez, Virginia R. "Exporting US Concepts of Race: Are There Limits to the US Model?" *Social Research* 65, no. 2 (1998): 369–99.

Domínguez, Virginia R. *White by Definition: Social Classification in Creole Louisiana.* New Brunswick, NJ: Rutgers University Press, 1986.

Douglass, Frederick. *The Education of Frederick Douglass.* New York: Penguin Books, 1995 [1847].

Duany, Jorge. *The Puerto Rican Nation on the Move: Identities on the Island and in the United States.* Chapel Hill: University of North Carolina Press, 2002.

Du Bois, W. E. B. *Against Racism: Unpublished Essays, Papers, Addresses, 1887–1961, by W. E. B. Du Bois.* Edited by Herbert Aptheker. Amherst: University of Massachusetts Press, 1985.

Du Bois, W. E. B. "The Twelfth Census and the Negro Problems." *Southern Workman* 29, no. 5 (1900): 305–309.

Du Bois, W. E. B., ed. *The Health and Physique of the Negro American.* Atlanta: Atlanta University Press, 1906.

Duncan, Joseph W., and William C. Shelton. *Revolution in United States Government Statistics, 1926–1976.* Washington, DC: GPO, 1978.

Durand, E. Dana. "Memoirs of Edward Dana Durand." Unpublished MS, 1954. Bureau of the Census Library, Suitland, MD, Papers of Census Officials, file no. 5477.

Einhorn, Robin L. *American Taxation, American Slavery.* Chicago: University of Chicago Press, 2006.

Einhorn, Robin L. "Slavery and the Politics of Taxation in the Early United States." *Studies in American Political Development* 14, no. 2 (October 2000): 156–83.

Farland, Maria. "W. E. B. Du Bois, Anthropometric Science, and the Limits of Racial Uplift." *American Quarterly* 58, no. 4 (2006): 1017–45.

Farley, Reynolds. "Racial Identities in 2000: The Response to the Multiple-Race Response Option." In Perlmann and Waters, *The New Race Question*, 33–61.

Feeney, Patrick Gerard. "The 200 Years' War and Counting: Power Politics and Census Controversies, 1790–1990." PhD diss., Temple University, 1994.

Finger, John R. *The Eastern Band of Cherokees: 1819–1900.* Knoxville: University of Tennessee Press, 1984.

FitzPatrick, Paul J. "Leading American Statisticians in the Nineteenth Century." *Journal of the American Statistical Association* 52, no. 279 (September 1957): 301–21.

Fogel, Robert, and Stanley Engerman. *Time on the Cross.* Vol. 1, *The Economics of American Negro Slavery*; Vol. 2, *Evidence and Methods.* Boston: Little, Brown, 1974.

Fohlen, Claude, Jean Heffer, and François Weil. *Canada et États-Unis depuis 1770.* Paris: PUF, 1997.

Foner, Eric. *Reconstruction: America's Unfinished Revolution, 1863–1877.* New York: Perennial Classics, 2002.

Franklin, John Hope, and Alfred A. Moss, Jr., *From Slavery to Freedom: A History of African Americans*, 8th ed. New York: Knopf, 2003.

"The Fraudulent Census: Porter and His Democratic Allies." *The News (Washington, DC)*, 2 August 1891.

Fredrickson, George M. *The Black Image in the White Mind: The Debate on Afro-American Character and Destiny, 1817–1914.* New York: Harper & Row, 1971.

Fuchs, Lawrence H. *The American Kaleidoscope: Race, Ethnicity, and the Civic Culture.* Middletown, CT: Wesleyan University Press, 1990.

Garcia, Mario T. *Mexican Americans: Leadership, Ideology and Identity, 1930–1960.* New Haven, CT: Yale University Press, 1989.

Gigerenzer, Gerd, et al. *The Empire of Chance: How Probability Changed Science and Everyday Life.* Cambridge: Cambridge University Press, 1989.

Goldenweiser, E. A. "The Mother Tongue Inquiry in the Census of Population." *Journal of the American Statistical Association* 13, no. 104 (1913): 648–55.

Gould, Stephen Jay. *The Mismeasure of Man*. New York: W. W. Norton, 1993 [1981].

Graham, Hugh. "The Origins of Official Minority Designation." In Perlmann and Waters, *The New Race Question*, 288–99.

Grant, Madison. *The Passing of the Great Race*. New York: Charles Scribner's Sons, 1916.

Gratton, Brian, and Myron P. Gutman. "Hispanics in the United States, 1850–1990: Estimates of Population Size and National Origin." *Historical Methods* 33, no. 3 (Spring 2000): 137–53.

Green, Kellee. "The Fourteenth Numbering of the People: The 1920 Federal Census." *Prologue* 23, no. 2 (Summer 1991): 130–45.

Grob, Gerald. *Edward Jarvis and the Medical World of Nineteenth Century America*. Knoxville: University of Tennessee Press, 1978.

Grob, Gerald. *Mental Illness and American Society, 1875–1940*. Princeton, NJ: Princeton University Press, 1983.

Gross, Ariela J. "Litigating Whiteness: Trials of Racial Determination in the Nineteenth-Century South." *Yale Law Journal* 108, no. 1 (1998): 109–88.

Gutman, Herbert, and Richard Sutch. "Victorians All? The Sexual Mores and Conduct of Slaves and Their Masters." In *Reckoning with Slavery: A Critical Study in the Quantitative History of American Negro Slavery*, edited by Paul A. David et al., 134–62. New York: Oxford University Press, 1976.

Gutman, Myron P., W. Parker Frisbie, and K. Stephen Blanchard. "A New Look at the Hispanic Population of the United States in 1910." *Historical Methods* 32, no. 1 (Winter 1999): 5–19.

Hacker, J. David. "Civil War and the Census." In Anderson, *Encyclopedia of the US Census*, 72–73.

Haines, Michael R., Lee A. Craig, and Thomas Weiss. "The Short and the Dead: Nutrition, Mortality, and the 'Antebellum Puzzle' in the United States." *Journal of Economic History* 63 (2003): 382–413.

Haizlipp, Shirley Taylor. *The Sweeter the Juice: A Family Memoir in Black and White*. New York: Simon & Schuster, 1994.

Haller, John S., Jr. *Outcasts from Evolution: Scientific Attitudes of Racial Inferiority, 1859–1900*. Urbana: University of Illinois Press, 1971.

Haller, John S., Jr. "Race, Mortality, and Life Insurance: Negro Vital Statistics in the Late Nineteenth Century." *Journal of the History of Medicine and Allied Sciences* 25 (July 1970): 247–61.

Hamilton, Alexander, John Jay, and James Madison. *The Federalist: A Commentary on the Constitution of the United States*. Edited by Robert Scigliano. New York: Modern Library, 2000.

Haney López, Ian F. *White by Law: The Legal Construction of Race*. New York: New York University Press, 1996.

Harris, Cheryl. "Whiteness as Property." *Harvard Law Review* 106 (1993): 1710–91.

Hatch, L. W. "Foreign Parentage and Foreign Born." *Publications of the American Statistical Association* 4, nos. 28–29 (December 1894–March 1895): 116–18.

Helper, Hinton Rowan. *The Impending Crisis of the South: How to Meet It*. New York: Burdick Brothers, 1857.

Herzog, Tamar. *Defining Nations: Immigrants and Citizens in Early Modern Spain and Spanish America*. New Haven, CT: Yale University Press, 2003.

Higham, John. *Strangers in the Land: Patterns of American Nativism, 1865–1925*. 2d ed. New Brunswick, NJ: Rutgers University Press, 1988 [1955].

Hill, Joseph A. "Composition of the American Population by Race and Country of Origin." *Annals of the American Academy of Political and Social Science* 188 ("The American People: Studies in Population") (November 1936): 177–84.

Hindsdale, Burke A., ed. *The Works of James Abraham Garfield*. Freeport, NY: Books for Libraries Press, 1970 [1882].

Hobson, C. F., et al., eds. *The Papers of James Madison*. Vol. 13. Charlottesville: University Press of Virginia, 1981.

Hochschild, Jennifer L., and Brenna M. Powell. "Racial Reorganization and the United States Census 1850–1930: Mulattoes, Half-Breeds, Mixed Parentage, Hindoos, and the Mexican Race." *Studies in American Political Development* 22 (2008): 59–96.

Hollerith, Herman. "The Electrical Tabulating Machine." *Journal of the Royal Statistical Society* 57, no. 4 (December 1894): 678–89.

Hollinger, David A. *Postethnic America: Beyond Multiculturalism*. New York: Basic Books, 1995.

Hormann, Bernhard L. "'Racial' Statistics in Hawaii." *Social Process in Hawaii* 12 (1948): 27–35.

Horsman, Reginald. *Dr. Nott of Mobile: Southerner, Physician and Racial Theorist*. New Orleans: Louisiana State University Press, 1987.

Hughes, J. S. "Labeling and Treating Black Mental Illness in Alabama, 1861–1910." *Journal of Southern History* 58, no. 3 (August 1992): 435–60.

Hutchinson, Edward P. *Immigrants and Their Children, 1850–1950*. New York: John Wiley & Sons, 1956.

Hutchinson, Edward P. *Legislative History of American Immigration Policy, 1798–1965*. Philadelphia: University of Pennsylvania Press, 1981.

Hutchinson, Edward P. "Population Data: Fact and Artifact." Undated, unpublished typescript, US Citizenship and Immigration Services Historical Library, Washington, DC.

Ignatiev, Noel. *How the Irish Became White*. New York: Routledge, 1995.

INSEE. *Pour une histoire de la statistique*. Vol. 1: *Contributions*; Vol. 2: *Matériaux*. Edited by Joëlle Affichard. Paris: Economica-INSEE, 1987.

Jacobs, Harriet. *Incidents in the Life of a Slave Girl, Written by Herself*. Boston: By the Author, 1861.

Jacobson, Matthew Frye. "History, Historicity, and the Census Count by Race." In Perlmann and Waters, *The New Race Question*, 259–68.

Jacobson, Matthew Frye. *Whiteness of a Different Color: European Immigrants and the Alchemy of Race*. Cambridge, MA: Harvard University Press, 1998.

Jarvis, Edward. *The Autobiography of Edward Jarvis (1803–1884)*. Edited by Rosalba Davico. Medical History, Suppl. 12. London: Wellcome Institute for the History of Medicine, 1992.

Jarvis, Edward. "Insanity among the Coloured Population of the Free States." *American Journal of the Medical Sciences* 7 (1845): 71–83.

Jarvis, Edward. "Statistics of Insanity in the United States." *Boston Medical Journal* 27 (1842): 116–21.

Jenkins, Robert M. *Procedural History of the 1940 Census of Population and Housing*. Madison: University of Wisconsin Press, 1985.

Jenks, Albert Ernest. "The Legal Status of Negro-White Amalgamation in the United States." *American Journal of Sociology* 21, no. 5 (March 1916): 666–78.

Jensen, Joan. *Passage from India: Asian Indian Immigrants in North America*. New Haven, CT: Yale University Press, 1988.

Johnson, Walter. "The Slave Trader, the White Slave, and the Politics of Racial Determination in the 1850s." *Journal of American History* 87, no. 1 (June 2000): 13–38.

Johnson, Walter. *Soul by Soul: Life Inside the Antebellum Slave Market*. Cambridge, MA: Harvard University Press, 2000.

Keeling, John R. "The Role of Academic Social Science and the Dillingham Commission in American Immigration Restriction, 1890–1917." MA thesis, University of Southwestern Louisiana, 1992.

Kettner, James H. *The Development of American Citizenship, 1608–1870*. Chapel Hill: University of North Carolina Press, 1978.

King, Miriam L. "The Quantum of Happiness: The Politics of American Population Debates, 1850–1930." PhD diss., University of Pennsylvania, 1990.

King, Miriam L., and Diana L. Magnuson. "Perspectives on Historical US Census Undercounts." *Social Science History* 19, no. 4 (Winter 1995): 455–66.

Klinkner, Philip, and Rogers Smith. *The Unsteady March: The Rise and Decline of Racial Equality*. Chicago: University of Chicago Press, 1999.

Kolchin, Peter. *American Slavery, 1619–1877*. Rev. ed. New York: Hill and Wang, 2003.

Kolchin, Peter. "Whiteness Studies: The New History of Race in America." *Journal of American History* 89, no. 1 (June 2002): 154–73.

Kosmin, Barry. "Ethnic and Religious Questions in the 2001 UK Census of Population Policy Recommendations." *Jewish Policy Research Policy Papers* 2 (1999). Accessed online: http://www.bjpa.org/Publications/details.cfm?PublicationID=4103

Kraut, Alan M. *Silent Travelers: Germs, Genes, and the "Immigrant Menace."* Baltimore: Johns Hopkins University Press, 1994.

Kruger, Lorenz, Lorraine Daston, and Michael Heidelberger, eds. *The Probabilistic Revolution.* Cambridge, MA: MIT Press, 1987.

Kull, Andrew. *The Color-Blind Constitution.* Cambridge, MA: Harvard University Press, 1992.

Lewis, Lloyd. *Sherman: Fighting Prophet.* New York: Harcourt Brace, 1932.

Lind, Andrew W. "Economic Succession and Racial Invasion in Hawaii." PhD diss., University of Chicago, 1931. Published as *An Island Community: Ecological Succession in Hawaii.* Chicago: University of Chicago Press, 1938.

Lind, Andrew W. *Hawaii's People.* 4th ed. Honolulu: University Press of Hawaii, 1980 [1955].

Litwack, Leon F. "The Federal Government and the Free Negro, 1790–1860." *Journal of Negro History* 43, no. 4 (October 1958): 261–78.

Loveman, Mara. "The US Census and the Contested Rules of Racial Classification in Early Twentieth-Century Puerto Rico (1910–1920)." *Caribbean Studies* 35, no. 2 (July–December 2007): 79–114.

Loveman, Mara, and Jeronimo O. Muniz. "How Puerto Rico Became White: Boundary Dynamics and Intercensus Racial Reclassification." *American Sociological Review* 72, no. 6 (2007): 915–39.

Magnuson, Diana L. "The Making of a Modern Census: The United States Census of Population, 1790–1940." PhD diss., University of Minnesota, 1995.

Magnuson, Diana L. "US Census of Population Office Culture, 1902–1928." Unpublished article, Social Science History Association Conference, Fort Worth, November 1999.

Mayo-Smith, Richmond. "Statistical Data for the Study of the Assimilation of Races and Nationalities in the United States." *Publications of the American Statistical Association* 3, no. 24 (December 1893): 429–49.

McMillen, David. "Apportionment and Districting." In Anderson, *Encyclopedia of the US Census,* 34–42.

McPherson, James M. *Ordeal by Fire: The Civil War and Reconstruction.* New York: Alfred A. Knopf, 1982.

Mezey, Naomi. "Erasure and Recognition: The Census, Race, and the National Imagination." *Northwestern University Law Review* 97 (2003): 1701–68.

Mills, Gary B. "Miscegenation and the Free Negro in Antebellum 'Anglo' Alabama: A Reexamination of Southern Race Relations." *Journal of American History* 68, no. 1 (June 1981): 16–34.

Morris, Thomas D. *Southern Slavery and the Law, 1619–1860.* Chapel Hill: University of North Carolina Press, 1996.

"Mortality and Insurance of Colored Persons." *Publications of the American Statistical Association* 3, nos. 21–22 (March–June 1893): 350–52.

Munroe, James Phinney. *A Life of Francis Amasa Walker.* New York: Henry Holt, 1923.

Nash, Gary B. "The Hidden History of Mestizo America." *Journal of American History* 82, no. 3 (December 1995): 941–64.

Nash, Gerald. "The Census of 1890 and the Closing of the Frontier." *Pacific Northwest Quarterly* 71 (July 1980): 98–100.

Ngai, Mae M. "The Architecture of Race in American Immigration Law: A Reexamination of the Immigration Act of 1924." *Journal of American History* 86, no. 1 (June 1999): 67–92.

Ngai, Mae M. *Impossible Subjects: Illegal Aliens and the Making of Modern America.* Princeton, NJ: Princeton University Press, 2004.

Nobles, Melissa. "Racial Categorization and Censuses." In *Census and Identity: The Politics of Race, Ethnicity, and Language in National Censuses,* edited by David I. Kertzer and Dominique Arel, 43–70. Cambridge: Cambridge University Press, 2002.

Nobles, Melissa. *Shades of Citizenship: Race and the Census in Modern Politics.* Stanford, CA: Stanford University Press, 2000.

Ohline, Howard. "Republicanism and Slavery: Origins of the Three-Fifths Clause in the United States Constitution." *William and Mary Quarterly* 28 (October 1971): 563–84.

Omi, Michael, and Howard Winant. *Racial Formation in the United States from the 1960s to the 1990s.* New York: Routledge, 1994 [1986].

Pascoe, Peggy. "Miscegenation Law, Court Cases, and Ideologies of Race in Twentieth-Century America." *Journal of America History* 83, no. 1 (June 1996): 44–69.

Pascoe, Peggy. *What Comes Naturally: Miscegenation Law and the Making of Race in America.* New York: Oxford University Press, 2009.

Patterson, J. Stahl. "Increase and Movement of the Colored Population I." *Popular Science Monthly* 19 (September 1881): 665–75.

Pedraza, Silvia. "Beyond Black and White: Latinos and Social Science Research on Immigration, Race, and Ethnicity in America." *Social Science History* 24, no. 4 (Winter 2000): 697–726.

Perlmann, Joel. *"Race or People?": Federal Race Classifications for Europeans in America, 1898–1913.* Working Paper 320. Annandale-on-Hudson, NY: Bard College, Levy Economics Institute, 2001.

Perlmann, Joel, and Mary Waters, eds. *The New Race Question: How the Census Counts Multiracial Individuals.* New York: Russell Sage Foundation, 2002.

Porter, Robert P. "The Eleventh Census." *Publications of the American Statistical Association* 2, no. 15 (September 1891): 321–79.

Porter, Theodore M. *The Rise of Statistical Thinking, 1820–1900.* Princeton, NJ: Princeton University Press, 1986.

Porter, Theodore M. *Trust in Numbers: The Pursuit of Objectivity in Science and Public Life.* Princeton, NJ: Princeton University Press, 1995.

Prewitt, Kenneth. *What Is Your Race? The Census and Our Flawed Efforts to Classify Americans.* Princeton, NJ: Princeton University Press, 2013.

Quételet, Adolphe. *Congrès international de statistique.* Brussels, 1873.

Ransom, Roger L. *Conflict and Compromise: The Political Economy of Slavery, Emancipation, and the American Civil War.* Cambridge: Cambridge University Press, 1989.

Regan, Opal G. "Statistical Reforms Accelerated by Sixth Census Error." *Journal of the American Statistical Association* 68, no. 343 (September 1973): 540–46.

Reuter, Edward Byron. "The Superiority of the Mulatto." *American Journal of Sociology* 23, no. 1 (July 1917): 83–106.

Ripley, William Z. "Colored Population of African Descent." In *The Federal Census: Critical Essays*, edited by the American Economic Association, 38–48. New York: Macmillan, 1899.

Rodriguez, Clara E. *Changing Race: Latinos, the Census, and the History of Ethnicity in the United States.* New York: New York University Press, 2000.

Rodriguez, Clara E. "Latinos and the Census." In *The Oxford Encyclopedia of Latinos and Latinas in the United States*, edited by Suzanne Oboler and Deena J. González, 288–93. New York: Oxford University Press, 2005.

Roediger, David R. *The Wages of Whiteness: Race and the Making of the American Working Class.* London: Verso, 1991.

Rosales, F. Arturo. "Shifting Self Perceptions and Ethnic Consciousness among Mexicans in Houston, 1930–1946." *Aztlan* 16, nos. 1–2 (1985): 71–94.

Ross, Edward A. "The Causes of Race Superiority." *Annals of the American Academy of Political and Social Sciences* 18 (1901): 67–89.

Ross, Rodney A. "A Centennial Celebration of Federal Employment: Charles E. Hall (1868–1952), 'Specialist in Negro Statistics' with the Census Bureau." Unpublished presentation at the annual meeting of the Organization of American Historians, St. Louis, 1 April 2000.

Rossignol, Marie-Jeanne. "La Révolution américaine et l'abolition de l'esclavage: d'une ambition des Lumières à l'échec constitutionnel fédéral (1765–1808)." In *Les empires atlantiques entre Lumières et libéralisme (1763–1865)*, edited by Federica Morelli, Clément Thibaud, and Geneviève Verdo, 21–38. Rennes: Presses Universitaires de Rennes, 2009.

Russel, Kathy, Midge Wilson, and Ronald Hall. *The Color Complex: The Politics of Skin Color among African-Americans*. New York: Harcourt Brace Jovanovich, 1992.

Russell, Archibald. *Principles of Statistical Inquiry*. New York: D. Appleton, 1839.

Saada, Emmanuelle. *Les enfants de la colonie: Les métis de l'Empire français entre sujétion et citoyenneté*. Paris: La Découverte, 2007. US edition: *Empire's Children: Race, Filiation, and Citizenship in the French Colonies*. Chicago: University of Chicago Press, 2012.

Sabbagh, Daniel. *L'égalité par le droit: Les paradoxes de la discrimination positive aux États-Unis*. Paris: Economica, 2003.

Sabbagh, Daniel. "La normalisation juridique des rapports sexuels interraciaux aux États-Unis." *Tocqueville Review/Revue Tocqueville* 21, no. 2 (2000): 9–30.

Schmitt, Robert C. *Demographic Statistics of Hawaii: 1778–1965*. Honolulu: University of Hawaii Press, 1968.

Schor, Paul. "Compter et classer: Histoire des catégories de la population dans le recensement américain, 1790–1940." PhD diss., EHESS, 2001.

Schor, Paul. "Compter et classer par race: Hawaii, les Îles Vierges et le recensement américain, 1900–1940." *Histoire et Mesure* 13, nos. 1–2 (1998): 113–14. Available online: http://www.persee.fr/doc/hism_0982-1783_1998_num_13_1_893

Schor, Paul. "Origines nationales, race et ethnicité dans le recensement américain, de l'indépendance à 1920." MA thesis, EHESS, 1994.

Schor, Paul. "Un prisme en noir et blanc: L'invisibilité des familles multiraciales dans le recensement américain au début du vingtième siècle." In *Faire figure d'étranger: Regards croisés sur la production de l'altérité*, edited by C. Cossée, E. Lada, S. Lamri, and I. Rigoni, 39–56. Sociétales series. Paris: Armand Colin, 2004.

Schor, Paul. "The View from Below and the View from Above: What US Census-Taking Reveals about Social Representations in the Era of Jim Crow and Immigration Restriction." In *A World of Populations: Transnational Perspectives on Demography in the Twentieth Century*, edited by Heinrich Hartmann and Corinna R. Unger, 19–35. New York: Berghahn Books, 2014.

Schor, Paul, and Alexis Spire. "Les statistiques de la population comme construction de la nation: La mesure des origines nationales dans les recensements français et américains (1850–1920)." In *Les codes de la différence: Race—Origine—Religion; France—Allemagne—États-Unis*, edited by Riva Kastoryano. 91–121. Paris: Presses de la FNSP, 2005.

Seltzer, William. "Excluding Indians Not Taxed: Federal Censuses and Native Americans in the Nineteenth Century." Presentation at the 1999 Joint Statistical Meetings, Baltimore, 9 August. Online: https://pantherfile.uwm.edu/margo/www/govstat/ind.pdf

Skerry, Peter. *Counting on the Census? Race, Group Identity and the Evasion of Politics*. Washington, DC: Brookings Institution, 2000.

Skipper, Otis Clark. "J. D. B. DeBow and the Seventh Census." *Louisiana Historical Quarterly* 22 (April 1939): 479–91.

Smith, James McCune. "The Influence of Climate on Longevity, with Special Reference to Insurance." *Merchant's Magazine and Commercial Review* 14 (1846): 319–29, 403–18.

Smith, Shawn Michelle. "'Looking at One's Self Through the Eyes of Others': W. E. B. Du Bois's Photographs for the 1900 Paris Exposition." *African American Review* 34, no. 4 (Winter 2000): 581–99.

Smith, Tom W. "Ethnic Measurement and Identification." *Ethnicity* 7, no. 1 (March 1980): 78–95.

Sollors, Werner, ed. *Interracialism: Black-White Intermarriage in American History, Literature, and Law*. New York: Oxford University Press, 2000.

Sollors, Werner, ed. *Theories of Ethnicity: A Classical Reader*. New York: New York University Press, 1996.

Stanton, William R. *The Leopard's Spots: Scientific Attitudes Towards Race in America, 1815–1859*. Chicago: University of Chicago Press, 1960.

Steckel, Richard H. "Miscegenation and the American Slave Schedules." *Journal of Interdisciplinary History* 11, no. 2 (1980): 251–63.

Steckel, Richard H. "Stature and Living Standards in the United States." Working Paper Series on Historical Factors in Long Run Growth. Working Paper No. 24. National Bureau of Economic Research. Cambridge, April 1991.

Stone, Alfred. *Studies in the American Race Problem.* New York: Doubleday, 1908.

Stringfellow, Thornton. *Scriptural and Statistical Views in Favor of Slavery.* 4th ed. with additions. Richmond, VA: J. W Randolph, 1856.

Takaki, Ronald. *A Different Mirror: A History of Multicultural America.* Boston: Little, Brown, 1993.

Tehranian, John. "Performing Whiteness: Naturalization Litigation and the Construction of Racial Identity." *Yale Law Journal* 109, no. 4 (2000): 817–48.

Thomson, Charles A. H. "Public Relations of the 1940 Census." *Public Opinion Quarterly* 4, no. 2 (June 1940): 311–18.

Topalov, Christian. "L'individu comme convention: Le cas des statistiques professionnelles du XIXᵉ siècle en France, en Grande-Bretagne et aux États-Unis." *Genèses* 31 (June 1998): 48–75.

Truesdell, Leon E. *The Development of Punch Card Tabulation in the Bureau of the Census, 1890–1940. With Outlines of Actual Tabulation Programs.* US Department of Commerce, Bureau of the Census. Washington, DC: GPO, 1965.

Truesdell, Leon E. "Methods Involved in the Federal Census of Population." In *Methods in Social Science,* edited by Stuart A. Rice, 197–209. Chicago: University of Chicago Press, 1931.

Truesdell, Leon E. "Value of the Population Census for Research." *Annals of the American Academy of Political and Social Science* 188 ("The American People: Studies in Population") (November 1936): 329–39.

Turner, Frederick Jackson. "The Significance of the Frontier in American History." *Annual Report of the American Historical Association* (1893): 199–227.

Tushnet, Mark V. *The American Laws of Slavery, 1810–1860: Considerations of Humanity and Interest.* Princeton, NJ: Princeton University Press, 1981.

US Bureau of Immigration. *Annual Report of the Commissioner General: 1920–1921/1924–1925.* Washington, DC: GPO.

US Congress. "Ninth Census." House Reports, 41st Congress, 2d Session. Report 3. 18 January 1870.

US Congress. *Journals of the Continental Congress, 1774–1789,* edited by Worthington C. Ford et al. Washington, DC, 1904–37.

US Congress. *Statement of Mr Joseph A. Hill, Chief Statistician, Revision and Results, Bureau of the Census, December 28. Hearings before the Committee on the Census on H.R. 14498, 15021, 15158, 15217, December 28, 29 1920, January 4, 5, 6 1921. Apportionment of Representatives. Chairman: Isaac Siegel.* Washington, DC: GPO, 1921.

US Department of War. *Census of Porto Rico, Taken under the Direction of the War Department, U.S.A.* Bulletin no. 1. Washington, DC: GPO, 1900.

US Immigration Commission. *Dictionary of Races or Peoples: Reports of the Immigration Commission.* Vol. 5. Washington, DC: GPO, 1911.

Vacher, Dr. "Considérations sur le Census Américain de 1890." Extract from *Journal de la Société de statistique de Paris* (October 1891). Nancy: Berger-Levrault, 1891.

Walker, Francis A. "The Colored Race in the United States." *Forum* 11 (1891): 501–509.

Walker, Francis A. *Discussions in Economics and Statistics.* Edited by Davis R. Dewey. 2 vols. New York: Henry Holt, 1899.

Walker, Francis A. "Immigration and Degradation." *Forum* 11 (1891): 634–43.

Walker, Francis A. *The Indian Question.* Boston, 1874.

Walker, Francis A. "Statistics of the Colored Race in the United States." *Journal of the American Statistical Association* 2 (September–December 1890): 91–106.

Washington, Mary Lynn. "White, Black, or Mulatto: A Sociological Exploration of the Meaning of Racial Classification in the United States Census of 1880." PhD diss., Johns Hopkins University, 1997.

Watkins, Susan Cotts, ed. *After Ellis Island: Newcomers and Natives in the 1910 Census.* New York: Russell Sage Foundation, 1994.

Weil, Patrick. "Races at the Gate: A Century of Racial Distinctions in American Immigration Policy (1865–1965)." *Georgetown Immigration Law Journal* 15, no. 4 (Summer 2001): 625–48.

Weil, Patrick. "Le statut de la femme en droit de la nationalité: Une égalité tardive." In *Les Codes de la différence: Race–origine–religion; France, Allemagne, États-Unis,* edited by Riva Kastoryano, 123–43. Paris: Presses de Sciences-Po, 2005.

W[illcox], W. F. "Migration of Negroes." *Publications of the American Statistical Association* 5, no. 40 (December 1897): 371–72.

Willcox, Walter F. "The Probable Increase of the Negro Race in the United States." *Quarterly Journal of Economics* 19, no. 4 (August 1905): 545–72.

Williamson, Joel. *New People: Miscegenation and Mulattoes in the United States.* New York: Free Press, 1980.

Wirth, Louis. *The Ghetto.* New Brunswick, NJ: Transaction Publishers, 1998 [1928].

Wright, Carroll D., and William C. Hunt. *The History and Growth of the United States Census.* Washington, DC: Government Printing Office, 1900.

Zolberg, Aristide. *A Nation by Design: Immigration Policy in the Fashioning of America.* Cambridge, MA: Harvard University Press, 2006.

INDEX

Note: *Numbers in italics refer to illustration pages*

9 780190 092474